The SHSAT Is Changing!

A redesigned SHSAT will debut in the Fall of 2017. While much of the old format remains the same, especially in the Mathematics section, there are several brand new types of questions that will appear for the first time.

In this supplement, you will be introduced to all of the specific changes in format as announced by the New York City Department of Education (NYCDOE). This supplement includes:

- detailed descriptions of all of the new types of questions
- illustrative sample problems with full solutions and explanations
- additional practice problems, helpful strategies, and tips for success

ABOUT THIS BOOK

Barron's SHSAT book—the book now in your hands—continues to be widely recognized as a significant aid in helping students master the skills necessary to achieve success on the SHSAT. This book offers an enormous quantity of high-quality practice material and test-taking strategies that fully apply to the new SHSAT. We have been very pleased with the overwhelming number of positive, glowing responses received over the past fifteen years from students, parents, teachers, test prep centers, learning centers, tutors, and others who have used this book.

HOW TO USE THIS BOOK *NOW*

- Carefully read this entire supplement. Familiarize yourself with all of the content and format changes. Review the illustrative examples and sample problems. Do all of the new practice problems and study the accompanying solutions, tips, strategies, and suggestions.
- Nearly all of the material in this book still applies to the redesigned test. However, a few small modifications may be helpful. Specifically, Logical Reasoning questions and Scrambled Paragraphs will no longer appear on the redesigned test, so you may choose to skip over those sections in this book. However, we still recommend that you do the mind-stretching Logical Reasoning puzzles and enjoy the challenges posed by the Scrambled Paragraphs. This can be both fun and beneficial. Practicing these question types can help provide you with powerful analytical tools and insights, and help hone and polish your skills.
- Read and study the Test-Taking Strategies chapter, paying attention to applicable sections, especially Mathematics.
- Do the Math questions in the mini tests and model tests.

- Be sure to complete the Math Skills "Diagnosers." They help you locate and correct weaknesses.
- Do the Model Test Reading Comprehension Questions and review the associated "Skillbuilder."

Tools for Success

One of our main goals has been to provide you with the tools and techniques with which you may successfully confront the unfamiliar. Rather than only repeating and drilling specific problem types and hoping the same type may appear on the day of the test, you will acquire a more permanent and flexible set of approaches to problem solving that places you in a position of confidence and command—ready for anything!

Always Do More!

It is valuable to augment your test prep with enrichment. Always do more. Tackle the unfamiliar. Identify and eliminate weaknesses while fortifying your strengths. Do non-routine math problems such as those found on math competitions and contests.

Read with focus and write often. Always pay careful attention to details. Edit and revise your written work. Read with a critical, analytical eye and carefully write about what you have read. Remember that familiarity instills confidence; good rehearsals make for good performances.

When studying, avoid bad habits such as listening to music while trying to concentrate. Work with a full sense of commitment to the task at hand. Avoid distractions. Remember, you will likely get used to whatever you practice, including bad habits!

Abundant Rich Resources

This book is filled with excellent advice and proven powerful techniques regarding mathematical problem solving. There are more than 450 practice math problems together with full solutions and detailed explanations. In addition, this book contains a vast amount of useful Verbal related materials (now referred to as English Language Arts on the redesigned exam) that engage you in the good reading practices necessary for critical analyses of written passages.

You should still use the Model Tests for practice, especially the Mathematics sections. Work through the problems and review the solutions with care.

WHY IS THE SHSAT CHANGING?

According to the New York City Department of Education (NYCDOE), the SHSAT redesign is motivated by an attempt to more closely reflect, within the test, the type of classroom instruction and curricula that presently conform to the New York State Learning Standards.

The new, redesigned version will be administered for the first time in the Fall of 2017. Consequently, some of the traditional types of questions will no longer appear and several new types of questions will be introduced. The test will still be very challenging. The SHSAT will still be the critical determining factor upon which entrance to the specialized high schools is based.

THE STRUCTURE OF THE REDESIGNED SHSAT

Content and Format

The redesigned SHSAT retains the two-section format: Verbal, now called English Language Arts (ELA), and Mathematics. However, the new ELA section has been dramatically restructured. There are changes in both the types and number of questions, as well as in the skills that are being tested. In particular, Logical Reasoning questions and Scrambled Paragraphs will no longer appear. Two new types of questions will replace them as discussed in the next section.

There will now be 57 questions in the ELA section and 57 questions in the Math section. The type and distribution of questions is summarized on page 4.

New Time Limit

The new time limit will be **180 minutes** for the entire test, rather than the former time limit of 150 minutes. There are no breaks between sections. You may distribute your time in any way you choose.

TYPES OF ELA QUESTIONS

Revising/Editing Questions

The redesigned ELA section will feature two new types of questions—*Revising/Editing in a Passage* and *Revising/Editing Stand-Alone Items*. These questions will test your mastery of grammar and usage and your ability to revise and edit other people's writing.

Reading Comprehension Passages with Corresponding Questions

These will be the same types of Reading Comprehension questions that are presented in this book. The main difference will be that there will now be six reading comprehension passages instead of five, with five to seven questions per passage.

> **NOTE**
>
> All ELA questions will be in multiple-choice format with four possible answer choices. See pages 7–19 for complete details and illustrative examples of all the ELA question types.

TYPES OF MATH QUESTIONS

The Math section will consist of both computational questions and word problems that address a wide range of mathematical skills and analytical reasoning abilities. **Calculators are not permitted and no reference formulas will be supplied.**

Grid-in Questions

The only new type of question included in the Mathematics section will be the "grid-in" question. There will be five such questions. Each will require that you produce your own correct numerical answer without the help of answer choices. You will then enter your answer on the appropriate grid on the answer sheet.

Multiple-Choice Questions

Other than the grid-in questions, the remaining math questions will be multiple-choice. However, the new multiple-choice format will only have **four** choices from which to select the correct answer. This is in contrast to the old format of five choices.

See pages 24–32 for complete details and illustrative examples of all Math question types.

SUMMARY OF BASIC CHANGES

English Language Arts (formerly called "Verbal")		
Question Type	Old SHSAT	Redesigned SHSAT
Reading Comprehension Passages with associated questions	YES	YES
Revising/Editing in a Passage questions	NO	YES
Revising/Editing Stand-Alone questions	NO	YES

Mathematics		
Question Type	Old SHSAT	Redesigned SHSAT
Multiple-choice questions	YES	YES
Grid-in questions	NO	YES

SUMMARY OF THE NUMBERS AND TYPES OF QUESTIONS ON THE REDESIGNED SHSAT

The ELA and Mathematics sections of the test will each contain 57 questions, distributed as follows:

English Language Arts Section	
Type of Question	Number of Questions*
Revising/Editing in a Passage questions	2 reading passages each with 6–8 associated multiple-choice questions (with 4 answer choices)
Revising/Editing Stand-Alone questions	5–8 multiple-choice questions (with 4 answer choices)
Reading Comprehension Passages with associated questions	6 reading passages each with 5–7 associated multiple-choice questions (with 4 answer choices)

*There will be 20 Revising/Editing questions and 37 Reading Comprehension questions.

Mathematics Section	
Type of Question	Number of Questions
Multiple-choice questions	52 questions
Grid-in questions	5 questions

SCORING THE SHSAT

The basic scoring system has not changed.

- The total number of correct responses is called the **raw score**. The maximum raw score for each section is 47.
- The raw score for each section is converted into a **scaled score**.
- The scaled scores for both sections are combined to form the **composite score**.
- The composite score, together with your school preferences and the number of available seats in each school, will be used to determine your admission eligibility.

TIPS AND STRATEGIES

- Obtain a copy of the *Official DOE 2017–2018 Specialized High Schools Student Handbook* from your guidance counselor or online. This should provide you with the latest information and any possible updates.
- Determine how to best manage your time. A full 180 minutes is allowed for the entire test. There are no breaks between the sections of the test. You may distribute the time you spend on any part of the test as best suits your own needs. How best to do this may be realized after practicing several model tests under strict SHSAT conditions.
- Pace yourself—be sure to keep track of elapsed time!
- Do the practice questions in this supplement and in the book itself. Although the multiple-choice questions will now offer four answer choices instead of five, you should continue to practice the old style questions that have five answer choices. This is especially true for the math questions. The multiple-choice questions in this book are especially rich in scope and content, and have been designed to enrich and amplify your mathematical problem-solving skills.
- Remember that only correct responses will count toward your score. There is no penalty for an incorrect answer. Thus, don't leave any questions unanswered! Refer to the General Test-Taking Advice section in this book for more details on this.
- It may prove strategic to start the test with your strongest section. For example, if you feel strongest in Math, then start with the Math section. This will likely leave you more time to spend on the ELA section.

- Practice the old style Scrambled Paragraphs and Logical Reasoning questions. This practice will be beneficial because working on these types of questions can sharpen a multitude of valuable and transferable reading and writing skills.
- Refer to the "Skillbuilder" sections in this book, especially for Mathematics, for essential information, review and practice material, and valuable problem-solving strategies.

The Redesigned ELA Section

RECAP: WHAT'S NEW IN THE ELA SECTION

The English Language Arts (ELA) section, formerly called the Verbal section, will now consist of 57 questions, all of which are multiple-choice with four answer choices instead of five. The Scrambled Paragraphs and Logical Reasoning questions have been removed. They will be replaced with **20 Revising and Editing questions**. Five to eight of these will be stand-alone questions that ask about individual sentences or paragraphs. There will also be two passages with six to eight questions for each that ask how to best revise certain sections of the passage. While these new "revising/editing" questions may be challenging, they are based on the New York State Learning Standards and they focus on content that students should be familiar with from their classwork.

There will also now be **six Reading Comprehension passages, instead of five, with five to seven questions for each passage. There will be a total of 37 Reading Comprehension questions.** As far as the kinds of passages and questions that will be in the Reading Comprehension section of the redesigned test, they will be largely the same as those on the old test.

All graded questions in the ELA section are now worth one point each. Keep in mind that the new ELA section will also include **10 "field test items"** or ungraded questions. This means that out of 57 questions, only 47 questions will be scored. The other ten will be "test" questions designed to help the makers of the SHSAT plan new question types for future exams.

REVISING/EDITING IN A PASSAGE QUESTIONS

Because so many of the Revising/Editing in a Passage questions focus on how ideas in the passage fit together, *we strongly recommend that you **read the entire passage** before answering **any** of the questions*. Also, **process of elimination** will be critical for these new question types; even if you're not sure which answer is best for a certain question, you can probably eliminate one or more answer choices that are definitely wrong.

Four Steps to Success for the Revising/Editing in a Passage Questions

1. **READ THE PASSAGE.** Read through the whole passage and really try to get a sense of what the author is trying to say. Also, look for what the author is trying to accomplish in each paragraph and how the paragraphs fit together.
2. **READ THE QUESTIONS AND PREDICT AN ANSWER.** Once you've finished the passage, read each question stem, the part that comes before the answer choices. Then, before you look at the choices, try to predict what you think the correct answer will look like. You might not get it exactly, but predicting first will help you select the right choice later on.

3. **USE THE PROCESS OF ELIMINATION.** Look through the answer choices and make a small dash with your pencil through any choices you think are wrong.

4. **PICK THE BEST OF THE REST.** If at this point you have more than one answer choice that has not been eliminated, pick the best of what is left. Think about what makes one answer choice better and what makes the others worse.

REVISING/EDITING STAND-ALONE QUESTIONS

The stand-alone items focus more on grammar and involve improving or identifying errors in sentences and paragraphs.

Four Steps to Success for the Stand-Alone Questions

1. **READ.** Read the sentence or paragraph inside the black box.

2. **READ THE QUESTION AND PREDICT AN ANSWER.** Read the question stem and predict what the answer will look like before you look at the answer choices.

3. **USE THE PROCESS OF ELIMINATION.** Look through the answer choices and make a small dash with your pencil through any choices you think are wrong.

4. **PICK THE BEST OF THE REST.** If at this point you have more than one answer choice that has not been eliminated, pick the best of what is left. Think about what makes one answer choice better and what makes the others worse.

REVISING/EDITING IN A PASSAGE—PRACTICE QUESTIONS

Sample Passage 1

> **DIRECTIONS:** Read the passage below and answer the following questions. You will be asked to improve the writing quality of the passage and to correct errors so that the passage follows the conventions of standard written English. You may reread the passage if you need to. Mark the **best** answer for each question.

Kraftwerk

(1) If asked to make a list of the most influential musicians of the 20th Century most people wouldn't include a German electronic music band from Düsseldorf. (2) Kraftwerk, started in 1969 by Ralf Hütter and Florian Schneider as an experimental rock band, would go on to influence a wide array of artists and change the sound of popular music.

(3) Kraftwerk was a pioneer in electronic instrumentation, including the use of synthesizers, drum machines, and "vocoders," devices that convert the human voice into electronic data and distort it. (4) Vocoders were originally used in the U.S. Navy to encrypt voice communications from ships. (5) Kraftwerk's style was completely original when it first came out and, over the years, the band experimented with a multitude of sounds in their music. (6) On their 1975 album

Autobahn, the band used synthesizers to mimic the noises made by speeding cars and blaring horns. (7) By combining these technical innovations with minimalist lyrics, Kraftwerk created an entirely new sound, one that would change the landscape of popular music.

(8) In 2013 one critic wrote, "No other band since The Beatles has given so much to pop culture." (9) Kraftwerk's influence can be heard in music genres as diverse as synth-pop, techno, and industrial. (10) They also had an effect on rock-and-roll and hip-hop. (11) Musicians as diverse as Depeche Mode, Madonna, David Bowie, Björk, Daft Punk, Kanye West, and Jay-Z have all sampled Kraftwerk.

1. Which transition should be added to the beginning of sentence 2?

   (A) So,
   (B) Apparently,
   (C) Nonetheless,
   (D) Eventually,

2. Which edit is needed to correct sentence 5?

   (A) add a comma after *style*
   (B) add a comma after *completely*
   (C) add a comma after *out*
   (D) add a comma after *experimented*

3. What sentence would best follow sentence 6 to support the argument presented in the passage?

   (A) This technique would be commonplace by the 1990s.
   (B) No one had successfully incorporated sounds from daily life into popular music like this before.
   (C) *Autobahn* went on to become Kraftwerk's most commercially successful album.
   (D) Although *Autobahn* was groundbreaking, it did not break into the top 25 on any pop charts.

4. Which of the following sentences is irrelevant to the passage as a whole and, thus, should be deleted?

   (A) 2
   (B) 4
   (C) 6
   (D) 10

5. What is the best way to combine sentences 9 and 10 in order to make the passage more concise?

(A) Kraftwerk's influence can be heard in music genres as diverse as synth-pop, techno, and industrial, as well as more mainstream genres like rock-and-roll and hip-hop.

(B) Because Kraftwerk influenced more mainstream genres like rock-and-roll and hip-hop, we are less aware of its impact on synth-pop, techno, and industrial music.

(C) Kraftwerk has influenced a large number of very diverse types of music such as synth-pop, techno, and industrial, and they also influenced more mainstream types of music like rock-and-roll and hip-hop.

(D) Even though Kraftwerk has influenced styles like synth-pop, techno, and industrial, they also have had an impact on other styles of music like rock-and-roll and hip-hop.

6. Which conclusion should be added to the end of the passage to strengthen its argument?

(A) In recognition of their impact on modern music, Kraftwerk won a Lifetime Grammy Award in 2014, and the band's work continues to influence musicians to this day.

(B) Many musicians have joined and left Kraftwerk since it was founded, but Hütter is the only original member still active in the band today.

(C) Commercially, Kraftwerk was never as successful as many of the bands it influenced.

(D) Little is known about the private lives of the band members because they never grant interviews.

Sample Passage 2

> **DIRECTIONS:** Read the passage below and answer the following questions. You will be asked to improve the writing quality of the passage and to correct errors so that the passage follows the conventions of standard written English. You may reread the passage if you need to. Mark the **best** answer for each question.

Funding for Arts Education

(1) Proponents of the arts have long protested the fact that art education is usually the first thing eliminated when schools need to cut their budgets. (2) Critics of art education argue that the arts are not a necessary part of an elementary and high school curriculum, unlike English, Math, Science, and History, which are thought of as more critical subjects and are tested on state and national exams. (3) However, art education had been shown to lead to many benefits, including higher overall student performance and higher graduation rates.

(4) The amount of emphasis given to art education in public schools varies, and the art subjects taught can include music, dance, and theater, as well as visual arts. (5) The value of art education, however, is not only found in the fact that students

learn these disciplines. (6) Art education also seeks to promote self-expression and increase student engagement. (7) It has also been shown to improve students' judgment and problem-solving abilities. (8) For very young students, art education can have beneficial, favorable, and advantageous effects, such as improvement in dexterity and enhancement of language abilities.

(9) The unfortunate result of cutting art education from public school budgets is that this often cuts off access to these programs for the students who need it most. (10) While many schools can find additional community funding to pay for art education, schools that serve predominantly low-income students rarely have that luxury. (11) Not only do students from these schools lose access to creative expression when art funding is cut, but they are the ones an art education would benefit the most in terms of higher college admissions rates and increased cognitive ability.

1. Which edit should be made to correct sentence 3?

   (A) change *However* to *Still*
   (B) change *had* to *has*
   (C) change *including* to *among which are*
   (D) change *overall* to *median*

2. Which of the following is the best way to combine sentences 5 and 6?

   (A) The value of art education, however, is not only found in the fact that students learn these disciplines and in that it promotes self-expression and increases student engagement.
   (B) The value of art education, however, is not only found in the fact that students learn these disciplines but also in that it promotes self-expression and increases student engagement.
   (C) The value of art education, however, is not only found in the fact that students learn these disciplines, but it is also true that it promotes self-expression and increases student engagement.
   (D) The value of art education, however, is not only found in the fact that students learn these disciplines, and more importantly it promotes self-expression and increases student engagement.

3. Which revision of sentence 8 uses the most concise and precise language?

   (A) For very young students, art education can have beneficial, favorable, and advantageous effects such as improvement in dexterity and enhancement of language abilities.
   (B) Art education can improve dexterity and language ability, sometimes in young students.
   (C) It has been the case that sometimes very young students will also benefit from an art education and also in language abilities.
   (D) In cases of very young students, art education can improve both dexterity and language abilities.

4. Which sentence, if true, would best follow sentence 8?

   (A) More study should be given to which art forms lead to the largest increases in language ability for younger students.
   (B) Athletics is another part of schools' budgets that is often affected when schools try to save money.
   (C) Despite these benefits, many administrators still fail to prioritize art education in their budgets.
   (D) We can see from the many benefits provided by art education that the arts are, in fact, more important than English, Math, Science, and History.

5. Which of the following is the best revision of the underlined portion of sentence 10?

   (A) predominantly low-income students
   (B) predominantly, low-income students
   (C) predominantly low-income student's
   (D) predominantly, low-income students'

6. Which sentence would best serve as a conclusion to this passage?

   (A) Far from being dispensable or frivolous, art education funding provides material benefits to students, especially those students who need it most.
   (B) More research is needed to determine whether art education is more beneficial to students than other subjects.
   (C) It is clear that schools will dedicate more money to art education in the future.
   (D) Without art education, it is certain that most low-income students will fail to reach college.

Answers Explained

> **NOTE**
>
> We think that the process of elimination is such an important part of the Revising/Editing section of the SHSAT that, for most of the explanations, we will explain not only why the right answers are correct, but also why the other choices are incorrect.

PASSAGE 1: KRAFTWERK

1. **(C)** The first paragraph of this passage is about the contrast between the reader's expectations about and the reality of Kraftwerk's influence. In choice A, "So," implies a causal relationship between the first and second sentence that isn't there, so choice A is wrong. In choice B, "Apparently," implies that the author is unsure about the second sentence. Since that is not the case, choice B is wrong. In choice C, "Nonetheless," does capture the apparent contradiction between the first two sentences, so choice C is correct. In choice D, "Eventually," suggests that the transition between the first two sentences is about time, which it isn't, so we can eliminate choice D as well.

2. **(C)** Sentence 5 has two independent clauses (clauses with a subject and an active verb) linked with the coordinating conjunction *and*. When you link two independent clauses

with a coordinating conjunction, you need to put a comma before the coordinating conjunction. Therefore, choice C is the correct answer.

3. **(B)** Paragraph 2 is about the groundbreaking nature of Kraftwerk's sound. Therefore, to emphasize this, the sentence that follows sentence 6 should be about the newness of the techniques described there. It may be true that the technique would be commonplace by the 1990s, but that fact is irrelevant to the passage, so choice A is wrong. Choice B talks about the newness of the sounds from sentence 6, so choice B is the correct answer. Choice C is about the financial success of an album, a fact that doesn't have anything to do with the paragraph, so we can eliminate choice C. Choice D changes the subject of the paragraph to popularity, so we can eliminate choice D.

4. **(B)** Sentence 2 introduces the point of the passage and therefore should not be eliminated, so choice A is not the correct answer. Sentence 4 talks about the original use of a technology that Kraftwerk employs, but this is not related to the purpose of the passage. This sentence can be eliminated without compromising the meaning of the passage, so choice B is the correct answer. Sentence 6 further develops the point of the second paragraph, that Kraftwerk is a groundbreaking band, so it cannot be eliminated. Therefore, choice C is not the correct answer. Sentence 10 further establishes the breadth of Kraftwerk's influence that was introduced in sentence 9 and is the point of the last paragraph. That sentence does not need to be eliminated, so choice D is not the correct answer.

5. **(A)** Sentences 9 and 10 both discuss the genres of music that Kraftwerk has influenced. The best answer will be the one that combines the information in sentences 9 and 10 concisely without distorting it. Choice A does this, and is thus the correct answer. Choice B discusses the level of awareness about the band's influence, a topic that is not in the original sentences, so choice B is not the correct answer. Choice C does combine the information in sentences 9 and 10, but in an overly wordy way. Eliminate choice C. Choice D introduces an element of contrast between sentences 9 and 10 that is not in the original passage, so choice D is incorrect.

6. **(A)** This passage has been about Kraftwerk's influence, so its concluding sentence should reflect that fact. Choice A does this and is thus the correct answer. Choice B talks about the band members who make up Kraftwerk, a topic that is briefly introduced in the first paragraph but is not important enough to merit being the last sentence of the passage. Rule out choice B. Choice C introduces the topic of how much money Kraftwerk made, a topic that is never discussed in the passage, so choice C is not the correct answer. Choice D changes topics again to the private lives of the band members. Since this is not relevant to the rest of the passage, eliminate choice D.

PASSAGE 2: FUNDING FOR ARTS EDUCATION

1. **(B)** Choice A involves the transition between sentences 2 and 3. Since sentence 3 contrasts with sentence 2 rather than flowing from it, *However* is the correct word where it is. Eliminate choice A. Choice B involves verb tense, and the verb should be in present perfect tense rather than past perfect, so choice B is the correct answer. (Hint: Don't worry too much about the names of the different verb tenses. "Art education *has* been shown to lead to many benefits" establishes a fact and supports the point of the passage. "Art education *had* been shown to lead to many benefits" sounds like something that used to be true until someone came along to disprove it.) For choice C, the issue is concision. *Among*

which are is just a wordier way to say *including*, so *including* is better. We can eliminate choice C. For choice D, *median* changes the meaning of the sentence, so choice D is not the right answer.

2. **(B)** This question is about combining two sentences into one and determining the best way to compare two ideas in a sentence. Since all of the answer choices for this question have "not only" before the first idea, the correct way to format the sentence is to compare the ideas with "not only X but also Y." Choice B does this and is thus the correct answer. Choice A uses "not only … and" to link the two phrases, so it is wrong. Choice C uses "not only … but it is also true," which is unnecessarily wordy, so it too is wrong. Choice D uses "not only … and" again, so it is incorrect. Also, choice D introduces the phrase "more importantly," which changes the meaning of the sentence.

3. **(D)** For question 3, we need to find the best revision for a sentence in the passage. Choice A is the same sentence that appears in the passage with no changes made. While it is grammatically correct, it is too wordy. If you were doing process of elimination on an actual test, you would want to hold on to this answer for now, but look for another that is more concise. Choice B changes the meaning of the sentence. As written in the passage, the benefits were specifically for young people. In choice B, the benefits are only *sometimes* for young people. We can eliminate choice B. Choice C also changes the meaning of the sentence by adding "sometimes" before "very young students." It is also too wordy. Choice D is concise and preserves the meaning of the original sentence, making it the correct answer.

4. **(C)** The sentence that follows sentence 8 will end a paragraph that discusses the benefits of art education and introduce a paragraph that discusses the negative effects of cutting art education. Therefore, this sentence must facilitate the transition between these two ideas. Choice A shifts the topic from the benefits of art education to a need for more research as to the effects of art education. It also does not facilitate the transition between the two paragraphs. Eliminate choice A. Choice B completely changes the topic of the paragraph from the arts to athletics. Eliminate choice B. Choice C addresses the benefits of art education and reintroduces the fact that art education still does not always receive adequate funding. Choice C is the correct answer. Choice D takes the argument of paragraph 2 too far. The passage makes the case that art education is important, but it does not state that it is more important than other subjects. Eliminate choice D.

5. **(A)** The grammar issue in the underlined portion of sentence 10 is the use of commas and apostrophes. There is no reason for there to be a comma after "predominantly," so we can eliminate choices B and D. "Students" should be neither singular possessive, as in choice C, nor plural possessive, as in choice D, so we can eliminate both of them. Therefore, choice A is the correct answer.

6. **(A)** This passage is about the benefits of art education, not just for its own sake, but also for the sake of enhancing other aspects of the educational experience. Choice A reflects this and is thus the correct answer. Choice B changes the point of the passage and introduces the new topic of added research. Choice C shifts from the value of art education to the inevitability of the arts receiving more funding in the future, a prediction that is not supported by the passage. Choice D takes the negative effects of funding cuts for the arts too far. We know that low-income students see higher college admissions rates with art education. We do not know that most of them will fail to reach college without it.

> **DIRECTIONS:** Read and answer each of the following questions. You will be asked to recognize and correct errors in sentences or short paragraphs. Mark the **best** answer for each question.

1. Sputnik 1 was the first man-made satellite to be put into orbit. The Soviet Union launched Sputnik 1 into space using an R-7 rocket on October 4, 1957. Having achieved a low Earth orbit, Russian scientists were able to study radio signals sent back to Earth by Sputnik 1. The Sputnik 1 mission started the Space Race between the United States and the Soviet Union, which would go on to include other space missions like Sputnik 2, Sputnik 3, the Mercury Program, and the Apollo Moon landings.

    Which sentence should be revised to correct a misplaced modifier?

    (A) Sentence 1
    (B) Sentence 2
    (C) Sentence 3
    (D) Sentence 4

2. Beijing the capitol of modern China is located north of Shanghai.

    Which edits should be made to the preceding sentence?

    (A) There should be a comma after "Beijing."
    (B) There should be a comma after "China."
    (C) There should be a comma after "Beijing" and after "China."
    (D) There should be a comma after "Beijing," after "China," and after "north."

3. Casablanca is renowned as one of the most quoted movies of all time, <u>and as many people fail to know</u> its cast and crew didn't have a completed script when filming on it began.

    Which of the following is the best revision of the underlined portion of this sentence?

    (A) <u>, and as many people fail to know</u>
    (B) <u>, but what many people don't know is that</u>
    (C) <u>, however what many people don't fail to know is that</u>
    (D) <u>, so what many people don't know is that</u>

4. In order to better understand the world and their place in it, high school students should read a reputable newspaper every day. High schools should make newspapers available in their libraries.

    To clarify the relationship between the two sentences above, which transition should be added to the beginning of the second sentence?

    (A) For this reason,
    (B) Of course,
    (C) Moreover,
    (D) Ultimately,

5. Jedediah often referred to music history textbooks when he was learning to play the piano; whenever he practices a new style, he would read about the performers who pioneered it.

   In the preceding sentence, which verb should be changed?

   (A) referred
   (B) was
   (C) practices
   (D) read

Questions 6 and 7 refer to the following passage:

From 1154 to 1485, kings from the Plantagenet family ruled England. In general, the Plantagenets tried to retain as much power for the monarchy as possible, but on occasion they were forced to negotiate compromises with England's nobles and the Catholic Church. In the 1160s, conflict between Henry II and the Archbishop of Canterbury; Thomas Becket, helped establish the independence of the Catholic Church from the king's control. In 1215, rebel Barons forced another Plantagenet king, John I, to sign the Magna Carta, a document that limited the power of the king to impose taxes and imprison his enemies without trial.

6. The first underlined portion of the above passage should be changed to read:

   (A) possible, but on occasion
   (B) possible. Consequently, on occasion
   (C) possible, and occasionally
   (D) possible, and also they occasionally

7. The second underlined portion of the above passage should be changed to read:

   (A) the Archbishop of Canterbury Thomas Becket,
   (B) the Archbishop of Canterbury, Thomas Becket
   (C) the Archbishop of Canterbury, Thomas Becket,
   (D) the Archbishop of Canterbury Thomas Becket

8. Unfortunately Megan lost her job so she was forced to move into an older smaller house.

   Which edits should be made to the preceding sentence?

   (A) There should be a comma after "Unfortunately" and after "older."
   (B) There should be a comma after "job" and after "older."
   (C) There should be a comma after "Unfortunately," after "job," and after "older."
   (D) There should be a comma after "job," after "older," and after "forced."

9. After landing at the airport, <u>our hotel sent a cab to pick us up</u>.

   The underlined portion of the sentence should be changed to read:

   (A) our hotel sent a cab to pick us up.
   (B) a cab from our hotel picked us up.
   (C) a cab from our hotel was picking us up.
   (D) we found that our hotel had sent a cab to pick us up.

10. As he (1) <u>excitedly waited</u> for his girlfriend's plane to land, (2) <u>John decided</u> (3) <u>buying</u> a gift for her (4) <u>at</u> the airport gift shop.

    Which underlined portion of the sentence above needs to be changed?

    (A) 1
    (B) 2
    (C) 3
    (D) 4

11. The road manager packed up the instruments. The instruments belonged to the musicians.

    Which of the following is a correct way to combine the two sentences above?

    (A) The road manager packed up the musicians instrument's.
    (B) The road manager packed up the musician's instruments.
    (C) The road manager packed up the musicians' instruments.
    (D) The road manager packed up the musician's instrument's.

Answers Explained

> ### NOTE
> We think that the process of elimination is such an important part of the Revising/Editing section of the SHSAT that, for most of the explanations, we will explain not only why the right answers are correct, but also why the other choices are incorrect.

1. **(C)** This question is about finding a misplaced modifier. Misplaced modifiers occur when a modifying word or phrase is not placed next to the word it is meant to modify. Sentence 3 begins, "Having achieved a low Earth orbit, Russian scientists were able to … " Did Russian scientists achieve a low Earth orbit? No, Sputnik did. Sentence 3 has the misplaced modifier.

2. **(C)** This is a question about commas. A dependent clause that doesn't change the meaning of a sentence is called appositive and needs to be set off by commas. "Beijing, the capitol of modern China, is located north of Shanghai" and "Beijing is located north of Shanghai" have the same essential meaning, so "the capitol of modern China" is appositive and should have commas around it. Also, there is no need to put a comma after "north."

3. **(B)** This question is about choosing the correct conjunction and avoiding awkward words or phrases. Coordinating conjunctions (you can remember which words are coordinating conjunctions with the acronym FANBOYS: for, and, nor, but, or, yet, and so) link two independent clauses (clauses with a subject and an active verb). In this sentence, the clause "Casablanca is renowned as one of the most quoted movies of all time" contrasts with the second clause, which establishes the fact that Casablanca didn't have a completed script when filming began. The coordinating conjunction we use to link these two independent clauses should reflect this contrast. For choice A, "and" implies two independent clauses that express ideas that complement one another, making choice A incorrect. Also, the phrase "fail to know" is awkward, creating another reason why choice A is incorrect. For choice B, "but" captures the contrast between the two clauses. Also, "don't know" is less awkward than "fail to know." Therefore, choice B is the correct answer. For choice C, "however" does capture the contrast between the clauses, but "however" is not a coordinating conjunction, and it should be preceded by a semicolon, not a comma. Also, "don't fail to know" is a double negative. Eliminate choice C for these reasons. Choice D avoids awkward phrasing, but "so" incorrectly implies a casual relationship between the clauses. Reject choice D.

4. **(A)** This question is about finding the right word or phrase to facilitate a smooth transition between two sentences. The fact that students should read a newspaper every day is the reason why high schools should make them available in their libraries. Choice A, "For this reason," reflects this causal relationship and is the correct answer. None of the other answer choices reflect causality.

5. **(C)** This question is about verb tense. All of the verbs in the answer choices are appropriate for describing events that happened in the past except for "practices." Therefore, choice C is the verb that should be changed.

6. **(A)** This is another question about joining two independent clauses. Here, we have two contrasting clauses, one about kings trying to retain power and the other about how sometimes those kings had to compromise. Choice A uses the coordinating conjunction "but," which reflects this contrast, so choice A is the correct answer. Choice B breaks the two independent clauses into two distinct sentences, which is an acceptable way to deal with two independent clauses. However, choice B is wrong because "consequently" implies that one clause caused the other, not that they contrast. Choices C and D use "and," which implies continuity between the clauses, not contrast, so we can eliminate choices C and D. Also, choice D is unnecessarily wordy.

7. **(C)** This question is about commas and the right way to use them to set off a dependent clause. Here, the name "Thomas Beckett" does not change the meaning of the sentence. It is therefore an appositive dependent clause and should be set off with commas. Choices A and B only put commas on one side of the name, so both are wrong. Choice C uses commas on both sides of the name and is thus correct. Choice D has no commas at all and is therefore wrong.

8. **(C)** This question tests a number of issues involved in proper comma use. There are three places we need to use commas in this sentence. The first place is after the introductory word "Unfortunately." The second is before the coordinating conjunction "so." The third place is between the two adjectives that modify "house," "older" and "smaller." Choice A includes "Unfortunately" and "older" correctly, but forgets "job," so we can eliminate this

answer choice. Choice B includes "job" and "older," but misses "Unfortunately," so we can eliminate this choice as well. Choice C includes "Unfortunately," "job," and "older," so it is the correct answer. Choice D adds an unnecessary comma after "forced."

9. **(D)** This is another question about misplaced modifiers. The modifying clause "After landing at the airport" should be placed next to the word it is modifying, namely, the people who landed at the airport. Choice A places "hotel" after the modifying clause, so choice A is incorrect. (It would be absurd if the hotel had landed at the airport, right?) In choices B and C, "cab" comes immediately after the modifying clause, so we can eliminate these choices as well. Choice D places the people who landed at the airport after the modifying phrase, making it the correct answer.

10. **(C)** Here, we have four underlined sections of a sentence and we must evaluate each of them individually to find the one that needs to be changed. In choice A, "excitedly" is an adverb that modifies the verb "waited," which is correct. Also, "waited" is in the past tense, which is appropriate for this sentence. Therefore, portion 1 does not need to be corrected. In choice B, we have the subject and the active verb of the sentence. They agree and are in the correct tense, so portion 2 does not need to be corrected. Choice C uses a gerund, "buying," when an infinitive such as "to buy" is needed. Portion 3 should be changed. (Hint: Don't worry too much about the names of the verb tenses, but pay attention when you see a verb. Ask yourself if it sounds right with the rest of the sentence.) Choice D is about the use of the preposition "at." One can buy things "at" a gift shop or one can buy things "from" a gift shop, but "at" is acceptable, so portion 4 does not need to be changed.

11. **(C)** In this question, we are combining two sentences, but the grammar issue being tested is the use of apostrophes in plural and possessive nouns. The rules here are pretty simple:

- If a noun is plural and nothing in the sentence belongs to it, it takes an **s** but no apostrophe (i.e., *Five* **cats** *sat on the shelf.*).
- If a noun is singular, but something in the sentence does belong to it, it takes an **s** with an apostrophe before it (i.e., *The* **cat's** *ball of yarn fell on the floor.*).
- If a noun is plural and a thing or things in the sentence belong to it, it takes an **s** with an apostrophe after it (i.e., *The 5* **cats'** *saucers of milk sat on the floor.*).

In this question, are the musicians plural? Yes. Do they own something? Yes, the instruments. Therefore, "musicians'" is correct for this sentence. Are the instruments plural? Yes. Do they own something? No. Therefore, "instruments" is correct for this sentence. Choice C uses "musicians' instruments," so choice C is the correct answer.

The Redesigned Math Section

NEW MULTIPLE-CHOICE QUESTION FORMAT

The multiple-choice questions on the redesigned SHSAT will now offer **only four choices** from which to select an answer in contrast to the five choices offered on previous versions of the test. Of the 57 questions on the Math section, 52 are multiple-choice questions.

Sample Multiple-Choice Question and Solution

The area of a rectangle is 105. If the width is 15, what is the perimeter of this rectangle?

(A) 7
(B) 22
(C) 44
(D) 88

Solution:

(C) The area, A, of a rectangle is the product of its length, l, and its width, w, expressed as the formula $A = l \times w$. Therefore, $105 = l \times 15$, leading to $l = 7$. The perimeter is the sum of the lengths of the four sides. In general, the perimeter, p, of a rectangle is given by the formula $p = 2l + 2w$. Thus, the perimeter is $2(7) + 2(15) = 44$.

Reminders and Suggestions

- **Calculators are not permitted. No reference formulas will be supplied.**
- Carefully review the Mathematics "Skillbuilder" section in this book. Pay particular attention to the "Mathematical Problem Analysis" section.

Additional practice multiple-choice questions are located on pages 24–29.

NEW GRID-IN QUESTIONS

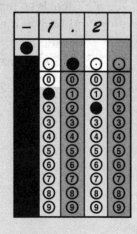

A "grid-in question" requires that you solve a problem by computing a numerical answer and placing that answer on an answer grid. This is different from a "multiple-choice question," which requires that you select the correct answer from among a given set of choices.

For example, if a problem asks you to compute the product of -3×0.4, then the answer, -1.2, would be correctly entered as shown on the grid on the right.

The official directions that you will see on the actual exam appear as follows:

Directions: Solve each problem. On the answer sheet, write your answer in the boxes at the top of the grid. Start on the left side of each grid. Print only one number or symbol in each box. **DO NOT LEAVE A BOX BLANK IN THE MIDDLE OF AN ANSWER.** Under each box, fill in the circle that matches the number or symbol you wrote above. **DO NOT FILL IN A CIRCLE UNDER AN UNUSED BOX.**

Additional practice grid-in questions are located on pages 30–32.

GENERAL TIPS

(1) ***No calculators are permitted, so do not practice with them!***

(2) *Immediately after solving (and checking) a problem:*

- Enter the answer in the boxes in the top line of its grid.
- If you skip a problem, be sure to also skip the grid for that problem.

(3) *When entering your answer in the top line of the grid, note that:*

- The first box is **only** used if the answer has a minus (–) sign.
- For accuracy and consistency, the rest of your answer should be entered starting at the second box, with each box you use getting either a digit (from 0 to 9) or a decimal point (.).
- Do not leave any blank boxes **within** the answer.

(4) *Under each box in the top line:*

- Fill in the circle that matches the number or symbol you entered at the top.
- If you change the top boxes later, be sure to erase and correct the filled in circles below.
- **If there is no entry in a top box, do not fill in any circles below that box.**
- **Be accurate:** Grading is based on the filled in circles, not on your entries in the top line.

(5) *Additional suggestions:*

- Be sure to place your answer in the top line before filling in the circles; this helps ensure accuracy and helps prevent gridding errors.
- There is no penalty for wrong answers, so when you finish the problems you know, go back and enter your best guess for the questions you skipped. **Answer every question!**
- Review the material in the Mathematics "Skillbuilder" section in this book.

Samples of Correct and Incorrect Gridding*

Suppose the answer is –3.2:

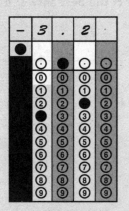

acceptable

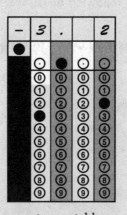

not acceptable
(has blank box
within answer)

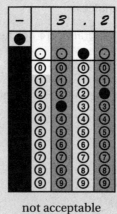

not acceptable
(has blank box
within answer)

Suppose the answer is 602:

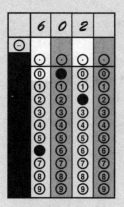

acceptable

not acceptable
(the filled in 0 in
the last column
changes the
answer to 6020)

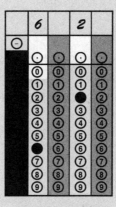

not acceptable
(has blank box
within answer)

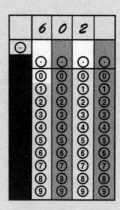

not acceptable
(column numbers
not filled in)

*The Department of Education may make additional revisions regarding "acceptable" and
"not acceptable" answers. Be sure to obtain the latest copy of the DOE Handbook.

MULTIPLE-CHOICE—PRACTICE QUESTIONS

DIRECTIONS: For each of the following questions, select the best answer from the given choices.

NOTE: Diagrams are not necessarily drawn to scale.

1. Which of the following numbers is closest to $\frac{3}{4}$?

   (A) $\frac{31}{40}$

   (B) $\frac{61}{80}$

   (C) 0.76

   (D) 0.741

2. The mean of x and y is 6. The mean of 1, 3, $5x$, and $5y$ is

   (A) 8.5
   (B) 12
   (C) 16
   (D) 32

3. The cost of purchasing some items is calculated as follows: Each item costs $13, and there is an initial fee of $7. For example, if 2 items were ordered, the total cost would be $33. The total cost of Tony's order was $$T$. It follows that T could be

   (A) 113
   (B) 123
   (C) 137
   (D) 146

4. Amy, Betty, and Carlos together received a sum of money, which was distributed among them as follows: First Amy took $\frac{1}{2}$ of the total money, then Betty took $\frac{1}{4}$ of the remaining money, and finally Carlos took $6. If no money was left, how much was originally received?

   (A) $8
   (B) $16
   (C) $24
   (D) $32

5. Let x, y, and z be positive numbers such that $2x = 5y = 3z$. Then, it must be true that

   (A) $x < y < z$
   (B) $x < z < y$
   (C) $y < x < z$
   (D) $y < z < x$

6. On the number line below, point A is located at –4 and point B is located at 20. AQ is $\frac{3}{8}$ of the distance from A to B, while BR is $\frac{3}{8}$ of the distance from B to A. Find the length of QR.

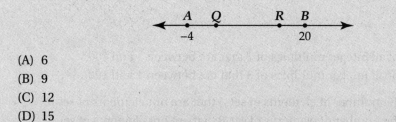

(A) 6
(B) 9
(C) 12
(D) 15

7. In the diagram below, three of the four straight lines intersect in a single point. Certain angles have their degree measures indicated. The value of x is

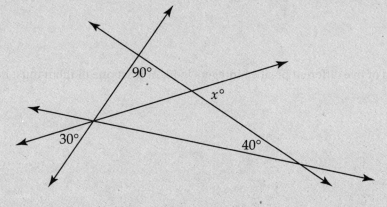

(A) 50
(B) 60
(C) 70
(D) 80

8. If $x < x^3 < x^2$, which of the following could be a possible value for x?

(A) $-\frac{1}{2}$

(B) 0.1

(C) 0.5

(D) $\frac{2}{3}$

9. The mean (average) of Sophia's five test grades is 80. The only possible test grades are integers between 0 and 100 inclusive. She will take one more test. The mean of *all six grades* can be any of the following numbers EXCEPT

(A) 70
(B) 76
(C) 83
(D) 85

10. If 8 times 10^{11} is $\dfrac{5}{9}$ of K, then the value of K expressed in scientific notation is

    (A) 1.44×10^{12}
    (B) 14.4×10^{9}
    (C) 1.44×10^{13}
    (D) 14.4×10^{10}

11. Let A be the set of all integer multiples of 7 that are between 1 and 100.
Let B be the set of all integer multiples of 3 that are between 1 and 100.

Let x represent the number of elements of set A that are not elements of set B.
Let y represent the number of elements of set B that are not elements of set A.

Compute the *sum* $x + y$.

    (A) 28
    (B) 29
    (C) 39
    (D) 43

12. The sum of five different positive integers is 40. At least one of them must be greater than

    (A) 9
    (B) 10
    (C) 11
    (D) 12

13. Square $ABCD$, whose sides are parallel to the axes, is located in the coordinate plane as shown in the diagram below.

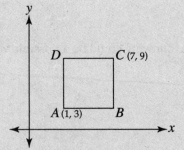

The coordinates of vertex A and vertex C are indicated. The square is first reflected in the x-axis and then that image is rotated 180° counterclockwise about the origin. After that rotation, the image of vertex B is $B'(h, k)$. The value of k is

    (A) 1
    (B) 3
    (C) 7
    (D) 10

14. Lily is unable to solve two multiple-choice questions, each question having exactly four answer choices. She decides to randomly guess. Each choice has the same chance of being selected, and her choice selection on one question does not influence her choice selection on the other question. What is the probability that Lily answers at least one of the two questions correctly?

(A) $\dfrac{7}{16}$

(B) $\dfrac{1}{2}$

(C) $\dfrac{9}{16}$

(D) $\dfrac{15}{16}$

15. The mean of four numbers, a, b, 60, and 70, is 46. The numbers a and b are positive *even* integers. What is the largest possible value of the median of this set of four numbers?

(A) 56

(B) 57

(C) 58

(D) 60

Answers Explained

1. **(D)** Note that $\dfrac{3}{4} = 0.75 = \dfrac{30}{40} = \dfrac{60}{80}$. To determine which number is closest, find the difference between $\dfrac{3}{4}$ and each choice as follows:

   (A) $\dfrac{31}{40} - \dfrac{30}{40} = \dfrac{1}{40}$

   (B) $\dfrac{61}{80} - \dfrac{60}{80} = \dfrac{1}{80}$

   (C) $0.76 - 0.75 = 0.01 = \dfrac{1}{100}$

   (D $|0.741 - 0.750| = |-0.009| = \dfrac{9}{1000}$

   The smallest difference comes from choice D.

2. **(C)** We have $\dfrac{(x+y)}{2} = 6$, so $x + y = 12$. Now $\dfrac{5(x+y)+4}{4} = \dfrac{5(12)+4}{4} = \dfrac{64}{4} = 16$.

3. **(C)** If Tony bought x items, where x is a positive integer, then the total cost, T, would be $13x + 7$. Thus, $T = 13x + 7$. Subtracting 7 from both sides of this equation produces $T - 7 = 13x$ (note that $13x$ is a multiple of 13 since x is an integer). Subtract 7 from each of the given choices to determine which difference is a multiple of 13. Doing that leads to the answer, which is 137.

4. **(B)**

   Method I: After Amy took her share of the money, $\dfrac{1}{2}$ of the original amount remained. Betty then took $\dfrac{1}{4}$ of $\dfrac{1}{2}$ of the money, which is equivalent to $\dfrac{1}{8}$ of the original amount

$\left(\frac{1}{4} \text{ times } \frac{1}{2} \text{ is } \frac{1}{8}\right)$. This left $\frac{1}{2} - \frac{1}{8}$ or $\frac{3}{8}$ of the original amount of money for Carlos.

Carlos took \$6, implying that \$6 is $\frac{3}{8}$ of the original amount of money. If \$6 is $\frac{3}{8}$ of the original amount of money, then \$2 is $\frac{1}{8}$ of the original amount. Therefore, the original sum of money was \$16.

Method II: Use Algebra.
Let x represent the total amount of money originally received.

Amy took $\left(\frac{1}{2}\right)x$; therefore, $\left(\frac{1}{2}\right)x$ remained.

Betty then took $\frac{1}{4}$ of what remained, which is $\left(\frac{1}{4}\right)\left(\frac{1}{2}\right)x = \left(\frac{1}{8}\right)x$.

Carlos then took all that was left, which is \$6.
Adding together what each person took gives us the original amount of money received,

which is x. Therefore, $\left(\frac{x}{2}\right) + \left(\frac{x}{8}\right) + 6 = x$. We now clear all the fractions by multiplying

each side by 8, producing $4x + x + 48 = 8x$. Thus, $48 = 3x$, which means that $x = 16$ or \$16.

Method III: The correct answer may also be quickly revealed by testing each of the answer choices.

5. **(D)** Method I: $2x = 5y$ leads to $x = \left(\frac{5}{2}\right)y$, which is $\left(2\frac{1}{2}\right)y$

                    $5y = 3z$ leads to $z = \left(\frac{5}{3}\right)y$, which is $\left(1\frac{2}{3}\right)y$

Now, we see that $(1)y < \left(1\frac{2}{3}\right)y < \left(2\frac{1}{2}\right)y$, so $y < z < x$

Method II: To gain some leverage in solving this problem, we may first attempt to assign some values to x, y, and z that satisfy the given conditions. Notice that in the equation $2x = 5y = 3z$, all of the numerical coefficients, namely, 2, 5, and 3, are factors of 30. If we let $2x = 5y = 3z = 30$, then $x = 15$, $y = 6$, and $z = 10$. Thus, $y < z < x$ as in choice D. More generally, we may set $2x = 5y = 3z = k$, where k is any positive number. This leads to $x = \left(\frac{1}{2}\right)k$, $y = \left(\frac{1}{5}\right)k$, and $z = \left(\frac{1}{3}\right)k$. Since k is positive, the inequality in choice D is correct.

6. **(A)** $AB = 20 - (-4) = 24$, so $AQ = \left(\frac{3}{8}\right)(24) = 9$.

Similarly, $BR = \left(\frac{3}{8}\right)(24) = 9$.

Finally, $QR = AB - AQ - BR = 24 - 9 - 9 = 6$.

7. **(B)** When two lines intersect, the vertical angles formed are equal. In the small right triangle formed, the lower left angle and the given 30° angle are vertical angles, so the lower left angle is also equal to 30°. Consequently, the third angle of that right triangle is 60°. That "third angle" and the angle whose degree measures x are vertical angles. Therefore, $x = 60$. Note that the 40° angle is not needed for this solution and is given as a "distractor."

8. **(A)** $-\frac{1}{2} < -\frac{1}{8} < \frac{1}{4}$ (choice A is right) $0.5 > (0.5)^2 = 0.25$ (choice C is wrong)

  $0.1 > (0.1)^3 = 0.001$ (choice B is wrong) $\frac{2}{3} > \left(\frac{2}{3}\right)^2 = \frac{4}{9}$ (choice D is wrong)

9. **(D)** Let t be Sophia's grade on the sixth test, and let M be the mean of all 6 tests. Note that the <u>sum</u> of the first 5 test grades is 400 (that is, 80×5). Then, $\frac{(400+t)}{6} = M$, leading to $t = 6M - 400$. Remember that t must be an integer between 0 and 100 inclusive. Expressing this as an inequality, we have $0 \le 6M - 400 \le 100$ or equivalently $400 \le 6M \le 500$. Therefore, $66\frac{2}{3} \le M \le 83\frac{1}{3}$. Thus, the mean of *all six grades* cannot be 85.

10. **(A)** $8 \times 10^{11} = \frac{5K}{9}$, so $K = 72 \times \frac{10^{11}}{5}$. To simplify the right side, write it as $72 \times 10^{10} \times \frac{10}{5}$. Then, divide the 5 into the 10. We now have $K = 72 \times 10^{10} \times 2$, which is 144×10^{10}. To change to scientific notation, we write this as 1.44×10^{12}.

11. **(C)** Set A consists of the numbers $7 \bullet 1, 7 \bullet 2, 7 \bullet 3, \dots, 7 \bullet 14$, which is 14 elements. We must remove from this set any multiples of 3 (namely $7 \bullet 3, 7 \bullet 6, 7 \bullet 9, 7 \bullet 12$), which is 4 elements. Therefore, $x = 14 - 4 = 10$ elements.

    Set B consists of the numbers $3 \bullet 1, 3 \bullet 2, 3 \bullet 3, \dots, 3 \bullet 33$, which is 33 elements. We must remove from this set any multiples of 7 (namely $3 \bullet 7, 3 \bullet 14, 3 \bullet 21, 3 \bullet 28$), which is 4 elements. Therefore, $y = 33 - 4 = 29$ elements.

    The final answer is $10 + 29 = 39$. You may try doing this using Venn diagrams.

12. **(A)** If none of the integers is greater than 9, the maximum possible sum would be $5 + 6 + 7 + 8 + 9 = 35$. Therefore, at least one of the integers must be greater than 9 [for example: $6 + 7 + 8 + 9 + 10 = 40$]. Thus, choice A is correct. This example also shows that none of the integers need be greater than 10.

13. **(B)** First, determine the coordinates of point B. Using the fact that $ABCD$ is a square whose sides are parallel to the axes, the coordinates of B are quickly found to be $(7, 3)$. A reflection in the x-axis transforms $(7, 3)$ into $(7, -3)$. The rotation then transforms $(7, -3)$ in $(-7, 3)$. The value of k is therefore 3.

14. **(A)** Note that p, the probability of guessing a correct answer to a question having four choices, is $\frac{1}{4}$. The probability of getting a question wrong is $\frac{3}{4}$. We may approach this problem by first computing the probability that Lily answers *both questions incorrectly*. This is computed by multiplying $\frac{3}{4}$ by $\frac{3}{4}$ since the events are independent. Thus, the probability that Lily answers *both questions incorrectly* is $\frac{9}{16}$. Subtracting $\frac{9}{16}$ from 1 gives us the probability that Lily does *NOT answer both questions incorrectly*, meaning that she had to answer at least one of the two questions correctly. The correct answer to this problem is $1 - \frac{9}{16} = \frac{7}{16}$. Try doing this problem directly by listing all possible favorable outcomes or by making a tree diagram.

15. **(A)** The mean is $\frac{(a+b+60+70)}{4} = 46$. Simplifying this equation leads to $a + b = 54$.

    Suppose that $a < b$, then the largest possible value for b is 52 (remember that both a and b must be positive, even integers). In order to determine the median, the four numbers must be placed in increasing order: a, b, 60, 70. The median is halfway between b and 60, so we choose the largest possible value for b, which is 52. That makes the median equal to $\frac{(52+60)}{2} = \frac{112}{2} = 56$.

GRID-IN—PRACTICE QUESTIONS

> **DIRECTIONS:** Solve each of the following problems by computing a numerical answer and placing that answer on the appropriate answer grid. Grids are provided at the end of this section.
>
> **NOTE:** Diagrams are not necessarily drawn to scale.

1. The square root of 1,000 lies between the two consecutive integers N and $N + 1$. Compute the value of N.

2. A survey of a large sample of people revealed that:

   (i) 1 out of 3 people surveyed have medical condition X

   (ii) 9 out of 10 people who have medical condition X don't know that they have it

   Based only on this information, if there were 6,600 people in the sample, how many don't know that they have medical condition X?

3. It takes 3 hours to completely fill Demarco's empty tank. Water is pumped at a constant rate. During the first 40 minutes, 800 gallons of water was pumped into the tank. How many gallons does it take to completely fill his tank?

4. The diagram to the right shows a scale drawing of a room as part of a floor plan. The lengths are indicated in centimeters (cm). In this drawing, 5 cm represents 8 feet. What is the perimeter, *in feet*, of the actual room that is represented in this scale drawing? Note that all "corners" meet at right angles.

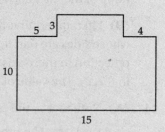

5. Solve for x if $\dfrac{2.8}{0.14} = \dfrac{x}{0.09}$.

6. How many even, two-digit numbers do not contain the digit 6? (Reminder: The tens digit of a two-digit number cannot be zero (0).)

7. The number 8,406 has precisely one three-digit prime factor. Compute that factor.

8. In the figure below, the sum of the areas of congruent squares *DHKG* and *IEBF* is equal to the area of square *ABCD*. If the area of square *GLFC* is 100, what is the area of square *IJKL*?

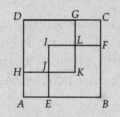

9. After $-\frac{1}{2}$ is divided by $-\frac{2}{3}$, the result obtained is multiplied by -3. Compute the final result.

10. The mean of five consecutive integers is M. The number 18 is one of the five integers. When 18 is removed, the mean of the remaining four integers is 16.75. What is the smallest of the original set of five consecutive integers?

Grid in your answers for questions 1–10 below.

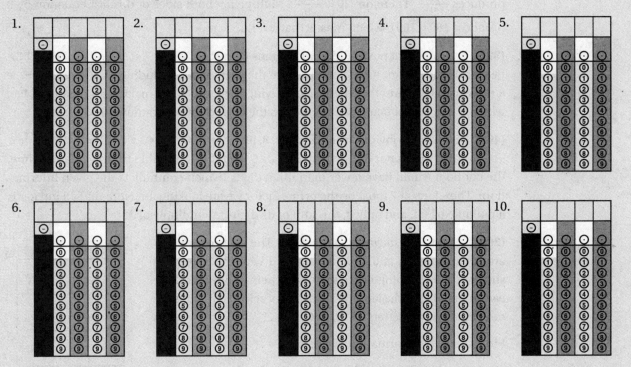

Answers Explained

1. **(31)** The problem indicates that N^2 would be less than 1,000, but $(N+1)^2$ would be more than 1,000. Testing well-chosen numbers, $30^2 = 900$, $31^2 = 961$, and $32^2 = 1,024$, so $N = 31$.

2. **(1,980)** Based on the given information, $\frac{1}{3}$ of the 6,600 people have medical condition X. Therefore, 2,200 people have medical condition X. Of those 2,200 people, $\frac{9}{10}$ of them don't know they have it. Finally, $\frac{9}{10}$ of 2,200 is 1,980. More directly,

$$\left(\frac{1}{3}\right)\left(\frac{9}{10}\right)6{,}600 = 1{,}980$$

3. **(3,600)** 3 hours = 3 • 60 minutes = 180 minutes. Every 40 minutes, 800 gallons is pumped into the tank. Compute how many times 40 minutes goes into 3 hours, then multiply that by 800. Our final answer will be $\left(\frac{180}{40}\right)$ • 800, which is 3,600 gallons.

4. **(89.6)** The sum of the lengths of the horizontal line segments is $15 + 15 = 30$. The sum of the lengths of the vertical line segments is $10 + 3 + 3 + 10 = 26$. Thus, the perimeter, P, as represented on the scale drawing, is 56 cm. The scaling factor is $\frac{8}{5}$. Using the proportion $\frac{8}{5} = \frac{P}{56}$ produces $P = 89.6$ feet.

5. **(1.8)** Multiplying both the numerator and the denominator of the fraction on the left side of the equation by 100 produces $\frac{280}{14}$, which is equal to 20. Multiplying both the numerator and the denominator of the fraction on the right side of the equation by 100 produces $\frac{100x}{9}$. Therefore $20 = \frac{100x}{9}$. Multiplying both sides of this last equation by 9 produces $180 = 100x$, which means that $x = 1.8$.

6. **(32)** There are eight possibilities for the tens digit (1, 2, 3, 4, 5, 7, 8, 9) and four possibilities for the units digit (0, 2, 4, 8; these are the even digits, excluding 6), so the answer is $8 \cdot 4$, which is 32. Another method of solving this problem is making an organized list, which is not very difficult and will lead to the correct answer rather quickly.

7. **(467)** Dividing by obvious prime factors, $8{,}406 = 2 \cdot 4{,}203 = 2 \cdot 3 \cdot 1{,}401 = 2 \cdot 3 \cdot 3 \cdot 467$. The number 467 is not divisible by 2, 3, or 5, and if it is divisible by any greater prime, the quotient would have fewer than three digits (which contradicts the given information). Therefore, 467 must be the prime factor we are looking for. Note that an integer is a multiple of 3 if, and only if, the sum of its digits is a multiple of 3.

8. **(200)** Refer to the diagram to the right. The sides of congruent squares *DHKG* and *IEBF* are marked with the letter x as shown; the remaining outer segments, being congruent, are each marked with the letter y. The areas of selected regions are designated by the letters *M*, *N*, *P*, *Q*, and *Z*.

   From the given information, we have:

   $$(M + Z) + (P + Z) = M + N + P + Q + Z$$

   Simplifying gives us:

   $$2Z = N + Q + Z$$
   $$Z = N + Q$$

   $N = y^2 = Q$. Thus, $Z = N + N = 2N = 200$.

9. **(−2.25)** $\left(-\frac{1}{2}\right)$ divided by $\left(-\frac{2}{3}\right)$ is equal to $\left(-\frac{1}{2}\right)$ times $\left(-\frac{3}{2}\right)$, which equals $\frac{3}{4}$.

   Next, $\left(\frac{3}{4}\right) \cdot (-3) = -\frac{9}{4}$. Because this must be placed on a grid, it must be changed to decimal form, which is −2.25.

10. **(15)** Let the original set of numbers be x, $x + 1$, $x + 2$, $x + 3$, and $x + 4$. Their mean is their sum divided by 5, which is $\frac{(5x+10)}{5}$, which is $x + 2 = M$. If we remove 18, the mean of the remaining four numbers is their sum divided by 4, which is $\frac{(5x+10-18)}{4}$ or $\frac{(5x-8)}{4}$. Setting this equal to 16.75 and multiplying both sides by 4, we get $5x - 8 = 67$. Solving for x, we get $x = 15$.

BARRON'S

NEW YORK CITY

SHSAT

SPECIALIZED HIGH SCHOOLS ADMISSIONS TEST

4TH EDITION

LAWRENCE ZIMMERMAN, M.A.
GILBERT KESSLER
ANNE VILLEPONTEAUX, M.A.

BARRON'S

Note: *Barron's New York City SHSAT, 4th Edition* includes 32 blue-tinted pages at the beginning of the book that highlight recent changes made to the Specialized High Schools Admissions Test. These changes will be reflected in the Fall 2017 exam. For more information on this test, and for news and updates, please visit *http://schools.nyc.gov/accountability/resources/testing/shsat.htm*.

Barron's would like to thank Lawrence Zimmerman and Gilbert Kessler, the writers of the Supplement, and Eric Schlosser, who contributed the ELA section. Barron's greatly appreciates their invaluable advice regarding the redesigned SHSAT.

All inquiries should be addressed to:
Barron's Educational Series, Inc.
250 Wireless Boulevard
Hauppauge, New York 11788
www.barronseduc.com

ISBN: 978-1-4380-1072-4

ISSN: 2168-8249

Printed in the United States of America
9 8 7 6 5 4 3 2 1

Contents

The Barron's Advantage

You have already made TWO very good decisions!

You have decided to attend one of the best high schools in the country, and you have chosen the right test prep book.

Here's why Barron's *SHSAT* for New York City Specialized High Schools gives you the ADVANTAGE.

- **More than 600 practice problems** cover every aspect of the actual test.
- **Three full-length** practice tests and **four minitests** written in the style and at the level of the actual test offer plenty of practice to test what you know.
- **Detailed solutions to every practice test problem are given.** These solutions feature useful TIPS and FACTS that provide topical review as you go.
- **Study guides,** powerful and productive **test-taking strategies,** and lots and lots of **model problems** solved and analyzed in detail let you proceed at your own pace.
- **Skillbuilders** that carefully guide you through each type of test question with additional practice exercises give you even more opportunities to test your knowledge. The unique **Math Diagnosers** find and correct any weaknesses while reinforcing your strengths.
- **Logical Reasoning** examples and explanations help you master this traditionally difficult part of the test.

Students have told us that much of the other test prep materials they have used in the past was too easy—that when it came time for the actual test, they were in for a big surprise. The questions you find in Barron's test prep materials accurately reflect the level of difficulty of the actual test. The Barron's authors are experts in their fields, with more than forty years of experience.

Preface

Admission to the New York City Specialized High Schools has become increasingly competitive. Now more than ever, good test preparation is essential.

The Admissions Test is a challenging test that calls for logical thinking and strong ability in both English and mathematics. To be successful, you must be very well prepared. That means you must have your mathematical and reading skills in top working order, you should be thoroughly familiar with the test format and types of questions that will be asked, and you should be aware of test-taking tips that will help you score well. A major approach to all of this is practicing with well-written, comprehensive test prep materials.

This book has been written with these aims in mind. You will find a wealth of carefully crafted material to help you achieve your goal. In addition to practice tests with detailed solutions and explanations, there are sections devoted to strengthening your skills in each of the four major areas covered by the test. The design of the book allows you to work at your own pace. Care has been taken to ensure accuracy, especially regarding mathematical concepts and terminology. Topical review is actually contained within the solutions and the Skillbuilders, where important information, facts, and tips have been highlighted and explained.

We would especially like to thank Peter Mavrikis, Editorial Director, Test Prep Division and Samantha Karasik, Editor, Test Prep Division for their very insightful advice and valuable assistance in preparing this latest edition.

INSIDE THE SHSAT

Introduction

AN OVERVIEW

The specialized high schools of New York City offer a wide range of excellent academic programs. Whereas some emphasize mathematics, science, technology, and engineering, others stress social science and the humanities.

Admission to these schools is based entirely on one single exam—the New York City Specialized High Schools Admissions Test, often referred to as the SHSAT. Basing admission on a single exam may seem unfair, but it is prescribed by New York State law. More than 20,000 students compete for the limited number of places available in these specialized schools each year, so to have a real advantage, you must adequately prepare for this annual test. Even if you are the best and the brightest, and many of you are, you can significantly enhance your chances of admission to the school of your choice with good test prep and guided practice and review.

When Should You Begin to Prepare?
What Do You Have to Do?

The sooner you begin, the more time you will have to prepare. Some students begin more than a year in advance. This book allows you to proceed at your own pace and provides you with all the material you need to perform well on the exam.

What's on the Test?

The test consists of two major sections

> **Verbal** (three parts)
> > Scrambled Paragraphs
> > Logical Reasoning
> > Reading

> **Mathematics**

Both sections are made up of multiple-choice questions. Each section is worth 50 points. There is a time limit of 150 minutes, with no break. It is recommended that you allow 75 minutes for each of the two sections, but you are permitted to allocate the time however you wish. There is no penalty for wrong answers or omissions (questions left blank), so it is to your advantage to bubble in an answer to every question, even if you must guess. Detailed descriptions of each section are found on pages 6–11.

The number of correct answers you get is converted into a so-called scaled score that is used to determine your standing. The conversion formulas vary from year to year.

When Is the Test Administered?

The test has traditionally been given in late October. It is for admission in the following September. For example, you would take the October 2013 exam for admission in September 2014. Be sure to verify this year's test dates and locations. The test is administered to current eighth graders seeking admission to the ninth grade, and another form of the test is given to current ninth graders seeking admission to the tenth grade. The overwhelming number of applicants are eighth graders.

How and When Do I Obtain Information and Application Forms?

You must get information regarding applications and test sites from your guidance counselor. Do this early in September. In addition, you should obtain a copy of the *Specialized High Schools Student Handbook.* This is available from your guidance counselor or online from the Department of Education Office. The *Handbook* contains additional current information regarding the test sites and any special rules that may apply.

All procedures and dates are subject to change. Be sure to obtain current information from your counselor or the handbook.

What Decisions Do I Have to Make?

You have to decide, in advance, which will be your first, second, etc., choice of schools. Where you actually take the exam does not affect your indicated choice of schools. You may take the exam only once in any given year. Violation of this rule will disqualify you from attending any of the specialized schools.

> **IMPORTANT:** If your score on the exam is high enough to gain admission to your first-choice school, you are fully expected to attend that school.

What Score Do I Need?

Your total number of correct answers is your raw score. The raw score is converted to a scaled score by means of a special formula. This process converts your raw score into an integer between 200 and 800. (The Department of Education does not publicly release the conversion formulas.) The scaled scores are not directly proportional to the raw scores. For example, at the middle range of scores, a difference of one correct answer may change the scaled score by only a few points, whereas at higher and lower ranges, a difference of one correct answer may change the scaled score by 10 to 20 points. The cut-off score (minimum scaled score needed) for each of the schools is determined by how many places each school has available.

Although we can prepare you for the test, there are some things we cannot do. We cannot predict the cut-off scores and we cannot tell you precisely how many questions you have to answer correctly to achieve a particular cut-off score.

Trends over the years indicate that the number of students taking the test is increasing and that cut-off scores are rising.

The Summer Discovery Program

Certain applicants whose scores are just short of the cut-off score may qualify for the Summer Discovery Program. Successful completion of this program allows qualifying students to gain admission. The eligibility requirements for admission to this program include

- scoring just below the cut-off score.
- recommendation from counselor, and documentation of special circumstances and needs. See your counselor and the *Handbook* for details.

THE SPECIALIZED HIGH SCHOOLS

Bronx High School of Science
75 West 205th Street; Bronx, New York 10468
Telephone: (718) 817-7700   Website: www.bxscience.edu

Brooklyn Latin School
325 Bushwick Avenue; Brooklyn, New York 11206

Brooklyn Technical High School
South Elliot Place at DeKalb Avenue; Brooklyn, New York 11217
Telephone: (718) 804-6400   Website: www.bths.edu

High School for Mathematics, Science and Engineering at City College
138th Street and Convent Avenue; New York, New York 10031
Telephone: (212) 220-8179   Website: www.hsmse.org

High School of American Studies at Lehman College
2925 Goulden Avenue; Bronx, New York 10468
Telephone: (718) 329-2144   Website: www.lehman.cuny.edu/hsas

Queens High School for the Sciences at York College
94-50 159th Street; Jamaica, New York 11451
Telephone: (718) 657-3181   Website: www.qhssyc.org

Staten Island Technical High School
485 Clawson Street; Staten Island, New York 10306
Telephone: (718) 667-5725   Website: www.siths.org

Stuyvesant High School
345 Chambers Street; New York, New York 10282-1099
Telephone: (212) 312-4800   Website: www.stuy.edu

THE TEST: A DETAILED DESCRIPTION

Overview

The SHSAT consists of two major sections: Verbal and Mathematics. The time limit is 150 minutes total for both sections with no break. The suggested time is 75 minutes for each section.

Verbal Section: 45 multiple-choice questions, total value 50 points

- 5 Scrambled Paragraph sets
- 10 Logical Reasoning questions
- 5 Reading passages, each followed by 6 related questions

Mathematics Section: 50 multiple-choice questions, total value 50 points

- 50 Mathematics questions covering a range of topics and testing a variety of skills and abilities

There is no penalty for wrong or omitted answers.

The Details

Scrambled Paragraphs

DESCRIPTION

In each Scrambled Paragraph set, you are presented with an initial sentence followed by five sentences in random order. You must arrange these five sentences to form a paragraph that is well organized, logical, and grammatically correct.

POINT VALUE

Each set of six sentences is worth two points. There is NO partial credit granted for partially correct ordering. The five sets of questions are worth a total of 10 points.

DIRECTIONS

The usual directions instruct you to select the order of the five given sentences that will create the **best** paragraph, one that is both well organized and grammatically correct. You should certainly make notes in your test booklet as you work on ordering the sentences. You cannot do this all in your head! Some students find that, rather than beginning by assigning numbers to the sentences, it makes sense to arrange the letters visually, in some blank space on the page in your test booklet. For instance, you may know that S comes before Q without knowing the number of either sentence yet, so you might write an S in the margin before a Q, leaving space to put the other letters on either side as needed. Working through the practice problems in this book will help you find a notation system that works for you. Finally, transfer your answers to the answer grid.

EXAMPLE

Paragraph 1

Most people are more familiar with butterflies than moths because butterflies are diurnal and moths nocturnal.

_____ (Q)   One obvious difference is the antennae, which in butterflies are slender, long, and knobbed and in moths are thicker and furry-looking.

_____ (R)   Another difference is that the resting butterfly folds its wings up, closing them, whereas the wings of the resting moth are held straight out or folded down.

_____ (S)   They are similar insects, but in addition to their habits, there are ways to distinguish between them on sight.

_____ (T)   A final visible difference is that a butterfly's body is slender and smooth-looking and a moth's is thick and sometimes, like the antennae, furry-looking.

_____ (U)   Distinguishing between these two insects is, therefore, not a difficult task—if you can get a close look at one before it flies away.

The Grid

Paragraph 1

The second sentence is   Ⓠ Ⓡ Ⓢ Ⓣ Ⓤ

The third sentence is   Ⓠ Ⓡ Ⓢ Ⓣ Ⓤ

The fourth sentence is   Ⓠ Ⓡ Ⓢ Ⓣ Ⓤ

The fifth sentence is   Ⓠ Ⓡ Ⓢ Ⓣ Ⓤ

The sixth sentence is   Ⓠ Ⓡ Ⓢ Ⓣ Ⓤ

The Answer

The correct order of the sentences is S Q R T U. This example is discussed in Skillbuilder A: Scrambled Paragraphs. A full explanation of the answer is given there. *All the examples that follow here are selected from the Skillbuilders beginning on page 41.*

Logical Reasoning

DESCRIPTION

Each multiple-choice question asks you to **draw a logical conclusion or conclusions based only on given information.** Among the question types are those requiring you to determine the relative positions of people or objects, decipher simple codes, interpret clues to help draw a valid conclusion, and so on. There are many variations of this type of question. Usually present are some linked questions (two or more questions based on the same given information).

POINT VALUE

Each of 10 Logical Reasoning questions is worth one point, for a total of 10 points.

DIRECTIONS

The usual directions instruct you to read the given information and, **based only on the information given**, choose the **best** answer to each question. You are cautioned to read the words very carefully and not read into the question information that is not actually present. For example, the phrase "the green book is below the red book" does not necessarily mean that the green book is directly below the red book (with no other books in between). Thus, there could be one or more books between the red and green books.

EXAMPLE

11. Five different-colored blocks are stacked one above the other. They are numbered 1, 2, 3, 4, and 5 from *bottom to top*.

    (1) One of the blocks is red.
    (2) Below the white block are precisely two other blocks, one of which is the blue block.
    (3) Between the blue block and the green block are exactly three other blocks.

    Which color block is on the top?

    A. Blue
    B. Green
    C. Red
    D. White
    E. Cannot be determined from the given information

The Grid

11 Ⓐ Ⓑ Ⓒ Ⓓ Ⓔ

The Answer

The correct answer is B. This example is fully discussed in Skillbuilder B: Logical Reasoning, in the section "Put 'Em in Their Places" on page 54.

The Logical Reasoning questions test your ability to

- read carefully and accurately
- discriminate between relevant (important) and irrelevant (unimportant) information
- analyze and process information
- reject answers that are too broad or too narrow, and answers that present outside information that may be true, but is not found in the passage

Reading

DESCRIPTION

You are presented with a prose passage of about 350 to 450 words in length. The subject matter may include descriptions of historical events, information about natural or scientific phenomena, discussions of topics relating to music, art, or sports, and so on. In each passage, there is a central unifying theme, and points of view are often expressed or implied. Following each passage there is a set of six multiple-choice questions. The first question asks you to identify the central theme or main idea of the passage. Other questions pertain to factual information contained in the passage, inferences that may be drawn, the meaning of words and phrases, points of view expressed or implied, and so on.

POINT VALUE

There is one point for each of the six questions associated with each of the five reading passages, for a total of 30 points.

DIRECTIONS

The usual directions instruct you to read the passage and answer the six questions following that passage. You are cautioned to base your answers **only on what is contained in the passage.** Choose, from among the answer choices, the **best** answer for each question.

EXAMPLE

Antonio Stradivari was born in 1644 in Cremona, Italy, a town noted for the production of excellent violins. Although Stradivari made cellos and violas as well as violins, it is violins for which he is renowned. His teacher, Nicolo Amati, passed on to him the techniques of violin making as these were practiced in Cremona. The pupil Stradivari employed these techniques but went on to surpass his teacher, making violins whose excellence has never been exceeded or even fully understood.

What makes a Stradivarius such a fine instrument? Stradivari did alter the proportions of the violin, but this change alone does not explain their superiority. Some think that the special varnish he used is responsible for the wonderful sound of the instruments, but not every expert agrees with this idea. A relatively recent theory concerns the unusually cold weather in Europe during this period of history. Lower-than-usual temperatures would have slowed the growth rate of the trees whose wood was used in the violins, resulting in a very dense wood. Perhaps the magnificent Stradivarius sound derives from the density of the wood rather than from the composition of the varnish.

The only violin maker whose instruments rival those of Antonio Stradivari is Giuseppe Antonio Guarneri, who lived at the same time. This fact does not give conclusive proof, but it does seem to bolster the cold-weather theory of the secret of the Stradivarius.

21. Which of the following best expresses the purpose of the author of the passage?

    A. To discuss the excellence of the violins produced by Stradivari
    B. To indicate a surprising result of climate change
    C. To explain what makes a violin superior
    D. To compare the violins of Stradivari and Guarneri
    E. To summarize the career of Antonio Stradivari

22. Which of the following is **not** mentioned as a possible factor influencing the quality of a Stradivarius violin?

    F. Special varnish
    G. Dense wood
    H. Experience gained through making violas and cellos
    J. Changes in proportions
    K. Methods used by Cremonan violin makers

The Grid

21 Ⓐ Ⓑ Ⓒ Ⓓ Ⓔ

22 Ⓕ Ⓖ Ⓗ Ⓙ Ⓚ

The Answers

The correct answers are 21 A and 22 H. This example is fully discussed in Skillbuilder C: Reading.

   The Reading questions test your ability to read carefully and understand what you have read. This is gauged by your ability to distinguish between stated fact and implication, as well as your ability to draw valid inferences based on the passage.

Mathematics

DESCRIPTION

There are 50 multiple-choice questions covering a broad range of topics and assessing a wide range of abilities. Topics include arithmetic, basic algebra, elementary geometry, probability, and statistics. On the ninth year version of the test, there is also some trigonometry. Many questions assess your knowledge of basic concepts. Others test your ability to think creatively and apply what you know in what may be new or unfamiliar situations.

IMPORTANT:
- Calculators are **not** permitted.
- No formulas are provided.

POINT VALUE

There is one point for each of the 50 questions, for a total of 50 points.

DIRECTIONS

The usual directions instruct you to solve each problem and choose the **best** answer from among the given choices. You are directed to do your work in the test booklet or on scratch paper (if provided). Formulas and definitions of technical terms are not given. Diagrams are not necessarily drawn to scale, but graphs are drawn to scale. You are told that lines that appear to be straight are indeed straight and lines that appear to be parallel or perpendicular may be assumed to be so, and so on. Reduce fractions to lowest terms when appropriate and do not do any figuring on your answer sheet.

EXAMPLES

51. The value of $\frac{9090}{90}$ is

   A. 11
   B. 100
   C. 101
   D. 111
   E. 1010

52. For positive numbers x and y, define $x \circledR y$ to mean $x^2 - 2y$. Find the value of $5 \circledR 3$.

   F. 69
   G. 19
   H. 16
   J. 13
   K. 4

53. The sides of a square are each multiplied by 3 to form a new square. If the area of the original square was K, then the area of the new square is

    A. K^3
    B. $3K$
    C. $6K$
    D. $9K$
    E. $12K$

The Grid

51 Ⓐ Ⓑ Ⓒ Ⓓ Ⓔ

52 Ⓕ Ⓖ Ⓗ Ⓙ Ⓚ

53 Ⓐ Ⓑ Ⓒ Ⓓ Ⓔ

The Answers

The correct answers are 51 C, 52 G, and 53 D. These examples are fully discussed in Skillbuilder D, Section 1 on page 104.

Summary

	Scrambled Paragraphs	Logical Reasoning	Reading	Mathematics
number of questions	5	10	5 passages, 6 questions each	50
total point value	10	10	30	50
percentage of test	10%	10%	30%	50%

Total time: 150 minutes without a break. You may return to any section at any time. You may do the sections in any order you wish. Recommended time is 75 minutes for the (entire) Verbal Section and 75 minutes for the Mathematics Section.

Marking the Grid

Bring to the test three to five well-sharpened #2 pencils, a good eraser, and a noncalculator watch to keep track of time.

When you bubble in an answer on the answer sheet, make sure your mark is clear and dark and completely fills the circle.

Be careful where you bubble in each answer. If you enter answers on the wrong line, you not only lose credit for those answers, but you waste a tremendous amount of time because you must eventually erase those answers and enter them correctly. This is a costly mistake, yet it is an **easily avoidable error**. *Each time* you bubble in an answer, say the question number to yourself and be sure the grid number matches it. Make this automatic. This is especially important if you skip a question.

If you change an answer, erase the old mark **completely**. Do not bubble in more than one answer to a problem, or no credit will be given for either answer.

When to bubble in your answers:

- For Scrambled Paragraphs, you must decide on the order of the five sentences before you bubble in that set of answers.

- For Reading, some people prefer to answer all six questions for a passage before transferring the six answers to the answer sheet; others prefer to bubble in each answer as they do each question. Try both systems when you do the practice tests. Decide which system works best for you.

- For Logical Reasoning and Mathematics, bubble in the answer *immediately after you do each question.* Do *not* solve several problems before entering their answers.

A few minutes before the test ends, look over your answer sheet to be sure **every** question has some answer bubbled in. You cannot get credit for an empty space, so simply guess if necessary. On this test you do not lose credit if an answer is wrong, but you do get credit for a correct guess.

Make sure there are no stray marks on the answer sheet. Do not fold or tear that sheet.

> The test information in this book is accurate as of the date of publication. However, some aspects of the test have varied over the years. It is important that you check with your school counselor for the latest information and instructions.

HOW TO USE THIS BOOK

This book is designed to help you improve your score on the SHSAT by

- Providing you with sample tests in the style and at the level of the actual test.
- Providing detailed solutions featuring TIPS AND FACTS. Review of material is provided through the solutions.
- Helping you find and correct weaknesses while sharpening your skills. "Skillbuilders" for each part of the exam provide you with detailed analyses and methods for solving each type of question.
- Providing you with test-taking strategies and suggestions that will bring you to peak performance.

The successful test taker should follow several important principles.

- **Know your basics.**
  You already have basic math and verbal skills. Practice will sharpen them to the degree needed to help you attain a high score.

- **Know the test format.**
  This includes types of questions, time limits, directions, and gridding procedures.

- **Know the strategies.**
  Familiarity with general test-taking techniques, as well as strategies that are specific to each type of question, will give you the test-taking advantage.

- **Practice!**
  Taking the actual test is like preparing for a performance, or getting ready for the big game of the season. A good performance depends on good rehearsals. You want to give a **great** performance on test day.

> **EXTREMELY IMPORTANT:** Whenever you practice, work under test-like conditions.

- **Do practice exams under strict time limits.**
- **Review solutions in detail.** These contain important and informative review material.
- **Don't cram.**

A Suggested Plan of Study

The time necessary to accomplish this plan will vary from individual to individual. Some students will spread this over months; others may do it in much less time. However, we suggest that you set up a regular schedule of study and try to do some practice every day.

1. Be sure you have read the detailed description of the test beginning on page 6 in order to acquaint yourself with the test format.
2. Next, take Minitest 1 under strict test-like conditions. This will give you an idea of what the actual test is like.
3. Now grade the test (there is an answer key following the minitest) and *enter the results on the Progress Charts* found at the end of the book. Then carefully review the Answer Explanations to this minitest (they follow the answer key). Look at the Analysis that follows the Answer Explanations.
4. Begin with the opening section ("General Advice"), which is followed by the Skillbuilders. Skillbuilders are detailed "how-to" sections; the Scrambled Paragraphs, Logical Reasoning, Reading, and Mathematics portions of the test are each treated in a separate Skillbuilder. You may do these Skillbuilders in any order you choose. In fact, it is advisable to start with your weakest area, especially if the time you have to prepare before the exam is limited.

   Skillbuilder D, Section 2 contains a Math Skills Diagnoser, which consists of six "Workouts" focused on specific areas of math skill such as arithmetic, algebra, geometry, and graphs. After you grade each "Workout" (the Solutions immediately follow the Workout), enter the results on the last page of the Progress Charts in the back of the book. Then review those Solutions. After you finish each "Follow-Up," grade it (the answers appear after Follow-Up F) and enter those results on the last page of the Progress Charts.
5. Do the rest of the sample tests. For maximum benefit, leave ample time between taking these practice tests. It is best not to do and review more than one test on any given day. *It is absolutely necessary that each practice test be done in a single sitting, under strict time limits.* After each test, check the answer key

and enter your results on the Progress Charts. Then study the solutions. Return to the appropriate Skillbuilders for any needed review.

6. If you are a ninth-grade student applying for admission to the tenth grade, do the ninth-grade math supplement.

7. When you have completed all the tests in the book, redo each one, beginning with Minitest 1. Again, enter the results on the Progress Charts for the purpose of comparison. As those charts indicate, review those problems that were answered incorrectly both times.

8. For additional practice, redo the math Workouts and Follow Ups in Skillbuilder D, Section 2. Enter the results on the Progress Charts for the purpose of comparison.

9. *Be sure to make a photocopy of the answer sheets in case you retake any of the tests.*

Answer Sheet
DIAGNOSTIC MINITEST 1

Part I   Verbal

Scrambled Paragraphs

Paragraph 1

The second sentence is ⓠ ⓡ ⓢ ⓣ ⓤ
The third sentence is ⓠ ⓡ ⓢ ⓣ ⓤ
The fourth sentence is ⓠ ⓡ ⓢ ⓣ ⓤ
The fifth sentence is ⓠ ⓡ ⓢ ⓣ ⓤ
The sixth sentence is ⓠ ⓡ ⓢ ⓣ ⓤ

Paragraph 2

The second sentence is ⓠ ⓡ ⓢ ⓣ ⓤ
The third sentence is ⓠ ⓡ ⓢ ⓣ ⓤ
The fourth sentence is ⓠ ⓡ ⓢ ⓣ ⓤ
The fifth sentence is ⓠ ⓡ ⓢ ⓣ ⓤ
The sixth sentence is ⓠ ⓡ ⓢ ⓣ ⓤ

Paragraph 3

The second sentence is ⓠ ⓡ ⓢ ⓣ ⓤ
The third sentence is ⓠ ⓡ ⓢ ⓣ ⓤ
The fourth sentence is ⓠ ⓡ ⓢ ⓣ ⓤ
The fifth sentence is ⓠ ⓡ ⓢ ⓣ ⓤ
The sixth sentence is ⓠ ⓡ ⓢ ⓣ ⓤ

Logical Reasoning

10 Ⓐ Ⓑ Ⓒ Ⓓ Ⓔ
11 Ⓕ Ⓖ Ⓗ Ⓙ Ⓚ
12 Ⓐ Ⓑ Ⓒ Ⓓ Ⓔ
13 Ⓕ Ⓖ Ⓗ Ⓙ Ⓚ

Reading

14 Ⓐ Ⓑ Ⓒ Ⓓ Ⓔ
15 Ⓕ Ⓖ Ⓗ Ⓙ Ⓚ
16 Ⓐ Ⓑ Ⓒ Ⓓ Ⓔ
17 Ⓕ Ⓖ Ⓗ Ⓙ Ⓚ
18 Ⓐ Ⓑ Ⓒ Ⓓ Ⓔ
19 Ⓕ Ⓖ Ⓗ Ⓙ Ⓚ
20 Ⓐ Ⓑ Ⓒ Ⓓ Ⓔ
21 Ⓕ Ⓖ Ⓗ Ⓙ Ⓚ
22 Ⓐ Ⓑ Ⓒ Ⓓ Ⓔ
23 Ⓕ Ⓖ Ⓗ Ⓙ Ⓚ
24 Ⓐ Ⓑ Ⓒ Ⓓ Ⓔ
25 Ⓕ Ⓖ Ⓗ Ⓙ Ⓚ

Part II   Mathematics

26 Ⓐ Ⓑ Ⓒ Ⓓ Ⓔ
27 Ⓕ Ⓖ Ⓗ Ⓙ Ⓚ
28 Ⓐ Ⓑ Ⓒ Ⓓ Ⓔ
29 Ⓕ Ⓖ Ⓗ Ⓙ Ⓚ
30 Ⓐ Ⓑ Ⓒ Ⓓ Ⓔ

31 Ⓕ Ⓖ Ⓗ Ⓙ Ⓚ
32 Ⓐ Ⓑ Ⓒ Ⓓ Ⓔ
33 Ⓕ Ⓖ Ⓗ Ⓙ Ⓚ
34 Ⓐ Ⓑ Ⓒ Ⓓ Ⓔ
35 Ⓕ Ⓖ Ⓗ Ⓙ Ⓚ

36 Ⓐ Ⓑ Ⓒ Ⓓ Ⓔ
37 Ⓕ Ⓖ Ⓗ Ⓙ Ⓚ
38 Ⓐ Ⓑ Ⓒ Ⓓ Ⓔ
39 Ⓕ Ⓖ Ⓗ Ⓙ Ⓚ
40 Ⓐ Ⓑ Ⓒ Ⓓ Ⓔ

41 Ⓕ Ⓖ Ⓗ Ⓙ Ⓚ
42 Ⓐ Ⓑ Ⓒ Ⓓ Ⓔ
43 Ⓕ Ⓖ Ⓗ Ⓙ Ⓚ
44 Ⓐ Ⓑ Ⓒ Ⓓ Ⓔ
45 Ⓕ Ⓖ Ⓗ Ⓙ Ⓚ

46 Ⓐ Ⓑ Ⓒ Ⓓ Ⓔ
47 Ⓕ Ⓖ Ⓗ Ⓙ Ⓚ
48 Ⓐ Ⓑ Ⓒ Ⓓ Ⓔ
49 Ⓕ Ⓖ Ⓗ Ⓙ Ⓚ
50 Ⓐ Ⓑ Ⓒ Ⓓ Ⓔ

Diagnostic Minitest 1

PART 1—VERBAL

19 QUESTIONS

SUGGESTED TIME: 35 MINUTES

Scrambled Paragraphs

Paragraphs 1–3

> **Directions:** Below are six sentences that can be arranged to form a well-organized and grammatically correct paragraph. The first sentence is provided, but the other five are listed in random order. Choose the order that will form the **best** paragraph. Each correct paragraph is worth two points, with no partial credit given.
>
> You may wish to put numbers in the blanks at the left of each sentence to help keep track of the order. When you finish the set, mark your answers on the answer sheet.

PARAGRAPH 1

Living in the harsh Southwest, the Navajo Indians have survived the poverty and deprivation of the desert as well as the violent persecution of the United States government.

_____ (Q) The weaving of blankets and rugs, for example, is one tradition that has been passed on from mother to daughter for hundreds of years.

_____ (R) On the other hand, the Navajo have proved adaptable, incorporating over the years valuable aspects of other cultures, Indian and non-Indian.

_____ (S) In spite of these hardships, they have managed to retain their language as well as many of their customs and much of their native tradition.

_____ (T) The Navajo tribe's main source of wealth, however, is their reservation's abundant resources of coal, oil, and uranium; these riches make them the wealthiest American Indian tribe.

_____ (U) Many Navajos speak English, and from other Indian tribes these former warriors have learned trades that have given them a measure of prosperity.

PARAGRAPH 2

In the nineteenth century, a French fabric called *serge de Nimes* after Nimes, its city of origin, became a favorite material for work trousers.

_____ (Q) The first Levi's riveted work pants, called "waist overalls," were an immediate success and sold well for several decades with only minor changes.

_____ (R) They became a symbol of teenage rebellion in the 1950s, but today a pair of jeans can be found in almost every closet across the country.

_____ (S) Other companies began making similar work pants from denim, and in the 1940s denim pants called "dungarees" became the popular casual wear called *jeans*.

_____ (T) It was exported to other European countries and also to the United States, where it came to be called by the shorter name *denim*.

_____ (U) A dry-goods wholesaler named Levi Strauss sold the fabric to Gold Rush miners in California, so he was already familiar with its strength and comfort when inventor Jacob Davis suggested using rivets to reinforce the pockets of work pants.

PARAGRAPH 3

Europe hopes to achieve a first in space exploration when the European Space Agency lands on the comet Wirtanen in 2012.

_____ (Q) At that great distance from the sun, Wirtanen will be a frozen mass that is not yet trailed by the characteristic comet's tail.

_____ (R) The climax of the mission will come when *Rosetta* makes contact with the comet by means of a 220-pound landing vehicle, which will anchor itself to the comet's surface with a harpoon fired just before impact.

_____ (S) The Wirtanen mission will send a spacecraft called *Rosetta* to rendezvous with Wirtanen and subsequently collect matter from the surface of the comet.

_____ (T) The rendezvous will take place when the comet is approaching the sun but is still 420 million miles from it.

_____ (U) *Rosetta* will orbit Wirtanen for about a month as it hurtles toward the sun at 81,000 miles per hour, beginning to develop its streaming tail of frozen matter.

LOGICAL REASONING

Questions 10–13

> **Directions:** For each of the following questions, select the **best** answer from the given choices. Bubble in the letter corresponding to your answer on the answer sheet. Your answer should be based **only on the given information.**
>
> Read the words carefully. For example, "The red book is **to the right** of the blue book" does not necessarily mean that there is no other book between them. Similarly, be careful when reading words such as **between, below, above, after, before, behind,** and **ahead of.**

10. Matthias and Shawna together are stronger than Carlos and Gary together. Matthias and Gary together are stronger than Shawna and Carlos together. It **must** be true that

    A. Matthias is stronger than Shawna
    B. Matthias is stronger than Carlos
    C. Matthias is stronger than Gary
    D. Shawna is stronger than Carlos
    E. Gary is stronger than Carlos

Questions 11 and 12 refer to the following information.

Alan, Barbara, and Simionee play the piano, oboe, and violin, but not necessarily in that order. Each plays only one instrument. Also:

1) Alan is not the piano player.
2) The piano player and the oboe player are teachers.
3) Barbara is not a teacher.

11. Who plays the oboe?

    F. Alan
    G. Barbara
    H. Simionee
    J. Either Alan or Barbara, but there is not enough information to determine which one
    K. Could be Alan, Barbara, or Simionee, but there is not enough information to determine which one

12. Who plays the violin?

    A. Alan
    B. Barbara
    C. Simionee
    D. Either Alan or Barbara, but there is not enough information to determine which one
    E. Could be Alan, Barbara, or Simionee, but there is not enough information to determine which one

13. If a student took the Math Contest, then that student was on the Team. No student in the Algebra class took the Math Contest.

    Based only on the information above, which of the following **must** be true?

    F. If a student was on the Team, then that student took the Math Contest.
    G. No student who took the Math Contest was in the Algebra class.
    H. If a student did not take the Math Contest, then that student was in the Algebra class.
    J. If a student did not take the Math Contest, then that student was not in the Algebra class.
    K. No student in the Geometry class took the Math Contest.

READING

Questions 14–25

> **Directions:** Read each passage and answer the questions that follow it. Base your answers **only on the material contained in the passage.** Select the one **best** answer for each question. Bubble in the letter corresponding to that answer on the answer sheet.

I. Today a growing number of parents are practicing infant massage and finding it a rewarding experience. To give infant mas-
Line sage, the parent usually lays the baby on a
(5) blanket on the floor. Having rubbed a little canola oil onto his or her index finger, the parent begins lightly stroking the baby's skin. Parents report that infants usually lie quiet, seeming to enjoy the experience.
(10) Furthermore, they claim that massaged infants are less colicky—that is, less tense and fussy.

Just a few decades ago in this country meditation was seen as a practice only for
(15) monks and other recluses; hypnotism was viewed as a parlor trick; and acupuncture was considered Far Eastern quackery. Today these "alternative health" methods are recognized by the medical community as valu-
(20) able tools for maintaining wellness and for managing health problems. Now comes infant massage. In other cultures it has been used for hundreds of years as a way to promote the emotional and physical health of
(25) babies. In the United States, however, it is still in the process of gaining general acceptance as a useful technique.

Proponents of infant massage say that massaged babies are more relaxed and less irrita-
(30) ble. Such babies, they maintain, sleep better and even tend to be healthier. Studies support these claims. Research data indicate that massage improves digestion, aids brain and muscle development, and boosts immune
(35) function. Premature and drug-addicted babies who are massaged have fewer motor difficulties, better neurological development, more favorable weight gain, and fewer hospitalizations. There is even some evidence that
(40) massage may improve IQ.

With minimum instruction anyone can successfully practice this valuable technique. The ideal person to administer the massage, however, is the child's parent. The
(45) reason for this is that a major benefit of this shared experience is a closer bonding. The gentle, loving touch administered to the tiny body communicates caring and promotes a sense of security. Moreover, the
(50) communication is two-way. The parent learns to interpret and respond to the baby's cues—for example, which are the baby's favorite massage spots, and whether the baby would prefer not to be massaged at a
(55) given time. Thus, the interpersonal bond is strengthened even more.

14. Which of the following best expresses the topic of the above passage?

   A. Resistance to change in the American medical community
   B. A treatment for colic in infants
   C. Nonverbal communication—a key to physical and emotional well-being
   D. A short history of infant massage
   E. The benefits of infant massage

15. According to the passage, which of the following is **not** a possible benefit of infant massage for the parents?

   F. They may have fewer medical bills.
   G. They may be more rested.
   H. They may learn about other alternative health practices.
   J. They build a stronger bond with their babies.
   K. Communication with the baby is improved.

16. The passage suggests that

    A. infant massage guarantees a healthy baby.
    B. doctors do not approve of infant massage.
    C. hypnotism is best reserved for purposes of entertainment.
    D. the skin is an important medium of nonverbal communication.
    E. infant massage involves difficult techniques.

17. With which of the following would the author of the passage **not** agree?

    F. Parents should take their babies to professional massage therapists.
    G. Most babies can benefit from massage.
    H. A baby may not always want massage when it is convenient for the parent.
    J. Massage can make a parent and infant emotionally closer to each other.
    K. Some benefits of infant massage have been scientifically verified.

18. In the context of this passage, what is the significance of meditation, hypnotism, and acupuncture?

    A. Like infant massage, they are Asian in origin.
    B. They are "alternative" and thus not practiced by health professionals in this country.
    C. Like massage, they rely on touch.
    D. They are useful in promoting infant well-being.
    E. They are examples of health practices that had slow acceptance in this country.

19. All of the following are mentioned as possible benefits of infant massage **except**

    F. improved brain development.
    G. higher IQ.
    H. better motor skills.
    J. addiction cure.
    K. better digestion.

II. Earthworms are familiar creatures, although most people don't encounter them every day. Fishing enthusiasts use them for
Line bait, and biology students dissect them in
(5) the laboratory. But most of the time they stay out of sight unless rain has soaked the soil, driving them above ground. Squeamish gardeners probably wince when their bare hands suddenly feel a telltale cool wiggle,
(10) but they have ample reason to appreciate the little reddish dirt dwellers.

There are five families of earthworms (class *Oligochaeta* of phylum *Annelida*) distributed across every continent except
(15) Antarctica. Although most of the species found in North America are only a few inches in length, some tropical areas boast worms 11 feet long. Earthworms have no eyes or ears, but the lack is no hindrance, as
(20) vision and hearing are unnecessary for finding food—these underground dwellers can actually eat their habitat! And they can even communicate with each other in a limited way. When disturbed, their bodies exude an
(25) oily film that serves as a warning to nearby fellows.

The cylindrical bodies of earthworms bear tiny external structures called *setae*. In combination with an elongated, tapered shape
(30) and an efficient muscular system, these tiny bristles enable earthworms to burrow easily through soil. As they burrow, they stir up and loosen the soil, creating tiny pockets of air that they breathe through their skin. This
(35) tilling makes for a healthy medium for vegetative growth. Underground cultivation is not their only service, for these helpful creatures also process and excrete decaying vegetation called humus, which directly fertilizes
(40) the earth. And when they die, their decomposing bodies perform a last act of service.

A healthy acre of land may contain up to three million earthworms, which together can till about eighteen tons of soil per year.
(45) Regrettably, modern farming methods often decrease earthworm population through the

overuse of pesticides. Persistent heavy applications of toxins over a period of years can actually result in "dead" soil, which no (50) longer contains the earthworms necessary to make it productive. By contrast, land that is farmed with earthworm-friendly methods can continue its optimum productivity for thousands of years—and then thousands (55) more after that.

20. Which of the following is the best title for this passage?

    A. "How to Have a Healthy Garden"
    B. "Annelids Worldwide"
    C. "Meet a Friend of the Soil"
    D. "Pesticides and the Death of the Soil"
    E. "An Eyeless, Earless Mystery"

21. What is the "last act of service" that an earthworm provides?

    F. It warns its neighbors by exuding an oily film.
    G. It excretes processed humus.
    H. It aerates the soil.
    J. Its decaying body fertilizes the soil.
    K. It ceases to feed upon its habitat.

22. What is the most likely reason why earthworms come to the surface when it rains?

    A. They are attracted to the moisture above.
    B. Their air supply is replaced by water.
    C. Raindrops striking the ground trigger their "warning" systems.
    D. The underground temperatures drop too low.
    E. They seek decaying vegetation floating on the layer of water above.

23. What is the meaning of the word "setae" (line 28)?

    F. Setae are the earthworm's rudimentary lungs.
    G. It refers to the shape of the earthworm's body.
    H. It is the name of the earthworm's projecting bristles.
    J. It refers to the peculiarly shaped mouth of the earthworm.
    K. It denotes efficient muscles.

24. Which of the following best explains the earthworm's beneficial effect on the soil?

    A. The earthworm cultivates and enriches the soil.
    B. The earthworm digs burrows that provide air passages.
    C. The earthworm is a scavenger that cleans the soil.
    D. Dwindling numbers of earthworms can warn of toxic conditions in the soil.
    E. They "till" the soil and remove excess oxygen.

25. According to the passage, which of the following statements is true concerning pesticide use?

    F. It is "earthworm friendly."
    G. Too much can kill off earthworms.
    H. It is an essential part of modern farming.
    J. Properly applied, pesticides guarantee productive land for thousands of years.
    K. It is a way of controlling earthworm overpopulation.

PART 2—MATHEMATICS

QUESTIONS 26–50

SUGGESTED TIME: 40 MINUTES

Directions: For each of the following questions, select the **best** answer from the given choices. Bubble in the letter corresponding to your answer on the answer sheet. **DO NOT PUT ANY OTHER WORK ON THE ANSWER SHEET.** All necessary work can be done in your test booklet or on scrap paper that is provided.

NOTE: Diagrams other than graphs might not be drawn to scale. Do not assume any relationships that are not specifically stated unless they are implied by the given information.

26. $\frac{1}{2} + \frac{1}{3} - \frac{1}{4} =$

   A. $\frac{1}{20}$

   B. $\frac{7}{12}$

   C. $\frac{3}{4}$

   D. 1

   E. $\frac{13}{12}$

27. In the diagram, $AC = BD = 17$ and $BC = 3$. The length of segment $\overline{AD}$ is

   F. 20
   G. 24
   H. 28
   J. 31
   K. 34

$$A \quad\quad\quad\quad B \quad\quad C \quad\quad\quad\quad D$$

28. What is the value of $|x - y| + |y - x|$ if $x = -3$ and $y = -7$?

   A. −14
   B. −6
   C. 0
   D. 8
   E. 20

29. The product of the first ten prime numbers must be divisible by

   F. 16
   G. 18
   H. 20
   J. 22
   K. 24

30. $4^3 + 4^3 + 4^3 + 4^3 =$

   A. 4^4
   B. 4^9
   C. 4^{12}
   D. 16^3
   E. 16^{12}

31. If the mean of 4 and x is the same as the mean of 4, 10, and x, what is the value of x?

   F. 16
   G. 10
   H. 7
   J. −6
   K. No value of x will make this true.

32. If $x = 3$, what is the value of $\dfrac{5(4+x)}{2x}$?

    A. 15

    B. $\dfrac{25}{2}$

    C. 10

    D. $\dfrac{20}{3}$

    E. $\dfrac{35}{6}$

33. $.\overline{3} \times .\overline{3} =$

    F. .09

    G. $.\overline{09}$

    H. $.\overline{1}$

    J. $.\overline{6}$

    K. $.\overline{9}$

34. In the diagram, figure I is a square, and figures II and III are equilateral triangles. What is the value of x?

    A. 10

    B. 15

    C. 30

    D. 45

    E. 60

35. Two years ago, Esther was 3 years younger than Miguel is now. Let Miguel's present age be represented by M. Esther's age 10 years from now will be

    F. $M + 7$

    G. $M + 9$

    H. $M + 10$

    J. $M + 11$

    K. $M + 13$

36. All of the students in Mr. Jacobs's class are taking either French or algebra or both subjects. Exactly 16 students are taking French, exactly 18 students are taking algebra, and exactly 6 are taking both subjects. What is the total number of students in Mr. Jacobs's class?

    A. 22

    B. 28

    C. 31

    D. 34

    E. 40

37. Which of the following could be the sum of exactly three consecutive integers?

    F. 98

    G. 198

    H. 298

    J. 398

    K. 998

38. Five hamburgers and one order of fries together cost $10.24, whereas one hamburger and five orders of fries together cost $5.84. What is the total cost of three hamburgers and three orders of fries?

    A. $13.20

    B. $12.72

    C. $8.04

    D. $3.30

    E. None of the previous choices are correct.

39. Circles A and B touch but do not overlap, as shown. The area of circle A is 9π and the area of circle B is 16π. What is the area of the smallest circle that can contain the entire shaded figure?

    F. 25π

    G. 36π

    H. 49π

    J. 64π

    K. 196π

40. Which of the following numbers is closest to 1?

   A. $\dfrac{49}{50}$

   B. $\dfrac{99}{100}$

   C. $\dfrac{197}{200}$

   D. $\dfrac{499}{500}$

   E. $\dfrac{1003}{1000}$

41. Referring to the diagram, find the value of $(x + y)$.

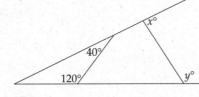

   F. 200
   G. 180
   H. 160
   J. 140
   K. Cannot be determined from the information given

42. If the notation $q*r$ means $\dfrac{q+r}{2}$, then $(a*b)*c$ will be equal to $a*(b*c)$

   A. always
   B. never
   C. only if $a = b$
   D. only if $b = c$
   E. only if $a = c$

43. $X: \dfrac{3}{7} > \dfrac{11}{24}$ $Y: \dfrac{2}{5} < \dfrac{9}{22}$ $Z: (.1)^2 > .1$

   F. X, Y, and Z are all true
   G. Z is true
   H. X, Y, and Z are all false
   J. Y is false
   K. X is false

44. Let n be a fixed integer between 1 and 50. If the number 100 is decreased by n%, and this result is then increased by n%, the final value obtained

   A. must be more than 100
   B. must be exactly 100
   C. must be less than 100
   D. will sometimes be less than 100 and sometimes more than 100, depending on the value of n
   E. will never be an integer

45. If x is a positive number, then $\dfrac{12+x}{2+x}$

   F. must be less than 6
   G. must equal 6
   H. must be greater than 6
   J. must equal 7
   K. is sometimes less than 6 and sometimes greater than 6, depending on the value of x

46. One of the following numbers is the product of a three-digit number and a four-digit number. Which is it?

   A. 22,146
   B. 745,691
   C. 10,000,001
   D. 803,024,559
   E. 257,654,228,931

47. If p is a prime, which one of the following *could* be a prime also?

   F. $23p + 45$
   G. $23p + 46$
   H. $23p + 47$
   J. $23p + 48$
   K. $23p + 49$

48. Which of the following is equivalent to the inequality $9 - x < 7 < 15 - x$?

   A. $x > 2$
   B. $x < 8$
   C. $1 < x < 4$
   D. $2 < x < 8$
   E. $2 > x > 8$

49. When the spinner shown in the diagram is spun once, the probability that the arrow will land on any one of the numbers 1, 2, 3, 4, or 5 is $\frac{1}{5}$. (Assume that the arrow never lands on a line.) The spinner is spun exactly twice. What is the probability that the *product* of the two numbers that occur is a prime number?

F. $\frac{4}{25}$

G. $\frac{5}{25}$

H. $\frac{6}{25}$

J. $\frac{7}{25}$

K. $\frac{8}{25}$

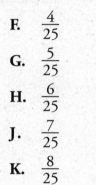

50. The area of trapezoid *ABCD* is

A. 48

B. 36

C. 30

D. 18

E. Cannot be determined from the information given

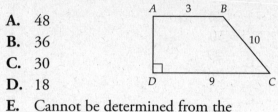

Answer Key
DIAGNOSTIC MINITEST 1

Scrambled Paragraphs	Logical Reasoning	Reading	
Paragraph 1 SQRUT	10. B	14. E	20. C
Paragraph 2 TUQSR	11. F	15. H	21. J
Paragraph 3 STQUR	12. B	16. D	22. B
	13. G	17. F	23. H
		18. E	24. A
		19. J	25. G

Mathematics

26. B	31. F	36. B	41. F	46. B
27. J	32. E	37. G	42. E	47. J
28. D	33. H	38. C	43. K	48. D
29. J	34. B	39. H	44. C	49. H
30. A	35. G	40. D	45. F	50. A

ANSWER EXPLANATIONS
MINITEST 1

Scrambled Paragraphs

Paragraph 1 SQRUT

Careful attention to clues will guide the test taker through paragraphs like this one. In S, the second sentence, the transitional phrase "these hardships" refers to the list of hardships in the first sentence and stresses the Navajos' maintenance of language and tradition. Sentence Q provides an example of one of these traditions. R offers the contrast of adaptability introduced by the transition "On the other hand." U further develops the idea of adaptability by giving examples, and it also mentions prosperity. The concluding sentence, T, continues the discussion of prosperity; this final sentence starts with a clear transition referring to wealth, and uses "however" to indicate a contrasting thought about wealth.

Paragraph 2 TUQSR

T starts with the pronoun "It" referring to the fabric and "other European countries," a clue linking T to the sentence naming France. U comes next, giving a development in the history of denim. U does not use the word *denim* but instead refers to "the fabric" and brings up the detail of rivets. Q continues the story with the success of the "riveted work pants." S continues the paragraph by starting at a time somewhat later than the invention of Levi's riveted work pants and then moving forward to the 1940s and then to the present. R concludes the paragraph by bringing the story through the 1950's and into the present time.

Paragraph 3 STQUR

This paragraph abounds in content clues. S refers to the initial sentence with "The Wirtanen mission" and a brief description of its task. The next three sentences give stages of the mission. T has the noun clue "rendezvous" referring to S and Q refers back to the distance mentioned in T." U moves from rendezvous to orbit, when Wirtanen is "beginning to develop its streaming tail. . . ." After establishment of orbit comes actual contact in R, introduced by the clue noun "climax."

Logical Reasoning

Solutions in this section frequently involve techniques discussed in Skillbuilder B, on page 53.

10. **(B)** This problem is most easily done by expressing the given information using inequality symbols. Using the first letter of each name to represent the people, we have $M + S > C + G$ and $M + G > S + C$. Adding these inequalities produces $2M + S + G > 2C + S + G$. Subtracting $S + G$ from both sides, then dividing both sides by 2, produces $M > C$. This is answer B.

11,12. **(F, B)** Make a chart whose rows are labeled A, B, and S (for the people) and whose columns are labeled p, o, v (for the instruments), and t (for teacher). Mark the chart according to given facts (1) and (3).

	p	o	v	t
A	X			
B				X
S				

Now (2) tells you that two people are teachers, so they must be A and S. Furthermore, A and S must play the piano and the oboe. Since A does not play piano, he must play oboe. Therefore the piano player must be S. That leaves B to play the violin, and the chart is complete.

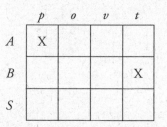

	p	o	v	t
A	X	✓		✓
B			✓	X
S	✓			✓

We can now answer the questions.

Question 11: **(F)**

Question 12: **(B)**

13. **(G)** Look at the second statement. It is equivalent to "If you are in the Algebra class, then you did not take the Math Contest." An alternative phrasing is "If you took the Math Contest, then you are not in the Algebra class." Therefore no student who took the Math Contest was in the Algebra class. That is choice G. Notice that the original first statement does not contribute to the final answer.

Reading

Passage I

14. **(E)** Main Idea   All of the other choices are too narrow because they involve only small parts of the passage. Every paragraph discusses the benefits of massage, so E is correct.

15. **(H)** Detail and Inference   The wording of the question (a "possible" benefit) does not require a direct statement. F is suggested by the indication of improved health (line 31), and G is stated in line 30. The last paragraph states both J and K. H is not suggested or stated in the passage.

16. **(D)** Inference   A is too extreme. Claims are made that massaged babies "tend to be healthier" (line 31). B also is too extreme. The passage says that the procedure is "gaining general acceptance" (lines 26–27) in the medical community, which indicates that at least some doctors approve of it.

17. **(F)** Detail   The last paragraph names the parent as the ideal infant massager (lines 43–44). The passage is clearly promoting infant massage as a generally beneficial practice, so G is incorrect. The last paragraph says that a baby may not want to be massaged at a particular time, so the author would agree with H (line 54). J and K are stated in the passage.

18. **(E)** Detail   None of the other choices are stated or suggested in the passage. The second paragraph states the slow acceptance of these practices and likens it to the slow acceptance of infant massage.

19. **(J)** Detail   All of the other choices are mentioned in the third paragraph.

Passage II

20. **(C)** Main Idea   A and D are too narrow. B is too broad, as the passage discusses only earthworms, not all Annelida (line 13). E is off the topic of the passage, as no mystery is stated or suggested. C is broad enough and accurate, for the passage introduces the reader to the earthworm and indicates its benefits to the soil.

21. **(J)** Inference   F, G, and H are all inaccurate since the "last act of service" (line 41) occurs after death, and these choices concern actions of the living worm. K is incorrect because their eating decaying vegetation in the soil is part of a beneficial process (line 38). The last two sentences in the third paragraph link decaying matter with fertilization (line 39) and attribute the "act of service" to the worm's "decomposing" body (lines 40–41). Thus J is the correct choice.

22. **(B)** This question involves information from two paragraphs. The third paragraph states that the worms breathe air in soil pockets (lines 33–34). The first paragraph states that they come to the surface when driven above ground by a rain that has soaked, or filled, the soil (lines 6–7). B is the correct choice. None of the other choices is suggested or stated in the passage.

23. **(H)** Detail   The first two sentences of the third paragraph define *setae*.

24. **(A)** Detail   The beneficial cultivation and enriching, or fertilization (line 36), are directly stated in the passage. B and D are not presented as directly beneficial effects on soil. C and E are not stated or suggested in the passage.

25. **(G)** Detail   The last paragraph says that pesticides can kill off earthworms (line 46). None of the other choices are stated or suggested.

Mathematics

26. **(B)** Getting a common denominator of 12 produces $\frac{6}{12}+\frac{4}{12}-\frac{3}{12}=\frac{7}{12}$.

27. **(J)** Adding AC and BD counts the overlapped segment BC twice. Therefore we subtract it once, getting $17 + 17 - 3 = 31$.

28. **(D)**

> **TIP:** Combine the terms inside the absolute value signs before you compute the absolute value.

We have $|-3 + 7| + |-7 + 3| = |4| + |-4| = 4 + 4 = 8$.

29. **(J)** Two of those ten primes are 2 and 11, so the correct answer is 22. Each other choice contains some prime factor at least twice.

30. **(A)** This is 4×4^3, which is 4^4.

31. **(F)**

> **TIP:** If the mean of n numbers is A, then the numbers add up to $n \times A$.

$\frac{4+x}{2}=\frac{4+10+x}{3}$, leading to $3(4 + x) = 2(14 + x)$. This gives us $x = 16$.

32. **(E)** After substituting 3 for x, be sure to combine terms in the parentheses before multiplying or dividing.

33. **(H)** Changing the repeating decimals to fractions, we have $\frac{1}{3}\times\frac{1}{3}=\frac{1}{9}$. Changing $\frac{1}{9}$ back to a decimal results in $.\overline{1}$.

> **FACT:** $\frac{1}{9}=.\overline{1}$, $\frac{2}{9}=.\overline{2}$, $\frac{3}{9}=.\overline{3}\left[=\frac{1}{3}\right]$, and so on. Surprisingly, $.\overline{9}=\frac{9}{9}=1$!

34. **(B)** The angles around the central point must add up to 360°, so the vertex angle of the bottom isosceles triangle is 150°. Each base angle is then 15°.

35. **(G)** Two years ago, Esther's age was $M - 3$. Her age now is $(M - 3) + 2 = M - 1$. Ten years from now, her age will be $(M - 1) + 10 = M + 9$.

36. **(B)** Draw a Venn diagram, one circle representing students who take French and the other representing students who take algebra. The overlapping section represents students who take both. In the overlap, put the number 6. That leaves $16 - 6 = 10$ for the other part of the French circle, and $18 - 6 = 12$ for the other part of the algebra circle. We can now add the numbers in these three separate sections, getting the final answer $10 + 6 + 12 = 28$.

37. **(G)** Think of the consecutive integers as being represented by k, $k + 1$, and $k + 2$. Notice that the sum of these, $3k + 3$, must be divisible by 3. Now check the choices for divisibility by 3. Only choice G works.

> **TIP:** An even nicer representation for three consecutive integers is $k - 1$, k, and $k + 1$, because their sum is so simple.

38. **(C)** Using single letters to represent the types of food, we have $5H + 1F = 10.24$ and $1H + 5F = 5.84$. We can find $3H + 3F$ very easily by adding the two equations and then dividing by 2. This gives $3H + 3F = 8.04$.

> **TIP:** It is not always necessary to solve for H and F individually. See if the problem requires the individual values or not.

39. **(H)** Since the radii of the small circles are 3 and 4, the diameter of the enclosing circle is 14. Since its radius is 7, its area is 49π.

40. **(D)** Convert each fraction to an equivalent fraction with a denominator of 1000. The choices then become

$$\frac{980}{1000}, \frac{990}{1000}, \frac{985}{1000}, \frac{998}{1000}, \text{ and } \frac{1003}{1000}.$$

The closest to 1 is $\frac{998}{1000}$ or $\frac{499}{500}$.

41. **(F)** In the small triangle, the missing angle must be 20°. Then in the large triangle, the sum of the other two interior angles must be 160°. Those last two angles plus x and y form two straight angles, which total $180° + 180° = 360°$. Therefore we have $160 + x + y = 360$, so $x + y = 200$.

> **TIP:** It is not always possible to obtain x and y individually (and problems may not call for that).

42. **(E)** According to the $*$ notation, $(a*b)*c$

means $\dfrac{\dfrac{a+b}{2}+c}{2}$, and $a*(b*c)$ means

$\dfrac{a+\dfrac{b+c}{2}}{2}$. Equating the two expressions, then multiplying both sides by 2 produces

$\dfrac{a+b}{2}+c = a+\dfrac{b+c}{2}$.

Again multiplying both sides by 2, we get $a + b + 2c = 2a + b + c$. This leads to $c = a$. The fact that the position of the parentheses is important here means that this new operation is not associative. This is not an easy problem.

43. **(K)**

> **FACT:** For positive numbers a, b, c, and d, $\frac{a}{b} > \frac{c}{d}$ if and only if $ad > bc$. Also, for positive numbers a, b, c, and d, $\frac{a}{b} < \frac{c}{d}$ if and only if $ad < bc$.

Inequality X is equivalent to $72 > 77$, which is false. Inequality Y is equivalent to $44 < 45$, which is true. After squaring (.1), inequality Z produces $.01 > .1$, which is false. Thus the answer is K.

44. **(C)**

> **TIP:** It is sometimes easiest to choose a simple but specific value of a variable to work with.

For example, let $n = 10$. Note that 10% of 100 is 10. Subtracting that from 100 leaves us with 90. Now 10% of 90 is 9. Adding that to 90 brings the total to 99, which is less than the original 100. Other choices for n will produce a similar result. Use of algebra would prove that this result is always true.

45. **(F)** One possible beginning is to try a convenient number for x, such as 8; this produces the value $\frac{20}{10} = 2$. That eliminates all but F and K as possible answers (good progress so far), but now only guessing or trying lots of other values for x seems to finish the problem. The problem can be fully solved without guessing by actually dividing $12 + x$ by $2 + x$ using algebraic long division. This gives a quotient of 6 and a remainder of $-5x$. Therefore $\frac{12+x}{2+x} = 6 + \frac{-5x}{2+x}$. Since x is positive, this is always less than 6.

46. **(B)** The product of the smallest three-digit and four-digit numbers is $100 \times 1{,}000 = 100{,}000$. The product of the largest three-digit and four-digit numbers is *less than* $1{,}000 \times 10{,}000 = 10{,}000{,}000$. Thus, the answer is between these results, so it must have at least six digits and *fewer than* 8 digits. The only possible choice is 745,691. Notice that the problem does not ask for the factors of that number. Finding those factors in a limited time period could be a very difficult problem.

47. **(J)**

> **FACT:** The product of two odd numbers is odd. The sum of two odd numbers is even.

If p is an odd prime, answers F, H, and K will be even numbers. These could not be primes. Answer G must be a multiple of 23, since 23 is a factor of both terms. Therefore $23p + 46$ is not prime. The only possible choice is J (which actually becomes prime, for example, when $p = 5$).

> **FACT:** The number 2 is a prime (the smallest prime, and the only even one).

Checking to see if F, G, H, or K becomes prime when $p = 2$, we see that this does not occur.

48. **(D)** We can work with all three parts of the inequality at the same time, being sure to do the same thing to *all* parts (never to only two of the parts). Adding x to each of the three parts gives $9 < 7 + x < 15$. Subtracting 7 from each part gives $2 < x < 8$.

49. **(H)** There are $5 \times 5 = 25$ possible outcomes. (It is instructive to draw a tree or make a list to see them all.) The only products that are prime numbers come from 1×2, 2×1, 1×3, 3×1, 1×5, and 5×1. Thus the desired probability is $\dfrac{6}{25}$.

> **FACT:** A prime number is a positive integer greater than 1 whose only factors are itself and 1.

50. **(A)** Drop a perpendicular line from B, meeting $\overline{DC}$ at E. Then $DE = 3$, so $EC = 6$. Now in right triangle BEC, BE must equal 8 (by the Pythagorean Theorem).

> **FACT:** The area of a trapezoid is $\frac{1}{2}h(b_1 + b_2)$, where h is its height, and b_1 and b_2 are the lengths of its bases.

We now have the area of the trapezoid = $\left(\dfrac{1}{2}\right)(8)(3 + 9) = 48$.

ANALYSIS

On the chart below, circle the number of any question you got wrong or omitted. The numbers have been grouped by type of problem.

VERBAL

Scrambled Paragraphs	P1	P2	P3								
Logical Reasoning	10	11	12	13							
Reading	14	15	16	17	18	19	20	21	22	23	24	25

MATHEMATICS

Arithmetic	26	29	30	31	33	36	40	43	46	47
Algebra	28	32	35	37	38	44	45	48		
Geometry	27	34	39	41	50					
Miscellaneous	42	49								

Look at the circled questions to get an idea of where you may have weaknesses. For additional practice in any area, go to the appropriate Skillbuilder in the section on Test-Taking Strategies. In particular, Skillbuilder D (mathematics) contains Diagnosers arranged by topic.

TEST-TAKING STRATEGIES

General Advice

The suggestions that follow apply to the overall test. Special tips that apply to the individual sections of the test are given in the Skillbuilders.

Know the Test Site

Be sure you know how to get there. Perhaps you should try going there once to be familiar with the travel route.

Know the Format of the Test

Verbal Section	
Scrambled Paragraphs	5 paragraphs
Logical Reasoning	10 questions
Reading	30 questions
(5 passages with 6 questions about each passage)	
Mathematics Section	
Mathematics	50 questions

There is a 150-minute time limit for the entire test. Try not to spend more than 75 minutes on either the Math section or the (entire) Verbal section. You may take the parts of the test in any order. Read on for more details.

Know the Test Directions

Look over the practice tests in this book. Completely familiarize yourself with the directions for each part of the test. There is no reason to lose time on the actual exam by having to carefully reread directions. On the actual test, just spend a few seconds glancing at the directions to be sure there are no changes.

Remember, for the Mathematics section, that no reference formulas are given and calculators are **not** permitted.

Develop a Plan

Choose the order in which you wish to do the different parts of the test.

1. If you are especially good in English, choose Scrambled Paragraphs, Reading, Logical Reasoning, Mathematics.
2. If you are especially good in Math, choose Mathematics, Logical Reasoning, Scrambled Paragraphs, Reading.
3. If you prefer to finish the short sections first, choose Scrambled Paragraphs and Logical Reasoning (in either order), then Reading and Mathematics (in either order).

To find the best approach for you, try using different orders when doing the practice tests in this book.

Pace Yourself

Don't spend too much time on any one question. Getting bogged down on a single question is one of the greatest time wasters. You are aiming to get as many correct answers as possible, so **keep moving**. To help you do this, use the **? X** system.

The ? X system

As you do each test, you may find some questions that you are unsure of and some that you cannot do at all. This system keeps track of those problems, making it easier to find them and return to them later. When using the **? X** system, put these marks only in your test booklet, never on the answer sheet.

1. If you try a problem but are not sure of the answer, put a **?** next to the problem number **in your test booklet**. Because you have already spent some time analyzing the problem, choose an answer now and mark it on the grid, even if it is a guess. (See the next section for suggestions on eliminating choices.) You will go back to these problems later.
2. If you have no idea how to do a problem, put an **X** next to the problem number **in your test booklet**. Do not grid in an answer at this time. You may go back to these problems later if you have time.
3. When you finish the problems you are sure of, go back to the **?** problems. That mark in your test booklet makes them easy to locate. You may find that you now remember things that will help with the solution.
4. When you finish looking over the **?** problems, try your **X** problems. Because there is no penalty for guessing, enter some answer for **every** question, even if it is a random guess! But try to eliminate some of the choices first.

Eliminating Choices: If you must guess at an answer, try to reduce the number of choices first. If you can eliminate choices that are obviously wrong, your chances of guessing correctly are improved. Lightly cross out the choices that you eliminate. That way, when you return to the problem later, you need only concentrate on the reduced set of choices.

Try to get an idea of how much time you spend on each part of the test. This will identify those parts on which you may be going too slowly. In particular, for the Reading part, determine how much time it takes you to read a single passage. To do this, go to a test you have done previously, such as Minitest 1, and reread a passage. Note the time it takes to read the **passage**, not the questions. Do this for several passages. You should aim for about 3 to 4 minutes per passage on average to allow for ample time to answer the 6 associated questions.

Keep track of the question numbers and the corresponding answer numbers on the answer sheet. **Each time** you bubble in an answer, say the question number to yourself and be sure the grid number matches it. Make this automatic. This is especially important if you skip a question.

Leave no blanks. Use the last few minutes of the test to look over your answer sheet and simply **fill in answers for any skipped questions**. At this point, do not even look back at the test booklet itself. Remember that there is no penalty for incorrect answers.

Read the Questions with Focus and Purpose

Focus on the words of each question. Always determine precisely what is being called for.

More specific tips and strategies for each type of question appear in the Skillbuilder sections of this book.

Rehearse for the Test: Be in Control

Familiarity instills confidence. Good rehearsals make good performances. If you follow a good plan of study, you will be prepared. This confidence will allow you to be more relaxed during the test. Don't panic if there are questions you cannot do at first. Remember that you don't have to get every question right. (See page 4 for information regarding scoring and scaling.) Of the more than 20,000 students taking the test, probably no one will get a perfect score.

Simulate test conditions by strictly adhering to the time limits and working under test-like conditions. Work for the **full time** and check your work if you finish early, just as you would on the actual exam.

Maintain a steady pace. Don't rush. Don't skip around wildly.

Concentrate on what you are doing at the moment. Don't think about what's coming up later in the test. Focus on one question at a time.

Do all of the practice tests in this book carefully. Working under the proper time limits and test conditions will make you ready for the actual test. You will then have a plan and a sense of self-assuredness that will enable you to do your best.

Keep track of your progress by using the charts in the Appendix.

Anxiety control: It is likely that there will be some questions you cannot answer. Don't let this make you panic. Everyone feels nervous at times. Don't let this take control of you. If you start to get anxious, close your eyes for a moment and take a few slow, deep breaths to help you relax. Remind yourself that you need think about only one question at a time. Remember that each individual question you answer adds to your total score. Then open your eyes and continue with the test, one question at a time.

Use the Test Booklet and Scratch Paper Wisely

Work in the test booklet and on scratch paper if provided. Be **neat** and **organized**. This helps keep you focused and provides a means for checking. Organize your scrap work. If you are all over the place, you leave yourself open to careless errors and are less likely to be mentally focused.

Number the scrap work for each problem by putting the problem number in a circle at the start of the work. It is very difficult to go back over any work you have done if that work is not orderly and numbered according to each problem.

Use the **? X** system.

Mark the test booklet in any way that is comfortable for you. The test booklet is not graded. Only your answer sheet will be graded. For example, on the Math section of the test, make helpful marks directly on diagrams, graphs, and charts.

THE NIGHT AND MORNING BEFORE THE TEST

- Prepare your supplies: admission ticket, 3 to 5 well-sharpened #2 pencils, a good eraser, and a noncalculator watch.
- Review directions for getting to the site.
- Get a good night's sleep.
- Get up early and have a good breakfast.
- Take all your supplies.
- Leave home extra early. That way, if any mishaps occur, you will still be on time and not feel rushed.

You have done your practicing. You're very well prepared for this test! All the past hints and skills will come to you automatically.

SOME ADDITIONAL IDEAS AND SUGGESTIONS

Read

Read regularly and read a wide variety of works. Be an alert, focused reader. Try to be aware of the writer's purpose and tone. Look up and learn new words. Try to improve your reading speed without sacrificing comprehension.

Write

Practice writing. Write often and write with care. Widen your vocabulary. Incorporate new words and phrases into your writing. Don't be sloppy or haphazard. Be careful not to practice poor habits.

Do Challenging Math Problems

If your school has a math team, try to join or attend practices and math contests. Do extra math problems on a daily basis. Try to add nonroutine problems to your daily practice.

Write Your Own Problems

Try writing your own test-style questions. This task can provide great insight and dramatically improve your own problem-solving skills. Write some multiple-choice style questions, but be sure to include the best wrong answers. Be precise. Try the problems out on friends.

Design your own Scrambled Paragraphs using passages from books and articles that you read. Write some reading comprehension questions based on a passage from a book or article.

Don't Cram!

Spread out your practice over time. Cramming for this exam will not be beneficial because it is unlikely to improve your score. Some students begin their preparation more than a year in advance.

Skillbuilder A: Scrambled Paragraphs

Scrambled Paragraph problems test your ability to find a logical order in a series of sentences. You do this in part by reading and understanding the sentences, of course, but you will find that your ability to succeed at Scrambled Paragraphs will improve dramatically once you learn to recognize *transitional words and phrases* that link one sentence to another, much like links in a chain.

This Skillbuilder will provide you with information on the kinds of links or hooks you can expect, as well as practice in recognizing and using the hooks. In addition, it will make you familiar with a variety of types of idea development that are common on the test. For instance, some paragraphs (once "unscrambled") tell a history in chronological order, some present contrasting opinions on a single subject, and some present a misconception about a subject followed by the truth on that subject. These are just some of the progressions of ideas that will become more familiar to you as you work through the problems in this book.

WHAT'S BEING TESTED?

A Scrambled Paragraph presents an initial sentence followed by five sentences listed in random order. Your task is to **unscramble these five sentences** to form a well-organized, grammatically correct paragraph.

To become a skilled unscrambler, you must learn to recognize certain key features of paragraphs. You must also master some key skills. These keys will open the door to the correct paragraph order. They include the following:

- Recognizing **paragraph development**. This means identifying the underlying structure of the paragraph, such as contrasting one idea with another, or telling a story in time order.
- Locating **hooks** (transitional words and phrases). These provide clues about how to order the sentences. For instance, a sentence beginning with "Next" would not be the opening sentence of a paragraph. Many more hooks will be covered in this Skillbuilder, including some that may be new to you.
- **Connecting** the sentences. This is our final aim. Each sentence contains clues about why it *must* connect with the sentences directly before and/or after it.
- Verifying the **logical order**. This is your final check.

NOTE: The SHSAT has used two forms of Scrambled Paragraphs. This Skillbuilder includes work on both types, but emphasizes the most recent form because this is the form you are most likely to encounter when you take the test.

Recognizing Paragraph Development

A paragraph has a pattern of development that leads the reader from the opening sentence to the concluding sentence. This includes

Sequence of events. A brief historical narrative, similar events widely separated in time, a description of a process, and the like

Description. Details about a place, a person, a thing, an action, and so on

Explanation. Details that clarify the significance of an opening statement

Comparison-contrast. Details pointing out how people, things, and events are similar and/or different

PRACTICE

Quickly read the following scrambled paragraphs to determine the kind of development. At this point, you don't need to fully understand the content of the sentences.

PRACTICE 1

Most people are more familiar with butterflies than moths, because butterflies are diurnal and moths nocturnal.

_____ (Q) One obvious difference is the antennae, which in butterflies are slender, long, and knobbed and in moths are thicker and furry-looking.

_____ (R) Another difference is that the resting butterfly folds its wings up, closing them, while the wings of the resting moth are held straight out or folded down.

_____ (S) They are similar insects, but in addition to their habits, there are ways to distinguish between them on sight.

_____ (T) A final visible difference is that a butterfly's body is slender and smooth-looking and a moth's thick and sometimes, like the antennae, furry-looking.

_____ (U) Distinguishing between these two insects is, therefore, not a difficult task—if you can get a close look at one before it flies away.

Development pattern: _____

PRACTICE 2

A 60,000-year-old grave in Iraq has been discovered to contain a heavy sprinkling of pollen.

_____ (Q) The funeral offering suggests love, and the medicinal value of the plants reflects some knowledge of both healing and botany.

_____ (R) Evidently the remains of a funeral offering, the pollen is for the most part from plants used today as medicinal herbs.

_____ (S) Anthropologists speculate that the Neanderthal mourners surrounded the body of the deceased with plants to strengthen it on its journey to immortality.

_____ (T) Instead, this contemporary of early man must have had the ability to form close emotional bonds and to understand many aspects of its environment.

_____ (U) They point out that this discovery gives further evidence that Neanderthal Man was not the brutish, unintelligent creature he is often depicted to be.

Development pattern: _____

It probably was pretty easy to immediately see that the first paragraph uses **comparison-contrast**, discussing similarities and differences between butterflies and moths. The second is not so obvious, but even in skimming you probably noticed the words *suggests, evidently, evidence,* and *speculate* that indicate that the paragraph gives an **explanation** that has something to do with Neanderthals and pollen.

Skimming will give you a general idea of the content and pattern, and this is enough to get you started.

Now for the next step.

Recognizing Transitional Clues

Train yourself to recognize different kinds of clues that **hook** one sentence to another. There are several different kinds of these clues, and becoming familiar with them will not only help you hook sentences together logically but often indicate the kind of pattern you're trying to follow.

COMMON TRANSITIONAL CLUES ("HOOKS")

Expressions indicating *more of the same*

also	moreover	likewise
consequently	indeed	similarly
for example	in addition	therefore
furthermore	in fact	as a result

Expressions indicating *contrast*

although	nevertheless	on the other hand
even so	nonetheless	otherwise
however	on the contrary	

The lists are not complete, but being familiar with these common expressions will help you recognize other, similar transitions. A hook from one of these two groups usually links its sentence to a previous one.

Some of the words in the lists above may not yet be part of your regular vocabulary. If you are unsure of the precise usage of any of these words, be sure to look them up in a dictionary!

PRACTICE

Read the following sentences. Circle the transitional expressions and label them (for *more of the same*) or *contrast*. Note that not every sentence contains a "hook."

PRACTICE 3

The White House has announced that all government agencies have completed the upgrading of their computer software.

_____ (Q) Therefore there should be no major slowdowns or interruptions in service when the new mainframe systems are installed.

_____ (R) On the contrary, service should for the most part run smoothly and eventually be faster than ever.

_____ (S) These problems, though, should be minor and easily resolved by built-in correction features.

_____ (T) In fact, they are not expected to cause any significant delays in delivery of services.

_____ (U) It is to be expected, however, that some unforeseen problems will arise.

PRACTICE 4

Scientists are telling us that modern cleaning habits in homes, businesses, and hospitals depend too much on the use of antibacterial products.

_____ (Q) They also accuse patients and doctors of relying too heavily on antibiotics, even for viral illnesses, which antibiotics can't help.

_____ (R) Although most "tough microbe" cases have been manageable by the use of "super" antibiotics, the threat of ever more dangerous germs lies ahead.

_____ (S) There have been reported cases of serious and even fatal illnesses caused by these tough new microbes.

_____ (T) As a result of these two unhealthful practices, highly resistant strains of bacteria have developed.

_____ (U) These strains have adapted to antibiotics and antibacterial products and are no longer affected by them.

Did you label *therefore* and *in fact* in (3) and *also* and *as a result* in (4) as "same"? And did you label *on the contrary, though* and *however* in (3) and *although* in (4) as "contrast"? Good! You've got the hang of it.

ADDITIONAL COMMON TRANSITIONAL CLUES

Time-sequence expressions

afterward	finally	next
at that time	first . . . second	years later
earlier	later	in 1762 . . . in 1770

Pronouns

he	their	<u>Newton</u> was . . . *He* wrote
her	these	
his	they	<u>Einstein</u> developed . . . *His* theory states . . .
she	this	

In the examples about Newton and Einstein above, it is important to note that subjects are usually introduced for the first time by their full names. Therefore, a sentence referring to a person by his or her last name alone will almost certainly follow a sentence providing that person's full name. This also applies to subjects other than people. For instance, a sentence mentioning "the election of 1824" would likely come before a sentence referring to simply "the election."

PRACTICE

Read the following sentences and circle the hooks, labeling them *time* or *pronoun*. Ignore pronouns that are not hooks. Note that not every sentence contains a "hook."

PRACTICE 5

The Native American Mayans of Guatemala have an elaborate way of welcoming every new child to the community.

_____ (Q) Thirty-two days later, when he or she is 40 days old, there is another ceremony at which the little child becomes a full-fledged member of the community.

_____ (R) They are also present to represent the village at the baby's birth; furthermore, for a period of eight days after the birth, neighbors visit with gifts of food, although they do not see the baby yet.

_____ (S) As this youngster grows and eventually has children of his or her own, the welcoming ceremony is repeated, and the strong community bond valued by the Mayans is extended to yet another generation.

_____ (T) After the eight days, the neighbors come to kiss and welcome the newcomer, and candles are lighted to symbolize that the baby must respect his community.

_____ (U) When a couple first know that they are to have a baby, they visit the village leaders, who formally promise that the community will uphold the parents in their task of raising the child.

PRACTICE 6

On July 14, 1904, Isaac Bashevis Singer was born in Radzymin, Poland, into a long line of rabbis renowned for their piety and knowledge.

_____ (Q) In the decades following his arrival in this country, he produced a number of widely acclaimed novels that reflected the pre-World War II Jewish culture of Eastern Europe.

_____ (R) As a young man he broke with his family's rabbinical tradition, however, by choosing a career in writing.

_____ (S) When he was 31 he came to the United States to write for the *Jewish Daily Forward,* a Yiddish-language newspaper based in New York.

_____ (T) Three of his most popular novels are *The Manor, The Family Moskat,* and *Enemies, A Love Story.*

_____ (U) These and his short stories won him the Nobel Prize for Literature in 1978 for his "impassioned narrative art."

In Practice 5, pronoun hooks include *they* in R and *he or she* in Q. The *they* in U is not a hook. Time clues include *first* in U, *after the eight days* in T and *thirty-two days later* in Q. In Practice 6, pronoun hooks include *he* in R, *he* in S, *his* and *he* in Q, and *his* and *him* in U. Time clues include *as a young man* or just *young* in R, *when he was 31* in S, *In the decades following . . .* in Q, and *in 1978* in U.

ANOTHER IMPORTANT TRANSITION CLUE, REPETITION

- repeated words and phrases
- paraphrased details—that is, details repeated in different words

Look at the following two sentences taken from Practice (4). (The sentences are presented in unscrambled order.)

_____ (S) There have been reported cases of serious and even fatal illnesses caused by these tough new microbes.

_____ (R) Although most "tough microbe" cases have been manageable by the use of "super" antibiotics, the threat of ever more dangerous germs lies ahead.

In this case the sentences are hooked together by the same words.
Now look at the other three unscrambled sentences from Practice (4).

_____ (U) Scientists are telling us that modern cleaning habits in homes, businesses, and hospitals depend too much on the use of antibacterial products.

_____ (Q) They also accuse patients and doctors of relying too heavily on antibiotics, even for viral illnesses, which antibiotics can't help.

_____ (T) As a result of *these two unhealthful practices,* highly resistant strains of bacteria have developed.

In this case two examples of undesirable behavior are referred to in a third sentence by a descriptive phrase. Therefore T must follow Q and U.

PRACTICE

In the following Scrambled Paragraphs (5 and 6, which you viewed previously) circle the repetition clues, both the first mention and the second, the hook.

PRACTICE 5

The Native American Mayans of Guatemala have an elaborate way of welcoming every new child to the community.

_____ (Q) Thirty-two days later, when he or she is 40 days old, there is another ceremony at which the little child becomes a full-fledged member of the community.

_____ (R) They are also present to represent the village at the baby's birth; furthermore, for a period of eight days after the birth, neighbors visit with gifts of food, although they do not see the baby yet.

_____ (S) As this youngster grows and eventually has children of his or her own, the welcoming ceremony is repeated, and the strong community bond valued by the Mayans is extended to yet another generation.

_____ (T) After the eight days, the neighbors come to kiss and welcome the newcomer, and candles are lighted to symbolize that the baby must respect his community.

_____ (U) When a couple first know that they are to have a baby, they visit the village leaders, who formally promise that the community will uphold the parents in their task of raising the child.

PRACTICE 6

On July 14, 1904, Isaac Bashevis Singer was born in Radzymin, Poland, into a long line of rabbis renowned for their piety and knowledge.

_____ (Q) In the decades following his arrival in this country, he produced a number of widely acclaimed novels that reflected the pre-World War II Jewish culture of Eastern Europe.

_____ (R) As a young man he broke with his family's rabbinical tradition, however, by choosing a career in writing.

_____ (S) When he was 31 he came to the United States to write for the *Jewish Daily Forward,* a Yiddish-language newspaper based in New York.

_____ (T) Three of his most popular novels are *The Manor, The Family Moskat,* and *Enemies, A Love Story.*

_____ (U) These and his short stories won him the Nobel Prize for Literature in 1978 for his "impassioned narrative art."

Did you find in (5) *period of eight days* and its hook (after) *the eight days;* and *candles are lighted to symbolize . . .* and the hook *another ceremony*? And in (6) did you spot *long line of rabbis* and *family's rabbinical tradition* and also *came to the United States* and the hook *following his arrival in this country*? Good for you.

You're now ready for some practice in putting the techniques together.
Briefly, they are

1. **Skim** for development pattern.
2. Read to find the **hooks** that tie sentences together.
3. Find the most likely **second sentence**, the sentence that hooks most logically to the initial sentence. Then use the remaining hooks to put the rest of the sentences in order.
4. **Double-check** your arrangement for logical sense.

Work in pencil in an orderly manner. Make notes in the available space in your test booklet, indicating which sentences are linked and in what order. For instance, if you are certain that R comes directly before U, you might note "RU" in the margin, leaving space to put other letters before and after RU as required. Using a pencil makes it easy to make changes.

In this practice, when you are satisfied with the order of the sentences, circle your answers in the answer section that follows. On the actual exam, you will fill in those answers on the answer sheet's grid.

PRACTICE

Unscramble the two scrambled paragraphs below by using all the techniques that you've been working on. (The correct answers are given at the end of the wrap-up that follows these test items.)

PRACTICE 7

Years ago, tenant farmers were supposed to pay their landlords rent in the form of a portion of all they produced.

_____ (Q) The expression *let the cat out of the bag* still means to accidentally reveal troublesome information.

_____ (R) A farmer could cheat the landlord by going to market with a baby pig concealed in a bag and selling it to a cooperative butcher.

_____ (S) They would frequently get caught, however, when the butcher opened the bag too soon and the cat clawed its way out.

_____ (T) The landlord would never know about the baby pig sold this way and could not count it among the total of all that the farmer had produced.

_____ (U) Not content with cheating the landlord, a few farmers would cheat the butcher also by selling him a bag containing a cat instead of a piglet.

PRACTICE 7 ANSWERS:

The second sentence is	Ⓠ	Ⓡ	Ⓢ	Ⓣ	Ⓤ
The third sentence is	Ⓠ	Ⓡ	Ⓢ	Ⓣ	Ⓤ
The fourth sentence is	Ⓠ	Ⓡ	Ⓢ	Ⓣ	Ⓤ
The fifth sentence is	Ⓠ	Ⓡ	Ⓢ	Ⓣ	Ⓤ
The sixth sentence is	Ⓠ	Ⓡ	Ⓢ	Ⓣ	Ⓤ

PRACTICE 8

If taken one step at a time, a research paper is not actually hard to produce.

_____ (Q) To avoid later frustration, the researcher should next search a library and the Internet for available sources of information on the chosen topic.

_____ (R) The researcher must remember, however, to give credit in his paper to all of the sources from which he/she included information, even in paraphrased form.

_____ (S) If there is plenty of useful material available, the researcher should outline the questions he/she needs to answer and then seek the answers in the identified sources.

_____ (T) The crucial first steps are to find a subject—preferably an interesting one—and then to narrow the subject down to a manageable topic.

_____ (U) Paraphrasing the answers on note cards will make the final step— the actual writing of the paper—an easy snap of the fingers.

PRACTICE 8 ANSWERS:

The second sentence is	Ⓠ	Ⓡ	Ⓢ	Ⓣ	Ⓤ
The third sentence is	Ⓠ	Ⓡ	Ⓢ	Ⓣ	Ⓤ
The fourth sentence is	Ⓠ	Ⓡ	Ⓢ	Ⓣ	Ⓤ
The fifth sentence is	Ⓠ	Ⓡ	Ⓢ	Ⓣ	Ⓤ
The sixth sentence is	Ⓠ	Ⓡ	Ⓢ	Ⓣ	Ⓤ

Wrap-up

Here are some useful hints and reminders.

When you are taking the Practice Tests, be sure to practice the four techniques:

- *skim* for an idea of content and development (*skim:* don't read word-for-word).
- *read* to find the hooking clues.
- *identify* the second sentence, and then put the others in order.
- *double-check* for logic.

The double-check is crucial because *no credit is given for an answer that is only partly correct.* Be sure all the sentences are placed correctly!

Use the blanks provided to keep track of numbering; it won't take much time and will make the double-check easier. *Always write the numbers down*; don't rely on memory.

If you have trouble deciding on the best arrangement, take an educated guess and move on. It doesn't pay to spend too much time on one item.

Answers: Practice 7—RTUSQ; Practice 8—TQSUR

You're now ready for the Scrambled Paragraph sections of the Practice Tests.

Remember to work methodically, and always to double-check before recording your answer!

Another Form of Scrambled Paragraph

Before you leave this Skillbuilder, you should be aware of another form of Scrambled Paragraph. Although it has not appeared recently, it did appear on prior exams. In this form, the first sentence is *not* provided. You are given five randomly arranged sentences to put in the best order to form a well-organized paragraph. The previous suggestions in this Skillbuilder apply. However, you now have to decide which sentence should be the first in the paragraph.

FINDING THE FIRST SENTENCE

As you look for the transition clues, be alert for the sentence with **no apparent hook** to another sentence. Does this sentence introduce the paragraph's topic? If so, you have found the first sentence.

PRACTICE

For each of the following pairs of sentences, decide whether sentence Q or sentence R is more likely to be an opening sentence. Write a number 1 in the blank at its left. (Answers follow Practice A4.)

PRACTICE A1

_____ (Q) You know it's worth the effort when you finally taste the scrumptious mingling of flavors and textures.

_____ (R) Concocting a trifle can be a complicated and lengthy task.

PRACTICE A2

_____ (Q) A recent discovery in the mountains of North Carolina has stunned geologists and set the gem world buzzing.

_____ (R) It is no wonder the world is paying attention, for events like this one are few and far between.

PRACTICE A3

_____ (Q) Indeed, items worth thousands of dollars are routinely auctioned off, sometimes for only a fraction of their real value.

_____ (R) In a tiny village in New England, tucked between a hardware store and a barber shop, is one of the best sources of bargains in the world.

PRACTICE A4

_____ (Q) His favorite activity was scouring the mountainous countryside for interesting-looking rock formations.

_____ (R) Peter Raschfield of Boone, North Carolina, recently realized the dream of his lifetime—he discovered a cave full of rubies and other precious stones.

In each case, the lack of a hook identifies the first sentence.
Answers: Practice A1—R; Practice A2—Q; Practice A3—R; Practice A4—R.

PRACTICE A5

Unscramble the following paragraph by deciding which should be the first sentence, which should be second, and so forth.

_____ (Q) Early cans were opened by hammer and chisel—a clumsy approach—and later by sharp-edged levers and claws that were less clumsy but could inflict nasty cuts.

_____ (R) Finally, in 1930, an efficient and convenient can opener became available, one with a fairly simple design that is still the basis for most can openers.

_____ (S) The tin can for preserving food was a revolutionary invention of the early eighteenth century.

_____ (T) For more than a hundred years, however, it was difficult and sometimes even dangerous to get at the stored food.

_____ (U) This useful machine has a sharp circular blade that cuts into the lid of the can as a toothed wheel under the lip of the can moves the can forward to enable a smooth, continuous cut.

Answers follow Practice A6.

PRACTICE A6

Unscramble the following paragraph by deciding which should be the first sentence, which should be second, and so forth.

_____ (Q) Once the track is removed, however, only minimal maintenance is required.

_____ (R) The *Rails to Trails* movement has become an influential force in many communities.

_____ (S) This is achieved by converting old, unused railway beds into pathways for hiking, running, and biking.

_____ (T) The purpose of the movement is to turn useless eyesores into useful and attractive spaces.

_____ (U) The transformation requires an initial investment to pay for the removal of the track.

Answers: Practice A5—The best order is STQRU; Practice A6—The best order is RTSUQ.

Skillbuilder B: Logical Reasoning

Logical Reasoning questions are basically puzzles and games that challenge you to draw logical (valid) conclusions based upon some given conditions or relationships. If you have solved puzzles, played computer games, or tried to figure something out from clues, then you are already somewhat familiar with the kind of thinking that is called for by the Logical Reasoning section of the test.

This Skillbuilder will get you familiar with the major types of questions that are asked, strengthen your understanding of them, and provide you with techniques for their solution. Some types of Logical Reasoning questions may seem simple and others rather complicated, but by practicing them carefully, you will gain confidence and expertise. *Practice is the key to success.* Familiarity instills confidence!

WHAT'S BEING TESTED?

A Logical Reasoning question requires you to draw logical conclusions based upon a set of given conditions or relationships. It tests your ability to

- read carefully and accurately
- discriminate between relevant (important) and irrelevant (unimportant) information
- analyze and process information

We will group these questions by frequently occurring types, including lots of examples for study and practice.

In General, What Do I Do?

Whenever possible, organize the material into a diagram, chart, or helpful symbols. This changes the information from verbal to visual, making it easier to focus on the material. Be sure to include all the conditions, but *keep it simple.* Often there is some easy fact that you can start with (you do not have to use the information in the order in which it is given).

Some Things to Remember

1. Use *only* the information given or implied in the passage. Be careful not to read into the passage information that is not present.
2. Be neat! A sloppy diagram or carelessly drawn figure could cause you to miss an otherwise easy question.
3. Combine good analysis with common sense. Dismiss unreasonable choices. Pick the *best* of the choices available (only one will be correct). If you determine the correct answer and it is among the given choices, don't bother checking all the other choices.
4. Don't waste time. Don't dwell on any one question, but don't panic if you must skip a question.
5. Preview the choices. A brief look can help you focus on what is called for.

Most Logical Reasoning questions fall into certain categories, each with its own attributes. Study one type at a time, carefully going through the examples and their analyses. Then try the Follow-up Problems.

Logical Reasoning Problem 1

Put 'Em in Their Places

The clues describe relative sizes or places, and our task is to put things in the right order. **The Key:** Reformulate the information into a diagram or use inequality symbols for compact comparison.

EXAMPLE 1.1

Five different colored blocks are stacked one above the other. They are numbered 1, 2, 3, 4, and 5 from bottom to top.

1. One of the blocks is red.
2. Below the white block are precisely two other blocks, one of which is the blue block.
3. Between the blue block and the green block are exactly three other blocks.

Which color block is on the top?

(A) Blue
(B) Green
(C) Red
(D) White
(E) Cannot be determined from the information given.

ANALYSIS:

Carefully **read** the question, especially noting what is being called for: Which color block is on the top?

Organize the information into a diagram of some kind. A set of vertical boxes seems logical here.

Analyze the information.

Statement (2) implies that the white block must be in box 3, and the blue block is somewhere below it. We mark that as shown.

Statement (3) implies that the blue and green blocks must occupy the top and bottom boxes. Since the blue cannot be on top, the green must be there. The answer to the question is **B**. Statement (1) is irrelevant.

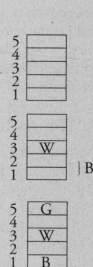

Notice how using a diagram makes the problem easy to analyze.

EXAMPLE 1.2

(In this example there are three questions.) *P, Q, R,* and *S* represent four different integers. You are given that

1. *P* is not the largest.
2. *Q* is less than *P.*
3. *R* is not the smallest.
4. *S* is greater than *R.*

If these integers are placed in numerical order from left to right, *with the smallest on the left,* then

Question 1: The next-to-smallest integer

(F) must be *P.*
(G) must be *Q.*
(H) must be *R.*
(J) must be *S.*
(K) cannot be determined.

ANALYSIS

Carefully **read** the question, especially noting what is being called for: The next-to-smallest integer . . .

Organize the information into a diagram of some kind. A set of horizontal spaces seems logical.

— — — —

Analyze the information.
Statements (1) and (2) tell us that *P* is not in the last space, and *Q* is somewhere to the left of *P.* This leads to three possible diagrams.

$$\underline{Q} \quad \underline{P} \quad \underline{} \quad \underline{}$$
or $\underline{Q} \quad \underline{} \quad \underline{P} \quad \underline{}$
or $\underline{} \quad \underline{Q} \quad \underline{P} \quad \underline{}$

Now statements (3) and (4) tell us that *R* is not in the first space, and *S* is somewhere to the right of *R.* This eliminates the third diagram, and allows us to fill in the other two, both of which are possible. We can now answer the question. The next-to-smallest integer could be either of two letters, so the answer is **K**.

$$\underline{Q} \quad \underline{P} \quad \underline{R} \quad \underline{S}$$
or $\underline{Q} \quad \underline{R} \quad \underline{P} \quad \underline{S}$

(continued)

Question 2: We can determine the exact position of

(A) none of the letters.
(B) only one letter.
(C) *P* and *Q* only.
(D) *Q* and *S* only.
(E) all four letters.

ANALYSIS

The final two diagrams in the analysis of Question 1 answer this question also. Looking at the two possibilities, we see that we can determine the exact positions of *Q* and S only, so the answer is **D**.

$$\underline{Q} \quad \underline{} \quad \underline{} \quad \underline{S}$$

Question 3: If we also know that *P* is greater than *R*, we can determine the exact positions of

(F) *Q* and *S* only.
(G) *P, Q,* and *S* only.
(H) all four letters.
(J) none of the four letters.
(K) It is impossible for *P* to be more than *R*.

ANALYSIS

Only one of those two final diagrams agrees with this additional information. Thus we know the position of all four letters. The answer is **H**.

$$\underline{Q} \quad \underline{R} \quad \underline{P} \quad \underline{S}$$

EXAMPLE 1.3

If Lawrence weighs more than Bob and Chuck together, but Lawrence weighs less than Chuck and Julio together, which one of the following must be true?

(A) Lawrence is heavier than Julio.
(B) Chuck is heavier than Bob.
(C) Julio is heavier than Lawrence.
(D) Julio is heavier than Bob.
(E) Julio is heavier than Chuck.

ANALYSIS

Carefully **read** the question, especially noting what is being called for: Which of the following *must* be true? Be very careful about the difference between *must* and *may*.

Organize (reformulate) the information. This time it is helpful to use mathematical symbols. It is also easier if we use single letters to represent each person (we will use the first letter of each name).

$$L > B + C \text{ and } L < C + J$$

Analyze the information.

This is most easily done when the inequality symbols go in the "same direction."

$$L > B + C \text{ and } C + J > L$$

We can now add the two inequalities (there are other approaches), then subtract L and C from both sides. It is now clear that the answer is **D**.

$$L + C + J > B + C + L \text{ so}$$
$$J > B$$

ALTERNATE ANALYSIS

Carefully read the question, especially noting what is being called for: Which of the following *must* be true?

Organize (reformulate) the information, putting B and C in a box, and C and J in a box, as shown.

Analyze the information. We see that $B + C < C + J$.

Since both boxes contain C, it must be true that $B < J$. This is the same as $J > B$. The answer is **D**.

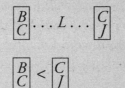

$$\boxed{\begin{matrix}B\\C\end{matrix}} \cdots L \cdots \boxed{\begin{matrix}C\\J\end{matrix}}$$

$$\boxed{\begin{matrix}B\\C\end{matrix}} < \boxed{\begin{matrix}C\\J\end{matrix}}$$

$$B < J$$

Follow-Up Problems

Answers are on page 86.

EXAMPLE 1.4

Bill, Depesh, Ming, Robert, and Sergei collected money for charity. Robert collected the most money; Bill collected $12 more than Ming; neither Ming nor Sergei collected the least. We can be sure that

(F) Sergei collected more than Bill.
(G) Sergei collected more than Ming.
(H) Sergei collected less than Ming
(J) Depesh collected less than Ming.
(K) no two people collected the same amount of money

EXAMPLE 1.5

There are 5 people (*A, B, C, D,* and *E*) in a room, and a table with 4 chairs around it. Four of the people are seated, one to a chair. *A* is not sitting next to *B, B* is not sitting next to *C, C* is not sitting next to *D,* and *D* is not sitting next to *E.* Who is standing?

(A) *A*
(B) *B*
(C) *C*
(D) *D*
(E) *E*

Logical Reasoning Problem 2

Breaking the Code

Artificial language and nonsense words are the elements of this puzzle. Can you *decipher* the scrambled message? With a little practice, these become easy. **The Key: Good organization and the process of elimination.**

Most of the test examples involve several sentences. The following example (with three questions) will show you the two simple steps that solve these problems. In this type, *you must check all of the choices* in order to find out which choice corresponds to the given word (whether that's the English word or the nonsense word). After a short time, you'll get very good and very quick at doing these!

EXAMPLE 2.1

In the code below, (1) each nonsense word represents the same English word in all three sentences, (2) each English word is represented by only one nonsense word, and (3) in any given sentence, the nonsense words may or may not be presented in the same order as the English words.

cal tig ba ru pla	means	"Alan is very happy today."
ba mul cal jah tig	means	"Judy is also very happy."
pla cal ru ko ba	means	"Today Alan is very confident."

Question 1: Which nonsense word represents "confident"?

(A) *ru*
(B) *ba*
(C) *ko*
(D) *mul*
(E) Cannot be determined from the information given.

ANALYSIS

Put a **mark** next to each sentence that contains the given word ("confident").

> *cal tig ba ru pla* means
> "Alan is very happy today."
>
> *ba mul cal jah tig* means
> "Judy is also very happy."
>
> *pla cal ru ko ba* means
> —"Today Alan is very confident."

Only one sentence contains "confident." **Check** each choice to see which one is in all the marked sentences, but not in any other sentence. Only *ko* satisfies this, so the answer is **C**. If another choice also worked, the answer would be **E**.

Question 2: Which English word is represented by *cal*?

(F) Alan
(G) happy
(H) very
(J) is
(K) Cannot be determined from the information given.

(continued)

ANALYSIS

Put a **mark** next to each sentence that contains the given word (*cal*). Don't use the same mark you used before, or you might get confused.

     cal tig ba ru   pla   means
☐ "Alan is   very happy today."

     ba   mul cal jah tig   means
☐ "Judy is also very happy."

     pla   cal ru ko ba   means
☐ "Today Alan is very confident."

All three sentences contains *cal*. **Check** each choice to see which choice is in all the marked sentences. Both "very" and "is" work, so the answer is **K**.

Question 3: Which nonsense word represents "happy"?

(A) *ba*

(B) *tig*

(C) *pla*

(D) *jah*

(E) Cannot be determined from the information given.

ANALYSIS

Put a **mark** next to each sentence that contains the given word ("happy"). Again, use a different mark.

     cal tig ba ru   pla   means
● "Alan is   very happy today."

     ba   mul cal jah tig   means
● "Judy is   also very happy."

     pla   cal ru ko ba   means
"Today Alan is very confident."

Only the first two sentences contain "happy." **Check** each choice to see which one is in all the marked sentences, but not in any other sentence. Only *tig* satisfies this, so the answer is **B**.

NOTE: Don't worry about translating every word. Just focus on the words that are called for.

EXAMPLE 2.2

In the following code, each nonsense word represents the same English word throughout the sentence, but is **never** in the same position as that English word. We will call this a **restricted** code.

pon gur bal bal gur   means   "He waits and he waits."

What does *pon bal* mean?

ANALYSIS

pon occurs only once in the sentence. The only English word that appears just once is "and," so *pon* means "and."

bal occurs twice in the sentence. It could mean "he" or "waits." But the instructions say that the nonsense word is never in the same position as the English word. Because of that restriction, we must eliminate "he," so *bal* means "waits."

pon bal = "and waits"

Sometimes a different form occurs in these problems, using symbols instead of nonsense words. This is no harder than the other form.

EXAMPLE 2.3

In the code below, (1) each symbol represents the same word in all 3 sentences, (2) each word is represented by only one symbol, and (3) in any given sentence, the symbols may or may not be presented in the same order as the words.

* @ # $ means   "I can cook tomorrow."
& @ * #   means   "I can help tomorrow."
$ % & @   means   "I help cook vegetables."

   Question 1: Which symbol represents "help"?

   (F) @
   (G) #
   (H) $
   (J) &
   (K) Cannot be determined from the information given

(continued)

ANALYSIS

Put a **mark** next to each sentence that contains the given word ("help").

	* @ # $	means	"I can cook tomorrow."
—	& @ * #	means	"I can help tomorrow."
—	$ % & @	means	"I help cook vegetables."

Only the last two sentences contain "help." **Check** each choice to see which one is in all the marked sentences, but not in any other sentence. Only & satisfies this, so the answer is **J.**

Question 2: If we now **restrict** this problem by saying that the symbol representing a given word is **never** in the same position as that word, which symbol will represent "tomorrow"?

(A) @
(B) #
(C) *
(D) $
(E) Cannot be determined from the information given

ANALYSIS

Put a **mark** next to each sentence that contains the given word ("tomorrow").

●	* @ # $	means	"I can cook tomorrow."
●	& @ * #	means	"I can help tomorrow."
	$ % & @	means	"I help cook vegetables."

Only the first two sentences contain "tomorrow." Immediately eliminate choices B and D because # and $ occupy the same position as "tomorrow." Now **check** each of the other choices to see which one is in all the marked sentences, but not in any other sentence. Only * satisfies this, so the answer is **C.**

EXAMPLE 2.4

In the following code, each nonsense word represents the same English word in both sentences, but is **never** in the same position as that English word.

| *mon lu da sut po* | means | "Kenji gave David a dog." |
| *gor da fil po rab* | means | "Kenji asked David for help." |

(continued)

The nonsense word that represents the English word "Kenji" is

(F) *lu*
(G) *da*
(H) *sut*
(J) *po*
(K) not determined by the given information

ANALYSIS

Put a **mark** next to each sentence that contains the given word ("Kenji").

> *mon   lu   da   sut po*   means
> __ "Kenji gave David a dog."
> · *gor   da   fil   po rab*   means
> __ "Kenji asked David for help."

Both sentences contains *da* and *po,* so it would seem that the answer is K. However, look at "David." It also appears in both sentences, but cannot be represented by *da* (remember, this is a **restricted** code). Therefore *po* must represent "David," leaving only *da* for "Kenji"! The answer is **G.** This is a more difficult type of situation, because you must check a word other than the one called for in the question!

This can occur only in the **restricted** type of problem.

Follow-Up Problems

Answers are on page 86.

EXAMPLE 2.5

In the code below, (1) each symbol represents the same word in all 3 sentences, (2) each word is represented by only one symbol, and (3) in any given sentence, the symbols may or may not be presented in the same order as the words.

> @   means   "Matt likes Louisa."
> # @   means   "Louisa likes Matt."
> # $ means   "Louisa helped Matt."

Question 1: Which word is represented by @?

(A) Matt
(B) likes
(C) Louisa
(D) helped
(E) Cannot be determined from the information given

(continued)

Question 2: What symbol represents "Matt"?

(F) #
(G) >
(H) @
(J) $
(K) Cannot be determined from the information given.

Question 3: If we now **restrict** this problem by saying that the symbol representing a given word is **never** in the same position as that word, what symbol represents "Matt"?

(A) #
(B) >
(C) @
(D) $
(E) Either # or >, but cannot determine which one.

EXAMPLE 2.6

In the following code, each nonsense word represents the same English word throughout the sentence, but is **never** in the same position as that English word:

gak	lu	gak	ig	bor
"All's	well	that	ends	well."

The nonsense word that represents the English word "ends" could be

(F) *gak, lu, ig,* or *bor*
(G) *lu, ig,* or *bor* only
(H) *gak, lu,* or *bor* only
(J) *lu* or *bor* only
(K) *gak* or *ig* only

Logical Reasoning Problem 3

Ifs and Thens

If you practice these problems, *then* you'll do well on the test. A simple rule for manipulating *If-Then* logic statements puts you in total control. **The Key: Use a simple *logic* shorthand.**

> *If there is a snowstorm, then the schools will be closed.*

The above statement is called a *conditional statement* because closing the schools is conditional (dependent) upon there being a snowstorm. A conditional statement describes a cause (the IF part, or the Hypothesis) and an effect (the THEN part, or the Conclusion).

If we represent   *there is a snowstorm*   by *p*
and   *the schools will be closed*   by *q*

then we may abbreviate the entire statement simply as   **If *p*, then *q***

or even more briefly as   **$p \rightarrow q$** (*p* implies *q*).

From the statement, it also seems logical that if the schools are not closed, then we are not having a snowstorm. If you compare this second statement with the original, you will see that we have interchanged the IF with the THEN parts, and also negated both parts. This leads to Basic Principle 1.

BASIC PRINCIPLE 1

Given $p \rightarrow q$

the only other statement that *must* also be valid is **not *q* $\rightarrow$ not *p***. Using the symbol ~ to mean *the negative of,* this is finally abbreviated as

$$\sim q \rightarrow \sim p$$

This second statement is called the *Contrapositive* of the first statement.

EXAMPLE 3.1

Original statement: If there is a snowstorm, then the schools will be closed.
Contrapositive: If the schools are **not** closed, then there is **not** a snowstorm.
(Notice that some words in the original sentence may change a bit so that the grammar is correct.)

EXAMPLE 3.2

Original statement: If it is raining, then the streets are wet.
Contrapositive: If the streets are **not** wet, then it is **not** raining.

EXAMPLE 3.3

Original statement: If Graham passes math, then he will not go to summer school.
Contrapositive: If Graham **is** going to summer school, then he did **not** pass math.
(Notice that the **negative of a negative is positive**.)

Remember: To form the Contrapositive of a statement,

1. Interchange the IF with the THEN
2. Negate *both* parts of the new statement

As **Basic Principle 1** says, if you have an **If-Then** statement, the only other statement that *must* logically agree with it is its *Contrapositive*.

EXAMPLE 3.4

Let us suppose that the following statement is true: If you are rich, then you own *grackles*. Which is the only one of the following three statements that **must** also be true?

    (A) If you own grackles, then you are rich.
    (B) If you are not rich, then you do not own grackles.
    (C) If you do not own grackles, then you are not rich.

ANALYSIS

Make sure the original statement is in *If-Then* form.	*If* you are rich, *then* you own grackles.
Form the Contrapositive.	If you do not own grackles, then you are not rich.
Check which choice is the same as the Contrapositive. The answer is **C**.	

Notice that the original statement need not be true in reality. (Rich people may not really own grackles.) But the Contrapositive will still agree logically with that original statement.

Some people also think that if $p \rightarrow q$, then $q \rightarrow p$. This is not logically valid! *If there is a snowstorm, then the schools will be closed* $(p \rightarrow q)$ does not also tell you that *If the schools are closed, then there is a snowstorm* $(q \rightarrow p)$. Schools may be closed because it is the weekend, for example. Don't accidentally select that choice as a logical conclusion. (That was choice A in the previous problem.) Only the Contrapositive **must** be logically valid.

Sometimes the original statement is in a disguised **If-Then** form, and you must make sure you know where the IF and THEN are. Here are some typical disguises:

If you are smart, you will do well.	Put in the missing THEN: If you are smart, then you will do well. The Contrapositive is *If you do not do well, then you are not smart.*
People are intelligent if they read a lot.	Put in the missing THEN and rearrange; you must also fix up the wording: If people read a lot, then they are intelligent. The Contrapositive is *If people are not intelligent, then they do not read a lot.*
Dogs don't like cats.	Put in the missing IF and THEN: If an animal is a dog, then it does not like cats. The Contrapositive is *If an animal likes cats, then it is not a dog* OR *Animals that like cats are not dogs.*

EXAMPLE 3.5

Let us suppose that the following statement is true: You will be healthy if you eat spinach. Which is the only one of the following statements that **must** then be true?

(F) Spinach is an essential part of your diet.
(G) Only healthy people eat spinach.
(H) If you are not healthy, then you don't eat spinach.
(J) If you don't eat spinach, then you will not be healthy.
(K) In order to be healthy, you must eat leafy vegetables such as spinach.

ANALYSIS

Make sure the original statement is in *If-Then* form.	If you eat spinach, then you will be healthy.
Form the Contrapositive.	If you are not healthy, then you do not eat spinach.

Check which choice is the same as the Contrapositive. The answer is **H**. Notice that the original statement may not really be true! But the only other statement that logically follows from the original statement is its Contrapositive.

Sometimes two conditional statements are related, and can lead to a third.

EXAMPLE 3.6

First statement: If it snows heavily, then school will be closed.
Second statement: If school is closed, then Lynne will watch TV in the morning.

It seems logical therefore that: If it snows heavily, then Lynne will watch TV in the morning. This leads to Basic Principle 2.

BASIC PRINCIPLE 2

Given $p \rightarrow q$ and $q \rightarrow r$

we can conclude that $p \rightarrow r$

EXAMPLE 3.7

If Ray gets a good job, he will earn a lot of money. Ray will buy a dog if he earns a lot of money. Which is the only one of the following statements that **must** then be true?

(A) Ray likes dogs and money.
(B) People who get good jobs buy dogs.
(C) Ray will buy a dog if he gets a good job.
(D) If Ray does not get a good job, then he will not buy a dog.
(E) If Ray bought a dog, then he must have gotten a good job.

ANALYSIS

Make sure both original statements are in *If-Then* form. It is very helpful to use well-chosen letters to represent each part of the statements. Choose letters that remind you of the content.

Apply **Basic Principle 2**. Notice that the two given statements must have an identical element, in this case M (sometimes called a *connecting link*). That connecting link must be the conclusion of one statement and the hypothesis of the other.

Check which choice matches this final conclusion. The answer is **C**, although it is a bit disguised. We should stop there, but it is instructive to examine the other choices.

A. Ray likes dogs and money.

B. People who get good jobs buy dogs.

D. If Ray does not get a good job, then he will not buy a dog.

E. If Ray bought a dog, then he must have gotten a good job.

J → M
If Ray gets a good job, then he will earn a lot of money.

M → D
If Ray earns a lot of money, then he will buy a dog.

J → D
If Ray gets a good job, then he will buy a dog.

A. That may be true, but the example doesn't say so.

B. The example doesn't talk about people in general.

D. This is **~J → ~D**. That is not logically equivalent to the answer (it is not the contrapositive of the answer).

E. This is **D → J**. That is not logically equivalent to the answer (it is not the contrapositive of the answer).

EXAMPLE 3.8

If Teresa goes to the dance, then Danny will not go to the dance. If Sharon is away, then Danny will go to the dance. Which is the only one of the following statements that **must** then be true?

(F) If Sharon is away, then Teresa will go to the dance.
(G) If Teresa goes to the dance, then Danny will go to the dance.
(H) Teresa, Danny, and Sharon can all go to the dance.
(J)   If Teresa goes to the dance, then Sharon is not away.
(K) If Teresa doesn't go to the dance, then Sharon is away.

(continued)

ANALYSIS

Make sure both original statements are in *If-Then* form.

NOTE: It is best to let the single letters represent the *positive* versions of each part of the statements. Thus use D to represent *Danny will go,* and ~D to represent *Danny will not go.* This practice will make all your analyses both clear and consistent.

Before we can apply **Basic Principle 2**, we need an *identical* element (that connecting link). We can get a ~D into the second statement if we form its contrapositive. (According to Basic Principle 1, the contrapositive is logically equivalent to the statement.) So we must first change the second statement into its contrapositive.

Now we can apply **Basic Principle 2**.

Check which choice matches this final conclusion. The answer is **J**.

Another approach is to make D itself the connecting link. This requires forming the contrapositive of the first statement instead, and leads to S → ~T. This result is not one of the choices! Check its contrapositive (T → ~S). This is choice **J**.

T → ~D
If Teresa goes, then Danny will not go.
S → D
If Sharon is away, then Danny will go.

T → ~D
If Teresa goes, then Danny will not go.
~D → ~S
If Danny does not go, then Sharon is not away.

T → ~S
If Teresa goes (to the dance), then Sharon is not away.

Notice how hard it would be to do this problem without using the logic shorthand.

Follow-Up Examples

Answers are on page 86.

EXAMPLE 3.9

There are 4 people (*A, B, C,* and *D*) in a room, and only 3 chairs. Three of the people are to be seated, one to a chair. If *A* is seated, then *B* must be seated; if *B* is seated, then *C* must be seated; if *C* is seated, then *D* must be seated. Who **must** remain standing?

(A) *A*
(B) *B*
(C) *C*
(D) *D*
(E) These rules for seating cannot be followed successfully.

EXAMPLE 3.10

Steven will not buy a computer if Daniel buys a printer. If Vivian buys a flat-screen monitor, then Steven will buy a computer. Based on these statements, which of the following **must** be true?

(F) If Daniel does not buy a printer, Steven will not buy a computer.
(G) If Steven buys a computer, Vivian will buy a flat-screen monitor.
(H) If Vivian buys a flat-screen monitor, then Daniel will not buy a printer.
(J) If Steven does not buy a computer, Vivian will buy a flat-screen monitor.
(K) Vivian will buy a flat-screen monitor if Daniel buys a printer.

Logical Reasoning Problem 4

Who Does What

In this type of puzzle, the clues (conditions) lead to a matching game. We try to match one set of attributes with another, such as people with professions or hats with colors. **The Key: Make a chart.**

EXAMPLE 4.1

Two men (Matt and Evan) and two women (Betty and Linda) are teachers of history, physics, French, and Spanish, not necessarily in that order. Each person teaches only one subject. We know that

(1) Matt does not teach physics.
(2) The history teacher is not a woman.
(3) The French teacher is not a man.
(4) Betty teaches Spanish.

Who teaches physics?

(A) Matt
(B) Evan
(C) Betty
(D) Linda
(E) Cannot be determined from the information given.

(continued)

ANALYSIS

Carefully read the question. Make a **chart** with the people in the left-hand column and the attributes (subjects, in this case) across the top.

	HIST	PHYS	FR	SP
MATT				
EVAN				
BETTY				
LINDA				

Analyze each given piece of information, *one by one,* and **organize** it into your chart. Use a ✓ to represent *yes* and an X to represent *no.* If the information is not specific enough to enter yet, go on. Return to that information later.

(a) *Matt does not teach physics.* Put an X in the physics box for Matt.

(a)
	HIST	PHYS	FR	SP
M		X		
E				
B				
L				

(b) *The history teacher is not a woman.* Put Xs in the history boxes for Betty and Linda.

(b)
	HIST	PHYS	FR	SP
M		X		
E				
B	X			
L	X			

(c) *The French teacher is not a man.* Put Xs in the French boxes for Matt and Evan.

(c)
	HIST	PHYS	FR	SP
M		X	X	
E			X	
B	X			
L	X			

(d) *Betty teaches Spanish.* Put a ✓ in the Spanish box for Betty. We can now put Xs in all the other Spanish boxes, and in the other boxes in Betty's row.

(d)
	HIST	PHYS	FR	SP
M		X	X	X
E			X	X
B	X	X	X	✓
L	X			X

We can now enter ✓s showing that Matt teaches history and Linda teaches French. We can then put an X in the history box for Evan (or the physics box for Linda) so Evan must teach physics. The answer to the question is **B**.

	HIST	PHYS	FR	SP
M	✓	X	X	X
E			X	X
B	X	X	X	✓
L	X		✓	X

EXAMPLE 4.2

Eliot is strong and Justin has blue eyes. The tall person has black hair, but the person with brown eyes is not tall. We can definitely conclude that

(F) Justin has black hair and is strong.
(G) Eliot has black hair and is strong.
(H) Justin has black hair and is tall.
(J) Eliot has brown eyes and is tall.
(K) Eliot does not have black hair.

ANALYSIS

Carefully read the question. Make a **chart** with the people in the left-hand column and the attributes across the top. You do not need separate columns for blue eyes and brown eyes. Just have a column for blue eyes. A person with brown eyes would then get an X in the blue eyes column.

	STRONG	BLUE EYES	TALL	BLACK HAIR
ELIOT				
JUSTIN				

Analyze each given piece of information, *one by one*, and **organize** it into your chart. Use a ✓ to represent *yes* and an X to represent *no*. If the information is not specific enough to enter yet, go on. Don't forget to return to that information later.

(a) *Eliot is strong.* Enter a ✓ under "strong" for Eliot. (This does not mean that Justin is not strong!) Therefore leave Justin's "strong" box empty.

(b) *Justin has blue eyes.* Enter ✓ under "blue eyes" for Justin. Leave Eliot's "blue eyes" box empty for now (later you will have information about this).

(a) (b)

	STRONG	BLUE EYES	TALL	BLACK HAIR
E	✓			
J		✓		

(c) *The tall person has black hair.* This information is not specific enough to enter yet.

(d) *The person with brown eyes is not tall.* This tells us that someone's eyes are not blue. That must be Eliot, so we put an X under "blue eyes" for Eliot. We can now also put an X under "tall" for Eliot.

(d)

	STRONG	BLUE EYES	TALL	BLACK HAIR
E	✓	X	X	
J		✓		

(e) Finally, we return to part (c) and enter a ✓ under "tall" for Justin, and therefore also enter a ✓ under "black hair" for Justin. That completes what we know.

(e)

	STRONG	BLUE EYES	TALL	BLACK HAIR
E	✓	X	X	
J		✓	✓	✓

Now examine each choice. Remember that *we don't know* if Justin is strong or if Eliot has black hair. The answer is **H**. Also note that as soon as we realize that choice H is correct, we need not waste time by examining the rest of the choices.

Follow-Up Problems

Answers are on page 87.

EXAMPLE 4.3

You have a dog, a cat, and a bird in your house.

1. Two of these animals are brown, and the other is gray.
2. One of the brown animals is large and the other brown animal is small.
3. The bird is large.
4. The dog is gray.

Which of the following **must** be true?

(A) The dog is small.
(B) The cat is small.
(C) The dog is large.
(D) The cat is large.
(E) The size of the dog and the size of the cat cannot be determined from the given information.

EXAMPLE 4.4

Gus, Florence, and Hank are a banker, a computer scientist, and a teacher, but not necessarily in that order. Gus is not the banker or the teacher, and Hank is not the teacher. A correct conclusion based only on this information is that

(F) Gus is not the computer scientist.
(G) Hank is the computer scientist.
(H) Florence is the banker.
(J) Hank is the banker.
(K) Florence is the computer scientist.

EXAMPLE 4.5

Problems can often be done by different methods. The following problem was Example 1.2 of **"Put 'Em in Their Places."** Try this problem by the chart method illustrated in this section. (In this example there are three questions.) P, Q, R, and S represent four different integers. You are given that

(1) P is not the biggest.
(2) Q is less than P.
(3) R is not the smallest.
(4) S is greater than R.

Question 1: The next-to-smallest integer

(A) must be P.
(B) must be Q.
(C) must be R.
(D) must be S.
(E) cannot be determined.

(continued)

Question 2: We can determine the exact position of

(F) none of the letters.
(G) only one letter.
(H) *P* and *Q* only.
(J) *Q* and *S* only.
(K) all four letters.

Question 3: If we also know that *P* is greater than *R*, then we can determine the exact positions of

(A) *Q* and *S* only.
(B) *P, Q,* and *S* only.
(C) all four letters.
(D) none of the four letters.
(E) It is impossible for *P* to be more than *R*.

Logical Reasoning Problem 5

Analogies

Sun–Day; Moon–Night. Find the common **relationship** between the two word pairs. **The Key: Find common ties.**

A given word pair can be related in many ways. For example, *father–baby daughter* could be related as

adults and their young

OR   larger and smaller things   (different from *smaller and larger things* because of the order in the word pair.)

OR   male and female

Similarly, *motorcycle–bicycle* could be related as

faster and slower things

OR   motorized and nonmotorized things

OR   larger and smaller things

Of course, many other relationships may exist, but only a limited number of choices will be offered in a particular problem. Be sure to check all the choices, crossing off those that are clearly wrong.

EXAMPLE 5.1

Below are two word pairs. The words in each pair are related in some way. The relationship between the words in the first pair is similar to the relationship between the words in the second pair.

father–baby daughter

motorcycle–bicycle

What is the relationship displayed in both word pairs?

(A) older and younger things
(B) larger and smaller things
(C) parents and their children
(D) people and what they often travel in
(E) people and means of travel

ANALYSIS

Check each choice:

A. older and younger things	Doesn't apply to the second word pair.
B. larger and smaller related things	Looks good.
C. parents and their children	Doesn't apply to the second word pair.
D. people and what they often travel in	This may relate the words of one pair to the words of the other, but that's not what the instructions call for. The **relationship** must be within *each* word pair.
E. people and means of travel	Doesn't apply to either word pair.

The answer is **B.**

Here are some frequently used relationships:

type	examples
words and their opposites	bright–dull; happy–sad; slow–fast
words and their synonyms	bright–sunny; wet–damp; car–automobile
objects and their uses	pencil–write; nose–smell; scissors–cut
adults and their young	man–child; dog–puppy; lioness–cub
male and female	man–woman; bull–cow; king–queen
one out of many	page–book; card–deck; tree–forest
cause and effect	joke–laughter; pain–crying; practice–skill
related mathematical terms	algebra–equation; geometry–figure; arithmetic–number

EXAMPLE 5.2

Below are two word pairs. The words in each pair are related in some way. The relationship between the words in the first pair is similar to the relationship between the words in the second pair.

smell–odor

sight–view

What is the relationship displayed in both word pairs?

(F) parts of the body and what they do
(G) how our bodies warn us of danger
(H) senses and what they detect
(J) senses and how they develop as we grow older
(K) things that are pleasant to the senses

ANALYSIS

Check each choice:

F.	parts of the body and what they do	No parts of the body are indicated.
G.	how our bodies warn us of danger	No dangers are indicated.
H.	senses and what they detect	Looks good.
J.	senses and how they develop as we grow older	The first word of each pair is a sense, but the second word has nothing to do with how that sense develops.
K.	things that are pleasant to the senses	There is nothing to indicate that the odor or view is pleasant.

The answer is **H**.

Follow-Up Problems

Answers are on page 87.

EXAMPLE 5.3

Below are two word pairs. The words in each pair are related in some way. The relationship between the words in the first pair is similar to the relationship between the words in the second pair.

clouds–sky

fish–water

What is the relationship displayed in both word pairs?

(A) things that float
(B) objects with different shapes and places that appear blue
(C) objects that are very high or very low
(D) objects and where they are usually found
(E) things people like to watch

EXAMPLE 5.4

Below are two word pairs. The words in each pair are related in some way. The relationship between the words in the first pair is similar to the relationship between the words in the second pair.

policeman–cop

automobile–car

What is the relationship displayed in both word pairs?

(F) words and their synonyms
(G) words and their opposites
(H) vehicles people ride in
(J) people who enforce the law and what they travel in
(K) types of jobs and forms of transportation

Two Variations of Analogy Questions

EXAMPLE 5.5

Which one of the following word pairs shows a relationship similar to the relationship in *strong–weak*?

(A) clever–smart
(B) high–low
(C) feet–inches
(D) nose–smell
(E) run–jump

EXAMPLE 5.6

Which word could replace the *??* so that the two word pairs would show a similar relationship?

boat–water

car–*??*

(F) ocean
(G) air
(H) road
(J) racetrack
(K) auto

Logical Reasoning Problem 6

Miscellaneous

It is impossible to classify every type of Logical Reasoning question. The examples that follow represent some of the other types that occur with moderate frequency. Familiarize yourself with the form and style of these questions. There are often several approaches to solving them, including techniques you have already encountered in previous parts of this section.

Parallel Reasoning

Parallel reasoning is a game of imitation. **Analyze** what's given, then **match** the type of reasoning to the proper choice. In this kind of question, be especially sure to use *only* the information given or implied.

EXAMPLE 6.1

Every Biloxi High School teacher lives in the city of Biloxi. Susan lives in Biloxi. Therefore Susan is a Biloxi High School teacher.

Which of the following employs reasoning that is most similar to the reasoning used in the above passage?

(A) All doctors studied biology. Dr. Cohen is a doctor. Therefore Dr. Cohen studied biology.
(B) Every healthy dog eats Yum Yum dog food. Duchess the dog eats Yum Yum dog food. Therefore Duchess is a healthy dog.
(C) Every high school senior will be well prepared for college. Einstein is not well prepared for college. Therefore Einstein is not a high school senior.
(D) Every student in Mr. Spiegel's music class has a good voice. Carrie is a student in Mr. Spiegel's music class. Therefore Carrie has a good voice.
(E) No politician is dishonest. Therefore every politician is honest.

Brief solution: (Answer: **B**) This example is related to the Ifs and Thens of Section 3. Using T for *being a Biloxi High School teacher* and L for *lives in Biloxi*, the first statement is $T \rightarrow L$. The second and third statements together are equivalent to $L \rightarrow T$. We are looking for the choice that uses the same type of reasoning. That is choice **B**. Whether that type of reasoning is valid is immaterial. It is not necessary to analyze the remaining choices.

It is important to realize that the given passage may actually contain flawed reasoning. Our task is to find the choice that most closely parallels (matches) the reasoning illustrated in the passage.

Strengthening and Weakening Arguments

A typical detective puzzle. If we had some additional information, what deductions could we make?

EXAMPLE 6.2

A researcher decided that the fossilized bone fragment found on a recent South American expedition was *not* that of a saber-toothed cat.

Which one of the following statements, if true, would most **strengthen** her conclusion?

(F) The fossil does not exactly match other saber-toothed cat fossils found in the Natural History Museum.
(G) Saber-toothed cats are extinct.
(H) Saber-toothed cat fossils have never been found before in South America.
(J) The saber-toothed cat's range has been definitively established as being restricted to North America.
(K) The fossil that was found was only a bone fragment and was not complete.

Brief solution: (Answer: **J**) Choices F, G, and K do not link the find to the location. Choice H does not negate the possibility of a new find. But choice J eliminates the possibility of such a find outside of North America (the key word being *definitively*).

EXAMPLE 6.3

In a recent report, the XYZ Test Prep Center said that students enrolled in their classes were better prepared for the SHSAT than those who were not enrolled there. Which one of the following statements, if true, would most **weaken** the conclusion of the report?

(A) There were XYZ students enrolled in the test prep classes who did not do well on the exam.
(B) Students who used the Barron's test prep book did well on the exam.
(C) Students who were not enrolled in the XYZ test prep classes were not surveyed.
(D) There were only seventy-five students enrolled in the XYZ test prep classes.
(E) Students who prepare carefully usually perform better on the exam than those who do not prepare carefully.

Brief solution: (Answer: **C**) To produce a valid conclusion, the report would have to compare students in XYZ classes with students not in XYZ classes. If choice C is assumed true, then that comparison was not made. Thus choice C weakens the conclusion of the report. The other choices do not provide any information regarding comparing the two groups.

The Missing Piece

A key piece of information is missing that would enable a valid conclusion to be made.

EXAMPLE 6.4

Barry lives in town T, but works in town W. Stanley said that Barry always travels from home to work by train.

Of the following choices, which one **must** be true in order for Stanley's statement to be valid?

(F) Stanley also lives in town T.
(G) Barry and Stanley often travel to work together.
(H) Barry likes to travel on trains.
(J) Barry never drives to work.
(K) The only way to get from town T to town W is by train.

Brief solution: (Answer: **K**) If choice K is true, then Stanley's statement is fully supported. The other choices do not have any bearing on how Barry actually travels to work.

A Few Other Examples

EXAMPLE 6.5

All seniors at The Academy take calculus or physics. Some seniors take both courses. Rocky, a senior at The Academy, is not taking physics. Based only on the given information, which of the following **must** be true?

I. Rocky is taking calculus.
II. Marsha, who is a senior at The Academy, is taking calculus.
III. If John is taking calculus at The Academy, then John is a senior.

(A) I only
(B) II only
(C) I and II only
(D) II and III only
(E) I, II, and III

Brief solution: (Answer: A) As a senior, Rocky must take calculus or physics. Since she is not taking physics, she must be taking calculus. Thus I is true. Marsha could be taking physics instead of calculus. Therefore II need not be true. Finally, the original statement does not imply that taking calculus is restricted to seniors, so John might not be a senior. Thus III need not be true.

EXAMPLE 6.6

Louis attended some baseball games one summer. The last four games he attended were at Shea Stadium. All but five games he attended were at Yankee Stadium. At least three games he attended were at Yankee Stadium. What was the fewest number of games that Louis could have attended?

(F) 8
(G) 9
(H) 10
(J) 12
(K) Cannot be determined from the information given.

Brief solution: (Answer: F) Louis attended at least 3 games at Yankee Stadium. He also attended 5 games elsewhere. (The fact that 4 of these were at Shea Stadium does not affect the final count.) Therefore he attended at least 8 games.

EXAMPLE 6.7

Peter has seven files currently on his computer that he would like to "back up" on disks. Three of these files may together be put onto one disk. Each of the other files requires two disks. In addition, Peter wants to have duplicate copies on disks of everything he backs up. What is the minimum number of disks that Peter must use?

(A) 9
(B) 11
(C) 17
(D) 18
(E) 22

Brief solution: (Answer: **D**) Three files go onto 1 disk. The other four files require 8 disks. That is a total of 9 disks minimum. Duplication brings the count to 18.

Some Harder Logic Problems, Just for Fun

Solutions follow these three problems.

EXAMPLE 7.1

If only one of the following values is the answer (to an unknown question), that value must be

(A) $\sqrt{.25}$
(B) 1 1/4
(C) 125%
(D) 1/2
(E) 5^2

EXAMPLE 7.2

Five statements (I, II, III, IV, and V) were made, each statement being a comment about the other statements. Those five statements are listed below, but statements I, III, and IV were accidentally erased!

I. —
II. Statement V is true.
III. —
IV. —
V. Statements II and IV are each false.

We know that exactly one of those statements is true, and the other four are false. Which statement **must** be the true one?

(F) I
(G) II
(H) III
(J) IV
(K) V

EXAMPLE 7.3

Of the four views of the same cube (see diagram) whose faces are marked *A*, *B*, *C*, 1, 2, and 3, at **most** one view is incorrect. (NOTE: The letters/numbers are used only to identify specific faces of the cube. Those letters/numbers have not been rotated even if the face has undergone a rotation.)

(A) View *a* is incorrect.
(B) View *b* is incorrect.
(C) View *c* is incorrect.
(D) View *d* is incorrect.
(E) All four views are correct.

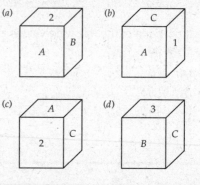

Brief solutions

Example 7.1: **(E)** Choices A and D are equal in value, so neither can be the correct answer. Choices B and C are equal in value, so that eliminates them. Only choice E is unique in value.

Example 7.2: **(J)** If II is true, then V must be true. That is not possible, so II must be false. That makes V false also. But if V is false, then one of the statements II or IV must be true. It's not II, so IV must be true.

Example 7.3: **(C)** This is a difficult problem. Solving the problem involves choosing a corner of a cube and visualizing the three faces that *surround* that corner, going (for example) in a clockwise direction around that corner.

Look at *b: A, C,* 1 occur going around one corner. Now look at *c: A, C,* 2 occur going around one corner. Therefore *b* and *c* cannot both be correct. Let's assume for the moment that *c* is correct and *b* is wrong. That means both *a* and *d* must be correct also.

Now compare *a* and *c:* In *a,* we have *A,* 2, *B* going around one corner. If we visualize that occurring in *c,* we realize that face *B* must be opposite face *C.* But that contradicts *d,* where *B* and *C* are not opposite each other. Therefore *d* would have to be wrong. That contradicts our previous statement that both *a* and *d* must be correct.

Something is wrong somewhere, and since we made only one assumption, that assumption (that *c* is correct) must be false. Therefore *c* cannot be correct.

Know Your Words

There are certain words whose precise meanings and implications you must know. Here is a brief list.

1. Words expressing comparison, relative size, or position:

   above/below
   before/after
   ahead of/behind
   to the right of/to the left of
   greater than/less than
   taller than/shorter than
   older than/younger than

ILLUSTRATION

If Jeff is standing to the right of Jo, **do not assume** that no one is standing between them. If a stack of blocks has a green block between the red block and the blue block, do not assume that the green block is the *only* block between the red and the blue. Similar cautions apply to the other words.

2. Words expressing quantity:

   one
   only one, or exactly one
   at least one
   at most one
   each
   every
   all

One implies the existence of at least one, but does not necessarily mean only one. If I say that I have a penny in my pocket, it does not necessarily mean that I have exactly one penny in my pocket. Consider the old riddle, "How many months have 28 days?" The answer is "They all do!"

---

3. Words expressing possibility:

must be
may be, or could be, or can be
cannot be

These words frequently appear. Be very careful to distinguish between what *must* be and what *may* be. This is often the key to successfully unraveling a logical reasoning puzzle.

All beagles are friendly dogs.

Based *only* on the information in the above statement, indicate whether each of the following

1. must be true.
2. may be true.
3. cannot be true.

(A) Muffin, a beagle, is a friendly dog.
(B) Misty, a beagle, is an unfriendly dog.
(C) Poodles are unfriendly dogs.
(D) No beagle is unfriendly.
(E) There is at least one unfriendly beagle.
(F) If a dog is friendly, then it is a beagle.
(G) No collie is friendly.

Answers: A1, B3, C2, D1, E3, F2, G2

ADVICE AND REMINDERS

READ	Read the questions carefully and accurately. It may prove helpful to mark important phrases. It always helps to identify specifically stated information, such as *All seniors take math* or *Tony is the tallest* or *Mary did not go to the dance with Joe.*
IS IT FAMILIAR	Note whether the question fits a category with which you are familiar.
JUST THE FACTS	Use only the actual information given or implied. Avoid adding information that you think should be part of the question, or making inferences without supporting facts. Avoid leaping to conclusions.
DISPLAY THE INFORMATION	Whenever possible, try to express the given verbal information in some convenient form, such as a diagram, a chart, or helpful symbols. Make the information work for you.
PREVIEW THE CHOICES	It is often helpful to skim the choices before attempting to answer the question.
MAKE REASONABLE CHOICES	Combine good analysis with common sense. Pick the *best* choice from among the given choices. Dismiss clearly ridiculous answers.
KEEP MOVING	If you determine the correct answer and you find it among the choices, don't bother checking the other choices. Move on.
PACE YOURSELF	Be aware of the time. Don't dwell on any one question. Use the **? X** system as you go.

Answers to Follow-Up Problems

Put 'Em in Their Places

Example 1.4   Answer: **(J)**

Example 1.5   Answer: **(C)**

Breaking the Code

Example 2.5   Question 1 = **(B)**

Question 2 = **(K)**

Question 3 = **(B)**

Example 2.6   Answer: **(J)**

Ifs and Thens

Example 3.9   Answer: **(A)**

Brief solution: If A is seated, then B must be seated. Now by Basic Principle 2, C must be seated. Continuing, D must then be seated. But that is impossible, since we have only three seats. Therefore A cannot be seated. If you picked choice E, you probably thought that *If A is seated, then B must be seated* is logically equivalent to *If B is seated, then A must be seated*. But that is *not* the Contrapositive, and need not be true. We can seat B without having to seat A. This is not the same type of problem as "Put 'Em in Their Places," Example 1.5.

Example 3.10   Answer: **(H)**

Brief solution: Use P for "Daniel buys printer," C for "Steven buys computer," and F for "Vivian buys flat-screen monitor." We are given P→ ~C and F→ C. Combining these requires an identical element (connecting link), so we use the Contrapositive of the second statement, which is ~C → ~F. Then Basic Principle 2 tells us that given P→ ~C and ~C → ~F, we can conclude that P→ ~F ("If Daniel buys a printer, then Vivian will not buy a flat-screen monitor"). But this is not one of the choices! Let's see if the Contrapositive of that last statement is one of the choices: F→ ~P ("If Vivian buys a flat-screen monitor, then Daniel will not buy a printer"). It is choice **H.**

Who Does What

Example 4.3   Answer: **(B)**
Brief solution: We do not have enough specific information from (1) and (2) to enter these in a chart at first. But if we enter (3), then (4), then (1), then (2), we get the chart shown here. Choice A can't be resolved. Choice **B** works, so stop there. The chart could also be made with just two columns (for example, "brown" and "large").

	BROWN	GRAY	LARGE	SMALL
DOG	X	✓		
CAT	✓	X	X	✓
BIRD	✓	X	✓	X

Example 4.4   Answer: **(J)**
Brief solution: *Gus is not the banker or the teacher* produces the chart shown. Now *Hank is not the teacher* allows us to complete the chart (not shown), producing answer **J**.

	BANKER	COMPUTER SCIENTIST	TEACHER
GUS	X	✓	X
FLORENCE		X	
HANK		X	

Example 4.5   Question 1 = **(E)**
Question 2 = **(J)**
Question 3 = **(C)**
Brief solution: The chart shows the four bits of given information. We can continue the chart (not shown) by putting a ✓ in the

	SMALLEST	NEXT TO SMALLEST	NEXT TO LARGEST	LARGEST
P	X			X
Q			X	X
R	X		.	X
S	X	X		

"largest" box for *S* and a ✓ in the "smallest" box for *Q* (since they are the only empty boxes left in those columns). Finally, we can put an X in the "next to smallest" box for *Q* and an X in the "next to largest" box for *S*. We now see that the first two answers are **E** and **J**. Adding the information from Question 3 fixes the positions of *P* and *R*, and therefore of all four letters. The third answer is **C**.

Analogies

Example 5.3   Answer: **(D)**

Example 5.4   Answer: **(F)**

Example 5.5   Answer: **(B)**
Brief analysis: The given relationship is one of opposites.

Example 5.6   Answer: **(H)**
Brief analysis: The relationship is *vehicles and what they travel on*. Note that answer J is too specific.

Skillbuilder C: Reading

Reading questions test your ability to read with understanding and to answer questions based on your reading. The reading section of the SHSAT consists of five passages of 350–450 words followed by six multiple-choice questions for each passage. The questions in this section are arranged in order of difficulty. They are not presented in the order in which the correct answer appears in the passage. The content of the passages is varied, with subject matter including (but not limited to) science, history, biography, anthropology, and the arts.

This Skillbuilder will provide you with techniques for more efficient reading, and will teach you what kinds of questions to expect and how to find their answers. By practicing the suggested methods, you will gain skill and confidence.

> **WHAT'S BEING TESTED?**
>
> A Reading question usually asks you to find a **main idea,** to answer a specific question about the **facts** of a passage, or to draw an **inference**—that is, to perceive an idea that is suggested rather than stated.

What Do I Do?

- Follow an **orderly procedure** that gives you a **purpose** in reading and a way to **focus** on important points in the passage.
- Identify the **key elements** in each question. Determine the **type of information** the question requires.
- **Find the answer** by using the **clues** provided by your focused method of reading.

Your first challenge is to master the best approach to reading the passages. If you learn and practice an orderly, efficient way to read, answering the questions will be easier.

Reading for Purpose and Focus

When you are reading a relatively short passage that you know you are going to be tested on, your reading technique should be different from the way you read a magazine article or a long chapter in a textbook. You want to read quickly, spending just two or three minutes on each passage, but you should read with purpose, and you should mark the passage to highlight major ideas and topics.

- *Reading the question.* Some people prefer to glance at the questions (ignoring the answer choices) before reading the passage. Others prefer to start by reading the passage. You are free to choose whichever strategy works best for you; however, you should try both before you decide.
- *Reading the passage.* Read the passage quickly, circling important words and phrases. Try to jot down the main idea of the passage. Don't reread any part of the material more than once—you will have a chance to go back and reread relevant portions again.

PRACTICE

Read and mark the following passage for **purpose** and **focus.**

The French Revolution, which began in 1789, ended the control of France by monarch and aristocracy, and launched the era of middle-class control. Business and financial leaders maintained their power even after a counter-revolution restored the monarchy in 1814. Although it regained its status and even some privilege, the aristocracy no longer dominated the affairs of the country.

1. Which of the following best tells what the passage is about?

   (A) The history of the French Revolution
   (B) The causes and results of the French Revolution
   (C) The end of the monarchy in France as a result of the French Revolution
   (D) Middle-class power as an outcome of the French Revolution
   (E) Revolution and counter-revolution

2. What does the passage suggest about the Revolution?

   (F) Changes brought about by the revolution were all reversed.
   (G) Some of the French people were dissatisfied with the outcome of the French Revolution.
   (H) The French Revolution was mainly a struggle of monarchy against aristocracy.
   (J) Business and financial control passed to the monarchy after the revolution.
   (K) The French Revolution was influenced by the American Revolution.

Look at the sample marked passage below. Note that no attempt has been made to mark *every* detail.

The (French Revolution), which began in 1789, ended the control of France by monarch and aristocracy, and launched the (era of middle-class control.) Business and financial leaders maintained their power even after a counter-revolution restored the monarchy in 1814. Although it regained its status and even some privilege, the (aristocracy no longer dominated) the affairs of the country.

The student who marked this passage circled what seemed most important. Another student might have circled different facts. Don't worry if your markings are different from this sample. *Marking the passage helps you to focus.* It also helps you find answers, but you can't expect to spot every answer on the first reading!

Try Another. Follow the same procedure to read this passage.

The transfer of power from aristocracy to middle class also occurred in England, but through a gradual evolution rather than a revolution. Although royalty and aristocracy held the high positions in early English history, the middle class in that country was important even in the Middle Ages. By the seventeenth century it was strong enough to unseat King Charles I in the Civil War. And even after the English Parliament restored the monarchy, placing Charles II on the throne, the power of the middle class continued to grow at the expense of the aristocracy and monarchy.

3. What is the main idea of the passage?

   (A) The outcome of the English Civil War
   (B) The evolution of the middle class
   (C) The growth in power of the English middle class
   (D) Social changes in Europe after the seventeenth century
   (E) The destruction of the aristocracy in England

4. What does the passage suggest about England's middle class?

   (A) It had little power before the Civil War.
   (B) It gained power mainly by peaceful means.
   (C) It was politically dominant during the Middle Ages.
   (D) It wished to restore the monarchy after the Civil War.
   (E) It launched the Civil War for financial and business motives.

5. Which of the following statements about Charles II is supported by the details of the passage?

   (A) He took power after a counter-revolution restored the monarchy.
   (B) He took the throne after his father died.
   (C) He passed laws that strengthened the middle class.
   (D) He was the last king of England.
   (E) He was the next king after Charles I.

6. Which of the following is **not** stated in the passage?

   (F) The power of the English aristocracy decreased after Charles II became king.
   (G) The middle class was responsible for the overthrow of Charles I.
   (H) Royalty and aristocracy had elevated status in early England.
   (J) Charles I influenced Parliament to restore the monarchy.
   (K) The English Civil War took place in the 1600s.

Check the passage below to see the way one student marked it.

The transfer of power from aristocracy to middle class also occurred in England, but through a gradual evolution rather than a revolution. Although royalty and aristocracy held the high positions in early English history, the middle class in that country was important even in the Middle Ages. By the seventeenth century it was strong enough to unseat King Charles I in the Civil War. And even after the English Parliament restored the monarchy, placing Charles II on the throne, the power of the middle class continued to grow at the expense of the aristocracy and monarchy.

Notice that the student who worked on this passage did more marking than the one who worked on the first passage. You may have circled different words and phrases. You may have marked more or fewer. That's okay. The important things are that you were reading attentively and that your markings will help you find the answers.

Now that you've had some practice reading and marking passages, let's move on to the paydirt part of the Reading test.

Key Elements

As you learned early in this Skillbuilder, Reading questions can be classified as **main idea** questions, **fact** questions, or **inference** questions. Knowing how to recognize the question types will make it easier for you to find the correct answers.

MAIN IDEA QUESTIONS

The first question on every passage asks for the main idea of the passage. It may ask

- what the passage is about, or
- what best states the author's purpose, or
- what is the best title for the passage.

Another kind of main idea question asks you

- to summarize some of the details in the passage, or
- to state a reason, or
- to make a generalization of some kind.

If you are not sure about the passage's main idea yet, you may wish to skip over the question for a moment and return to it after doing the other questions for the passage.

FACT QUESTIONS

A specific question about the content of the passage usually asks

- for a particular fact or detail stated in the passage, or
- what is or is **not** stated or is or is **not** true according to the passage.

Don't expect the correct answer to be stated in the exact words of the passage. Answers are more likely to be paraphrased—that is, worded differently.

INFERENCE QUESTIONS

Inference questions are unique in that they do not ask you directly about the material in the passage; instead, they ask you to make a leap or assumption from the information in the passage to a new conclusion—in other words, to *infer*. Be sure, though, that you do not leap too far—a correct answer to an inference question will still be supported or suggested by specific evidence in the passage.

An inference question most frequently asks

- what the passage suggests (implies),
- what a word means in a particular context (setting), or
- what the author's tone or attitude is. It may also ask you to
- infer a reason for some fact stated in the passage.

PRACTICE

Label the following questions *main idea, fact,* or *inference.*

1. What is the most likely reason that crows congregate at nightfall?
2. Which of the following best tells what the passage is about?
3. All of the following are properties of a liquid **except**
4. What are the favorite foods of the Baltimore Oriole?
5. What does the passage suggest about the origins of acupuncture?
6. What is the best title for the passage?
7. Which of the following best sums up the motivations of the Samurai warriors?
8. At what temperature will freezing water begin to sink?
9. What is the meaning of the word *arcane* as it is used in the passage?
10. Which of the following is a medical use of hypnotism?

SOLUTIONS

1. Inference. Words and phrases like *probable* and *most likely* usually indicate inference questions.
2. Main Idea. This wording is frequently used in the question asking for the main idea of a passage.
3. Fact. This question asks for a specific detail stated in the passage.
4. Fact. This question asks for a specific detail stated in the passage.
5. Inference. The question asks for something that has been *suggested* or inferred—not stated.
6. Main Idea. A good title refers to the main idea.
7. Main Idea. This question asks not for the main idea of the entire passage, but rather for the main idea of several separate pieces of information.
8. Fact. Like 3 and 4, this questions asks for a specific detail.
9. Inference. A word-definition question usually requires you to use stated information to figure out, or infer, the meaning of a word.
10. Fact. The question asks for a specific detail.

Now let's move on to the crucial part of your test-taking method.

Find the Answer

If you have read the passage quickly, you should have a minute or more to work on each question. It's important here to work carefully and not to rush yourself. Take one question at a time. Reread the question, and then go back to the passage and find the answer. Select the correct answer choice and record it. Do all this for each question before going on to the next.

Follow This Procedure

1. **Reread the question carefully, circling key words and phrases.** Circling the words and phrases that specify what you have to find in the passage will help you quickly determine the type of question, and it will also make it easier for you to locate the necessary information.

2. **Label the question according to the type of information it requires—main idea, detail, or inference.** After you have practiced with several passages, you may decide to omit the label. As a beginner, it may help to jot down the question type next to the question.

3. **Choose the answer.** First try to answer the question without looking at the choices. Remember, the incorrect answer choices are designed to look correct. They often contain, for example, a group of words taken directly from the passage. It is, therefore, very important to know what answer you are looking for **before** you look at the answer choices. This way you will not be tempted by incorrect choices and can more easily focus on the correct answer. Once you have your answer in mind, go through the answer choices and eliminate those that do not match up with it.

> Exceptions: Some questions ask you which of the choices is *not* mentioned in the passage. Some require that you examine each choice for some purpose. In these cases, you cannot formulate any answer without looking at the choices first.

If you cannot formulate an answer without looking at the choices, see if looking at the choices helps.

If looking at the choices does not help, return to the passage and find the answer. Your markings will help you. In some cases, you may have circled all or part of the answer. But even if the answer is not already neatly packaged for you, the markings should help steer you to the information you need.

If a question provides a line number, always read at least a few lines above and a few lines below the line referenced. The correct answer will rarely appear in the line specified in the question.

PRACTICE

Go back to the passages you marked. Reread and answer the questions, following the six-step method above. On the actual test, you will record your answers by blackening a bubble on the answer sheet, but right now just circle the correct answer. The solutions are below.

SOLUTIONS

1. Main idea. **(D)** A is inaccurate because the paragraph explains a result of the revolution. It does not tell of events making up a history. B is also inaccurate because the paragraph says nothing about causes and mentions only one result. C is incorrect because the paragraph says that the monarchy was later restored. Even if C were accurate, though, it would be an incorrect choice because it is too narrow. Most of the content concerns the middle class, not the monarchy. E is too broad. It does not limit the subject to a particular revolution, nor does it indicate the particular focus of the paragraph on the middle class after the revolution. D is both accurate and complete.

2. Inference. **(G)** F is incorrect because it is exaggerated. Only one reversal is mentioned. **Hint:** An exaggerated answer is always incorrect. H is inaccurate because the passage actually suggests that the monarchy and aristocracy were allies. J contradicts the information given in the passage. K is an example of an answer that is true but incorrect. It makes a correct statement, but nothing in the passage suggests it. **Hint:** An answer may be true yet be an incorrect answer choice. G is correct because although dissatisfaction is not stated, it is suggested by the fact of a counter-revolution.

3. Main idea. **(C)** A is inaccurate because no outcome is given except the removal and restoration of the monarchy. B is too broad. Only the English middle class is mentioned, and its evolution only in power. D is too broad; the passage doesn't discuss Europe as a whole, and only one social change. E is incorrect because it is exaggerated. The passage says that the aristocracy lost power, but not that it was eliminated. C accurately covers all the information in the passage.

4. Inference. **(B)** A contradicts information given in the passage. C is incorrect because it is exaggerated—"important" does not indicate nearly as much strength as "dominant." D is incorrect because, although Parliament did restore the monarchy, the passage does not suggest that the middle class controlled Parliament. E is incorrect because nothing in the passage states or suggests a reason. B is correct because of the statement that the English middle class gained power by "evolution rather than revolution."

5. Fact. **(E)** This question requires you to be sure that the passage states supporting information for the choice. A is incorrect because the passage makes no mention of a counter-revolution in England. B is incorrect because although Charles I was the father of Charles II, this fact is not stated in the passage. Also, the death of Charles I is not mentioned. Neither C nor D is mentioned in the passage. E is correct because Charles I is the king who was removed and Charles II was installed in the restoration of the monarchy. Therefore he must have been the next king after Charles I.

6. Fact. **(J)** This is an example of a question that requires you to use the answer choices to find the correct response. A quick rereading of the passage will verify every choice except J. Notice that the answer choices are *paraphrased.* That is, they are not word-for-word repetitions of the statements in the passage.

PITFALLS

The preceding explanations point out four pitfalls you may encounter on the SHSAT Reading test. Some incorrect answers may seem okay at first glance and so may trick you into a wrong choice. These bad answers include choices that say too much or too little and choices that are not actually stated or suggested in the passage.

Watch out for these kinds of incorrect choices.

- **Too broad.** This kind of wrong choice is most common in a main idea question but can be associated with the others also. It is an answer that includes, or covers, more than the passage does. 3B is an example of this type because it does not limit the subject enough.

- **Too narrow.** This type is also most likely to occur in a main idea question. Be sure that your choice for a main idea response is a subject that is important throughout the passage. 1C illustrates a response that includes only a minor aspect of the passage's content and so is too narrow.

- **Exaggerated.** Sometimes an answer would be okay if it didn't overstate the facts. Overstated choices are usually incorrect. For example, 4C errs in overstating the power of the middle class. Be wary when a choice uses strong language—especially words like *all, always,* and *every.* These words often indicate an exaggerated incorrect choice.

- **True but not given in the passage.** The instructions on the Reading test will tell you to base your answers only on the content of the passage. You need to be careful not to select an answer just because it seems true. Always look back at the passage to make sure it is mentioned (or, for an inference question, suggested) in the passage. 2K might trick an unwary student who has learned that ideas involved in the American Revolution did indeed influence the French Revolution. But K is an incorrect answer because the *passage* makes no such suggestion. It may seem strange to reject an answer that is factually correct! You must remember that you are being tested only on what is in the passage.

Apply what you know about bad answer types as you practice with the next passage and its questions.

First, review the steps for reading with purpose and focus and the steps for rereading and answering the questions. Then use the procedures in the following practice.

PRACTICE

Read the short passage below and carefully answer the questions that follow it. Be alert for answer choices that are too broad, too narrow, exaggerated, and true but not given in the passage. Solutions follow the passage.

Antonio Stradivari was born in 1644 in Cremona, Italy, a town noted for the production of excellent violins. Although Stradivari also made cellos and violas, it is his violins for which he is renowned. His teacher, Nicolo Amati,
Line passed on to him the techniques of violin making as it was practiced in
(5) Cremona. The pupil Stradivari employed these techniques but went on to surpass his teacher, making violins whose excellence has never been exceeded or even fully understood.

What makes a Stradivarius such a fine instrument? Stradivari did alter the proportions of the violin, but this change alone does not explain their supe-
(10) riority. Some think that the special varnish he used is responsible for the wonderful sound of the instruments, but not every expert agrees with this idea. A relatively recent theory concerns the unusually cold weather in Europe during this period of history. Lower-than-usual temperatures would have slowed the growth rate of the trees whose wood was used in the vio-
(15) lins, resulting in a very dense wood. Perhaps the magnificent Stradivarius sound derives from the density of the wood rather than the composition of the varnish.

The only violin maker whose instruments rival those of Antonio Stradivari is Giuseppe Antonio Guarneri, who lived at the same time. This
(20) fact does not give conclusive proof, but it does seem to bolster the cold-weather theory of the secret of the Stradivarius.

1. Which of the following best expresses the purpose of the author of the passage?

    (A) To discuss the excellence of the violins produced by Stradivari
    (B) To indicate a surprising result of climate change
    (C) To explain what makes a violin superior
    (D) To compare the violins of Stradivari and Guarneri
    (E) To summarize the career of Antonio Stradivari

2. Which of the following is **not** mentioned as a possible factor influencing the quality of a Stradivarius violin?

    (F) Special varnish
    (G) Dense wood
    (H) Experience gained through making violas and cellos
    (J) Changes in proportions
    (K) Methods used by Cremonan violin makers

3. Which of the following is suggested in the passage?

   (A) The cellos and violas of Stradivari are of inferior quality.
   (B) The violins of Guarneri are even more excellent than those of Stradivari.
   (C) There was an ice age in Europe during Stradivari's lifetime.
   (D) The wood in a Guarneri violin is very dense.
   (E) In later life Stradivari discarded the teachings of Amati.

4. According to the passage, how might a denser-than-usual wood affect a violin?

   (F) It would be more compact.
   (G) The bow would be stronger.
   (H) It would produce a deeper sound.
   (J) It would improve the quality of the sound.
   (K) It would lessen the importance of the varnish.

SOLUTIONS

1. Main idea. **(A)** Everything in the passage directly or indirectly concerns the excellence of the violins of Stradivari. B, C, and D are too narrow. E is too broad.

2. Fact. **(H)** Here is a question in which the *incorrect* answers are the ones stated in the passage. It is also an exception to the rule against looking at the answer choices. H is correct because although it is stated that Stradivari made these other instruments, it is not *suggested in the passage* that this experience is a possible factor in the excellence of his violins. The other answers are all stated in the passage, although K is mentioned in a different paragraph from the others. **Hint:** Sometimes you have to look in more than one place to find all the stated facts or suggested ideas.

3. Inference. **(D)** A, B, and C are exaggerated. E is not stated or suggested. D is correct because the Guaneri violins, rivals of the Stradivarius instruments, were made during the same period whose weather may have produced a denser wood. C is also an example of an answer that may seem true, but is an incorrect choice. You may remember reading about a "little ice age" in Europe during this period of history. The language of the passage, however, doesn't suggest weather extreme enough to be called an ice age.

4. Fact. **(J)** Although the passage uses the word *perhaps,* this can be considered a fact question because the reader does not have to draw an inference. The answer is stated in line 15.

The solution to question 2 points out an important aspect of answering the questions. In some cases a correct answer may involve information from different paragraphs. Your reading technique of circling important details can help you in this case.

WHAT IF A PASSAGE IS DIFFICULT TO READ?

You may find some of the passages on the SHSAT, especially the scientific ones, hard to read. Don't let difficult subject matter throw you. Remember, you don't have to master all the information in a passage. Your job is to answer the questions correctly. And you can do this by reading the passage with purpose and focus, and by answering the questions carefully and methodically.

Work on one more short passage, one that you may find a little difficult because of its technical subject matter.

PRACTICE

Use your orderly reading and answering procedures to find the correct answers to questions on the following passage. Be on guard for bad answer types, and remember that you may sometimes have to look in more than one place to find the correct answer.

The majority of our most familiar plants reproduce by means of seeds. There are two types of seed-bearing plants, angiosperm and gymnosperm. Angiosperms, the flowering plants, produce seed enclosed in an ovary that
Line eventually grows into a fruit. The seeds of gymnosperms, cone-bearers, and
(5) related plants, lie naked on the scales of cones.

In both groups, a structure called an ovule produces an egg cell, and a structure called the pollen tube contains two sperm cells. Fertilization occurs after the plant's pollen tube passes through a small opening in the ovule called the micropyle. One sperm nucleus unites with the egg cell to form a one-celled
(10) body called a *zygote.* This grows into the embryo, which develops an enclosing sac. In angiosperms two nuclei present in the embryo sac combine with the other sperm nucleus to form one nucleus that eventually produces a nutritive substance, endosperm tissue, around the embryo. Gymnosperm embryo sacs produce the endosperm from their own tissue, without the contribution of a
(15) second sperm nucleus.

The fertilized and mature ovule is called a seed. It is relatively tender, but it is surrounded by a strong, hard seed coat, called a *testa,* that develops from the outer covering of the ovule. In flowering plants the tegmen, a thin membrane, forms a second seed coat within the testa; gymnosperms lack this sec-
(20) ond coat as well as the surrounding fruit of the angiosperm seeds.

1. Which of the following best tells what this passage is about?

   (A) Differences between two categories of plants and how they are fertilized
   (B) How fertilization occurs in seed-bearing plants
   (C) How a seed becomes a new plant
   (D) Plant reproduction
   (E) The structure and production of seeds

2. What does the passage suggest about the testa?

   (F) It is not present in gymnosperm seeds.
   (G) It protects the mature ovule.
   (H) It develops from the embryo sac.
   (J) It is surrounded by the tegumen.
   (K) It produces the fruit of the angiosperm plants.

3. What structure contains the micropyle?

   (A) The embryo sac
   (B) The pollen tube
   (C) The sperm nucleus
   (D) The ovule
   (E) The zygote

4. All of the following are given as parts of the reproduction process **except**

   (F) combination of a cell and a nucleus.
   (G) production of an egg cell.
   (H) micropyle serving as passageway.
   (J) pollen tube entering ovule.
   (K) production of ovary by gymnosperms.

SOLUTIONS

1. Main Idea. **(E)** A is inaccurate; the content involves both similarities and differences. B is too narrow because only one part of the passage involves the actual fertilization. C is inaccurate, as the passage describes seed production, not plant production. D is too broad. Only seed-bearing plants are discussed, and every aspect of their reproduction is not included. E is correct, as it includes every part of the passage.

2. Inference. **(G)** This is an example of an inference question that requires you to work from the choices. F is incorrect because although the last paragraph (lines 16–20) says that the second coat is absent in the gymnosperm seed, no such suggestion is made about the testa. G is correct because the word *tender* is used to describe the seed, and the words *strong* and *hard* are used to describe the testa that covers the seed. H, J, and K all contradict information given in the passage. H contradicts the statement (lines 17–18) that the testa develops from the outer covering of the ovule. J contradicts the statement (line 19) that the tegumen is *within* the testa. K is wrong because the first paragraph (line 4) says that the ovary grows into the fruit.

3. Fact. **(D)** The correct answer is stated in lines 9–10.

4. Fact/Inference. **(K)** All of the other choices are stated in the second paragraph. The first paragraph mentions ovary production by angiosperms but implies that gymnosperms do not produce ovaries, so K doesn't correctly state the aspect of reproduction. Having verified that the other choices are given, you may have simply chosen K by the process of elimination. In a case like this, though, it's a good idea to double-check before recording the answer. The double-check takes you to a different paragraph from the other choices. Remember, you may have to look at more than one paragraph to find a given answer.

WRAP-UP AND PRACTICE

Before you leave the Reading Skillbuilder, let's have a final review, a few extra hints, and one full-length passage. Try timing yourself on this passage: Aim to read it in two to three minutes, and to spend about one minute answering each question.

Remember
- Set a goal.
- Read quickly, with purpose and focus.
- Circle key words and phrases.
- Read each question, circling key points.
- Answer each question, returning to the passage when necessary.
- Record your answer.

As you did for the short passages, circle the correct answer. When you are working the full Practice Tests, of course, you will record your answers on the answer sheet.

What If None of the Choices Match My Answer?
Lightly cross out clearly incorrect choices.
Select the best choice of those remaining.
Quickly double-check the passage to confirm your choice.

What If I Still Don't Have a Match?
In this case, make your best guess and move on. It doesn't pay to get hung up on one answer.

What If Time Is Running Short?
This is another situation where you should make an educated guess and move on.
  Now try this full-length passage. The solutions are at the end of this Skillbuilder.

The wild dogs of Africa, like New World wolves and eagles, have suffered a sustained human assault based in part on prejudice. Farmers and ranchers once sought to eradicate all three species because of their occasional raids on *Line* livestock, not understanding the importance of predators in controlling
(5) rodents and other pests. All three species have approached the edge of extinction because of this ill-founded human hatred. African wild dogs, however, have endured an especially virulent extermination campaign based on their undeserved reputation as vicious creatures whose demise would do the world good.

(10)   *Lycaon pictus,* a species distantly relative to the wolf, used to flourish on much of the African subcontinent, but eradication efforts have reduced its huge former range to a few widely scattered remnants. Only a few thousand of the dogs remain, and they face overwhelming threats to survival in spite of the fact that recent studies have restored to them the respect that they
(15) deserve.

It used to be thought that African wild dogs were brutal killing machines. They were thought of as hunters who preferred to kill slowly. Furthermore, they supposedly killed and ate indiscriminately not only their natural prey but humans and even their own kind. But recent first-person and filmed observa-
(20) tions have proved that a wild dog kill is just as clean and quick as the kill of most other predators. Furthermore, observers in close contact with the dogs report virtually no aggression against human beings—or each other.

With some exceptions, cooperative rather than competitive behavior is the norm within African wild dog packs. Young adults lavish attention on pup-
(25) pies and willingly stay home to babysit while mothers hunt. Feeding the young is a cooperative effort also, as adults will provide them with meals of regurgitated food. Even gorging on a fresh kill, which in some other species is punctuated by snarls and nips, is a quiet, orderly process. In feeding, a hierar-chy is observed without having to be enforced. And although there are some-
(30) times special circumstances that result in one pack member killing others, cannibalism is nonexistent among these animals.

Even with the tide of opinion running in its favor, *Lycaon pictus* faces a perilous future. Lions and other predators kill large numbers of the dogs every year, as do humans, especially farmers trying to protect their livestock.
(35) Recent large-scale commercial cattle ranching poses an even greater threat to the survival of this threatened species. As ranchers fence off huge parcels of land, it becomes harder and harder for predators to survive. The few remaining African wild dogs may not be able to overcome this last onslaught against their existence.

1. Which of the following is the best title for this passage?

   (A) "The Wild Dog—Misunderstood and Endangered"
   (B) "Why Humans Hate Predators"
   (C) "The Attractive Qualities of the Wild Dog"
   (D) "Rash Judgment and Encroachment—Humans against Nature"
   (E) "The Importance of Predators"

2. Which of the following is **not** mentioned in the passage as a fact of *Lycaon pictus* life?

   (F) The consuming of partially digested food
   (G) Caregiving by pack members other than parents
   (H) Infant care by both parents
   (J) A system of organization by rank
   (K) Killing of some dogs by others

3. Which of the following most precisely explains the function served by the mention of wolves and eagles in the passage?

   (A) A way of placing the African wild dog in the predator category
   (B) A sobering reminder of how various human activities can endanger other creatures
   (C) Pointing out that wolves and eagles have been hated even more than wild dogs
   (D) Comparison and contrast of New World species and *Lycaon pictus*
   (E) Showing how misunderstanding causes unreasoning hatred of humans against predators

4. Which of the following is the greatest present threat to the African wild dog?

   (F) Unreasoning human hatred
   (G) Predators, including lions
   (H) Farmers protecting their livestock
   (J) Reduction of open range
   (K) Presence of large numbers of cattle

5. Which of the following best expresses the author's attitude toward behaviors within the dog pack?

   (A) Disapproval of the killing within the pack
   (B) Admiration of the pack members' mutually supportive behaviors
   (C) Amusement at the idea of wild dog babysitters
   (D) Relief to know that cannibalism does not exist
   (E) Mild disgust of the practice of eating regurgitated food

6. According to the passage, which of the following best sums up the place of young in a pack of African wild dogs?

   (F) An unwelcome burden on younger pack members
   (G) Creatures to be protected, loved, and nurtured
   (H) Welcome but essentially disposable features of pack life
   (J) Creatures to be supported by any means, even by an adult's starvation
   (K) Weaker beings to be killed at will

You're now ready for the Reading Practice Tests. As you work through them, you may find yourself making some alterations to the procedure recommended in the Skillbuilder. This is fine! The techniques presented here work well for most test-takers, but you are an individual, and through practice you will find what works best for you.

SOLUTIONS

1. Main Idea. **(A)** B, C, and E are all too narrow. D is too broad because "nature" involves much more than the subject of the passage, one species only. A involves all the content of the passage and no more than that.

2. Fact. **(H)** All the other choices are stated in the fourth paragraph.

3. Inference. **(E)** A is incorrect because of the context, which does not stress classification. B is too broad because the context does not involve "various activities." C is inaccurate according to the last sentence of the first paragraph (lines 6–9). D is too broad, as only one aspect is compared and contrasted—not the entire species. E is correct in the context of the sentences that discuss wolves and eagles.

4. Fact. **(J)** The correct answer is given in lines 36–37.

5. Inference. **(B)** This is an inference question that requires you to recognize the author's tone, or attitude. B is correct because of the positive language used throughout the fourth paragraph, where wild dog behavior is discussed. There is no language expressing disapproval (A), amusement (C), or disgust (E). D is not necessarily untrue, but it is too narrow, involving only the last sentence in the paragraph.

6. Inference. **(G)** F contradicts the word "willingly" in line 25. H is incorrect because there is no suggestion that the young are considered disposable. J is exaggerated—there is no suggestion that the adults who give up food are harming themselves in the process. K is unsupported, and it also contradicts the overall pattern of behavior toward the young. G is correct because the words "loved" and "nurtured" describe the behavior depicted in lines 25–27.

Skillbuilder D: Mathematics

The SHSAT Mathematics section includes topics from arithmetic, basic algebra, some elementary geometry, and a little probability and statistics. (The ninth-year version also includes some trigonometry.) Many questions test your knowledge of basic concepts. However, there are also some challenging problems that test your ability to think creatively and apply what you know in what may seem to be new and unfamiliar situations.

This Skillbuilder is divided into three sections:

- **Mathematical Problem Analysis**

  Tips and strategies for the Mathematics section of the SHSAT

- **The Math Skills Diagnoser**

  A set of six "Diagnosers" to help you identify, correct, and eliminate some frequently made errors

- **Some Basic Terms and Concepts You Should Know**

  A compact review of important basic terms, concepts, and formulas

Section 1
Mathematical Problem Analysis

Tips and Strategies

The best way to become a confident problem solver is to carefully practice a lot of well-selected problems.

This book contains carefully constructed problems designed to help you succeed. Some problems are very challenging and will require you to really stretch. But like a good athlete in training, you won't improve without pushing yourself beyond what you think are your limits. Sometimes even the best of athletes can benefit from a little coaching. So we provide detailed solutions, tips, strategies, and advice.

In this section you will find practical guidance regarding the Mathematics section of the test, including

- General advice
- How to sharpen your problem solving skills
- Illustrative problems and solutions

General Advice
WORK CAREFULLY!

It's not only how much you practice, but also the quality of the practice.

A regular practice schedule will permit you to improve steadily. Don't cram! It simply won't work for this type of exam.

Rehearse for the actual test by doing the practice exams in this book *strictly according to the given instructions and time limits.*

When you study, avoid distractions such as TV, radio, and so on. Don't rush. Pay attention to details. Work neatly. Carefully review solutions. For extra practice, redo the problems you get wrong.

BE ORGANIZED—BE NEAT—BE ALERT

Don't be "out of control." Many errors can be avoided by simply being careful about how you write or draw. Be well organized both mentally and on paper. Remember that a careless error is still an error!

Familiarize yourself with the test directions and format. Diagrams may not be drawn to scale. Check the test directions on test day to be sure of this.

Read the questions carefully. Pay particular attention to what each question is asking.

CHALLENGE YOURSELF

The SHSAT is designed to be a challenging test. To really be prepared, practice on challenging problems.

MAKE THAT CALCULATOR DISAPPEAR

As of the date of publication of this book, calculators are NOT permitted on the SHSAT. Therefore, do not rely on your calculator. No test problem will require the use of a calculator.

KNOW THOSE BASIC FORMULAS

Formulas will NOT be provided in the SHSAT test booklet. Commit them to memory. Check Section 3 for a list of some of the basic formulas.

KNOW YOUR MATH VOCABULARY

You have to be familiar with basic math vocabulary. Technical terms such as *consecutive integers, highest common factor, prime number, absolute value, parallel lines, trapezoid,* and many other math terms must be at your fingertips. You are expected to know them. They will NOT be provided in the test booklet. Check Section 3 for some important basic terms and concepts.

USE THE CHOICES WISELY

Learn how to make the most of the given choices.

For many problems, it is best to solve the problem fully before looking at the choices.

For some problems, it is absolutely necessary to look at the choices and make them part of the problem-solving process. Be aware, however, that some choices typically reflect common errors made in problem solving.

More details about using the choices appear later in this section.

IS THE ANSWER REASONABLE?

Always ask yourself whether or not the result that you got makes sense. *More details regarding this appear later in this section.*

PACING

During the actual test, follow these general rules:

- When you find the correct choice, STOP! Don't waste time checking the other choices.
- Don't give up too soon on any one question, but also don't dwell on any one question for too long. Keep moving. You're aiming at achieving the greatest number of correct answers.
- Remember that the questions are not arranged in strict order of difficulty. There are some easy questions on the later part of the test.
- Use the **? X** system as you go (see page 38). At the end of the test, be sure you have not left any blanks. There is no penalty for wrong answers.

How to Analyze a Problem

There are four basic steps involved in solving problems.

1. **Determine precisely what the problem calls for.** Every problem calls for something specific. What do you have to find? What is the value of *x* that solves the equation? Which number has the largest value? It helps to *underline it, circle it,* or *write it down.* The value of this simple process cannot be overestimated. This forces you to focus on the specific goal of the problem and prepare a solution strategy.

2. **Determine what information is given.** Note carefully what is given or implied. What do you have to work with? This focuses your attention on the ingredients that will be used in solving the problem.

3. **Think about what additional information or mathematical tools you may need.** For example, do you need a special formula or do you need to know certain properties relating to a geometric figure? Math problem solvers often refer to their collection of facts, formulas, and skills as their "toolbox." In this step you start to think about the tools that may prove useful.

4. **Carry out a plan to solve the problem.** Decide specifically how to bridge the gap between what is given and what is called for.

In short, always think

- What do I want
- What do I have
- What do I need
- What do I do

Knowing the basic problem-solving steps provides you with a structured approach. Of course, your ability to solve problems will only improve with experience and practice.

Be an Active Problem Solver

Problems don't solve themselves. Just looking at a problem won't get it done. You usually have to do something to activate the problem-solving process.

Be an active problem solver. Put your pencil in motion.

Depending on the problem, you could

- use variables to represent unknown quantities
- translate verbal information into mathematical symbols (for example, writing an equation that expresses the words of the problem)
- replace variables with numbers
- try special cases
- note other information that may be needed (for example, formulas)
- mark diagrams (for example, labeling congruent segments or angles)
- transfer numerical information from the text of the problem to the diagram (for example, inserting the given degree measure of an angle)
- draw a well-labeled diagram if none is supplied

Actively doing something can launch thoughts and ideas that get your problem-solving engine started.

Examples

1. READING THE QUESTION

One of the most frequent reasons for making careless and avoidable errors is simply not reading a question or problem carefully.

In this first set of examples, you will see illustrations of how important it is to *determine precisely what the question calls for.* This is the first step in carefully reading, interpreting, and ultimately solving a problem.

EXAMPLE 1.1

If $x + y = 11$, what is the value of $4x + 4y$?

In this problem it is crucial to determine exactly what is being asked. By doing this, you are alerted to what is NOT being asked.

What do you want to find? It is easy to be distracted and think that you have to find the values of x and y individually before obtaining the sum of $4x$ and $4y$. You don't.

Since $x + y = 11$, simply multiply both sides of this equation by 4. This produces $4x + 4y = 44$. You are done!

That wasn't too difficult. Here is a slight variation on this theme. Remember to use those four basic steps.

EXAMPLE 1.2

If $x + 2y = 5$ and $2x + y = 31$, what is the value of $x + y$?

Once again in this problem it is crucial to determine exactly what is called for. By doing this, you are again alerted to what is NOT asked.

You have to find the value of $x + y$. Does this mean that you must necessarily find the individual values of x and y first? You could. However, it is easier to find the value of $x + y$ in two steps:

since	$x + 2y = 5,$
and	$2x + y = 31,$
adding produces	$3x + 3y = 36$

Dividing both sides by 3, $x + y = 12$. You are finished!

The fact that the problem calls for the value of $x + y$, and not for the value of either x or y, is a clue. Make it work for you.

EXAMPLE 1.3

After completing $\frac{1}{3}$ of a trip, Tony still had 12 miles to go. How long was the trip?

You are asked to find the length of the entire trip.

What do you know?

Tony has 12 miles to go after completing $\frac{1}{3}$ of the trip.

The 12 miles left to go is therefore the remainder of the trip, or $\frac{2}{3}$ of the trip. If 12 miles is $\frac{2}{3}$ of the trip, then 6 miles is $\frac{1}{3}$ of the trip. The entire trip must be 18 miles.

EXAMPLE 1.4

If $12x - 19 = 1999$, what is the value of

(a) $12x - 15$
(b) $12x + 19$?

(a) The question asks you to find the value of $12x - 15$. Most people would first solve for x and then substitute that value into the expression $12x - 15$. Normally this procedure is fine. But the problem did not call for x. It called for $12x - 15$. This may be a signal that you can find $12x - 15$ directly.

$12x - 15$ can be obtained from $12x - 19$ by simply adding 4. Then $12x - 15 = (12x - 19) + 4 = (1999) + 4 = 2003$.

(b) Notice this time that $12x + 19$ can be obtained from $12x - 19$ by adding 38. Therefore, $12x + 19 = 12x - 19 + 38 = 1999 + 38 = 2037$.

In each of the previous examples, notice how helpful it was to first identify and focus on precisely what was called for.

For extra practice, try these. *Answers are on page 119.*

EXAMPLE 1.5

If 53–2x = 1999, find the value of 65–2x.

EXAMPLE 1.6

If x + 2y + 3z = 53 and 3x + 2y + z = 52, what is the value of x + y + z?

EXAMPLE 1.7

Four hot dogs and a soft drink cost $6.30, whereas one hot dog and four soft drinks cost $4.20. What is the total cost of one hot dog and one soft drink?

EXAMPLE 1.8

(a) 30 is 20% of what number?
(b) 20% of 30 is what number?

In examples (a) and (b), accurately determining what is being asked is the key. It is easy to misinterpret the question.

(a) Using x to represent the "number" clarifies the question. "30 is 20% of what number" becomes 30 = 20% of x, or 30 = .2x. Note that "of" indicates multiplication (see chart on page 152). This equation is equivalent to 300 = 2x, so x = 150.
  It is wise to do a quick check. Is 30 equal to 20% of 150? A little arithmetic verifies the result.

(b) Use the same technique illustrated in (a). This time we have 20% of 30 is x. (.2)(30) = x, so x = 6.

As you read each problem, concentrate on what you are actually trying to find. In (a) the number is such that 30 is 20% of that number. We are looking for a number that is LARGER than 30. In (b), the number is 20% of 30, so the number is SMALLER than 30.

2. USING A SPECIAL CASE

Sometimes you find that you have no idea of what to do or where to begin. Perhaps the numbers are too large, or maybe the wording is just too complicated. Frequently it helps to consider a special case. Use some *well-selected* numbers. To get some idea of how to do this, look over the next group of examples.

EXAMPLE 2.1

The sum of an even number of odd numbers is

(A) always even.
(B) always odd.
(C) sometimes even, sometimes odd.

(continued)

First, try some appropriate numbers to get some insight into the problem. Since we want an *even* number of *odd* numbers, consider, for example, the special case $3 + 5 + 9 + 15$. There is no special reason for choosing these particular odd numbers. Just be sure to select an even number of them. Notice that their sum, 32, is even. If you had to guess at this point, you might pick choice A. However, one example may be insufficient for drawing a valid conclusion. Try a few more special cases. In each case, the resulting sum is even. There is mounting evidence that choice **A** is correct.

Here's the math. Recall that the sum of any two odd numbers must be even, and that the sum of any number of even numbers is also even. Therefore, by pairing the odd numbers, we obtain an even sum.

Using a special case quickly suggested what was happening.

TIP: When trying to determine whether some combination of integers is odd or even, you may always use 1 to typify any odd number and 0 to typify any even number. For example, the sum of three odd numbers and an even number is typified by $1 + 1 + 1 + 0 = 3$, which is odd.

EXAMPLE 2.2

What is 10% of 10^{10}?

(A) 1
(B) 10
(C) 10^5
(D) 10^9
(E) None of these

Here you may be thinking, "What can I gain by using a special case? The number given is a fixed number—it's already a special case!" The number 10^{10} is a very large number (a 1 followed by 10 zeros), and the presence of the exponent can also prove distracting.

Replace 10^{10} by any reasonably small number. Then let's see what's going on.

What is 10% of 80? What is 10% of 100?

It's easy to find 10% of a number. Just divide the number by 10. Apply this to finding 10% of 10^{10}. Divide 10^{10} by 10.

Since $10^{10} = 10 \times 10 \times 10 \times 10 \times 10 \times 10 \times 10 \times 10 \times 10 \times 10$, the result of dividing 10^{10} by 10 is 10^9 (one of the 10s cancels). The correct answer is **D.**

EXAMPLE 2.3

The sides of a square are each multiplied by 3 to form a new square. If the area of the original square was *K*, then the area of the new square is

(A) K^3
(B) $3K$
(C) $6K$
(D) $9K$
(E) $9K^2$

This example is perfect for using a special case. Try a few values for the side of the square. Don't worry about *K* at this point. For example, if the original side was 2, the original area was 4. Tripling the side to 6 results in an area of 36, which is 9 times the original area.

Using a starting value of 5 for the original side produces an original area of 25. But tripling 5 to 15 results in an area of 225. Once again this is 9 times the original area.

In each case the new area is 9 times the original area. The answer appears to be choice **D**. The math goes like this. Let s be the original side. The original area is $K = s^2$. Tripling the side to $3s$ produces a new area of $(3s)^2$, which is $9s^2$ or $9K$.

EXAMPLE 2.4

The smallest of five consecutive integers is represented by $y - 3$. What is the largest of these integers, in terms of y?

Don't be distracted by the presence of a variable. Look at any set of five consecutive integers. For example 4, 5, 6, 7, and 8, or 23, 24, 25, 26, and 27. The largest integer can always be obtained by simply adding 4 to the first integer. The answer is $y - 3 + 4$, which is $y + 1$.

EXAMPLE 2.5

N granola bars cost T cents. What is the cost of K of these granola bars?

It can be difficult to solve a problem when many variables are involved. But see how easy it is to do the following similar problem in which the variables have been replaced by numbers.
Three granola bars cost 90 cents. What is the cost of 8 granola bars?

Find the cost of 1 granola bar, $\frac{90}{3}$, and multiply the result by 8.

The answer to the original problem is $(\frac{T}{N})(K)$. When using numbers for a special case, leave all computations in unsimplified form. This reveals the underlying process.

EXAMPLE 2.6

How many integers are there from 11 to 111 inclusive?

It is surprising how many people get this wrong. The correct answer is 101. The point of using the special case in this problem is to check the soundness of your initial reasoning. Try some easy-to-check numbers. Certainly you can count the number of integers from 11 to 15 inclusive. Subtract 11 from 15, but add back 1 because subtracting fails to include the smaller number. The method that produced this correct answer of 5 will transfer to the original problem.
There is no reason to lose points when you can check using a simple special case.

Try these examples for extra practice. *Answers are on page 119.*

EXAMPLE 2.7

If a two-digit number is decreased by the sum of its digits, then the resulting difference *must* be divisible by

(A) 2
(B) 4
(C) 5
(D) 9
(E) 11

EXAMPLE 2.8

In the formula $A = bh$, if b is tripled and h is quadrupled, then A is multiplied by N. Compute N.

EXAMPLE 2.9

If y is an even integer, which of the following *may* be an even integer?

(A) $\dfrac{y}{2}$

(B) $y^2 + 3y + 5$

(C) $5y + 11$

(D) $6y - 7$

(E) $5(y + 3)$

EXAMPLE 2.10

The original price of an item is discounted by 10% for a sale. A week later the sale price is discounted an *additional* 30% for a clearance sale. What single discount applied to the original price would be equivalent to those two successive discounts?

3. USING THE CHOICES

How should you use the given choices to your best advantage?

- In certain cases, it is best not to look at the choices until you have first worked the problem.
- Sometimes the choices themselves can provide valuable insight into an otherwise difficult problem.
- Finally, there are some questions that require you to try each choice. In these questions, you must actually look at each choice and make decisions.

How can you recognize these different types of situations? When you do use the choices, where should you start? The following examples will answer these questions and provide you with helpful tips.

When It Is Best Not to Try the Choices First

EXAMPLE 3.1

The mean of 13, 17, and y is the same as the mean of 8, 14, 3, and $3y$. What is the value of y?

(A) $\dfrac{2}{3}$

(B) $\dfrac{5}{2}$

(C) $\dfrac{17}{3}$

(D) 5

(E) 9

(continued)

Recall that the mean (average) of a set of values is the sum of the values divided by the number of values. The mean of 13, 17, and y is $\dfrac{(30+y)}{3}$, and the mean of 8, 14, 3, and $3y$ is $\dfrac{(25+3y)}{4}$. This leads to the equation $\dfrac{(30+y)}{3} = \dfrac{(25+3y)}{4}$. Trying to finish this problem by trying each choice could prove very time consuming and could also lead to arithmetical errors. So it is best here not to check choices first. Solve the equation, producing an answer of $y = 9$. This is choice **E**.

> **TIP:** When a problem involves a lot of computation, or the offered choices are not simple to use, or one of the choices is "none of these," it may be wise to do the problem first before looking at the choices.

When It May Be Helpful to Try the Choices

EXAMPLE 3.2

The sum of five consecutive multiples of 7 is 350.

The smallest of these is

(A) 28
(B) 35
(C) 42
(D) 56
(E) 70

You want to find the smallest of five consecutive multiples of 7 such that their sum is 350. An algebraic solution would solve the problem. However, in this problem, it is fastest to simply try the choices. Pick a choice, list the next four consecutive multiples of 7, add, and see if the result is 350. The computations are quick and easy.

What guidelines should be followed when trying choices? Where should you begin?

> **TIP:** The choices are generally arranged in either increasing or decreasing order of size. When trying the choices, it is often best to begin with choice B, C, or D.

Let's start with choice C. If 42 were the smallest of the five multiples of seven, then the others would be 49, 56, 63, and 70. Their sum is 210. Choice C is incorrect. But we can learn much from this incorrect answer! It is too small. Try larger values. Thus, choices A and B are immediately eliminated. Try choice D. $56 + 63 + 70 + 77 + 84 = 350$. Choice **D** is the correct answer.

Here's one method using algebra. Let the smallest of the five consecutive multiples of 7 be represented by s. The next four are $s + 7$, $s + 14$, $s + 21$, and $s + 28$. The sum of all five is $5s + 70$. Setting $5s + 70 = 350$ and solving for s, we have $s = 56$.

When It Helps to Preview the Choices

EXAMPLE 3.3

The product $5 \times 6 \times 7 \times 8 \times 9 \times 10 \times 11 \times 12$ is divisible by

(A) 2^{11}
(B) 2^{10}
(C) 2^9
(D) 2^8
(E) 2^7

In this example, previewing the choices provides insightful clues. Without looking at the choices, we really have no idea of what to do.

The choices direct us to look for the indicated power of 2 that is a factor of the given product. We look at those numbers that contribute twos. In the original product, 6 contributes one factor of 2. 8, being $2 \times 2 \times 2$, contributes three factors. 10 contributes one, and 12 contributes two. All together, there is a net contribution of seven twos. Therefore 2^7, choice **E,** is the correct answer. Notice that no higher power of 2 will divide the original product.

When You Must Check the Choices

EXAMPLE 3.4

X: $.5 < (.5)^2$

Y: $\dfrac{3}{11} > \dfrac{8}{29}$

Z: $\dfrac{111}{333} = \dfrac{1}{3}$

(F) X, Y, and Z are all true.
(G) Z is true.
(H) X, Y, and Z are all false.
(J) X and Y are true.
(K) Y is true.

This example actually requires that you check the choices. Previewing the choices alerts us to the fact that we will have to test the validity of each numerical statement X, Y, and Z. Once this is done, we can select the appropriate choice. Doing the math reveals that

X is false.　　$(.5)^2 = .25$, and .5 is more than .25.

Y is false.　　If *a, b, c,* and *d* are positive numbers, then $\left(\dfrac{a}{b}\right) > \left(\dfrac{c}{d}\right)$ only if *ad > bc*. In this case 3×29 is *less than* 11×8. Notice how much easier it is to compare the sizes of fractions using this method rather than trying to express each fraction using a common denominator.

Z is true.　　$\dfrac{111}{333} = \dfrac{111(1)}{111(3)} = \dfrac{1}{3}$

The correct answer is choice **G.**

Try these for extra practice. *Answers are on page 119.*

EXAMPLE 3.5

Which of the following is *closest* to .14?

(A) $\dfrac{1}{6}$

(B) $\dfrac{1}{7}$

(C) $\dfrac{1}{8}$

(D) $\dfrac{1}{9}$

(E) $\dfrac{1}{11}$

EXAMPLE 3.6

The smallest positive integer value of N such that $\frac{3}{11} > \frac{8}{N}$ is

(A) 33
(B) 32
(C) 31
(D) 30
(E) 29

4. ESTIMATION

In some problems it is helpful to actually approximate numerical values.

EXAMPLE 4.1

Which of the following is *closest* to .18?

(A) $\frac{10}{61}$

(B) $\frac{10}{71}$

(C) $\frac{10}{81}$

(D) $\frac{10}{91}$

(E) $\frac{10}{101}$

You have to find some reasonable way to estimate the given values. Try to approximate each of the choices. In each case, the denominators of the given fractions are close to multiples of 10. To efficiently estimate the value of the fractions, use the following approximations:

(A) $\frac{10}{60}$ or $\frac{1}{6}$

(B) $\frac{10}{70}$ or $\frac{1}{7}$

(C) $\frac{10}{80}$ or $\frac{1}{8}$

(D) $\frac{10}{90}$ or $\frac{1}{9}$

(E) $\frac{10}{100}$ or $\frac{1}{10}$

Now look at the value .18, which is just a little less than .20 or $\frac{1}{5}$. The best choice appears to be A, which is close to $\frac{1}{6}$. The other choices are all smaller values, and therefore are not as close. Double-check, by expressing $\frac{1}{6}$ as .1666. . . .

EXAMPLE 4.2

Let $P = \sqrt{3} + \sqrt{5}$, $Q = \sqrt{5} + \sqrt{3}$, and $R = \sqrt{10} - \sqrt{2}$, then

(A) $P < Q < R$
(B) $P < R < Q$
(C) $Q < P < R$
(D) $R < Q < P$
(E) $R < P < Q$

This example looks more ferocious than it actually is. Let's do some estimation. First note that $\sqrt{5}$ is a little more than 2. Write this as $\sqrt{5} = 2+$. Similarly, we approximate $\sqrt{3}$ as 1+, and $\sqrt{2}$ as 1+. Keep in mind that $\sqrt{3}$ is greater than $\sqrt{2}$. With these we can write

$$P = \sqrt{5+}, \quad Q = \sqrt{6+}, \text{ and } R = \sqrt{8+}.$$

The answer is then **A.** $P < Q < R$

---

5. IS THE ANSWER REASONABLE?

When you finally arrive at what you think is the answer to a problem, you should always ask yourself whether that answer makes sense. This simple but critical part of problem solving is a powerful way to avoid careless wrong answers.

EXAMPLE 5.1

The value of $4^5 + 4^5 + 4^5 + 4^5$ is

(A) 4^{20}
(B) 16^5
(C) 16^{20}
(D) 4^6
(E) 80

This particular problem invites error! Let's first look at a commonly occuring wrong answer, namely choice A. We apply the "is the answer reasonable" test to choice A as follows:

$$4^5 = 4 \times 4 \times 4 \times 4 \times 4 = 16 \times 16 \times 4$$

which is about 1000 (actually 1024). The expression in the question is $4^5 + 4^5 + 4^5 + 4^5$, which is about 4000. Now consider the value of 4^{20}. This is an extremely large number, far more than 4000. It is not a reasonable answer.

Can you now determine which other choices are also not reasonable?

Here's the math. The expression $4^5 + 4^5 + 4^5 + 4^5$ is the sum of 4^5 four times. Therefore $4^5 + 4^5 + 4^5 + 4^5 = 4 \times 4^5 = 4^6$. The answer is choice **D.**

EXAMPLE 5.2

The value of $\dfrac{9090}{90}$ is

(A) 11
(B) 100
(C) 101
(D) 111
(E) 1010

This relatively simple arithmetic problem can easily lead to careless mistakes, especially if you are in a hurry. A common error is illustrated by choice A. Before you commit to choice A, ask yourself whether 11 is really a reasonable answer.

$\dfrac{9090}{90}$ is about $\dfrac{9090}{100}$, which is approximately 90. Choice A must be incorrect.

The actual answer obtained by dividing 90 into 9090 is 101. Be careful when cancelling. Don't neglect the middle zero. The correct answer is choice **C.**

6. PSEUDO-OPERATIONS

To test your ability to deal with new mathematical situations, a special type of question is often present. In this type of question, a new definition, symbol, or set of symbols is introduced.

The typical question appears more difficult than it actually is because there is something unfamiliar present.

EXAMPLE 6.1

For positive numbers x and y, define $x ® y$ to mean $x^2 - 2y$. Find the value of $5 ® 3$.

(A) 69
(B) 19
(C) 16
(D) 13
(E) 4

Simply compute $5 ® 3 = 5^2 - (2)(3) = 25 - 6 = 19$. This is choice **B**.

A variation on this theme employs a slightly more complicated set of options.

EXAMPLE 6.2

For all positive integers a and b, define $<a, b>$ to mean

I. ab if a and b are *both* even or *both* odd.
II. $a^2 - b^2$ if *one* is even and the *other* is odd.

Which of the following has the *largest* value?

(A) $<4, 4>$
(B) $<5, 4>$
(C) $<6, 4>$
(D) $<7, 2>$
(E) $<6, 5>$

You must evaluate each choice and compare. To compute the value of each choice, first decide which of the two rules applies.

$<4,4>$ requires rule I and has a value of $4 \times 4 = 16$
$<5,4>$ requires rule II and has a value of $25 - 16 = 9$
$<6,4>$ requires rule I and has a value of $6 \times 4 = 24$
$<7,2>$ requires rule II and has a value of $49 - 4 = 45$
$<6,5>$ requires rule I and has a value of $36 - 25 = 11$
The answer is choice **D**.

SUMMARY OF BASIC TIPS AND STRATEGIES

When Studying

- Practice under conditions that are similar to the actual test conditions. Good rehearsals make for good performances.

- Make your study time count. Be focused, alert, and attentive. Do your work in a neat, organized manner.

- Familiarize yourself completely with the test format, directions, and question types. Know your basics and math vocabulary. Do not use a calculator when you practice.

- Read problems with care. Use the four-step approach to problem solving. What do I want? What do I have? What do I need? What do I do? When you think you have solved a problem, ask whether your answer is reasonable.

- Practice under time limits. Learn to pace yourself.

- Practice challenging problems and repeat them to sharpen skills. Don't give up too soon. Persistence can inspire creative, productive thinking.

- For extra practice, redo problems you got wrong.

- Be confident! With proper study, you will be well prepared for the test.

When Taking the Test

- Work carefully. Be neat and well organized. Use the test booklet and the scratch paper for your work. Be in control.

- Do all calculations carefully the first time. Don't waste time correcting avoidable mistakes. It's sometimes helpful to quickly estimate before actually calculating to give yourself an idea of an approximate value.

- Read the questions carefully. Determine precisely what the problem calls for, what is given, what you may need, and what you have to do to answer the question. Always ask yourself whether the answer is reasonable.

- Be an active problem solver. Combine thought and action. Actively mark diagrams, use variables to represent unknown quantities, try numbers, look at a special case, and so on. Do something to get your problem-solving engine started.

- Remember that on this test, diagrams might not be drawn to scale.

- The questions are not necessarily in order of difficulty. Easy questions may appear in the later part of the test.

- Use the choices advantageously. Make the choices work for you.

    Many problems should first be solved completely. Then find your answer among the choices. This is often better and faster than testing each choice to determine if it can fit the question.

    Some problems actually require you to check the choices and/or use the choices as part of the problem-solving process. For some easy questions, checking the choices may prove the fastest. Quickly eliminate choices that are obviously unreasonable.

    In some questions, previewing the choices can offer a clue about how to approach the problem.

When you have found the correct choice, STOP! Don't waste time checking the other choices.

- Don't give up too soon. Some seemingly difficult questions may require extra concentration or insight. In many cases, complex problems combine several simpler steps. Give yourself a chance to fully think, try, and analyze. But don't dwell too long on any one question. Pace yourself. You want to answer as many questions as possible.

- Use the **?** **X** system as you go. When you have finished the test, be sure you have not left any blanks. Remember that there is no penalty for wrong answers. A guess may yield a correct answer, but a blank cannot.

ANSWERS TO THE EXTRA PROBLEMS

Example 1.5   2011

Example 1.6 $\dfrac{105}{4}$

Example 1.7 $2.10

Example 2.7   Choice **D**

Example 2.8 $N = 12$

Example 2.9   Choice **A**

Example 2.10   37%

Example 3.5   Choice **B**

Example 3.6   Choice **D**

Section 2
The Math Skills Diagnoser

Frequently Made Errors

The Workouts in this section will help you identify, correct, and eliminate some frequently made errors. There are six Workouts and accompanying Follow-ups for extra practice. The Workouts cover some of the basic skills you should know. Workout F contains some additional material for those currently in the ninth grade.

> Workout A Arithmetic I
> Workout B Arithmetic II
> Workout C Algebra
> Workout D Geometry
> Workout E Graphs and Charts
> Workout F 9th Grade Topics

After each Workout you will find detailed solutions that enable you to diagnose and correct any errors. You will then find a set of Follow-up exercises. Use these to check your progress and for additional practice.

Get Ready

For the Workouts to be effective, you must pay careful attention to the time limits. You should not do all of the Workouts in one session.

Get Set

Set proper study conditions.

Work quickly! Don't linger over any one problem. Since these workouts are diagnostic, *avoid random guessing*. Leave out questions you cannot do and return to them later when you review the solutions.

Be sure not to look at the solutions until after you have completed the Workout!

Workout A

Arithmetic I

Directions for Workout A: 10 Questions   15-Minute Time Limit
Place your answer (A, B, or C) in the answer space provided.

1. $\frac{1}{2} + \frac{1}{3} =$ **A.** $\frac{2}{5}$ **B.** $\frac{5}{6}$ **C.** $\frac{2}{6}$

2. $(7)(5) - 5(5 - 8) =$ **A.** 50   **B.** -90 **C.** 20

3. $\sqrt{16} + \sqrt{9} =$ **A.** $\sqrt{25}$ **B.** 25   **C.** 7

4. $(2^3)(3^3) =$ **A.** 6^3 **B.** 6^6 **C.** 6^9

5. In scientific notation, $387 \times 100{,}000$ is represented as   **A.** 3.87×10^3 **B.** 3.87×10^7 **C.** 387×10^5

6. $(-12)(-6) \div (-3) =$ **A.** -24 **B.** 8   **C.** -6

7. $(.\overline{3})(.\overline{6}) =$ **A.** $.\overline{18}$ **B.** $.\overline{2}$ **C.** 1

8. N granola bars cost 84 cents. At this price, 21 granola bars would cost   **A.** \$17.64   **B.** $4N$ **C.** $\frac{\$17.64}{N}$

9. $\frac{5}{6} \div \frac{3}{20} =$ **A.** $\frac{50}{9}$ **B.** $\frac{1}{8}$ **C.** $\frac{9}{50}$

10. $\frac{21+56}{7} =$ **A.** 59   **B.** 11   **C.** 29

STOP! This is the end of Workout A

1	2	3	4	5	6	7	8	9	10

Solutions A

#	A	B	C
1	Don't add the numerators and denominators separately. To combine fractions, first get a common denominator.	✓	When expressing the given fractions as equivalent fractions, be sure to adjust the numerators accordingly. $\frac{1}{2} + \frac{1}{3} = \frac{3}{6} + \frac{2}{6} = \frac{5}{6}$
2	✓	Be careful not to first subtract 5 from 35. Following the order of operations: $(7)(5) - 5(5 - 8)$ $= (7)(5) - 5(-3)$ $= 35 + 15 = 50.$	Watch the signs! You should be adding 15, not subtracting it.
3	In general, $\sqrt{a} + \sqrt{b}$ does *not* equal $\sqrt{a+b}$. $\sqrt{16} + \sqrt{9} = 4 + 3 = 7$	You neglected the radical signs.	✓
4	✓	Be careful not to add exponents when the bases are different. $2^3 \cdot 3^3 = 2 \cdot 2 \cdot 2 \cdot 3 \cdot 3 \cdot 3$ $= 6 \cdot 6 \cdot 6 = 6^3.$	Don't be tempted to multiply the exponents in this situation.
5	$387 \times 100{,}000 = 3.87 \times 10{,}000{,}000 = 3.87 \times 10^7.$ **TIP:** You can always rely on an easy example to help you to remember a procedure. For example, 456 is 4.56×10^2. This reminds you of how to move the decimal point.	✓	This expression is not in scientific notation. **FACT:** A number expressed in scientific notation must be written in the form $A \times 10^B$, where $1 \leq A < 10$, and B is an integer.
6	✓	You probably divided -12 by -3 AND -6 by -3, and then multiplied.	The -6 should be multiplied by -12 first.
7	Convert the repeated decimals to equivalent fractions first. $\left(\frac{1}{3}\right)\left(\frac{2}{3}\right) = \frac{2}{9} = .222\ldots$ **TIP:** $.111\ldots = \frac{1}{9}$, $.222\ldots = \frac{2}{9}$, $.333\ldots = \frac{3}{9} = \frac{1}{3}$, etc. Yes, $.999\ldots$ *does* equal 1.	✓	Did you *add* by mistake?

#	A	B	C
8	First find the cost of *one* item. It is 84/*N* (total cost divided by the number of items). Thus 21 bars would cost 21 × (84/*N*) = $17.64/*N*.	There is no logical reason to divide 84 by 21.	✓
9	✓	You forgot to "invert" before multiplying.	You inverted the wrong fraction before multiplying. $(\frac{5}{6}) \div (\frac{3}{20}) = (\frac{5}{6}) \times (\frac{20}{3}) = \frac{50}{9}$ after reducing.
10	When the numerator is a sum, you must either first combine the terms, or divide *each* term of the numerator by the denominator. You have only divided 21 by 7. TIP: $\frac{a+b}{c} = \frac{a}{c} + \frac{b}{c}$	✓	See Column A. You only divided the 56 by 7.

Follow-Up A

Answers are on page 147.

1. $\frac{1}{3} - \frac{1}{4} =$

2. Compute: $(5 - 3)(8) - 2$

3. Compute: $\sqrt{5^2} - \sqrt{4^2}$

4. Express in scientific notation: 5,430,000,000,000

5. $\frac{9}{50} \div \frac{3}{20} =$

6. Compute the value of x if $12^5 = (2)^x (3)^5$

7. Compute: $(14)(-8) \div (-2)$

8. Compute: $(.\overline{7})(.\overline{1})(90)$

9. $\frac{50 - 40}{-10} =$

10. The total cost of *G* granola bars is 90 cents. Express the total cost of 3 granola bars in terms of *G*.

Workout B

Arithmetic II

1. The sum of two odd numbers is   **A.** always odd. **B.** always even.
   C. sometimes even, sometimes odd.

2. The number of primes less than 12 is   **A.** 4   **B.** 5   **C.** 6

3. Which of the following is divisible by 6 but not by 9?   **A.** $2^8 \cdot 3^3 \cdot 5^2$ **B.** $2 \cdot 3 \cdot 5^4$ **C.** $3^4 \cdot 5^4$

4. How many integers are there from 17 to 111, including 17 and 111?   **A.** 94   **B.** 95   **C.** 96

5. What is the greatest common factor of $2^3 \times 3^2 \times 5^4$ and $2^2 \times 5^3 \times 7^5$?   **A.** $2^3 \times 3^2 \times 5^4$ **B.** $2 \times 3 \times 5$ **C.** $2^2 \times 5^3$

6. If 25**Q**781 is divisible by 3, then the number of different possible values for the digit **Q** is   **A.** 1   **B.** 2   **C.** 3

7. The least common multiple of 2, 3, 4, 5, and 6 is   **A.** 720   **B.** 120   **C.** 60

8. How many integers between 1 and 400 are multiples of 7?   **A.** 56   **B.** 57   **C.** 58

9. If $\frac{5}{7} > \frac{8}{N}$ then N *could* be   **A.** 10   **B.** 11   **C.** 12

10. If the number N is a 5-digit prime number, which one of the following *might* be a prime number?   **A.** $N-2$ **B.** $N+31$ **C.** $3N+18$

STOP! This is the end of Workout B.

1	2	3	4	5	6	7	8	9	10

Solutions B

#	A	B	C
1	**TIP:** When checking to determine whether some combination of integers produces an even or odd result, try using some simple numbers. For example, $3 + 5 = 8$ (even).	✓	See Column A and apply the TIP... **TIP:** The sum of two odd numbers is always even. The product of two odd numbers is always odd. **FACT:** 0 is an even number.
2	You neglected to include 2 in your count. **FACT:** The number 2 is the first prime number.	✓	The primes less than 12 are 2, 3, 5, 7, and 11. You may have inadvertently included 1 or 9.
3	$6 (= 2 \cdot 3)$ is a factor of the given expression, but so is $9 (= 3^2)$.	✓	The expression *is not* divisible by 6, and *is* divisible by 9.
4	Compute $111 - 17 = 94$. THEN add back 1 (because subtracting doesn't count the starting number) to get 95. **TIP:** Check your ideas using smaller numbers. For example, if you try to count the number of integers from 7 to 11 inclusive, it's easy to see that $11 - 7$ produces one number too few.	✓	You added back one too many numbers. Check using a smaller set of numbers. (See Column A)
5	The number 3 is not *common* to both of the given numbers. It cannot be part of the greatest common factor.	The number 3 is not a common factor. Furthermore, there are greater powers of 2 and 5 that are common factors. **FACT:** When integers are expressed as powers of their prime factors, the greatest common factor can be found by multiplying together the *lowest-appearing powers of their common primes.*	✓

#	A	B	C
6	One possible value for Q is 1. However, the question calls for the *number* of possible values.	**FACT:** An integer is divisible by 3 if the *sum of its digits is divisible by 3.* The sum of the digits is 23 + **Q.** Thus if **Q** = 1, 4, or 7, the sum of the digits (24, 27, or 30) is divisible by 3. There are three possibilities. You left out one of them.	✓
7	The LCM is not always found by multiplying the given numbers together. This works only when the individual numbers have no common factor other than 1.	120 is a common multiple since all of the given numbers go into 120. But there is a smaller common multiple.	✓
8	You undercounted.	✓	**TIP:** To count the number of multiples of 7 from 1 to 400, simply divide 400 by 7: *retain the quotient and discard the remainder.* The quotient is the answer.
9	One method is to convert $\frac{5}{7}$ and $\frac{8}{10}$ to equivalent fractions having the same denominator. Clearly $\frac{50}{70}$ is not greater than $\frac{56}{70}$.	You could change $\frac{5}{7}$ and $\frac{8}{11}$ to fractions having 77 as their common denominator, or you could use the powerful method indicated in the following tip. **TIP:** For positive numbers a, b, c, and d, $\frac{a}{b}$ is greater than $\frac{c}{d}$ only if ad is greater than bc. For $\frac{5}{7}$ to be greater than $\frac{8}{N}$, 5 times N must be larger than 7 times 8. For which of the given values of N is $5N > 56$? Choices A and B are thus incorrect.	✓
10	✓ All primes greater than 2 are odd. An unknown odd number, therefore, has the potential to be prime.	odd + odd = even. But 2 is the only even prime and $N + 31$ is clearly bigger than 2. (See Example 1)	The number $3N + 18$ is divisible by 3. It can be written as $3(N + 6)$, or it may be thought of as the sum of two multiples of 3, namely $3N$ and 18. The sum of multiples of 3 is a multiple of 3. The only multiple of 3 that is a prime is 3×1.

Follow-Up B

Answers are on page 147.

1. How many odd integers are there from 17 to 59 inclusive?

2. Find the smallest positive integer N such that $\dfrac{7}{16} < \dfrac{N}{9}$

3. What is the smallest positive integer that is a multiple of both $(2^2)(3)$ and $(2)(3^2)$?

4. If 25**Q**781 is a multiple of 9, what is the value of the digit **Q**?

5. How many prime numbers are there whose squares are less than 250?

6. The sum of an odd number of odd numbers is

   (A) always odd.
   (B) always even.
   (C) sometimes odd, sometimes even.

7. What is the greatest common factor of $2^3 \cdot 5^2 \cdot 7^5$ and $5^3 \cdot 7^3 \cdot 11^8$?

8. How many integers between 1 and 40 are multiples of 3 or 7?

9. If p, q, and r are all odd primes, which of the following *might* also be a prime?

   (A) $p^2 - q^2 + 1$
   (B) $pqr + 3$
   (C) $(p + 2)(r + 2) + 1$

10. How many distinct positive integer factors does the number 125 have? (Include 1 and 125.)

Workout C

Algebra

Directions for Workout C: 10 Questions   15-Minute Time Limit
Place your answer (A, B, or C) in the answer space provided.

1. $7x - x =$ A. $6x$ B. 7 C. 6

2. $(y^3)(y^5) =$ A. y^8 B. $2y^8$ C. y^{15}

3. If $x = 3$, then $-x^2 =$ A. -6 B. 9 C. -9

4. If n represents a number, then "5 less than twice a number" may be written as A. $5 < 2n$ B. $5 - 2n$ C. $2n - 5$

5. $(2x)^3 =$ A. $2x^3$ B. $6x^3$ C. $8x^3$

6. If $3 - x > 10$, then A. $x < -7$ B. $x > -7$ C. $x < 7$

7. $(5 + 4x) - (3 - 3x) =$ A. $2 + 7x$ B. $8 + 7x$ C. $2 + x$

8. $(x + 2)(x + 5) =$ A. $x^2 + 10$ B. $x^2 + 7x + 10$ C. $2x + 10$

9. $\dfrac{8x + 4}{2} =$ A. $4x + 2$ B. $4x + 4$ C. $6x$

10. Let $0 < x < 1$. Which of the following has the largest value? A. x^2 B. $2x$ C. x

STOP! This is the end of Workout C.

1	2	3	4	5	6	7	8	9	10

Solutions C

#	A	B	C
1	✓	$7x - x = 7x - 1x = 6x$. Don't "take away" the x.	Combining like terms produces terms of the same type.
2	✓	$(y^3)(y^5) =$ $(y \cdot y \cdot y)(y \cdot y \cdot y \cdot y \cdot y) =$ $y^{3+5} = y^8$ **FACT:** When multiplying expressions having the same base, *add* the exponents: $(y^a)(y^b) = y^{a+b}$	Be careful! $(y^a)(y^b)$ *does not* equal y^{ab}. **TIP:** When in doubt, try replacing the variable with a number. For example, $(2^3)(2^5) =$ $(2 \cdot 2 \cdot 2)(2 \cdot 2 \cdot 2 \cdot 2 \cdot 2) =$ 2^8, not 2^{15}.
3	x^2 means "x times x," not "2 times x".	This is a very common error! To evaluate $-x^2$, *first square x, then negate.* Thus, -3^2 is the negative of 3^2. Do not square -3 in this case. Consider, for example, $15 - 3^2 = 15 - 9$, not $15 + 9$. -3^2 is not the same as $(-3)^2$.	✓
4	$5 < 2n$ means 5 *is less* than $2n$.	Consider the phrase "4 less than 10" (which equals 6). This means $10 - 4$. Similarly $5 - 2n$ means $2n$ less than 5 or 5 decreased by $2n$.	✓
5	$(2x)^3$ means $(2x)(2x)(2x)$, which produces $8x^3$. Be careful not to limit the exponentiation to only one of the factors. **FACT:** $(ab)^t = a^t \times b^t$	2^3 is 8, not 6.	✓
6	✓	If you divide both sides of the inequality by a negative number, be sure to reverse the sense of the inequality. If $-x > 7$, then $x < -7$.	Pay proper attention to the signs when dividing.
7	✓	$-(3 - 3x)$ is $-3 + 3x$.	When removing parentheses preceded by a negative sign, be sure to change the signs of *all* the terms contained within the parentheses. $-(3 - 3x) = -3 + 3x$.

#	A	B	C
8	The most common error when multiplying binomials is to neglect the middle terms. Don't forget to include 2 times x and 5 times x.	✓	x times x is x^2 (not $2x$), and you neglected the middle terms. (See Column A)
9	✓	Be sure to divide *every* term in the numerator by the denominator.	$8x + 4$ is not $12x$.
10	If $0 < x < 1$, then x^2 will be less than x. **TIP:** Try several well-chosen numbers to reveal what actually happens. Using $x = .5$, for example, it is easy to see that x^2 is less than x.	✓	If x represents any positive number, then $2x > x$.

Follow-Up C

Answers are on page 147.

1. Simplify: $8x^2 - x^2$.

2. Multiply: $(x^4)(x^{12})$

3. If $x = -5$, compute the value of $-x^2 - 2x$

4. Simplify $(3x^2)^3$

5. $(y - 3)(y - 4) =$

6. Simplify: $\dfrac{7x + 14}{7}$

7. Translate into algebraic symbols: *11 less than the square of a number.* Use x to represent the number.

8. Simplify: $(3x + 5) - (3 - 5x)$

9. Solve for x if $-3x < -6$.

10. If $-1 < x < 0$, which of the following has the smallest value?

    (A) x^2
    (B) x^3
    (C) x^4

Workout D

Geometry

Directions for Workout D: 10 Questions   15-Minute Time Limit
Place your answer (A, B, or C) in the answer space provided.

1. Two sides of an isosceles triangle
   are 7 and 3. The perimeter of this
   triangle is

      A. 17   **B.** 13
      C. There is more than one possible answer.

2. If each side of a square is doubled,
   then its area is multiplied by

      A. 2   **B.** 4   **C.** 16

3. Which of the following could NOT
   be the length of a leg of a right triangle
   whose hypotenuse is 5?

      A. 1   **B.** $\sqrt{26}$ **C.** 4.1

4. The ratio of the circumference of
   a circle to its diameter is

      A. π **B.** twice its radius   **C.** 2

5. The value of $x + y$ is

      A. 210   **B.** 150   **C.** 180

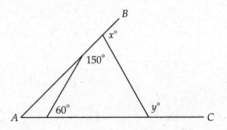

6. Line p is parallel to line q as shown
   in the figure. What is the value of z?

      A. Cannot be determined from the given information.
      B. 45°   **C.** 65°

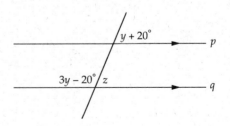

7. In the figure, angle *AOB* and angle *XOY* are right angles. Which angles must be equal?

A. *r* and *t*   **B.** *r, s,* and *t*
C. None of the angles *r, s,* and *t* must necessarily be equal.

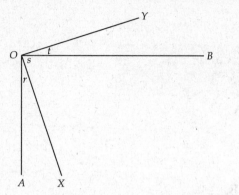

8. Triangle *ABC* contains an angle of 60° and a side whose length is 8. Which of the following additional pieces of information would allow you to uniquely determine the perimeter of the triangle? Triangle *ABC* is

A. scalene.   **B.** isosceles.
C. a right triangle.

9. $\overline{AOB}$, $\overline{COD}$, and $\overline{EO}$ are line segments. Which of the following must be true?

A. $d = b$ **B.** $a = d$ **C.** $c = b + d$

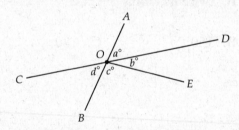

10. The area of triangle *ABC* is 20. The area of triangle *BDC* is

A. 8   **B.** 5   **C.** 4

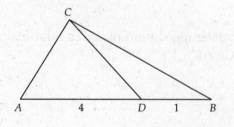

STOP! This is the end of Workout D.

1	2	3	4	5	6	7	8	9	10

Solutions D

#	A	B	C
1	✓	**FACT:** The sum of any two sides of a triangle must be greater than the third side. The sides cannot be 3, 3, and 7 since $3 + 3 < 7$.	The only possible cases are 3, 3, and 7—which is impossible—and 7, 7, and 3. The perimeter is 17.
2	The area is NOT doubled. It is multiplied by 4. Try several numerical values to convince yourself.	✓	Watch your arithmetic.
3	The only restriction is that any leg must be less than the hypotenuse.	✓ $\sqrt{26} > 5$, so it may *not* be a leg of the given right triangle.	4.1 is less than 5, and therefore permissible. The question *did not* imply that the sides had to be integers! Also, the fact that the hypotenuse is 5 does not mean that the legs must be 3 and 4.
4	✓	The circumference of a circle is $C = \pi d = 2\pi r$. Therefore $\frac{C}{d} = \frac{\pi d}{d} = \pi$.	You probably used an incorrect formula for the circumference of a circle.
5	✓	**FACT:** The sum of the interior angles of a quadrilateral is 360°. Therefore, the *sum* of the measures of the two angles adjacent to x and y is 150°. That is *not* the sum of x and y. The angles adjacent to x and y, together with x and y, form two straight angles. That total is 360°, so, $x + y$ must be 210°.	The sum of x and y would be 180° only if $\overline{AB}$ and $\overline{BC}$ were parallel.
6	**FACT:** When two parallel lines are cut by a transversal, the "corresponding angles" (angles that are in the same relative positions) are equal. So $z = y + 20$. Then $z + (3y - 20) = (y + 20) + (3y - 20) = 180$. Then, $y = 45$. But that is not the final answer. $z = y + 20 = 65°$.	Although 45° looks reasonable from the diagram, there is no logical support for this guess. Also, diagrams may not always be drawn to scale.	✓

#	A	B	C
7	✓	The information given does not lock the two right angles in position. Picture angle *XOY* pivoting around point *O*. Notice, for example, how the sizes of *s* and *t* change. They need not be equal.	$r + s = 90$, so $r = 90 - s$. Also, $t + s = 90$, so $t = 90 - s$. Thus, *r* and *t* are equal.
8	If the triangle is scalene, then the sides may assume an infinite number of lengths, regardless of the relative position of the 60° angle and the side whose length is 8.	✓ An isosceles triangle, one of whose angles is 60°, must be an equiangular triangle and therefore equilateral. The three sides are therefore equal and the perimeter is determined.	The fact that the triangle is a right triangle does not fix the position of the side whose length is 8. Being opposite the 60° angle produces a different perimeter from being opposite the 30° angle.
9	There is no reason for *d* and *b* to be equal.	✓ **FACT:** When two straight lines intersect, the "vertical angles" formed are equal.	Although $b + c + d = 180°$, the relative sizes of these angles are undetermined.
10	You most probably forgot to divide by 2.	Since the area of triangle *ABC* is 20, the altitude to side $\overline{AB}$ is 8. $[\frac{1}{2}(8)(5) = 20.]$ Triangle *BDC* shares that altitude, using $\overline{DB}$ as a base. Therefore its area is $\frac{1}{2}(8)(1) = 4$. You may have gotten 5 by thinking that triangle *BDC* was one quarter of triangle *ABC*, improperly using the lengths 1 and 4.	✓

Follow-Up D

Answers are on page 147.

1. All three sides of an isoceles triangle are integers. What is the smallest possible perimeter this triangle can have if one side has a length of 4?

2. What is the value of $a + b + c$?

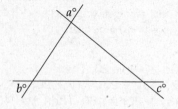

3. Compute the value of $x + y$.

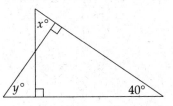

4. Find the value of w.

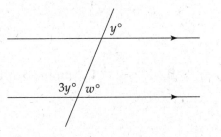

5. A circle of radius 3 passes through the center of and a point on the larger circle as shown. What is the ratio of the area of the shaded region to that of the unshaded region?

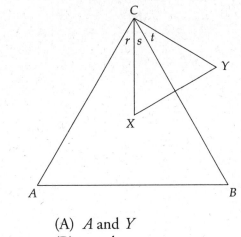

6. The area of triangle I is 36. What is the area of triangle II?

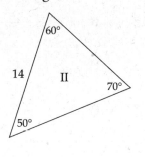

7. In the figure, $AB = BD$. Find the measure of angle x.

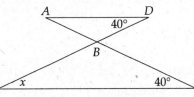

8. The area of triangle ACB is 28. What is the area of triangle XCY?

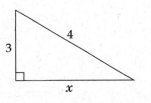

9. Compute x.

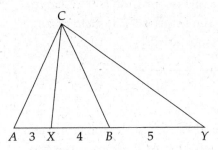

10. Triangle ABC and triangle XYC are both equilateral. Which pair of angles do not necessarily have the same measures?

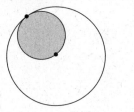

(A) A and Y
(B) r and t
(C) s and t

Workout E

Graphs and Charts

Directions for Workout E: 10 Questions   15-Minute Time Limit
Place your answer (A, B, or C) in the answer space provided.

1. A point T on the line is not shown. The length
of $\overline{RT}$ is 3 times the length of $\overline{RS}$. *How many*
such points T are possible?   **A.** 1   **B.** 2   **C.** more than 2

Questions 2, 3, and 4 refer to the following chart,
which shows the number of students achieving
a score of 0, 1, 2, 3, or 4 on a four-question quiz.

Number of Students	Score
5	4
3	3
4	2
7	1
1	0

2. The mean score is   **A.** 2   **B.** 2.2   **C.** 4

3. The median score is   **A.** 2   **B.** 2.2   **C.** 2.5

4. The mode is   **A.** 1   **B.** 2   **C.** 7

5. The straight line graph shows the total wages earned versus the number of days worked. What is the total amount earned for 7 days worked?

A. $300   **B.** $315   **C.** $1,575

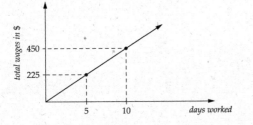

6. The pie chart displays each type of fruit sold at the GARDEN FRESH FARM during one week, as a percentage of the weight of all fruits sold during that week.

If 200 pounds of cherries were sold, how many pounds of melons were sold?

A. 30   **B.** 120   **C.** 800

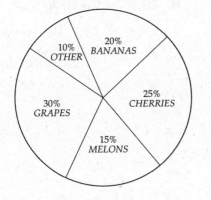

7. The grid shown is composed of 1 by 1 squares. What is the area, in square units, of the shaded figure?

A. 6   **B.** 7   **C.** 8

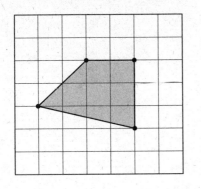

8. If *M* is the midpoint of $\overline{RT}$, then the value of *a* is   **A.** 6   **B.** 8   **C.** 13

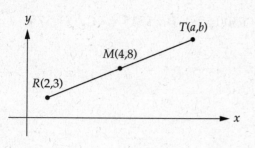

9. What is the distance between the points (−1, 7) and (5, 7)?   **A.** 0   **B.** 4   **C.** 6

10. The graph shows the number of students who selected each choice on a difficult question on the SHSAT. The correct choice was the one least frequently chosen. The percentage of students who selected that correct choice was   **A.** 40%   **B.** 20%   **C.** 10%

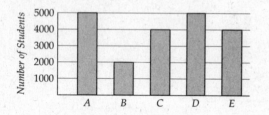

STOP! This is the end of Workout E.

1	2	3	4	5	6	7	8	9	10

Solutions E

#	A	B	C
1	You must consider points both to the right and to the left of *R*. There are two possible positions for point *T*.	✓	*T* may only be to the left of *S* or to the right of *S*.
2	The mean is the sum of all of the scores, counting all occurrences, divided by the total number of scores. In this case we have $\frac{44}{20} =$ 2.2. Do not simply add $0 + 1 + 2 + 3 + 4 = 10$, then divide by 5 to get 2.	✓	You may have chosen the "middle" number of students.
3	✓	The median score is the score in the middle when all the data is arranged in order. It is not necessarily the mean.	You may have computed the mean of 2 and 3 to arrive at 2.5.
4	✓	The mode is the score that occurs most frequently. Don't confuse it with the median.	The mode is the actual score, not the number of students achieving that score.
5	The daily wage is $\frac{\$225}{5} = \$45$. In 7 days the total amount earned is $45 \times 7 = \$315$. Don't rely upon visual estimation.	✓	Be careful to interpret the graph. First compute the daily wage. It is not $225.
6	Cherries are 25% of the total weight. Therefore the total weight is 800 pounds. Be careful not to take 15% of 200.	✓	The cherries represent 25% of the total weight sold. Therefore the total weight of all fruits sold is 800 pounds. This is not the weight of the melons alone.
7	You probably made an error in arithmetic. A quick visual estimation points to an area more than 6.	Don't try to simply count boxes. This could lead to an error. One way to compute the shaded area is to view it as a rectangle minus two triangles. This produces $(4 \times 3) - (\frac{1}{2})(4)(1) - (\frac{1}{2})(2)(2)$ $= 12 - 2 - 2 = 8$.	✓

#	A	B	C
8	✓	**FACT:** The coordinates of the midpoint of a line segment are the averages of the coordinates of the endpoints of that line segment. You may have tried to find *a* by doubling the 4.	13 is the value of *b*.
9	Since the *y*-coordinates are the same, the distance is found by subtracting the *x*-coordinates. $5 - (-1) = 6$.	Be careful when subtracting the negative value.	✓
10	The correct choice was B. The total number of students involved was 20,000. Therefore the percentage is $\frac{2000}{20000} \times 100 = 10\%$. Be careful not to use 5,000 as the total number of students.	Be careful not to simply associate 2,000 with 20%. You must do the necessary computations.	✓

Follow-Up E

Answers are on page 147.

1. If $AB = 4(BC)$, what is the coordinate of point C?

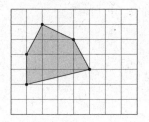

2. The grid shown is composed of 1×1 squares. What is the area of the shaded figure?

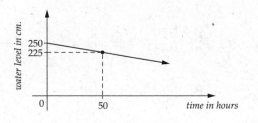

3. The midpoint of line segment $\overline{AB}$ is $(5, -3)$. The coordinates of point A are (m, n) and those of point B are (r, s). What is the value of $m + n + r + s$?

4. The straight line graph shows the water level in an open container over time as the water evaporates. What is the water level in cm. when the time is 300 hours?

Questions 5, 6, and 7 all refer to the following list:

3, 4, 7, 4, 5, 2, 2, 5, 12, 5

5. What is the mean?

6. What is the median?

7. What is the mode?

8. In 1999, 18% of the Martinez family budget went to clothing, and 22% more than that went to food. The total budget for the year was $20,000. How much was spent on food?

9. What is the distance between the points $(7, -1)$ and $(7, -9)$?

10. The bar graph shows the number of students who selected each choice (A, B, C, D, or E) on a particular question of a multiple choice test. The correct answer was the one chosen by 25% of the total number of students. What choice was the correct choice?

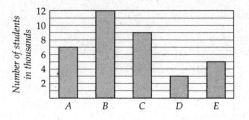

Workout F

Miscellaneous 9th Year Topics

Topics covered on the 9th-year test may vary as curricula change. Problems marked with an asterisk (*) represent topics that have not appeared recently.

Directions for Workout F: 10 Questions   15-Minute Time Limit
Place your answer (A, B, or C) in the answer space provided.

1. The inequality having the shaded region as its graph is

   A. $y > -3x + 12$
   B. $y \geq -3x + 12$
   C. $y < -3x + 12$

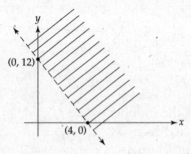

2. The area of an equilateral triangle whose side has a length of $4z$ is

   A. $z^2 \sqrt{3}$ **B.** $4z^2 \sqrt{3}$ **C.** $16z^2 \sqrt{3}$

3. The value of $6!/3!$ is

   A. $2!$ **B.** $3!$ **C.** 120

*4. In right triangle ABC, angle C is the right angle, $AC = 3$, and $BC = 4$. The value of $\sin A + \cos B$ is

   A. $\dfrac{7}{5}$ **B.** $\dfrac{8}{5}$ **C.** $\dfrac{6}{5}$

5. The figure is a cube whose edge is 4. What is the volume of the solid $ADCF$?

   A. $\dfrac{16\sqrt{3}}{3}$ **B.** $\dfrac{32}{3}$ **C.** 16

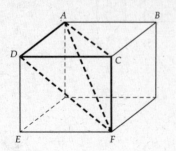

6. If $(10)(9)(8)(7)(6)(5)(4)(3)(2)(1) = (2^a)(y)$,
where y is an odd integer, then $a =$

A. 8   **B.** 6   **C.** 5

7. From an ordinary deck of 52 cards, a single
card is selected at random. What is the
probability that it is a 10 or is a red card?

A. $\dfrac{7}{13}$ **B.** $\dfrac{15}{26}$ **C.** $\dfrac{1}{26}$

8. A group of 30 people are in a room. Which
of the following *must* be true?

A. At least 5 of these people must have been
born on the same day of the week.
B. At least 7 of these people must have been
born on the same day of the week.
C. At least 24 of these people must have been
born on the same day of the week.

9. The ratio of a to b is 2:3, and the ratio
of b to c is 4:5. The ratio of a to c is

A. 8:15   **B.** 2:5   **C.** 5:6

10. If $|x - 3| + |y + 2| = 0$, then $(x + y)$

A. is 5.   **B.** is 1.
C. cannot be determined from the given
information.

STOP! This is the end of Workout F.

1	2	3	4	5	6	7	8	9	10

Solutions F

#	A	B	C
1	✓	The dashed line indicates that points on the line are not included as part of the shaded region. Thus, the type of inequality is strictly less than ($<$) or strictly greater than ($>$).	**TIP:** To check which inequality symbol is correct, first pick a convenient "test point" such as $(0, 0)$. Determine whether the test point is or is not part of the shaded region. Choose the correct inequality accordingly. Since $0 < -3(0) + 12$, the point $(0,0)$ lies in the "less than" region. Since $(0,0)$ is not in the shaded region, the correct inequality is $y > -3x + 12$ (the "greater than" region).
2	**FACT:** The area of an equilateral triangle having side s is $\frac{s^2}{4}\sqrt{3}$. The area of the given triangle is $\frac{(4z)^2}{4}\sqrt{3} = \frac{16z^2}{4}\sqrt{3} = 4z^2\sqrt{3}$. In squaring $4z$, be sure to square the 4 as well as the z.	✓	You may have neglected to divide by 4.
3	$a!/b!$ is not necessarily equal to $(\frac{a}{b})!$ $6! = 720$, while $3! = 6$. Thus, $\frac{6!}{3!} = \frac{720}{6} = 120$.	You cannot simply subtract the 3 from the 6.	✓
4	Sin $A = \frac{4}{5}$ and cos $B = \frac{4}{5}$. Don't confuse cos B with cos A $(= \frac{3}{5})$. This leads to the given incorrect answer.	✓	Remember the definitions of sine and cosine.
5	Figure $ADCF$ is a tetrahedron. **FACT:** The volume of a tetrahedron (or any pyramid) is one-third the area of a base times the height to that base. Use triangle ADC as a base and use $CF = 4$ as the height.	✓	Did you divide by 2 instead of 3?

#	A	B	C
	Note that triangle *ADC* is a right triangle with the right angle at *D*. Its area is 8, half the area of square *ABCD*. Mistaking it for an equilateral triangle produces this incorrect answer.		
6	✓	The desired exponent is the number of times 2 occurs as a factor in the given product. The numbers 10, 6, and 2 each contribute a single 2. The 8 contributes three 2s and the 4 contributes two 2s. That is a total of eight 2s.	Your count was inaccurate.
7	✓	There are four 10s and 26 red cards. However, two of the 10s are red. Be careful not to count them twice. Therefore, there are only 28 (= 26 + 4 − 2) favorable outcomes. The probability is $\frac{28}{52}$ or $\frac{7}{13}$.	Did you confuse the meaning of "or" with "and"? There are only two cards that are red and 10.
8	✓	It is possible for the 30 people to distribute themselves into 7 groups of 4, each group corresponding to one day of the week. Then fill in two more days with the remaining two people. Thus, no more than 5 people need share birthdays on any one day of the week.	If 30 objects are distributed among 7 boxes, it is relatively easy to see that at least one box must contain at least 5 of the original objects. By distributing as "evenly as possible" we manage to place no more than 5 objects in any one box.
9	✓	Try to make the numbers representing *b* equal. 2:3 becomes 8:12, while 4:5 becomes 12:15. Thus, *a:b:c* = 8:12:15. So *a:c* = 8:15. Failure to convert the ratios correctly could lead to the incorrect answer 2:5.	Several arithmetical errors can lead to this result.
10	**FACT:** The absolute value of a number cannot be negative. The sum of two absolute values can therefore be 0 only if *both* absolute values are 0. Thus $x = 3$ and $y = -2$, so $x + y = 1$. Letting *x* and *y* both be zero could lead to the incorrect answer 5.	✓	The information *is* sufficient.

Follow-Up F

Answers are on page 147.

1. What is the value of $5!/4!$?

2. If $|3x + y| + |y - z| = 0$, and $x = -7$, what is the value of z?

3. At the Ice Cream Store, ice cream cones are available in 9 different flavors. Sam buys one cone every day. What is the greatest number of days that Sam can buy cones without buying any one flavor three times?

4. The side of an equilateral triangle has length $6x$. What is the area of this equilateral triangle in terms of x?

5. The ratio of a to b is 2:3, and the ratio of a to c is 3:10. What is the ratio of b to c?

6. From an ordinary deck of 52 cards, a single card is selected at random. What is the probability that the chosen card is a 9 or a club?

7. The length of the edge of a cube is 6. A solid is formed whose vertices consist of the four vertices of one face of the cube together with the center of the opposite face. What is the volume of this solid?

8. If $(9)(8)(7)(6)(5)(4)(3)(2)(1) = 3^a(y)$, where y is not divisible by 3, compute the value of a.

*9. In right triangle ABC, with right angle at C, $AC = 5$ and $BC = 12$. Find the value of $(\sin A)^2 + (\sin B)^2$.

10. In right triangle ABC, angle C is the right angle, $AC = 3$, and $AB = 5$. Point D is on hypotenuse AB, such that $DB = 1$. Find the area of triangle DBC.

Answers to Follow-Ups

	Follow-up A	Follow-up B	Follow-up C	Follow-up D	Follow-up E	Follow-up F
1.	$\frac{1}{12}$	22	$7x^2$	9	0	5
2.	14	$N = 4$	x^{16}	180	10	21
3.	1	36	-15	100	4	18
4.	5.43×10^{12}	$Q = 4$	$27x^6$	45	100	$9x^2\sqrt{3}$
5.	$\frac{6}{5}$	6	$y^2 - 7y + 12$	$\frac{1}{3}$ or 1:3	4.9	9:20
6.	10	A	$x + 2$	144	4.5	$\frac{4}{13}$
7.	56	$5^2 \times 7^3$	$x^2 - 11$	$x = 40°$	5	72
8.	$\frac{70}{9}$	17	$8x + 2$	36	$8,000	4
9.	-1	A	$x > 2$	$\sqrt{7}$	8	1
10.	$\frac{270}{G}$	4	B	C	C	$\frac{6}{5}$

Section 3
Some Basic Terms and Concepts You Should Know

The SHSAT does not provide formulas or reference material for use during the test. You must know the formulas and be familiar with technical mathematical terms.

This section provides you with a brief reference guide. It is not intended to be a complete list. These, as well as many other terms and concepts, are found among the detailed solutions to the sample exam problems and in the "Diagnosers."

Arithmetic

Integers Positive and negative whole numbers together with zero.
. . . , $-3, -2, -1, 0, 1, 2, 3, 4, 5,$ . . .
$\sqrt{9}, 0, -\dfrac{12}{2}$ and 2.0 are integers.
$\sqrt{7}, \dfrac{4}{3}$ and 13.3 are not integers.

Even Integers . . . , $-6, -4, -2, 0, 2, 4, 6, 8,$ . . .
All even integers are multiples of 2.
Note that 0 is an even integer.

Odd Integers . . . , $-5, -3, -1, 1, 3, 5, 7,$ . . .
All odd integers are 1 more (or 1 less) than even integers.

Consecutive Integers $-1, 0, 1, 2, 3$ are five consecutive integers.
$-9, -8, -7$ are three consecutive integers.
$-2, 0, 2, 4, 6$ are five *consecutive even integers*.
$3, 5, 7$ are three *consecutive odd integers*.

Operations on Even and Odd Integers

Odd ± Odd = Even	Odd × Odd = Odd
Odd ± Even = Odd	Odd × Even = Even
Even ± Even = Even	Even × Even = Even

TIP: When checking for evenness or oddness you can use 0 and 1 to represent "typical" even or odd numbers. Example: even + odd = 0 + 1 = 1 = odd.

Factors A factor of a number is any positive integer that may be divided evenly into the number—that is, leaving a remainder of zero.
(Factors are considered to be positive integers unless otherwise noted.)
3 is a factor of 12.
Both 1 and 2001 are factors of 2001.
5 is *not* a factor of 19.
8 is a factor of both 24 and 80.
8 is called a *common factor* of 24 and 80.

Multiples   If a is a factor of b, then b is called a multiple of a.
15 is a multiple of 3.
15 is also a multiple of 5.
4, 8, 12, 16, 20, are five consecutive multiples of 4.

Prime Numbers   A prime (or prime number) is any positive integer having exactly two different integer factors. For example, the factors of 7 are 1 and 7 only. Thus, 7 is a prime.
The first ten primes are 2, 3, 5, 7, 11, 13, 17, 19, 23, and 29

- The number 1 is *not* a prime number.
- The only even prime number is 2.
- There is an infinite number of prime numbers.

Every positive integer be factored into primes.
$144 = 2 \times 2 \times 2 \times 2 \times 3 \times 3$
Often it is convenient to write the factorization in terms of powers of primes.
$144 = 2^4 \times 3^2$
$100{,}080 = 2^4 \times 3^2 \times 5 \times 139$

Composite Numbers   A composite is any positive integer with more than two different factors.
6 is composite. It has 1, 2, 3 and 6 as factors.
25 is composite. It has 1, 5, and 25 as factors.
1 is neither prime nor composite. It is called a *unit*.

Greatest Common Factor   The greatest common factor (also known as the greatest common divisor or highest common factor) of two numbers is the *largest* positive integer that is a *factor of both* numbers. Standard abbreviations are GCF, or GCD, or HCF.
The GCF of 24 and 30 is 6.
The GCF of 27 and 32 is 1.
The GCF of $2 \times 3 \times 3 \times 5 \times 7 \times 7 \times 7$ and $2 \times 2 \times 3 \times 5 \times 5 \times 7 \times 7 \times 11$ is $2 \times 3 \times 5 \times 7 \times 7$.

Least Common Multiple   The least common multiple (LCM) of two positive integers is the *smallest* positive integer having *both* of these integers as factors.
The LCM of two positive integers must be

(1) a positive multiple of both integers **and**
(2) the smallest of all of those positive multiples.

The LCM of 4 and 6 is 12.
The LCM of 9 and 18 is 18.
The LCM of 11 and 13 is 143 ($= 11 \times 13$).
The LCM of $2 \times 3 \times 3 \times 5 \times 7 \times 7 \times 7$ and $2 \times 2 \times 3 \times 5 \times 5 \times 7 \times 7 \times 11$ is $2 \times 2 \times 3 \times 3 \times 5 \times 5 \times 7 \times 7 \times 7 \times 11$.

Division   When 42 is divided by 8, the *quotient* is 5 and the *remainder* is 2. The number 42 is called the *dividend* and 8 is called the *divisor*.
This can be written as
$42 \qquad = \qquad 5 \times 8 \qquad + 2$
dividend $=$ quotient $\times$ divisor $+$ remainder

73 divided by 10 is 7 with a remainder of 3
73 = 7 × 10 + 3

Exponents   3 × 3 is written as 3^2.
The *base* is 3 and the *exponent* is 2.
$5^7 = 5 \times 5 \times 5 \times 5 \times 5 \times 5 \times 5$
$13^1 = 13$
$6^0 = 1$.
In general, if *n* is any nonzero number, then $n^0 = 1$.

Square Roots   Since $6^2 = 36$, 6 is the square root of 36.
The square root of 64 is 8.
The square root of 61 lies between 7 and 8.

Inequality Symbols   > means "is greater than." (5 > 3)
< means "is less than." (3 < 5)
≥ means "is greater than or equal to." (10 ≥ 6 is a true statement)
≤ means "is less than or equal to."
The age of every person in the room "is less than or equal to" 38 means that
   everyone in the room is 38 years of age or younger.

Order of Operations   When several types of operations are present, there is a
   designated order in which they should be performed.
Parentheses
Exponents
Multiplication   In Order from Left to Right
Division   In Order from Left to Right
Addition   In Order from Left to Right
Subtraction   In Order from Left to Right

$37 + (2 \times 4 - 3)^2 \div 5 =$ In the parentheses, do the multiplication before the
                                          subtraction.
$37 + (8-3)^2 \div 5 =$
$37 + (5)^2 \div 5 =$ Now do exponents.
$37 + 25 \div 5 =$ Next do division.
$37 + 5 =$
42

Averages   The mean (average, or arithmetic mean) is
           the *sum* of the values
                   divided by
           the *number* of values.

The mean age of four people whose ages are 13, 23, 17, and 27 is
   $\frac{13+23+17+27}{4}$ or $\frac{80}{4}$, which equals 20.

Often in solving problems involving averages, it is convenient to express the for-
   mula in an alternate but equivalent form:
   The *sum* of the values = (the number of values) × (the *average* of these values).
   Thus, if the average of 4 values is 20, their sum is 80.

Median
The median is the *middle value* of a set of values.
To find the median, first place the values in order.
CASE 1
When there is an odd number of values: 2, 4, 7, 9, 12, 38, 39
The median is 9.
CASE 2
When there is an even number of values: 1, 4, 9, 20
The median is the mean (average) of the two middle values.

$$\frac{4+9}{2} = 6.5$$

Mode
The mode of a set of values is the value that occurs most frequently.
2, 4, 5, 7, 7, 8, 9, 9, 9, 12, 23, 23   The mode is 9.
2, 4, 7, 9, 12, 38, 39   There is *no* mode.
2, 4, 4, 4, 5, 5, 5, 9, 9, 13   There are two modes, 4 and 5.

Absolute Value
The absolute value of a number expresses the undirected distance from that number to zero.
The absolute value of any number is always positive or zero.

$|5| = 5$
$|-7| = 7$
$\left|\frac{1}{3}\right| = \frac{1}{3}$
$|0| = 0$

Algebra

Exponents
When multiplying expressions involving the *same base:* add the exponents
$$t^3 \cdot t^7 = (t \cdot t \cdot t)(t \cdot t \cdot t \cdot t \cdot t \cdot t \cdot t) = t^{10}$$
When dividing expressions involving the *same base:* subtract the exponents
$$\frac{y^6}{y^2} = \frac{y \cdot y \cdot y \cdot y \cdot y \cdot y}{y \cdot y} = y^{6-2} = y^4$$
Be sure to subtract the denominator's exponent from the numerator's exponent.
When an expression involving an exponent is raised to a power, multiply the exponents.
$$(x^2)^3 = (x^2)(x^2)(x^2) = x^{2 \cdot 3} = x^6$$

Like Terms
Like terms are terms that differ, at most, in their numerical coefficients.
Like terms $6x^5$ and $13x^5$
Unlike terms $6x^5$ and $13x^4$
Like terms may be combined (added or subtracted) by simply combining their coefficients.
$6x^5 + 13x^5 = 19x^5$ Caution: Retain the same exponent.
$x^2 + x^2 = 2x^2$
$6x^5 + 13x^4$ cannot be combined into a single term.

Translating Words into Symbols
Examples:

5 more than a number or a number increased by 5:	$x + 5$
5 less than a number or a number decreased by 5:	$x - 5$
x less than 5 or 5 decreased by x:	$5 - x$

Be careful! $x - 5$ and $5 - x$ have different meanings.

4 more than twice a number:	$2x + 4$
Five times the quantity $(4y - 7)$:	$5(4y - 7)$
Half of a number:	$\left(\dfrac{1}{2}\right)x$ or $\dfrac{x}{2}$
75% of a number:	$.75x$ or $\dfrac{75}{100}x$

When attempting a direct translation of words into symbols, it is sometimes helpful to replace the "number" with some number of your choice. Using this chosen number, work through the expression and pay careful attention to what you did.

For example, for "five less than a number"
use "5 less than 17"; ["a number" is replaced by 17]
the result, of course, is 12.
Ask yourself, how did I get 12?
You translated "5 less than 17" into $17 - 5$
So "5 less than a number" is $x - 5$

Words	Indicated Operation	Symbols
sum, increased by, more than, total,	+	
The sum of twice a number and 7		$2a + 7$
Fifty-two more than three times a number		$3a + 52$
Milton is three years older than Irving		$M = I + 3$
difference, decreased by, less than, fewer	–	
The difference between x and y		$x - y$
Seven less than twice a number		$2x - 7$
Be careful not to confuse $2x - 7$ with $7 - 2x$		
Matt is three years younger than Louisa		$M = L - 3$
product, times, of	×	
The product of two consecutive integers		$x(x + 1)$
One-third of a number		$\left(\dfrac{1}{3}\right)x$
85% of the sum of Tim's age and Minna's age		$.85(T + M)$
quotient, divided by, ratio, over	/ or ÷	
12 divided by x		$\dfrac{12}{x}$
The ratio of 19 to y		$\dfrac{19}{y}$

Geometry

Triangles

The sum of the measures of the interior angles of a triangle is 180°.

$a + b + c = 180$

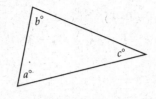

The measure of an exterior angle of a triangle is the sum of the measures of the two nonadjacent interior angles.

$e = a + b$

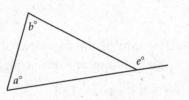

The sum of the lengths of any two sides of a triangle must be greater than the length of the third side.

$AB + BC > AC$

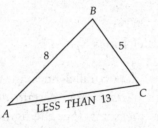

The length of any side of a triangle must be greater than the difference of the lengths of the other two sides.

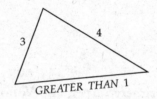

Pythagorean Theorem

In a right triangle, the square of the hypotenuse is equal to the sum of the squares of the legs.

$c^2 = a^2 + b^2$

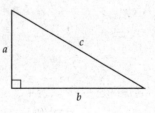

It is not necessary for the lengths of the sides of a right triangle to be integers.

Angle Sum for Quadrilaterals

The sum of the interior angles of a quadrilateral is 360°.

$a + b + c + d = 360$

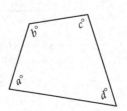

Lines and Angles

The sum of the measures of all of the angles about a point is 360°.

$a + b + c + d + e = 360$

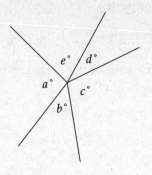

The sum of the measures of all of the angles about a point on one side of a straight line is 180°.

$a + b + c + d = 180$

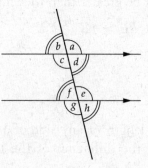

Parallel Lines

When two parallel lines are crossed by a third line, called a *transversal*, certain angles formed will have equal measures. (See the figure.)

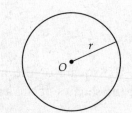

Perimeter, Area, and Volume

Circumference $C = 2\pi r$ or $C = \pi d$
Area $A = \pi r^2$

Perimeter $P = 2l + 2w$
Area $A = lw$

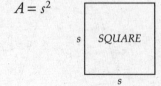

Area $A = s^2$

Area $A = \dfrac{1}{2}\, bh$

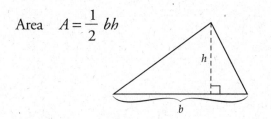

You may choose any vertex and draw a perpendicular line segment to the opposite side. The opposite side becomes a base (*b*) and the perpendicular becomes the height (*h*), or altitude, to that base.

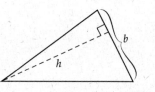

An altitude may fall outside of the triangle.

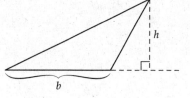

Area of a trapezoid $A = \dfrac{1}{2}h(b_1 + b_2)$

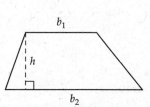

The volume of a rectangular solid is length × width × height.
$V = lwh$

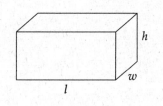

PRACTICE TESTS

Answer Sheet
MINITEST 2

Part I   Verbal

Scrambled Paragraphs

Paragraph 1

The second sentence is   Ⓠ Ⓡ Ⓢ Ⓣ Ⓤ
The third sentence is   Ⓠ Ⓡ Ⓢ Ⓣ Ⓤ
The fourth sentence is   Ⓠ Ⓡ Ⓢ Ⓣ Ⓤ
The fifth sentence is   Ⓠ Ⓡ Ⓢ Ⓣ Ⓤ
The sixth sentence is   Ⓠ Ⓡ Ⓢ Ⓣ Ⓤ

Paragraph 2

The second sentence is   Ⓠ Ⓡ Ⓢ Ⓣ Ⓤ
The third sentence is   Ⓠ Ⓡ Ⓢ Ⓣ Ⓤ
The fourth sentence is   Ⓠ Ⓡ Ⓢ Ⓣ Ⓤ
The fifth sentence is   Ⓠ Ⓡ Ⓢ Ⓣ Ⓤ
The sixth sentence is   Ⓠ Ⓡ Ⓢ Ⓣ Ⓤ

Paragraph 3

The second sentence is   Ⓠ Ⓡ Ⓢ Ⓣ Ⓤ
The third sentence is   Ⓠ Ⓡ Ⓢ Ⓣ Ⓤ
The fourth sentence is   Ⓠ Ⓡ Ⓢ Ⓣ Ⓤ
The fifth sentence is   Ⓠ Ⓡ Ⓢ Ⓣ Ⓤ
The sixth sentence is   Ⓠ Ⓡ Ⓢ Ⓣ Ⓤ

Logical Reasoning

10 Ⓐ Ⓑ Ⓒ Ⓓ Ⓔ
11 Ⓕ Ⓖ Ⓗ Ⓙ Ⓚ
12 Ⓐ Ⓑ Ⓒ Ⓓ Ⓔ
13 Ⓕ Ⓖ Ⓗ Ⓙ Ⓚ

Reading

14 Ⓐ Ⓑ Ⓒ Ⓓ Ⓔ
15 Ⓕ Ⓖ Ⓗ Ⓙ Ⓚ
16 Ⓐ Ⓑ Ⓒ Ⓓ Ⓔ
17 Ⓕ Ⓖ Ⓗ Ⓙ Ⓚ
18 Ⓐ Ⓑ Ⓒ Ⓓ Ⓔ
19 Ⓕ Ⓖ Ⓗ Ⓙ Ⓚ
20 Ⓐ Ⓑ Ⓒ Ⓓ Ⓔ
21 Ⓕ Ⓖ Ⓗ Ⓙ Ⓚ
22 Ⓐ Ⓑ Ⓒ Ⓓ Ⓔ
23 Ⓕ Ⓖ Ⓗ Ⓙ Ⓚ
24 Ⓐ Ⓑ Ⓒ Ⓓ Ⓔ
25 Ⓕ Ⓖ Ⓗ Ⓙ Ⓚ

Part II   Mathematics

26 Ⓐ Ⓑ Ⓒ Ⓓ Ⓔ
27 Ⓕ Ⓖ Ⓗ Ⓙ Ⓚ
28 Ⓐ Ⓑ Ⓒ Ⓓ Ⓔ
29 Ⓕ Ⓖ Ⓗ Ⓙ Ⓚ
30 Ⓐ Ⓑ Ⓒ Ⓓ Ⓔ

31 Ⓕ Ⓖ Ⓗ Ⓙ Ⓚ
32 Ⓐ Ⓑ Ⓒ Ⓓ Ⓔ
33 Ⓕ Ⓖ Ⓗ Ⓙ Ⓚ
34 Ⓐ Ⓑ Ⓒ Ⓓ Ⓔ
35 Ⓕ Ⓖ Ⓗ Ⓙ Ⓚ

36 Ⓐ Ⓑ Ⓒ Ⓓ Ⓔ
37 Ⓕ Ⓖ Ⓗ Ⓙ Ⓚ
38 Ⓐ Ⓑ Ⓒ Ⓓ Ⓔ
39 Ⓕ Ⓖ Ⓗ Ⓙ Ⓚ
40 Ⓐ Ⓑ Ⓒ Ⓓ Ⓔ

41 Ⓕ Ⓖ Ⓗ Ⓙ Ⓚ
42 Ⓐ Ⓑ Ⓒ Ⓓ Ⓔ
43 Ⓕ Ⓖ Ⓗ Ⓙ Ⓚ
44 Ⓐ Ⓑ Ⓒ Ⓓ Ⓔ
45 Ⓕ Ⓖ Ⓗ Ⓙ Ⓚ

46 Ⓐ Ⓑ Ⓒ Ⓓ Ⓔ
47 Ⓕ Ⓖ Ⓗ Ⓙ Ⓚ
48 Ⓐ Ⓑ Ⓒ Ⓓ Ⓔ
49 Ⓕ Ⓖ Ⓗ Ⓙ Ⓚ
50 Ⓐ Ⓑ Ⓒ Ⓓ Ⓔ

Minitest 2

PART 1—VERBAL

19 QUESTIONS
SUGGESTED TIME: 35 MINUTES

Scrambled Paragraphs

Paragraphs 1–3

> **Directions:** Below are six sentences that can be arranged to form a well-organized and grammatically correct paragraph. The first sentence is provided, but the other five are listed in random order. Choose the order that will form the **best** paragraph. Each correct paragraph is worth two points, with no partial credit given.
>
> You may wish to put numbers in the blanks at the left of each sentence to help keep track of the order. When you finish the set, mark your answers on the answer sheet.

PARAGRAPH 1

Ranging in length from 18 to 25 inches and with a wingspread of 36 to 60 inches, the Great Horned Owl is the largest North American owl.

_____ (Q) These include mammals like domestic cats and rabbits and large birds like ospreys, ducks, and herons.

_____ (R) The owl hunts these animals by waiting on a high perch until it detects the prey below; it then swoops down for the kill.

_____ (S) If the "Great" is accurate, however, the "Horned" is not, for the bird's head bears not horns, but prominent ear-tufts.

_____ (T) Aided by its size and strength, extremely acute hearing, and flying speeds of up to 40 miles per hour, this owl preys not only on small animals but also on larger ones.

_____ (U) These give it a fearsome appearance that is not at all deceiving, as this species is one of the most ferocious predators of the bird world.

161

PARAGRAPH 2

The main function of leaves is photosynthesis, which takes place in leaf tissue called *mesophyll*, where cells absorb carbon dioxide from air in the surrounding spaces, replacing it with expelled oxygen.

_____ (Q) In addition to this basic function, some plants have modified leaves that help the plant in special ways—for example, to defend the plant from predators, or to trap and digest insects.

_____ (R) In fact, all flowers are made up of modified leaves, with each part of the flower serving a specific reproductive function.

_____ (S) Other types of modified leaves, such as the tendrils of the pea plant, allow the plant to attach itself to and climb up structures like fences, trellises, and garden walls.

_____ (T) Other leaves may aid survival of the species by aiding reproduction, a function served by large and brightly colored leaves like those of the poinsettia, which attract pollinators to nondescript flowers.

_____ (U) Food produced by this process is circulated to other parts of the plant by a vascular system, which also transports water to the leaf.

PARAGRAPH 3

Until the Salk vaccine was developed in the 1950s, epidemics of poliomyelitis were a frequent summertime scourge that brought terror to parents, helpless frustration to physicians, and tragedy to many victims.

_____ (Q) The vaccine has been successful in eradicating poliomyelitis throughout much of the world, yet isolated outbreaks do still occur.

_____ (R) An Australian country nurse named Elizabeth Kenny developed an opposite approach: She used moist heat to relax the paralyzed muscle and physical therapy to stimulate and re-educate it.

_____ (S) Because no effective drug treatment has ever been developed, the management of the illness involves merely symptom alleviation, a poor answer to the sometimes devastating effects of the disease.

_____ (T) In spite of strenuous opposition from many in the medical community, her success rate gained the approval of the American Medical Association, and her methods became the standard treatment for paralytic poliomyelitis.

_____ (U) One of the most serious effects is permanent paralysis, which in the 1930s and 1940s was treated by immobilizing the affected limb in a rigid splint or cast.

LOGICAL REASONING

Questions 10–13

> **Directions:** For each of the following questions, select the **best** answer from the given choices. Bubble in the letter corresponding to your answer on the answer sheet. Your answer should be based **only on the given information.**
>
> Read the words carefully. For example, "The red book is **to the right** of the blue book" does not necessarily mean that there is no other book between them. Similarly, be careful when reading words such as **between, below, above, after, before, behind,** and **ahead of.**

Questions 10 and 11 refer to the following information.

Four plates are stacked one above the other. One plate is green. The blue plate does not touch the red or white plates.

10. The green plate

    A. must touch the red plate.
    B. must touch the white plate.
    C. must touch either the red or the white plate.
    D. must be above the blue plate.
    E. must be below the blue plate.

11. If the green plate is the next to lowest plate, which one of the following is **false?**

    F. The red plate could be highest.
    G. The white plate could be highest.
    H. The blue plate must be lowest.
    J. There could be 1 plate between the red and green plates.
    K. There could be 2 plates between the red and green plates.

Questions 12 and 13 refer to the following information.

In the code below, (1) each nonsense word represents the same English word in all 3 sentences, (2) each English word is represented by only one nonsense word, and (3) in any given sentence, the nonsense words may or may not be presented in the same order as the English words.

ni   ren   bul   means "Dogs chase cats."

pla   ni   ren   means "Cats chase birds."

shan   bul   ni   pla   means "Dogs chase birds also."

12. Which nonsense word represents "dogs"?

    A. *ni*
    B. *ren*
    C. *bul*
    D. *shan*
    E. *pla*

13. Which English word is represented by *ni*?

    F. dogs
    G. chase
    H. cats
    J. birds
    K. also

READING

Questions 14–25

I. Irish Travellers are an interesting ethnic group with a mysterious past. Called "Irish Tinkers" until recently, these people have
Line their own distinct beliefs and customs and
(5) even their own secret language, Shelta. Traditionally they have followed an itinerant lifestyle separate from their Irish compatriots, moving about in horse caravans or, more recently, motor-drawn trailers.

(10) There are several theories about the origins of the Travellers. It is possible that they are descended from ancient Celtic rivet-makers. Or they may be the vestiges of a class of vassals or servants who lost their
(15) homes when English conquerors confiscated the estates of their overlords. Some historians think it more likely that the group had its beginnings in the seventeenth-century invasion by the English gen-
(20) eral Cromwell, when many Irish were driven from their homes. The nineteenth-century potato famines, according to this theory, increased the numbers of those dispossessed and itinerant.

(25) The secret language Shelta, however, indicates a more romantic past. Greek, Hebrew, and ancient Gaelic elements in the language seem to be of scholarly origin. They suggest that Shelta probably arose several centuries
(30) ago among bands of wandering poets. If this is the case, it seems likely that in times of upheaval the original wanderers would accept uprooted families, who eventually adopted Shelta as their own tongue. The
(35) blended group, according to this theory, became the Irish Tinkers.

The traditional occupation of the Tinkers was metalworking. In fact, the name "Tinker" comes from the Celtic *tinceard,* or

(40) *tinsmith.* Tinkers could manage to support their families by mending spoons and pots and by crafting metal wares. With the introduction of plastics and of machine-made metal goods, however, they lost their
(45) chief means of livelihood along with the name "Tinker." Many turned to scrap-dealing to earn a living in the accustomed nomadic lifestyle, whereas others have continued to travel but subsist on odd jobs and
(50) begging. Some have left the road, settling into a mainstream job or "going on the dole," relying on the government for support instead of working.

Irish Travellers are not as distinct an ethnic
(55) group as they once were. In addition to lifestyle changes, intermarriage and emigration have blurred the identifying markers. Some have migrated to European countries and even Australia; others have moved to
(60) the southern United States. Typical Irish Traveller families in Georgia and South Carolina live in permanent homes, but the menfolk support their families as itinerant workers, frequently in roofing or other
(65) aspects of home repair. And although there is some intermarriage, the tendency of these communities is to maintain a degree of separation from their neighbors.

14. Which of the following best states the author's purpose?

A. To explain the origins of a mysterious language

B. To describe an extinct Irish class

C. To trace the history of uprooted Irish families

D. To explain the distinct features and evolution of an ethnic group

E. To make clear the distinction between "Tinkers" and "Travellers"

15. Which of the following is **not** given as a possible origin of the Irish Travellers?

    F. Great Irish lords who were driven from their lands
    G. People made homeless in a time of starvation
    H. Irish poets of long ago
    J. Celtic metal workers
    K. Irish people dispossessed by acts of war

16. Which of the following features of American Irish Traveller culture is according to ancient tradition?

    A. The family's nomadic lifestyle
    B. The occupation of the men
    C. The tendency of the Travellers to keep to themselves
    D. The stress placed on education
    E. Economic prosperity

17. What is meant by "going on the dole"?

    F. Changing one's occupation
    G. Receiving public financial assistance
    H. Depending on one's neighbors for emotional support
    J. Advertising for work
    K. Becoming an itinerant beggar

18. What does the passage suggest about Shelta?

    A. It has a literary origin.
    B. It is known by all Irish people.
    C. It is several thousand years old.
    D. It is no longer known to the younger Irish Travellers.
    E. It originated in ancient Greece or in biblical times.

19. All of the following are factors in the loss of distinctive "Irish Traveller" identity **except**

    F. modern technology.
    G. separation from the homeland.
    H. intermarriage with other groups.
    J. changes in occupation.
    K. loss of the secret language.

II. Those who are unfamiliar with the teachings of Muhammad, the founder of Islam, might be surprised to learn about his *Line* attitudes toward women and their rights. (5) His teachings are particularly striking in view of some of the rigid and even harsh restrictions placed on women in some Islamic cultures.

Muhammad's life was enriched by close (10) relationships with the female members of his family. His wife Khadija, a competent, successful businesswoman fifteen years older than her husband, was his adviser as well as his spouse and the mother of his (15) children. He seems to have been devoted also to his second wife, Aysha, and to have dearly loved his four daughters.

In the seventh-century Arabian city of Mecca, before Muhammad had the visions (20) that gave birth to Islam, the legal position of women was precarious. An unmarried woman whose father had died could only hope a brother would take her in. She had no legal right to protection and economic (25) support, as a man usually left his property to his male children. A married woman lived with her husband and his family and had little or no freedom or security. She was kept closely under their eye and could be (30) arbitrarily cast out by her husband.

Law and custom favored males in other ways as well. Unwanted female children could be killed, and women accused of adultery were customarily stoned to death, (35) a fate males similarly accused were likely to escape.

Islamic law as proclaimed by Muhammad made significant changes in the status of women. In the important area of economic (40) rights, Muhammad gave crucial guarantees to women. Not only did a bride receive a dowry from her bridegroom, but this dowry belonged to her to do with as she chose. She was also assured of a partial

(45) inheritance from her husband and from her
father, as well as support by her sons after
their father's death. Furthermore, a woman
was allowed to choose her own husband,
and in the case of divorce he was responsi-
(50) ble for her support.

The position of females improved in other
ways as well. Education was opened to girls,
and as a result the writers and scholars of
early Islam included women as well as men.
(55) Muhammad expected women to partici-
pate fully in religion, and in some cases
women even served as congregational leaders. Female infanticide was outlawed. The
penalty for adultery was changed from
(60) stoning to public whipping and applied to
men as well as women.

Although not all of these rights survived
Muhammad, laws concerning marriage and
financial security remained in place for cen-
(65) turies. These laws gave women not only
more security but also more status than
they had known before the establishment
of Islam.

20. Which of the following best expresses the
author's purpose?

    A. To show how Muhammad bettered the
       position of women
    B. To explain the dominant position of
       women in early Islam
    C. To explain current restrictions on
       women in some Islamic cultures
    D. To reveal the earlier injustices against
       women
    E. To demonstrate the misconceptions
       that some people have about Islam's
       origins

21. Which of the following was **not** true of
women in early Islam?

    F. They had a certain degree of economic
       security.
    G. They could enjoy the advantages of
       education.
    H. Their position in the practice of
       religion was fully equal to men's.
    J. They retained some financial protection
       in the case of divorce.
    K. A married woman owned and
       controlled a certain amount of wealth.

22. Why might some people be surprised to
learn about the position of women in early
Islam?

    A. They know nothing of Islam as it is
       today.
    B. All of the laws passed by Muhammad
       were changed within a few decades.
    C. They are more familiar with the history
       of pre-Islamic cultures.
    D. They are aware of current repression of
       Moslem women in some places.
    E. There are no written records of the
       laws passed by Muhammad.

23. What does the passage suggest about
Muhammad?

    F. He is the founder of a minor religious
       cult.
    G. He believed that religion was the
       exclusive function of men.
    H. He made divorce easier for both men
       and women.
    J. He was influenced by his regard for the
       women in his life.
    K. He knew how to influence people
       without using force.

24. Which of the following best states the position of women in pre-Islamic Mecca as described in the passage?

   A. They had financial security but no family security.
   B. They usually had to depend on men to take care of them.
   C. They had no rights under the law.
   D. According to law, they could not inherit property.
   E. They were frequently killed for little or no reason.

25. What does the passage indicate about the origins of Islam?

   F. It began with laws proclaimed by Muhammad.
   G. It developed through mystic experiences of Muhammad.
   H. It was based on the religion of seventh-century Mecca.
   J. It was inspired by his love for his daughters.
   K. It came to Muhammad in a dream.

PART 2—MATHEMATICS

QUESTIONS 26–50

SUGGESTED TIME: 40 MINUTES

> **Directions:** For each of the following questions, select the **best** answer from the given choices. Bubble in the letter corresponding to your answer on the answer sheet. **DO NOT PUT ANY OTHER WORK ON THE ANSWER SHEET.** All necessary work can be done in your test booklet or on scrap paper that is provided.

> **NOTE:** Diagrams other than graphs might not be drawn to scale. Do not assume any relationships that are not specifically stated unless they are implied by the given information.

26. $\dfrac{60 \times 30}{60 + 30} =$

   A. 2
   B. 20
   C. 200
   D. 2000
   E. none of these

27. Which of the following is closest in value to .213?

   F. $\dfrac{1}{2}$

   G. $\dfrac{1}{3}$

   H. $\dfrac{1}{4}$

   J. $\dfrac{1}{5}$

   K. $\dfrac{1}{6}$

28. In triangle *ABC*, $\overline{CD}$ bisects angle *ACB*. Compute the value of $x + y$, in degrees.

   A. 45
   B. 70
   C. 80
   D. 110
   E. 135

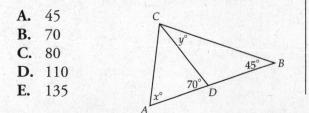

29. Two consecutive odd primes, such as 11 and 13, are called a pair of "twin primes." How many *pairs* of twin primes are there between 15 and 45?

   F. 2
   G. 3
   H. 4
   J. 5
   K. 7

30. For any number *x*, the symbol $\lceil x \rceil$ means the smallest integer that is greater than or equal to *x*. For example, $\lceil 3.2 \rceil$ is 4. What is $\lceil \sqrt{156.3} \rceil$?

   A. 11
   B. 12
   C. 13
   D. 156
   E. 157

31. Eight years from now, Oana will be twice as old as her brother is now. Oana is now 12 years old. How old is her brother now?

   F. 2
   G. 4
   H. 6
   J. 10
   K. 16

32. Suppose a snail crawls $\frac{2}{5}$ inch per second. At this rate, what is the total number of inches the snail crawls in 2 minutes?

    A. 48
    B. 30
    C. 24
    D. 5
    E. $\frac{4}{5}$

33. The straight line graph shows the relationship between the number of tickets sold and the amount of money in the cash register if the register contained $150 before any tickets were sold. What is the price of 1 ticket?

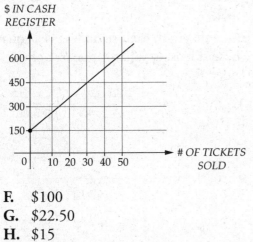

    F. $100
    G. $22.50
    H. $15
    J. $12.50
    K. $10

34. If $15 - 2x < 7$, then for all possible values of x that make the inequality true,

    A. $x < 8$
    B. $x > 8$
    C. $x > 4$
    D. $x < 4$
    E. $x > \frac{1}{4}$

35. Four congruent circles are enclosed in a square as shown. The perimeter of the square is 64. What is the circumference of *one* of the circles (in terms of π)?

    F. 4π
    G. 8π
    H. 16π
    J. 32π
    K. 64π

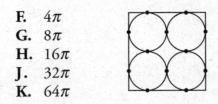

36. If $3x + 2y = 19$ and $2x + 3y = 91$, what is the value of $x + y$?

    A. 8
    B. 9
    C. 21
    D. 22
    E. 72

37. Kenny buys candy bars at 9 for $1 and sells them at 3 for $1. How many candy bars must he sell in order for him to make a profit of exactly $10?

    F. 27
    G. 30
    H. 45
    J. 60
    K. 90

38. Juan travels at the rate of 30 miles per hour for 4 hours. He then returns over the same route in 3 hours. What was his average rate for the return trip, in miles per hour?

    A. $22\frac{1}{2}$
    B. $34\frac{2}{7}$
    C. 35
    D. 36
    E. 40

39. The value of $3^5 + 3^5 + 3^5$ is

    F. 3^6
    G. 3^{15}
    H. 9^5
    J. 9^{125}
    K. 45

40. Lindsay has *P* dollars and Mark has $9 less than Lindsay. If Mark receives an additional $11, how many dollars will Mark now have, in terms of *P*?

    A. $P - 20$
    B. $20 - P$
    C. $P + 2$
    D. $2 - P$
    E. $P + 11$

41. $R = 2 \cdot 3 \cdot 3 \cdot 5 \cdot 7 \cdot 11 \cdot 11$ and $S = 3 \cdot 7 \cdot 13 \cdot 17$. What is the greatest common factor of *R* and *S*?

    F. $2 \cdot 3 \cdot 3 \cdot 3 \cdot 5 \cdot 7 \cdot 7 \cdot 11 \cdot 11 \cdot 13 \cdot 17$
    G. $2 \cdot 3 \cdot 3 \cdot 5 \cdot 7 \cdot 11 \cdot 13 \cdot 17$
    H. $3 \cdot 7$
    J. $3 \cdot 3 \cdot 7 \cdot 7$
    K. $3 \cdot 3 \cdot 3 \cdot 7 \cdot 7$

42. The counting numbers are placed in order in the chart, as shown. Assuming the pattern continues, in which column will the number 200 appear?

    A. *q*
    B. *s*
    C. *t*
    D. *u*
    E. *v*

p	q	r	s	t	u	v
		1	2	3	4	5
6	7	8	9	10	11	12
13	14	15	16	17	18	19
20	21	...				

43. The equation $2(3x + 6) = 3(2x + 4)$ is satisfied by

    F. no value of *x*.
    G. only negative values of *x*.
    H. only $x = 0$.
    J. only positive values of *x*.
    K. all values of *x*.

44. Wai Ling averaged 84 on her first three exams, and 82 on her next 2 exams. What grade must she obtain on her sixth test in order to average 85 for all six exams?

    A. 96
    B. 94
    C. 90
    D. 89
    E. 86

45. How many prime numbers between 8 and 60 leave a remainder of 2 when divided by 6?

    F. 0
    G. 1
    H. 4
    J. 6
    K. 7

46. In the diagram, each small box is a square whose side is 3. What is the area of the shaded figure?

    A. 108
    B. 54
    C. 36
    D. 18
    E. 6

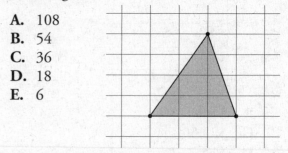

47. When expressed in scientific notation, the number 1,230,000,000 is 1.23×10^B. The value of *B* is

    F. 2
    G. 7
    H. 8
    J. 9
    K. 10

48. In the diagram, lines *m* and *n* are parallel. What is the value of *x*?

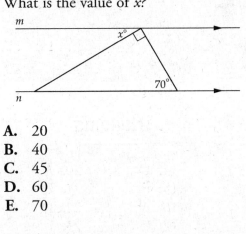

- **A.** 20
- **B.** 40
- **C.** 45
- **D.** 60
- **E.** 70

49. If $P = \sqrt{2 + \sqrt{10}}$, $Q = \sqrt{10 + \sqrt{2}}$, and

$R = \sqrt{5 + \sqrt{5}}$, then

- **F.** $P < Q < R$
- **G.** $P < R < Q$
- **H.** $Q < R < P$
- **J.** $R < Q < P$
- **K.** $P = Q$

50. The sides of a triangle *all* have integer lengths. Two sides have lengths 7 and 10. If the largest and smallest possible *perimeters* for the triangle are *L* and *S*, the value of $L + S$

- **A.** is 20.
- **B.** is 51.
- **C.** is 52.
- **D.** is 54.
- **E.** cannot be determined from the information given.

Answer Key
MINITEST 2

Scrambled Paragraphs

Paragraph 1 SUTQR
Paragraph 2 UQSTR
Paragraph 3 QSURT

Logical Reasoning

10. C
11. K
12. C
13. G

Reading

14. D   20. A
15. F   21. H
16. A   22. D
17. G   23. J
18. A   24. B
19. K   25. G

Mathematics

26. B	31. J	36. D	41. H	46. B
27. J	32. A	37. H	42. D	47. J
28. D	33. K	38. E	43. K	48. A
29. G	34. C	39. F	44. B	49. G
30. C	35. G	40. C	45. F	50. D

ANSWER EXPLANATIONS
MINITEST 2

Scrambled Paragraphs

Paragraph 1 SUTQR

S is the second sentence, with a reference to the "Great" size mentioned in the inital sentence and to the "horns" that are not really horns. U begins with the pronoun "These" referring to the horns and gives information about the ferocity of the owl's predation. T continues this subject with information on why the bird is so ferocious and about smaller and larger prey. Q with its transitional pronoun "these" gives examples of the larger prey and R shows how the bird hunts that prey.

Paragraph 2 UQSTR

U logically comes second, with the transitional "this process" referring to photosynthesis and telling what follows it. Q begins with a transition that indicates additions to the basic function of photosynthesis and goes on to give an example. Sentence S provides another example of plants with "modified leaves." T continues with the transition "Other leaves" and another example. R ends the paragraph with a comment on the fact that flowers are modified leaves, which refers to the poinsettia in T.

Paragraph 3 QSURT

Q is the second sentence since it continues the discussion of the vaccine introduced in the initial sentence. U could come next, except that the transitions after U would produce a paragraph with no logical place for S.

> **TIP:** Work through the entire paragraph before deciding upon your answer.

S must come after Q, introducing the factor of "symptom alleviation" and the effects of polio. U follows S, giving an example of one of the most serious effects and its treatment. R has the transitional phrase "opposite approach," and tells what the approach was and who developed it. T has the pronoun "her," a clue linking T to R. It continues the story of Elizabeth Kenny by telling

of early opposition to her method, followed by acceptance.

Logical Reasoning

Solutions in this section frequently involve techniques discussed in Skillbuilder B.

10,11. **(C,K)** Draw a set of four vertical boxes. Since the blue plate can only touch the green plate, the blue must either be the highest or the lowest plate (the inner plates each touch two others). Duplicate your set of boxes, marking the top box blue in one set, and the bottom box blue in the other set. For each set, the box next to the blue can now be marked green. We can now answer the questions.

10. **(C)**

11. **(K)** Each of the first four choices is possible, but the last choice would mean that the red and green plates occupy the top and bottom boxes.

12,13. **(C,G)** Remember to **mark your sentences** in this type of logical reasoning problem.

12. **(C)** The word "dogs" is in sentences 1 and 3 only. Only *bul* is in exactly those sentences.

13. **(G)** The nonsense word *ni* is in all three sentences. Only the word "chase" is in all three sentences.

Reading
Passage I

14. **(D)** Main Idea A is too narrow. B is inaccurate, as the Travellers are not extinct. C limits the subject to uprooted families, wheras the passage suggests a core of wandering poets. E is too narrow. Since the passage gives both history and description, and

the Travellers can be considered an ethnic group, D is correct.

15. **(F) Detail** All of the other choices can be found in the passage. F is not given. The passage states as a possible origin people who *served* lords, not the lords themselves (line 14).

16. **(A) Detail** The itinerant lifestyle as a tradition is specifically mentioned in lines 5–7. The other choices are either wrong or refer to the group as it exists today.

17. **(G) Detail** Usually definition questions require inference, but in some cases the definition is provided. In this case, it is given immediately following the phrase (lines 52–53).

18. **(A) Inference** The idea that Shelta arose among poets suggests that its origin may be in literature. All of the other choices contradict statements in the passage.

19. **(K) Detail** F is indicated as a factor in the fourth paragraph (line 44). G, H, and J are given as factors in the last paragraph. K, however, contradicts the second sentence in the passage, which says that the people have (present tense) their own language (line 5).

Passage II

20. **(A) Main Idea** A is the only answer both broad enough and also accurate. B is broad, but not accurate. The passage indicates that women achieved equality in some areas, but does not state or suggest a superior position for women. C and D are too narrow. D is both narrow and inaccurate, as the passage is not about how Islam began but rather certain early developments in Islam.

21. **(H) Detail** The word "fully" makes this choice inaccurate because it is too extreme. The passage states (lines 55–56) that women

sometimes led congregations, which indicates that a position of leadership for women was not the usual thing. Thus, women's position was not fully equal. The other choices are all stated.

22. **(D) Inference** D is suggested in the first paragraph (lines 2–3). B contradicts the information given in the last paragraph. Nothing in the passage supports C or E as a choice.

23. **(J) Inference** The fact that an entire paragraph is devoted to the important females in Muhammad's life suggests that he may have been influenced by his feelings about them. None of the other choices can be inferred. The words "minor" and "cult" make F incorrect because nothing in the passage suggests that Islam is either a cult or minor. G contradicts information given in the next-to-last paragraph (lines 56–57). Divorce is mentioned only once (line 49), and the information given does not suggest that divorce was made easier, so H is incorrect. K is not mentioned or suggested.

24. **(B) Main Idea** The answer is found in the third paragraph. A contradicts the statement that a woman had no "legal right to . . . economic support" (line 24). C is too extreme; the third and fourth paragraphs indicate a weak legal position but do not suggest that women had no rights at all. D is incorrect because of the word "usually" (line 25), which indicates that men could and sometimes did leave property to women. E is too extreme, as the paragraph gives reasons why females could be killed but does not say that they could be killed on a whim.

25. **(G) Detail** The answer is directly stated in the third paragraph (line 20).

Mathematics

26. **(B)** This is $\frac{1800}{90} = 20$.

27. **(J)** We must check each of the choices. Changing each to a decimal, they become .5, .333. . . , .25, .2, and .1666. . . . The closest to .213 is .2, which is J.

28. **(D)** Since $\overline{CD}$ bisects angle *ACB*, it must be true that angle *ACD* is also equal to $y°$. In triangle *ACD*, one angle measures 70°. Therefore the sum of the other two angles, $x + y$, must be 110°.

29. **(G)** The primes between 15 and 45 are 17, 19, 23, 29, 31, 37, 41, and 43. There are three pairs of twin primes (namely 17 and 19, 29 and 31, and 41 and 43).

30. **(C)** Since $12^2 = 144$ and $13^2 = 169$, $\sqrt{156.3}$ is a number between 12 and 13. The smallest integer that is greater than or equal to that number is 13.

31. **(J)** Oana is now 12 years old, so in eight years she will be 20. Since she will then be twice as old as her brother is now, her brother must now be 10.

32. **(A)** Two minutes is equal to 120 seconds. In that time, the snail crawls $120(\frac{2}{5}) = 48$ inches.

33. **(K)** Eliminating the initial $150 that was in the cash register, we see that 30 tickets sold for $300. Therefore each ticket sells for $\frac{300}{30} = \$10$.

34. **(C)** One method of solution is to subtract 15 from both sides of the inequality, getting $-2x < -8$. Then we divide both sides of the new inequality by -2, getting $x > 4$.

> **FACT:** When both sides of an inequality are multiplied or divided by a negative number, the sense of the inequality must be reversed.

35. **(G)** Each side of the square is 16. Therefore, each circle has a diameter of 8. The circumference of each circle is given by $C = \pi d = 8\pi$.

36. **(D)** Adding the two equations produces $5x + 5y = 110$. When we divide both sides of this equation by 5, we get $x + y = 22$.

> **TIP:** It is not always necessary to obtain x and y individually (and the problem may not call for that).

37. **(H)** Kenny is selling 9 bars for $3, but those 9 bars cost him only $1. Therefore he makes $2 for every 9 bars he sells. In order to make a profit of exactly $10, he must sell $(5)(9) = 45$ candy bars.

38. **(E)**

> **FACT:** *Distance = rate × time*

Juan's first trip covered $(30)(4) = 120$ miles. This formula can be rewritten in the form $rate = \frac{distance}{time}$. Therefore his return trip was done at the average rate of $\frac{120}{3} = 40$ miles per hour.

39. **(F)** Combining terms, this is 3×3^5, which is 3^6.

40. **(C)** Mark started with $P - 9$ dollars. Adding $11 gives him $P - 9 + 11 = P + 2$ dollars.

41. **(H)**

> **FACT:** The greatest common factor (also called the greatest common divisor) of R and S consists of the primes common to both R and S, with each such prime raised to the smaller of the exponents it had in R or S.

Since $R = 2 \cdot 3^2 \cdot 5 \cdot 7 \cdot 11^2$ and $S = 3 \cdot 7 \cdot 13 \cdot 17$, the greatest common factor is $3 \cdot 7$.

42. **(D)** Column q contains the multiples of 7. If we divide 7 into 200, we get a quotient of 28 and a remainder of 4. That means $200 = (7)(28) + 4$. The number $(7)(28)$, being a multiple of 7, will be in column q. The number 200 will appear 4 columns later, in column u.

43. **(K)** Carrying out the multiplications, we get $6x + 12 = 6x + 12$. Since both sides are identical, any value for x will satisfy the equation.

44. **(B)**

> **TIP:** If the mean of n numbers is A, then the numbers add up to $n \times A$.

Wai Ling's first three exam grades added up to $3 \times 84 = 252$. Her next two grades added up to $2 \times 82 = 164$. So far all her grades add up to 416. In order for six grades to average 85, they must add up to $6 \times 85 = 510$. Her sixth grade will have to be $510 - 416 = 94$.

45. **(F)** Any multiple of 6 is even. If a number is 2 more than a multiple of 6, that number is also even. There are no even primes between 8 and 60.

> **FACT:** The only even prime is the number 2.

46. **(B)** The base of this triangle is 9, and its height is 12. The area of the triangle is $\frac{1}{2}bh = \frac{1}{2}(9)(12) = 54$. If you chose 6 as your answer, you forgot that the side of each small box was 3, not 1. Even then, you could have found the correct area by using the fact

> **FACT:** If two figures are "similar" (same shape), then the ratio of their areas is the *square* of the ratio of their corresponding sides.

For example, if the corresponding sides are in the ratio 3:1, their areas are in the ratio 9:1. Thus, if the side of a square is tripled, its area is multiplied by 9.

47. **(J)**

> **FACT:** For a number to be in scientific notation, it must be of the form $A \times 10^B$, where $1 \le A < 10$ and B is an integer.

We start by placing the decimal point after the 1, getting 1.23. Now we count how many positions to the right the decimal point would have to be moved to produce the original number. It would have to move 9 places (the decimal point for the original number is actually after its final 0). That means the exponent B must be a 9.

> **TIP:** If you have difficulty remembering how to adjust the exponent of 10 when you move a decimal point, try using smaller numbers. For example, 25×10 (or 250) is equal to 2.5×100 (that is 2.5×10^2).

48. **(A)** The third angle of the right triangle is equal to 20°. Because of the parallel lines, that angle must also equal x.

> **FACT:** If two parallel lines are crossed by a transversal, the "alternate-interior" angles formed must be equal.

49. **(G)** $\sqrt{10}$ is a little more than 3, $\sqrt{2}$ is a little more than 1, and $\sqrt{5}$ is a little more than 2. Then P is a little more than $\sqrt{2+3}$ or $\sqrt{5}$, Q is a little more than $\sqrt{10+1}$ or $\sqrt{11}$, and R is a little more than $\sqrt{5+2}$ or $\sqrt{7}$. Therefore P is the smallest, R is next, and Q is the largest.

50. **(D)**

> **FACT:** The sum of the lengths of two sides of a triangle is greater than the length of the third side.

Since two sides are 7 and 10, the third side must be less than 17. Therefore the longest that the third side could be is 16, and $L = 7 + 10 + 16 = 33$. The shortest the third side could be is 4, because a side of 3 plus a side of 7 is not greater than a side of 10. Therefore $S = 7 + 4 + 10 = 21$. Then $L + S = 33 + 21 = 54$.

Answer Sheet
MINITEST 3

Part I   Verbal

Scrambled Paragraphs

Paragraph 1

The second sentence is Ⓠ Ⓡ Ⓢ Ⓣ Ⓤ
The third sentence is Ⓠ Ⓡ Ⓢ Ⓣ Ⓤ
The fourth sentence is Ⓠ Ⓡ Ⓢ Ⓣ Ⓤ
The fifth sentence is Ⓠ Ⓡ Ⓢ Ⓣ Ⓤ
The sixth sentence is Ⓠ Ⓡ Ⓢ Ⓣ Ⓤ

Paragraph 2

The second sentence is Ⓠ Ⓡ Ⓢ Ⓣ Ⓤ
The third sentence is Ⓠ Ⓡ Ⓢ Ⓣ Ⓤ
The fourth sentence is Ⓠ Ⓡ Ⓢ Ⓣ Ⓤ
The fifth sentence is Ⓠ Ⓡ Ⓢ Ⓣ Ⓤ
The sixth sentence is Ⓠ Ⓡ Ⓢ Ⓣ Ⓤ

Paragraph 3

The second sentence is Ⓠ Ⓡ Ⓢ Ⓣ Ⓤ
The third sentence is Ⓠ Ⓡ Ⓢ Ⓣ Ⓤ
The fourth sentence is Ⓠ Ⓡ Ⓢ Ⓣ Ⓤ
The fifth sentence is Ⓠ Ⓡ Ⓢ Ⓣ Ⓤ
The sixth sentence is Ⓠ Ⓡ Ⓢ Ⓣ Ⓤ

Logical Reasoning

10 Ⓐ Ⓑ Ⓒ Ⓓ Ⓔ
11 Ⓕ Ⓖ Ⓗ Ⓙ Ⓚ
12 Ⓐ Ⓑ Ⓒ Ⓓ Ⓔ
13 Ⓕ Ⓖ Ⓗ Ⓙ Ⓚ

Reading

14 Ⓐ Ⓑ Ⓒ Ⓓ Ⓔ
15 Ⓕ Ⓖ Ⓗ Ⓙ Ⓚ
16 Ⓐ Ⓑ Ⓒ Ⓓ Ⓔ
17 Ⓕ Ⓖ Ⓗ Ⓙ Ⓚ
18 Ⓐ Ⓑ Ⓒ Ⓓ Ⓔ
19 Ⓕ Ⓖ Ⓗ Ⓙ Ⓚ
20 Ⓐ Ⓑ Ⓒ Ⓓ Ⓔ
21 Ⓕ Ⓖ Ⓗ Ⓙ Ⓚ
22 Ⓐ Ⓑ Ⓒ Ⓓ Ⓔ
23 Ⓕ Ⓖ Ⓗ Ⓙ Ⓚ
24 Ⓐ Ⓑ Ⓒ Ⓓ Ⓔ
25 Ⓕ Ⓖ Ⓗ Ⓙ Ⓚ

Part II   Mathematics

26 Ⓐ Ⓑ Ⓒ Ⓓ Ⓔ
27 Ⓕ Ⓖ Ⓗ Ⓙ Ⓚ
28 Ⓐ Ⓑ Ⓒ Ⓓ Ⓔ
29 Ⓕ Ⓖ Ⓗ Ⓙ Ⓚ
30 Ⓐ Ⓑ Ⓒ Ⓓ Ⓔ

31 Ⓕ Ⓖ Ⓗ Ⓙ Ⓚ
32 Ⓐ Ⓑ Ⓒ Ⓓ Ⓔ
33 Ⓕ Ⓖ Ⓗ Ⓙ Ⓚ
34 Ⓐ Ⓑ Ⓒ Ⓓ Ⓔ
35 Ⓕ Ⓖ Ⓗ Ⓙ Ⓚ

36 Ⓐ Ⓑ Ⓒ Ⓓ Ⓔ
37 Ⓕ Ⓖ Ⓗ Ⓙ Ⓚ
38 Ⓐ Ⓑ Ⓒ Ⓓ Ⓔ
39 Ⓕ Ⓖ Ⓗ Ⓙ Ⓚ
40 Ⓐ Ⓑ Ⓒ Ⓓ Ⓔ

41 Ⓕ Ⓖ Ⓗ Ⓙ Ⓚ
42 Ⓐ Ⓑ Ⓒ Ⓓ Ⓔ
43 Ⓕ Ⓖ Ⓗ Ⓙ Ⓚ
44 Ⓐ Ⓑ Ⓒ Ⓓ Ⓔ
45 Ⓕ Ⓖ Ⓗ Ⓙ Ⓚ

46 Ⓐ Ⓑ Ⓒ Ⓓ Ⓔ
47 Ⓕ Ⓖ Ⓗ Ⓙ Ⓚ
48 Ⓐ Ⓑ Ⓒ Ⓓ Ⓔ
49 Ⓕ Ⓖ Ⓗ Ⓙ Ⓚ
50 Ⓐ Ⓑ Ⓒ Ⓓ Ⓔ

Minitest 3

19 QUESTIONS

SUGGESTED TIME: 35 MINUTES

Scrambled Paragraphs

Paragraphs 1–3

> **Directions:** Below are six sentences that can be arranged to form a well-organized and grammatically correct paragraph. The first sentence is provided, but the other five are listed in random order. Choose the order that will form the **best** paragraph. Each correct paragraph is worth two points, with no partial credit given.
>
> You may wish to put numbers in the blanks at the left of each sentence to help keep track of the order. When you finish the set, mark your answers on the answer sheet.

PARAGRAPH 1

Spain's great national epic, *El Cid,* is set in eleventh-century Spain just after the collapse of Muslim rule in that country.

_____ (Q) It tells the romantic adventures of the larger-than-life hero the Cid, a courageous knight of the Muslim South who conquers Valencia, establishes his own kingdom, and defeats his enemies.

_____ (R) He also found documents showing that Diaz died in 1099 defending the South against Muslim invaders from North Africa.

_____ (S) The epic, probably composed in the twelfth century, was thought to be pure legend until the twentieth-century Spanish scholar Ramon Menendez Pidal searched out evidence that the Cid was a real person.

_____ (T) Like most epics, the narrative *El Cid* embellishes and inflates the facts; however, unlike most epics, *El Cid* has solid documentary evidence to back up most of its story.

_____ (U) Pidal identified the epic's real-life protagonist as Rodrigo Diaz, an eleventh-century Castilian who left his native region to fight in the South and who really did conquer the kingdom of Valencia.

PARAGRAPH 2

Native American named Wa-tho-huck, or Bright Path, also known as Jim Thorpe, may well go down in history as the greatest all-around athlete of the twentieth century.

_____ (Q) Although he withdrew from school for two years to play semiprofessional baseball, he returned to Carlisle and a distinguished varsity career in football, track and field, basketball, swimming, boxing, baseball, and several other sports.

_____ (R) Three years before Jim Thorpe died, he was named by American sportscasters and sportswriters as the greatest all-around athlete and football player of the first half of the twentieth century, but it was 29 years after his death before the International Olympic committee restored his medals.

_____ (S) In 1912 he competed in the Olympic Games as a member of the U.S. track and field team and won both the decathlon and the pentathlon, only to have his victories revoked because of his two years of semiprofessional activity.

_____ (T) Born in Indian Territory in what is now Oklahoma in the late 1880s—the date of his birth is not precisely known—Thorpe distinguished himself early at Carlisle Indian School by his display of outstanding football and track talent.

_____ (U) Thorpe subsequently went on to a 16-year career in professional baseball and football; after this period he tried his hand at several different careers but no longer participated actively in professional sports.

PARAGRAPH 3

Ethology is sometimes called the behavioral branch of biology because it concerns the study of animal behavior, specifically that which is genetically programmed.

_____ (Q) With no prior learning this insect finds bees, one at a time, paralyzes each with a single precise sting, collects them in her hollow until she has exactly enough, and then lays an egg on one of the bees.

_____ (R) Ethologists maintain that many or most animal behaviors are determined by "nature," or genetics, rather than "nurture," or learning.

_____ (S) A pioneer in the study of this behavior was the famous ethologist Konrad Lorenz, who succeeded in getting baby geese to imprint on him.

_____ (T) In support of their theories, they offer examples of action patterns that are inexplicable otherwise, like the journeys of adult salmon back upstream to the place where they were hatched and the digger wasp's elaborate preliminary to egg-laying.

_____ (U) Another type of behavior studied by ethologists is imprinting, an instinctive response in some species, including ducks and geese, whose young immediately after hatching will follow the first object they see that produces the correct attracting sound.

LOGICAL REASONING

Questions 10–13

10. All violinists like pizza. No drummers like pizza. Everyone who likes pizza likes orange soda.

    Based only on the information above, which of the following **must** be true?

    A. No one who likes orange soda is a violinist.
    B. No one who likes orange soda is a drummer.
    C. If someone likes pizza, then that person must be a violinist.
    D. If someone is not a drummer, then that person likes pizza.
    E. Every violinist likes orange soda.

Questions 11 and 12 refer to the following information.

    Arthur, Giuseppe, Viola, and Rob each chose to participate in exactly two activities. These activities were chosen from chess, Ping-Pong, soccer, and tennis. Each activity was chosen by exactly two people. We also know that

    (1) Arthur chose chess, but not Ping-Pong.
    (2) Giuseppe did not choose soccer.
    (3) Viola and Rob both chose tennis.

11. Giuseppe must have chosen

    F. chess and tennis.
    G. chess and Ping-Pong.
    H. Ping-Pong and tennis.
    J. chess, and one other activity that cannot be determined from the information given.
    K. Ping-Pong, and one other activity that cannot be determined from the information given.

12. Viola and Rob

    A. both chose Ping-Pong.
    B. both chose soccer.
    C. chose Ping-Pong and soccer, respectively.
    D. chose soccer and Ping-Pong, respectively.
    E. chose Ping-Pong and soccer, but it cannot be determined who chose which activity.

13. Below are two word pairs. The words in each pair are related in some way. The relationship between the words in the first pair is similar to the relationship between the words in the second pair.

    hunger—eat
    thirst—drink

    What is the relationship displayed in both word pairs?

    F. Nutrition problems of the world
    G. Things we do at meals
    H. Ways to satisfy bodily needs
    J. Personal feelings and activities
    K. Needs common to both humans and animals

READING

Questions 14–25

I. The samurai were the warrior class of Japan during that country's feudal period, which lasted from the twelfth to the mid-
Line nineteenth century. Their position was
(5) much like that of the knights of medieval Europe: They were warriors dedicated to the service of a nobleman, and they followed a strict code of honor. Bushido—"the way of the warrior"—enjoined loyalty to lord and
(10) country, upright behavior, endurance, courage, courtesy, and truthfulness.

A unique feature of samurai culture was the practice of hara-kiri, or seppuku, a form of ritual suicide by disembowelment. Performed as
(15) a way of preserving honor, its earliest use was by warriors who faced the disgrace of capture by the enemy. Later it served as a way of acknowledging and being purged of guilt. In this context it could be practiced voluntarily,
(20) the more admired way, or involuntarily by order of the ruler, a death considered honorable if not wholly admirable.

Sometimes samurai lost their noble masters, in which case they became *ronin*, or
(25) unattached samurai. The most common reasons for such loss were punishment for some improper behavior, defeat in battle, or the master's death or deposition. Some ronin, apparently unable to lay aside their weapons,
(30) turned to a life of highway robbery. Others were able to successfully adopt a peaceful existence.

The most celebrated ronin were those who carried out the famous Ako vendetta in
(35) 1703. A nobleman named Lord Asano had assaulted an official named Lord Kira. Lord Kira's conduct had provoked the assault, but because he was an official of the shogun, or military dictator, he was under

(40) the protection of the ruler. As punishment Lord Asano was ordered to commit hara-kiri. After he carried out the fatal sentence, his 47 ronin acted according to their code of honor. They swore vengeance on Lord
(45) Kira, the official whose provocation had led to their master's violent act and subsequent downfall.

Lord Kira knew of their vow and exercised extreme caution. The ronin were forced to
(50) bide their time for two years, pretending that they had abandoned their oath. When they judged that their enemy had finally relaxed his guard, the band of 47 attacked and killed him. Their courageous deed of honor made
(55) them overnight heroes. Condemned to die for the murder, the faithful followers of Lord Asano were nevertheless deemed worthy to commit hara-kiri. Thus they preserved their honor even in death.

14. Which of the following is the best title for the passage?

   A. "The Shogun's Official"
   B. "Daily Life of a Samurai"
   C. "The Role of Hara-Kiri in Feudal Japan"
   D. "Samurai Honor"
   E. "Vengeance for Lord Asano"

15. What is the most likely reason why the author included the story of the ronins' vengeance?

   F. It is a good illustration of Bushido.
   G. It shows the injustice of involuntary hara-kiri.
   H. It explains how a samurai could become masterless through no fault of his own.
   J. It provides an example of patience.
   K. It illustrates how some ronin were unable to adjust to a peaceful lifestyle.

16. How did the practice of hara-kiri originate?

    A. As a way to atone for cowardice in battle
    B. As a way for a person guilty of some crime to preserve honor
    C. As a way for a ronin to remain with his master in death
    D. As a way to avoid becoming a prisoner of war
    E. As an original feature of Bushido

17. Why did Lord Asano's ronin desire to kill Lord Kira?

    F. He had insulted their master.
    G. He had ordered their master to commit hara-kiri.
    H. He was an official of the shogun who had ordered their master to commit hara-kiri.
    J. He had assaulted their master.
    K. His behavior had indirectly led to their master's death.

18. With which of the following statements would the author most likely agree?

    A. The ronin in the story were ideals of samurai virtue.
    B. Although they were courageous, the ronin should have followed legal means.
    C. The shogun overreacted in ordering such a severe penalty against Lord Asano.
    D. People of today should follow the example of the 47 ronin.
    E. Lord Kira deserved to die.

19. Which of the following is **not** a similarity between European knights and samurai?

    F. Ritual suicide
    G. A military career
    H. Attachment to a lord
    J. Binding rules of behavior
    K. Loyalty to someone of a higher rank

II. Emeralds, scarcer than diamonds, are a sort of geological miracle because they con-
Line tain elements that combine only under
(5) extraordinary conditions. They are classified as beryls, which are composed of the
elements beryllium, aluminum, silicon, and
oxygen. However, emeralds differ from
other beryls in that they also contain traces
of chromium or vanadium, which give
(10) them their distinctive green color.

A "miracle" is required to bring the heavier
chromium or vanadium together with the
lighter beryllium because they naturally
occur in different layers of rock. But when
(15) the movement of the earth's crust shoves an
oceanic layer onto a continental layer, the
heavier elements and the lighter ones are
brought together. With this mixture in
place, emeralds are a possibility, but not
(20) until another dramatic geologic event
occurs. If the shifting plates of the crust
create sufficient pressure, some rock may
be forced downward until it melts. This
process produces jets of superheated liquid
(25) which rise, leaching out elements in the
rock layer above. When these elements are
the essential ingredients of emeralds, and
the ingredients combine, the miracle is
complete.

(30) Emeralds occur in several regions of the
world, including South Africa, Egypt,
Pakistan, Brazil, and Colombia. Because of
their color, clarity, and size, those of
Colombia are the most prized. Their magnifi-
(35) cent difference is due to a difference in their
creation.

The basic processes—a combination of usually separated minerals and a bath of hot liquid—are the same as those that produced all
(40) other emeralds. But there are some differences. In the first place, in Colombia the
heavier and lighter elements were originally
mixed by the shifting of the earth's crust but
then were washed off and superimposed on
(45) the floor of an inland sea, where they formed

potentially emerald-bearing shales. With the
elements in place, plate tectonics—the
movement of the earth's crust—began to
play its crucial part. Tremendous pressure
(50) built up as the South American continent
was pushed westward. Undersea rock layers
folded and split, and hot water flowed
upward through layers of salt and shale,
leaching out the emerald components. Over
(55) a period of time, the solution collected in a
pocket in the earth's crust, where pressure
built to the exploding point. When the
pocket burst, the sudden eruption produced
instant emerald crystals, created so quickly
(60) that they had no time to mix with other
minerals. The purity of the crystals lends
Colombian emeralds their superior color
and clarity.

An intriguing feature of emeralds is that
(65) each one encloses a minute droplet of fluid,
fancifully dubbed a "garden." In Colombian gems the garden is a salt crystal, a
reminder of their unique origin.

20. Which of the following best states what this
passage is about?

    A. The superiority of Colombian emeralds
    B. Some unusual effects of plate tectonics
    C. The production of a rare mineral
    D. The function of chromium and
       vanadium
    E. The difference between an ordinary
       stone and a rare one

21. What is the meaning of "superimposed" as
it is used in the passage (line 44)?

    F. Absorbed throughout
    G. Deposited from above
    H. Melted because of geologic factors
    J. Applied as an effect of extreme heat
    K. Extracted through the action of salt
       water

22. Which of the following best explains why
Colombian emeralds are so clear?

    A. Each one contains a salt crystal.
    B. They don't contain adulterating elements.
    C. They were produced in a purifying
       explosion.
    D. They have not mixed with vanadium or
       chromium.
    E. They formed under extremely high
       pressure.

23. Which of the following is **not** true of
emeralds?

    F. They are beryls.
    G. Plate tectonics is involved in their
       creation.
    H. They occur only when shales form on a
       sea bed.
    J. Part of the production process always
       involves the action of fluid.
    K. They are rare.

24. What does the passage suggest about
emeralds from places other than Colombia?

    A. They are greener than Colombia's
       emeralds.
    B. They are more abundant than
       Colombian emeralds.
    C. They are considered more desirable
       than Colombian emeralds.
    D. They are closer in composition to other
       beryls than Colombian emeralds are.
    E. Their "gardens" do not consist of salt
       crystals.

25. What is the most likely reason why
chromium and vanadium do not occur in
the same rock layer as beryllium?

    F. They were produced on different parts
       of the earth's surface.
    G. They have been leached out of their
       original layer.
    H. The layers have been separated by plate
       tectonics.
    J. Their heavier weight caused them to
       settle in a lower layer.
    K. They were produced under different
       temperature conditions.

PART 2—MATHEMATICS

QUESTIONS 26–50

SUGGESTED TIME: 40 MINUTES

> **Directions:** For each of the following questions, select the **best** answer from the given choices. Bubble in the letter corresponding to your answer on the answer sheet. **DO NOT PUT ANY OTHER WORK ON THE ANSWER SHEET.** All necessary work can be done in your test booklet or on scrap paper that is provided.

> **NOTE:** Diagrams other than graphs might not be drawn to scale. Do not assume any relationships that are not specifically stated unless they are implied by the given information.

26. How many multiples of 3 between 1 and 22 are even?

    A. 7
    B. 5
    C. 3
    D. 1
    E. None

27. $2x(3y) =$

    F. $12xy$
    G. $6xy$
    H. $5xy$
    J. $6x + 6y$
    K. $5x + 5y$

28. In triangle ABC, $AB = AC$ and the measure of angle C is 70°. What is the measure of angle A, in degrees?

    A. 40
    B. 55
    C. 60
    D. 70
    E. 90

29. $\sqrt{36} \times \sqrt{9} + \sqrt{16} =$

    F. $\sqrt{340}$
    G. 22
    H. 30
    J. 42
    K. 150

30. At 9 A.M. it was 12 degrees *below zero.* By noon the temperature had dropped 7 degrees. Over the next two hours, the temperature rose 5 degrees. What was the temperature at 2 P.M.?

    A. 0°
    B. 10° below zero
    C. 14° below zero
    D. 24° below zero
    E. none of these

31. Bob's age is now 3 times Tom's age. Twelve years from now, Tom will be 15 years old. How many years old is Bob now?

    F. 3
    G. 5
    H. 9
    J. 27
    K. 45

32. In rectangle *ABCD*, point *E* is on side $\overline{AB}$. What is the measure of angle *DEC*?

    A. 10°
    B. 48°
    C. 60°
    D. 70°
    E. 90°

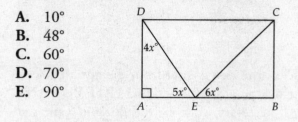

33. If $1 < 4n < 50$, and *n* is a positive integer, what is the largest possible value for *n*?

    F. 199
    G. 49
    H. 13
    J. 12.5
    K. 12

34. Which of the following is equal to $\dfrac{8x-8}{2}$?

    A. $8x - 4$
    B. $4x - 4$
    C. $4x - 8$
    D. $4x$
    E. 4

35. If $7x - 14 = 14 - 7x$, then $x =$

    F. −4
    G. −2
    H. 0
    J. 2
    K. 4

36. If *N* granola bars cost 3 dollars, then the cost of 3 granola bars is

    A. $\dfrac{9}{N}$ dollars
    B. *N* dollars
    C. 3*N* dollars
    D. 1 dollar
    E. 9 dollars

37. In Mr. Romano's class, the ratio of the number of girls to the number of boys is 3:2. A student is selected at random from the class. The probability that the selected student is a boy is

    F. $\dfrac{1}{6}$
    G. $\dfrac{1}{3}$
    H. $\dfrac{2}{5}$
    J. $\dfrac{3}{5}$
    K. $\dfrac{2}{3}$

38. Each of the integers from −3 to 5 inclusive is placed in the diagram, with one number going into each box. If the sum of the numbers in each row is the same, what is that sum?

    A. 0
    B. 3
    C. 5
    D. 6
    E. 7

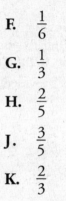

39. What is the median of the set of numbers {4, 16, 12, 10, 6, 8, 12, 12}?

    F. 9
    G. 10
    H. 11
    J. 12
    K. 13

40. If $\underline{X}$ means $\dfrac{X+3}{X}$ then the value of $(\underline{3})(\underline{6})$ is

    A. $\dfrac{7}{6}$
    B. $\dfrac{4}{3}$
    C. 3
    D. 16
    E. 18

41. What is the least common multiple of
    P and Q if $P = 3 \cdot 3 \cdot 11 \cdot 11 \cdot 13$ and
    $Q = 3 \cdot 5 \cdot 11 \cdot 11 \cdot 11$?

    F. $3 \cdot 11$
    G. $3 \cdot 5 \cdot 11 \cdot 13$
    H. $3 \cdot 11 \cdot 11$
    J. $3 \cdot 3 \cdot 11 \cdot 11 \cdot 11$
    K. $3 \cdot 3 \cdot 5 \cdot 11 \cdot 11 \cdot 11 \cdot 13$

42. What is the perimeter of figure *ABCDEF*?

    A. 33
    B. 34
    C. 35
    D. 36
    E. none of these

    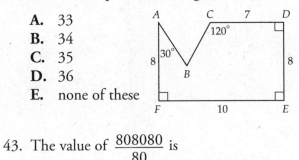

43. The value of $\frac{808080}{80}$ is

    F. 111
    G. 10101
    H. 101010
    J. 640
    K. 1000

44. From 7:00 P.M. to 8:00 P.M., José completed
    one-third of his homework. From 8:00 P.M.
    to 9:00 P.M., he completed $\frac{1}{4}$ of the
    remaining part of his homework. What
    fraction of his homework still remained to
    be completed after 9:00 P.M.?

    A. $\frac{1}{2}$

    B. $\frac{1}{3}$

    C. $\frac{1}{4}$

    D. $\frac{1}{5}$

    E. $\frac{1}{6}$

45. Which of the following represents the
    phrase "5 less than 8 times *n*"?

    F. $5 < 8n$
    G. $5 - 8n$
    H. $8n + 5$
    J. $8n - 5$
    K. $n - 3$

46. If $p = -3$ and $q = 2$, what is the value of
    $p^2 - (q - p)$?

    A. -14
    B. 14
    C. -4
    D. 4
    E. 11

47. What is the area of triangle *ABC*?

    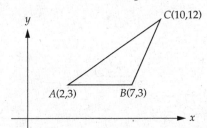

    F. 15
    G. 18
    H. $22\frac{1}{2}$
    J. 25
    K. 30

48. If $\frac{64}{x - 8} + 7 = 11$, what is the value of
    $\frac{64}{x + 8}$?

    A. 2
    B. 4
    C. 16
    D. 24
    E. 32

49. If the diameter of a circle is 6.4×10^8, then the radius of the circle is

   F. 3.2×10^8
   G. 3.2×10^4
   H. 3.2×5^8
   J. 6.4×10^4
   K. 6.4×5^8

50. When $\frac{1}{11}$ is expressed as a decimal, what digit appears in the 16th place to the right of the decimal point?

   A.   0
   B.   1
   C.   2
   D.   5
   E.   9

Answer Key
MINITEST 3

Scrambled Paragraphs	Logical Reasoning	Reading	
Paragraph 1 QSURT	10. E	14. D	20. C
Paragraph 2 TQSUR	11. G	15. F	21. G
Paragraph 3 RTQUS	12. E	16. D	22. B
	13. H	17. K	23. H
		18. A	24. E
		19. F	25. J

Mathematics

26. C	31. H	36. A	41. K	46. D
27. G	32. D	37. H	42. E	47. H
28. A	33. K	38. B	43. G	48. A
29. G	34. B	39. H	44. A	49. F
30. C	35. J	40. C	45. J	50. E

ANSWER EXPLANATIONS
MINITEST 3

Scrambled Paragraphs

Paragraph 1 **QSURT**
The opening sentence introduces the subject of *El Cid*. At first glance S might seem to come next, but it refers to "the Cid," who has not yet been introduced. Q comes after the opening sentence because the pronoun "It" refers to the epic and because it gives overall information, including the name of the hero, the Cid. S follows, giving information about old opinion and new knowledge, including the fact that the Cid really lived. U clearly refers to S, referring to the "Pidal" named in S and giving the name Diaz to the Cid. R refers back to U by naming Diaz and goes on to mention documents. T finishes the paragraph by referring to the documents mentioned in R.

Paragraph 2 **TQSUR**
The paragraph gives a thumbnail biography of Jim Thorpe and follows a chronological order. T follows the opening sentence, giving information of Thorpe's early life. Q comes next, "returned to Carlisle" connecting it to T. S comes next, with the reference to "semiprofessional activity" referring to Q. U follows with information on later life, and R ends with information on the end of his life.

Paragraph 3 **RTQUS**
R is the second sentence, giving the "nature" theory that refers to the genetic programming mentioned in the opening sentence. T mentions "their theories," referring to R, and mentions the digger wasp. Q describes the behavior of the digger wasp.

U gives another type of "instinctive" behavior, and S tells about a pioneer in the study of this other type.

Logical Reasoning

Solutions in this section frequently involve techniques discussed in Skillbuilder B.

10. **(E)** Let V represent "violinist," D represent "drummer," P represent "liking pizza," and O represent "liking orange soda." The given statements can now be written as V → P, D → ~P, and P → O.

The first and last of these statements lead (by Basic Principle 2) to V → O, which is choice E. [The other choices are (A) O → ~V, (B) O → ~D, (C) P → V, and (D) ~D → P, none of which is logically valid.]

11,12. **(G,E)** Make a chart whose rows are labeled A, G, V, and R (for the people) and whose columns are labeled c, p, s, and t (for the activities). Mark your chart according to the given information. You can then put X's in the remaining boxes of the tennis column, a check mark in the soccer box for A (that must be his second activity), check marks in the remaining boxes of G's row (he must choose two activities), and X's in the remaining boxes of the chess column (chess has already been chosen by two people). We can now answer the questions.

11. **(G)**

12. **(E)** Viola and Rob cannot choose the same activity, because that would result in 3 people choosing that activity.

13. **(H)** Choice K simply gives categories to each part of the word pair. Choice H indicates the **relationship** between the words of each pair.

Reading

Passage I

14. **(D)** Main Idea   D is the only choice broad enough. Every paragraph except the third discusses some aspect of honor, and that paragraph is necessary for understanding the story. A, B, and E are too narrow. E is too narrow because the story of the vengeance is used as an illustration of the overall main idea. B is inaccurate, as the passage does not relate a daily routine.

15. **(F)** Main Idea   The emphasis in the story is on the idea that the ronin acted according to their code of honor, Bushido. The other choices all miss the emphasis on honor.

16. **(D)** Detail   The correct answer is stated in the second paragraph (line 16).

17. **(K)** Inference   The passage indicates that the ronin blamed Lord Kira for their master's death (line 51). F is incorrect because the passage does not state or suggest how Lord Kira provoked the assault. G contradicts the information given in the fourth paragraph, which says that Lord Kira was under the protection of the ruler and thus Lord Asano was ordered to commit hara-kiri (lines 42–43). This suggests that the ruler gave the order. H and J contradict the details of the story.

18. **(A)** Inference   Since the story of the ronin is used as an example of honor, it can be inferred that the main characters of the story exemplify this quality.

> **NOTE:** Individual readers may agree with one or more of these incorrect choices, but no details in the story state or suggest them.

19. **(F)** Detail   All of the other choices are stated in the first paragraph.

Passage II

20. **(C)** Main Idea   The entire passage focuses on the geologic processes that produce emeralds, which are described as scarce. A, B, and D are too narrow. Only two sentences in the passage concern A. The production of emeralds involves other factors in addition to plate tectonics, so B is incorrect. D is wrong for the same kind of reason—the chemicals named are only a part of the production process. E is not mentioned at all in the passage.

21. **(G)** Inference   F is not a correct answer because the passage says that the elements were "superimposed *on*." The word *on* contra-

dicts the word *throughout* in F. No mention of melting, heat, or salt water is made in the context, so H, J, and K are incorrect. G is the only possible choice according to the context. The fact that the elements were superimposed on the *floor* of the ocean suggests that they came from above.

22. **(B)** Detail   The passage says that the Colombian emerald crystals did not mix with other elements (line 59); thus they are not adulterated. The following sentence says that this lack of adulteration is the reason for their clarity (line 61).

23. **(H)** Detail   H contradicts the explanation given in the second paragraph. Shales are involved only in the production of Colombian emeralds. All the other choices are true and stated in the passage.

24. **(E)** Inference   The last sentence in the passage makes a connection between the salt crystal in Colombian emeralds and the uniqueness of these stones, suggesting that the salt crystal is unique to Colombian emeralds. A is nowhere suggested or stated in the passage. B is not stated or suggested, and also is contra-indicated by the statement that the reasons Colombian emeralds are especially prized involve their color, clarity, and size (line 33). Rarity is not mentioned. D is not suggested or stated in the passage.

25. **(J)** Inference   The first sentence of the second paragraph says that chromium and vanadium are heavier than beryllium (lines 11–12) and that they "naturally" occur in different layers of rock (line 14). The inference can be made that weight caused them to sink. Leaching is mentioned as part of the process that brings the elements together, so G is incorrect. The same is true of plate tectonics (line 46), so H is also incorrect. K is incorrect because no mention is made of a temperature differential in the production of the elements themselves.

Mathematics

26. **(C)** Even numbers are multiples of 2. In order to also be a multiple of 3, the numbers must actually be multiples of $(2)(3) = 6$. Between 1 and 22 there are three multiples of 6.

27. **(G)** Rearranging terms, we have $2 \cdot 3 \cdot x \cdot y = 6xy$.

28. **(A)**

> **FACT:** The base angles (those are the angles opposite the equal sides) of an isosceles triangle are equal.

Angle B also measures 70°, so the third angle of the triangle is 40°.

29. **(G)** This is $6 \times 3 + 4$. The order of operations indicates that we do the multiplication first, so we have $18 + 4 = 22$.

30. **(C)** Numerically, the given changes are equivalent to $(-12) - (7) + (5) = -14$.

31. **(H)** Tom will be 15 years old in 12 years, so he is now 3. Bob is now 3 times Tom's present age, so Bob is 9.

32. **(D)** From right triangle *ADE*, $4x + 5x = 90$, so $x = 10$. Then $6x = 60$. Finally, $5x + 6x = 50 + 60 = 110$. That leaves 70° for angle *DEC*.

33. **(K)** Dividing *each* of the three parts of the inequality by 4, we get $\frac{1}{4} < n < \frac{50}{4}$. The largest integer that is less than $\frac{50}{4} (= 12\frac{1}{2})$ is 12.

34. **(B)** Dividing each term of the numerator by 2 produces $4x - 4$.

35. **(J)** Adding $7x$ to both sides produces $14x - 14 = 14$, so $14x = 28$. Then $x = 2$.

36. **(A)** If N granola bars cost 3 dollars, then 1 granola bar costs $\frac{3}{N}$ dollars. Therefore, 3 granola bars will cost $3 \times \frac{3}{N} = \frac{9}{N}$ dollars. If that first concept seems difficult, try using simple numbers: If 2 granola bars cost \$3, then 1 granola bar costs \$1.50. You had to divide the total cost by the number of bars.

37. **(H)** If we use $2x$ to represent the number of boys in the class, and $3x$ to represent the number of girls, then the total number of students is $5x$. Since there are $2x$ ways to pick a boy, the probability that the selected student is a boy is $\frac{2x}{5x} = \frac{2}{5}$. If it helps, try using simple numbers such as 20 for the number of boys and 30 for the number of girls.

38. **(B)** The sum of the numbers in the nine boxes is the sum of the integers from -3 to 5. That is 9. Since the sum of the numbers in each row is the same, that sum must be $\frac{1}{3}$ of 9, which is 3.

39. **(H)** Arranging the elements of the set in increasing order produces {4, 6, 8, 10, 12, 12, 12, 16}. The median is the middle number if there are an odd number of elements. When there are an even number of elements, we use the mean of the two central numbers. That is $\frac{10 + 12}{2} = 11$. Do not confuse this with the mean of all the numbers, which is $\frac{4 + 6 + 8 + 10 + 12 + 12 + 12 + 16}{8} = 10$.

Also do not confuse it with the mode of all the numbers, which is 12.

40. **(C)** The value of $(3)(6)$ is $\left(\frac{3 + 3}{3}\right)\left(\frac{6 + 3}{6}\right) = \left(\frac{6}{3}\right)\left(\frac{9}{6}\right) = 3$.

41. **(K)**

> **TIP:** The least common multiple of P and Q must contain every prime that is in *either P or Q*, and must contain each of those primes the greater number of times it appears in either P or Q.

In this case, the least common multiple will be $3 \cdot 3 \cdot 5 \cdot 11 \cdot 11 \cdot 11 \cdot 13$.

42. **(E)** Since AD must equal $EF (=10)$, the missing segment $\overline{AC}$ must equal 3. The missing angles of triangle ABC must be 60° and 60°, so that triangle is equilateral. That means $AB = BC = 3$. We now see that the perimeter of figure $ABCDEF$ is $3 + 3 + 7 + 8 + 10 + 8 = 39$.

43. **(G)** When dividing, be careful not to omit needed zeros. The answer is 10101.

44. **(A)** When José completed one-third of his homework, there was still $\frac{2}{3}$ to be done. He then completed $\frac{1}{4}$ of that, which means he completed $\frac{1}{4} \times \frac{2}{3} = \frac{1}{6}$ more. So far, he has done $\frac{1}{3} + \frac{1}{6} = \frac{1}{2}$ of his homework. That means there is still $\frac{1}{2}$ of his homework to go.

45. **(J)** "8 times n" is represented by $8n$. "Five less than n" is $8n - 5$. [For example, "Five less than 100" is $100 - 5$, or 95.] That is choice J.

Actually, the phrase "5 less than 8 times n" can really be interpreted in two different ways, producing two different representations. This can best be seen by putting parentheses into the text phrase! Thus the expression "5 less than (8 times n)" is clearly $8n - 5$. But the expression "(5 less than 8) times n" is $(8 - 5) \times n$, which is $3n$. This shows how mathematical language is usually clearer than plain words!

IMPORTANT: Since a phrase like "5 less than 8 times n" comes up so frequently, it is generally agreed that it will be interpreted as $8n - 5$.

46. **(D)** Substituting the numbers, the expression becomes $(-3)^2 - [(2) - (-3)] = 9 - [5] = 4$.

47. **(H)** Using $\overline{AB}$ as the base of the triangle, we have $AB = 7 - 2 = 5$. The length of the altitude from C to that base is $12 - 3 = 9$. The area of a triangle equals
$$\frac{1}{2}(\text{base})(\text{height}) = \frac{1}{2}(5)(9) = \frac{45}{2} = 22\frac{1}{2}.$$

48. **(A)** Subtracting 7 from both sides, we get $\frac{64}{x-8} = 4$. Clearly $x - 8$ must be 16. Then $x = 24$, so $x + 8 = 32$. The final answer is 2.

49. **(F)** The radius is half the diameter, which is $\frac{1}{2} \times 6.4 \times 10^8 = 3.2 \times 10^8$. Be careful not to take half of *both* terms of the product.

50. **(E)** $\frac{1}{11}$ is equal to .090909. . . . The digit in the 16th decimal place will be a 9.

Answer Sheet
MINITEST 4

Part I   Verbal

Scrambled Paragraphs

Paragraph 1

The second sentence is   Ⓠ Ⓡ Ⓢ Ⓣ Ⓤ

The third sentence is   Ⓠ Ⓡ Ⓢ Ⓣ Ⓤ

The fourth sentence is   Ⓠ Ⓡ Ⓢ Ⓣ Ⓤ

The fifth sentence is   Ⓠ Ⓡ Ⓢ Ⓣ Ⓤ

The sixth sentence is   Ⓠ Ⓡ Ⓢ Ⓣ Ⓤ

Paragraph 2

The second sentence is   Ⓠ Ⓡ Ⓢ Ⓣ Ⓤ

The third sentence is   Ⓠ Ⓡ Ⓢ Ⓣ Ⓤ

The fourth sentence is   Ⓠ Ⓡ Ⓢ Ⓣ Ⓤ

The fifth sentence is   Ⓠ Ⓡ Ⓢ Ⓣ Ⓤ

The sixth sentence is   Ⓠ Ⓡ Ⓢ Ⓣ Ⓤ

Paragraph 3

The second sentence is   Ⓠ Ⓡ Ⓢ Ⓣ Ⓤ

The third sentence is   Ⓠ Ⓡ Ⓢ Ⓣ Ⓤ

The fourth sentence is   Ⓠ Ⓡ Ⓢ Ⓣ Ⓤ

The fifth sentence is   Ⓠ Ⓡ Ⓢ Ⓣ Ⓤ

The sixth sentence is   Ⓠ Ⓡ Ⓢ Ⓣ Ⓤ

Logical Reasoning

10 Ⓐ Ⓑ Ⓒ Ⓓ Ⓔ

11 Ⓕ Ⓖ Ⓗ Ⓙ Ⓚ

12 Ⓐ Ⓑ Ⓒ Ⓓ Ⓔ

13 Ⓕ Ⓖ Ⓗ Ⓙ Ⓚ

Reading

14 Ⓐ Ⓑ Ⓒ Ⓓ Ⓔ

15 Ⓕ Ⓖ Ⓗ Ⓙ Ⓚ

16 Ⓐ Ⓑ Ⓒ Ⓓ Ⓔ

17 Ⓕ Ⓖ Ⓗ Ⓙ Ⓚ

18 Ⓐ Ⓑ Ⓒ Ⓓ Ⓔ

19 Ⓕ Ⓖ Ⓗ Ⓙ Ⓚ

20 Ⓐ Ⓑ Ⓒ Ⓓ Ⓔ

21 Ⓕ Ⓖ Ⓗ Ⓙ Ⓚ

22 Ⓐ Ⓑ Ⓒ Ⓓ Ⓔ

23 Ⓕ Ⓖ Ⓗ Ⓙ Ⓚ

24 Ⓐ Ⓑ Ⓒ Ⓓ Ⓔ

25 Ⓕ Ⓖ Ⓗ Ⓙ Ⓚ

Part II   Mathematics

26 Ⓐ Ⓑ Ⓒ Ⓓ Ⓔ

27 Ⓕ Ⓖ Ⓗ Ⓙ Ⓚ

28 Ⓐ Ⓑ Ⓒ Ⓓ Ⓔ

29 Ⓕ Ⓖ Ⓗ Ⓙ Ⓚ

30 Ⓐ Ⓑ Ⓒ Ⓓ Ⓔ

31 Ⓕ Ⓖ Ⓗ Ⓙ Ⓚ

32 Ⓐ Ⓑ Ⓒ Ⓓ Ⓔ

33 Ⓕ Ⓖ Ⓗ Ⓙ Ⓚ

34 Ⓐ Ⓑ Ⓒ Ⓓ Ⓔ

35 Ⓕ Ⓖ Ⓗ Ⓙ Ⓚ

36 Ⓐ Ⓑ Ⓒ Ⓓ Ⓔ

37 Ⓕ Ⓖ Ⓗ Ⓙ Ⓚ

38 Ⓐ Ⓑ Ⓒ Ⓓ Ⓔ

39 Ⓕ Ⓖ Ⓗ Ⓙ Ⓚ

40 Ⓐ Ⓑ Ⓒ Ⓓ Ⓔ

41 Ⓕ Ⓖ Ⓗ Ⓙ Ⓚ

42 Ⓐ Ⓑ Ⓒ Ⓓ Ⓔ

43 Ⓕ Ⓖ Ⓗ Ⓙ Ⓚ

44 Ⓐ Ⓑ Ⓒ Ⓓ Ⓔ

45 Ⓕ Ⓖ Ⓗ Ⓙ Ⓚ

46 Ⓐ Ⓑ Ⓒ Ⓓ Ⓔ

47 Ⓕ Ⓖ Ⓗ Ⓙ Ⓚ

48 Ⓐ Ⓑ Ⓒ Ⓓ Ⓔ

49 Ⓕ Ⓖ Ⓗ Ⓙ Ⓚ

50 Ⓐ Ⓑ Ⓒ Ⓓ Ⓔ

Minitest 4

19 QUESTIONS

SUGGESTED TIME: 35 MINUTES

Scrambled Paragraphs

Paragraphs 1–3

> **Directions:** Below are six sentences that can be arranged to form a well-organized and grammatically correct paragraph. The first sentence is provided, but the other five are listed in random order. Choose the order that will form the **best** paragraph. Each correct paragraph is worth two points, with no partial credit given.
>
> You may wish to put numbers in the blanks at the left of each sentence to help keep track of the order. When you finish the set, mark your answers on the answer sheet.

PARAGRAPH 1

In the nonbreeding season the American crow leads an interesting communal life, with thousands or even hundreds of thousands of birds roosting together.

_____ (Q) At this temporary station, still more flight lines come together, and the air is filled with acrobatic crows who appear to be greeting each other with enthusiastic swoops and dives.

_____ (R) There they spend most of the day; then the flocks retrace their pathways, their numbers increasing as pathways converge, until they arrive at a feeding "stopover."

_____ (S) After feeding, the birds embark on the final lap of the return flight to their roosting site, where they arrive together as daylight fades.

_____ (T) In the morning these thousands divide into numerous flocks and travel by established flight paths to widely dispersed feeding grounds as far as fifty miles away.

_____ (U) Spectators are amazed at the twilight spectacle of thousands of these gregarious birds converging on their communal roost.

PARAGRAPH 2

The material in the center of a lead pencil is actually a mixture of graphite and clay, not "lead," as it is commonly called.

_____ (Q) These are baked until they are dry and are then laid in grooves of a wooden block over which another grooved block of wood is placed.

_____ (R) Depending on whether the pencils are intended to produce a darker or a lighter mark, the proportions in the mixture vary, with a higher proportion of graphite resulting in a darker mark.

_____ (S) A machine then cuts the blocks into what we should probably call graphite-clay pencils.

_____ (T) The two materials are mixed and ground together into a substance that looks like a kind of dough.

_____ (U) The mixture is poured into a machine that has cylindrical holes the size of a pencil lead and is pushed through the holes from which it emerges in the form of long strings.

PARAGRAPH 3

Although greed has been the major force behind the destruction of the Amazon rain forests, this same force may, ironically, provide their salvation.

_____ (Q) For example, it should be possible to mine the vast reserves of gold, iron and tin ores, manganese, bauxite, and other minerals with a minimum of environmental disturbance.

_____ (R) Timber can be "mined" also, in a careful harvest of the forests' abundant variety instead of the wasteful burning and bulldozing currently used to extract only a few kinds of wood.

_____ (S) As the researchers and planners discuss these solutions, however, destruction continues; if the remaining rain forests are to be saved, the time to act is now.

_____ (T) Farming and ranching, which have been similarly wasteful and only marginally productive, can be improved through soil studies and the development of new seeds, so that smaller areas can support more livestock and produce bigger and better harvests.

_____ (U) As the devastation reaches catastrophic proportions, scientists and environmentalists are now proposing that the only way to save the Amazon region is to develop methods for using its riches without destroying their source.

LOGICAL REASONING
Questions 10–13

Directions: For each of the following questions, select the best answer from the given choices. Bubble in the letter corresponding to your answer on the answer sheet. Your answer should be based **only on the given information.**

Read the words carefully. For example, "The red book is **to the right** of the blue book" does not necessarily mean that there is no other book between them. Similarly, be careful when reading words such as **between, below, above, after, before, behind,** and **ahead of.**

Questions 10 and 11 refer to the following information.

The letters A, B, C, and D represent four books that are on a shelf. There **might** or **might not** be other books on the shelf. Exactly 2 books are between A and B. Exactly 1 book is between B and C. D is next to C.

10. We can conclude that between books A and D,

   A. there is only book C.
   B. there is only book B.
   C. there may be exactly 2 books.
   D. there may be exactly 3 books.
   E. there may be exactly 4 books.

11. If B is **not** next to D, then the minimum number of books that can be on the shelf is

   F. 4
   G. 5
   H. 6
   J. 7
   K. 8

12. Below are two word pairs. The words in each pair are related in some way. The relationship between the words in the first pair is similar to the relationship between the words in the second pair.

   cold—winter
   hot—summer

   What is the relationship displayed in both word pairs?

   A. Temperatures and the season in which they are often found
   B. Temperatures and seasons of the year
   C. Words and their opposites
   D. Words and their synonyms
   E. Words used in weather reports

13. Tim said that Uncle Ebeneezer is coming to dinner on Friday, so we are going to have roast beef.

   Of the following choices, which one must be true in order for Tim's statement to be valid?

   F. The only thing Uncle Ebeneezer ever eats for dinner is roast beef.
   G. We always serve roast beef on Fridays.
   H. Uncle Ebeneezer does not eat roast beef on any other day of the week.
   J. Uncle Ebeneezer always eats at our house on Fridays.
   K. Roast beef is Uncle Ebeneezer's favorite food.

READING

Questions 14–25

I. Folk epics—long narratives that relate the exploits of national heroes—are typically a mixture of history and fiction. The
Line *Iliad,* for example, tells the story of a war
(5) between the Trojans and Greeks that began when a Trojan prince abducted the most beautiful woman in the world from her Greek husband. The romantic story and probably most of the details of the
(10) subsequent siege of Troy are fictitious, but archeology has proved that there was indeed a war and a besieged city exactly where the epic places them.

The Anglo-Saxon folk epic *Beowulf* relates
(15) the deeds of the hero Beowulf, who comes to Denmark to save the followers of King Hrothgar from a monster named Grendel. The monster, who makes nightly raids on Hrothgar's communal hall, is never seen
(20) by the Danes. He attacks in the dark, wreaking bloody havoc upon the sleeping Danes and leaving only grisly remains for the daylight. In the daytime the Danes can sense his presence nearby, lurking in
(25) the shadows of the forest, but they never see him. The heroic visitor Beowulf battles the monster and mortally wounds him, but there is no dead body to be viewed, for Grendel flees to his
(30) underwater home to die, leaving behind only the clawed arm that Beowulf has ripped off.

Readers often speculate about the factual basis for the story. Did Hrothgar's tribe
(35) really suffer a long and bloody siege of unknown origin? Was there really a "monster," perhaps a marauding bear or other animal? Was Grendel a primitive humanoid, a Scandinavian Bigfoot who had some-
(40) how been provoked by Hrothgar's men? In his novel *Eaters of the Dead,* writer Michael Crichton speculates that Grendel was a band of invaders who came at night, carrying torches, which in the dark pro-
(45) duced a monstrous, serpentine effect.

Another explanation, possibly the most likely, has its basis in the blood-feud culture of that time and place. An injury to a tribe member by an outsider demanded
(50) vengeance in kind. The violent revenge required a similar response, so a bloody feud between neighboring tribes could go on for years, with murder after murder decimating both groups. It may be that
(55) Hrothgar's people were locked in a blood feud with a particularly vicious and cowardly enemy who attacked only in darkness, when all were asleep. There are lines in *Beowulf* that support the interpretation that
(60) the monster "[kept] the bloody feud/alive, seeking no peace, offering/no truce. . ." The hero Beowulf, who owed Hrothgar a debt of honor, may have come to help settle the disastrous vendetta that was crushing
(65) the old king's people.

14. Which of the following is the most likely purpose of the author of the passage?

A. To explain how epics originate
B. To offer an explanation for a legend
C. To examine the blood-feud culture of an earlier time
D. To prove that all epics are based in truth
E. To explain the motives of the hero Beowulf

15. What is a blood feud?

    F. A war between tribes in which there is no possibility of a truce
    G. An especially bloody battle between individuals
    H. An intertribal war based on revenge
    J. A series of violent raids by an outsider
    K. A vicious and cowardly war

16. In this passage, what is the function of the reference to the *Iliad*?

    A. It illustrates the statement that many epics have some basis in fact.
    B. It reveals the romantic aspect of epics.
    C. It demonstrates the influence of archeology.
    D. It explains why the *Iliad* cannot properly be called a "folk epic."
    E. It demonstrates that epics are mostly fact.

17. Which of the following most precisely explains why Grendel's nature is a mystery?

    F. Hrothgar's people never see him.
    G. He can cause inhuman destruction.
    H. He is able to carry on a feud for years.
    J. A monster would not be expected to carry a torch.
    K. His severed arm bears claws.

18. According to the passage, which of the following is the best definition of an epic?

    A. Mostly fact and a little fiction
    B. The story of a fictitious hero whose actions take place in a historical context
    C. The story of a country and its heroes
    D. A long story about the adventures of a heroic figure
    E. The story of a nation's heroic history

19. According to the passage, which of the following statements about the hero Beowulf is the most accurate?

    F. He comes to Denmark to settle a blood feud.
    G. He is a national hero of Denmark.
    H. He is the only one who gets a clear look at Grendel.
    J. After killing Grendel, he rips the monster's arm from his body.
    K. He is under obligation to Hrothgar.

II. The fishing industry is in worldwide trouble. Some fisheries, while cutting back on operations, and others are closing down
Line entirely. Large numbers of men and women
(5) who once earned their living from the sea are unemployed. Once-abundant fishing grounds are so barren that they are being put off-limits. The ocean, once considered an inexhaustible resource, is yielding smaller
(10) and smaller catches. In response, both environmentalists and industry leaders struggle to find ways to restore the former abundance. And many worry out loud that restoration efforts may be too feeble and too
(15) late.

Seafood has always been important to the human diet wherever people have had access to it, but in recent decades demand has soared as the earth's population has bur-
(20) geoned, transportation and refrigeration have broadened availability of seafood, and nutritionists have touted its benefits. To supply the demand, commercial fisheries have improved their efficiency and enlarged
(25) their operations. The result was by no means foreseen by every observer, although it was certainly inevitable. Overfishing, induced by demand, has reduced stocks so drastically that many formerly plentiful fish
(30) and shellfish are disappearing from the nets they used to fill. Some species that were once staple are so endangered that they can no longer be legally harvested.

In addition to taking too much from the
(35) earth's oceans, fishers have also been
unknowingly wreaking such havoc on the
bottom that the remaining populations are
deprived of the means to rebuild their
numbers. The most efficient way to gather
(40) large numbers of fish is to drag enormous
nets across the bottom. Unfortunately this
is an extremely destructive method. A drag-
net carries weights and rigid side-planks to
keep it open, and as it moves it scrapes
(45) away the upper layers of the bottom. Only
a few inches are removed, but those inches
are crucial to the ecology of the ocean, for
important invertebrate species live, feed,
and hide there.

(50) The scraped area does not quickly rebuild,
either. Sometimes recovery takes years—
years in which surviving fish populations
lack the food and the hiding places necessary to bounce back from overfishing. The
(55) area affected by dragging is so enormous—
two to three million square miles a year—
that it is easy to conceptualize oceans with
few or no fishing areas left undamaged.

One reason why this destruction has gone
(60) on for so long may be that people cannot
readily see it. Anyone can view the devastation that remains when a once-beautiful
mountain area has been strip-mined or a
once-beautiful forest clear-cut. But not even
(65) the experts can look out over the ocean and
see a ravaged bottom. Human beings have
been inflicting large-scale harm on the
oceans for more than a hundred years without knowing what they were doing. Only in
(70) recent years have marine biologists begun to
understand the complex impact of industries, especially commercial fishing, on the
oceans. And much remains to be learned.
We can only hope that the knowledge
(75) comes in time to save the oceans and their
bounty.

20. What is an apparent purpose of this
passage?

  A. To educate people about how the
  oceans can be saved
  B. To explain the necessity for banning
  commercial fishing
  C. To explain the mechanics of drag
  fishing
  D. To show the similarities among
  bottom-fishing, clear-cutting, and
  strip-mining
  E. To explain how the success of
  commercial fishing has led to its
  decline

21. Which of the following best states the
reason why overfished species cannot
quickly rebuild?

  F. They are too small in number.
  G. It naturally takes many years for a fish
  population to rebound.
  H. Only a few inches of ocean bottom
  remain.
  J. Their habitat has been altered.
  K. They are still being harvested.

22. What difference between damage to land
and damage to ocean is pointed out in the
passage?

  A. Damage to land is more quickly healed.
  B. Human beings can see the land but not
  the ocean bottom.
  C. Marine biologists have been less
  aggressive than other environmental
  scientists.
  D. Damage to the ocean is impossible to
  detect.
  E. Commercial fishing does more
  environmental damage than other
  industries.

23. What best states the effect of a net's being dragged across the ocean bottom?

   F. It destroys everything in its path.
   G. It damages the habitat and the food chain.
   H. It removes large quantities of fish.
   J. It scrapes away several feet of protective mud and sand.
   K. It resembles strip-mine damage.

24. All of the following are mentioned as causative factors in the fishing boom described in the second paragraph **except**

   A. more people to feed.
   B. ability to deliver goods to distant areas more quickly.
   C. promotion by nutritionists.
   D. better means of preserving freshness.
   E. discovery of the nutritive quality of seafood.

25. Which of the following is suggested by the passage?

   F. Commercial fishing should be banned.
   G. Much is still unknown about the impact of technology on the ocean.
   H. People should eat more meat and less seafood.
   J. Drag fishing causes irreparable damage to the ocean bottom.
   K. It is too late to alleviate the damage done to the ocean by commercial fishing.

PART 2—MATHEMATICS

QUESTIONS 26–50

SUGGESTED TIME: 40 MINUTES

Directions: For each of the following questions, select the **best** answer from the given choices. Bubble in the letter corresponding to your answer on the answer sheet. **DO NOT PUT ANY OTHER WORK ON THE ANSWER SHEET.** All necessary work can be done in your test booklet or on scrap paper that is provided.

NOTE: Diagrams other than graphs might not be drawn to scale. Do not assume any relationships that are not specifically stated unless they are implied by the given information.

26. $(7)(6) - 6 =$

    A. 0
    B. 1
    C. 7
    D. 36
    E. 42

27. Fred and Michael collected money for the school trip. Fred collected 50% more than Michael. If Michael collected $150, how much did Fred and Michael collect all together?

    F. $150
    G. $225
    H. $375
    J. $450
    K. $475

28. 5.835×10^4 is equal to

    A. .0005835
    B. .005835
    C. 58,350
    D. 583,500
    E. 58,350,000

29. What is the value of $|x - y| + |y - x|$ if $x = 9$ and $y = 2x$?

    F. 18
    G. 9
    H. 4.5
    J. 0
    K. −9

30. When 54 is divided by the positive integer N, the quotient is 13 and the remainder is R. The value of R is

    A. 0
    B. 1
    C. 2
    D. 3
    E. 4

31. If $N = \sqrt{36 + 49}$, then N is

    F. a number between 9 and 10.
    G. a number between 10 and 11.
    H. a number between 11 and 12.
    J. a number between 12 and 13.
    K. 13.

32. Susan is 5 years older than Phen is now. In *N* years, Susan will be twice as old as Phen is now. If Susan is now 22 years old, what is the value of *N*?

    A. 5
    B. 12
    C. 17
    D. 22
    E. 34

33. The number of integer values of *n* for which $1 \leq \sqrt{n} \leq 3$ is

    F. 3
    G. 9
    H. 7
    J. 1
    K. 0

34. In right triangle *ABC*, angle *ACB* is 90°. The number of degrees in angle *BEC* is

    A. 80
    B. 70
    C. 60
    D. 50
    E. 40

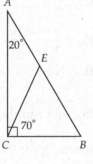

35. If it is now 12:00 noon, what time was it 40 hours ago?

    F. 4 A.M.
    G. 6 A.M.
    H. 8 A.M.
    J. 4 P.M.
    K. 8 P.M.

36. The mean of all the odd integers between 6 and 24 is

    A. 11
    B. 12
    C. 13
    D. 14
    E. 15

37. Let *x* be an element of the set {.2, 1.2, 2.2, 3.2, 4.2}. For *how many* values of *x* is $\frac{10x}{3}$ an integer?

    F. 0
    G. 1
    H. 2
    J. 3
    K. 4

38. George has just enough money to buy 3 chocolate bars and 2 ice cream cones. For the same amount of money, he could buy exactly 9 chocolate bars. For the same amount of money, how many ice cream cones could George buy?

    A. 3
    B. 5
    C. 6
    D. 7
    E. 9

39. The length of $\overline{AB}$ is twice the length of $\overline{RS}$, where *S* is a point (not shown) to the right of *R*. The coordinate of the midpoint of $\overline{RS}$ is

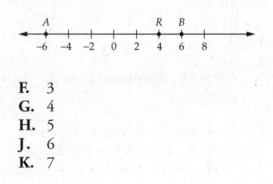

    F. 3
    G. 4
    H. 5
    J. 6
    K. 7

40. *ABCD* and *PQRS* are squares, as shown. The area of *PQRS* is

    A. 3
    B. 4
    C. 5
    D. 6
    E. 7

41. If $x = 10$ and $y = 8$, what is the value of $y(3x - 2y)$?

    F. 112
    G. 224
    H. 1792
    J. −144
    K. 140

42. One-third the product of two numbers is 24. One-half the product of these same two numbers is

    A. 72
    B. 54
    C. 48
    D. 36
    E. 12

43. The area of rectangle *ABCD* is 72. Point *F* is on $\overline{AB}$ such that $BF = 4$. What is the *sum* of the areas of triangles *CBF* and *DAF*?

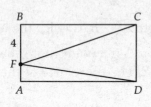

    F. 18
    G. 24
    H. 36
    J. 42
    K. Cannot be determined from the given information.

44. Ms. Brady has 28 students in her class. The ratio of boys to girls in the class is 2 to 5. How many new boys must be added to the class to make the ratio of boys to girls 1:2?

    A. 1
    B. 2
    C. 4
    D. 12
    E. 32

45. The vertices of rectangle *ABCD* all lie on the same circle as shown. The circumference of the circle is 64π. What is the length of $\overline{AC}$?

    F. 8
    G. 16
    H. 32
    J. 64
    K. 128

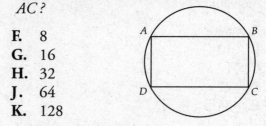

46. Ten cards are numbered 10, 11, 12, . . . , 19, one number per card. Brian removes three cards whose numbers are primes, and puts the remaining cards in a hat. If one card is then drawn at random from the hat, what is the probability that its number is a prime?

    A. $\dfrac{1}{10}$

    B. $\dfrac{1}{9}$

    C. $\dfrac{1}{5}$

    D. $\dfrac{2}{5}$

    E. None of these

47. For any number *N*, we define ■ *N* ■ to mean $\dfrac{N}{2}$ if *N* is even and $(5N - 1)$ if *N* is odd. The value of ■ 9 ■ + ■ 10 ■ is

    F. $9\dfrac{1}{2}$
    G. 19
    H. 29
    J. 49
    K. $53\dfrac{1}{2}$

48. In the figure, all line segments meet at right angles. What is the area enclosed by the figure?

    A. 84
    B. 72
    C. 70
    D. 68
    E. 64

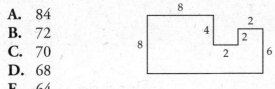

49. Apu has some nickels and some pennies. If the pennies were nickels and the nickels were pennies, he would have 80¢ less than he has now. The difference between the number of nickels and the number of pennies that he has

    F. is 12.
    G. is 20.
    H. is 24.
    J. is 28.
    K. cannot be determined.

50. Wei Jing has between 70 and 150 baseball cards in his collection. When he arranges them in groups of 10, he has 3 left over. When he arranges them in groups of 9, he has 5 left over. If he arranges them in groups of 8, how many will he have left over?

    A. 1
    B. 3
    C. 5
    D. 7
    E. 0

Answer Key
MINITEST 4

Scrambled Paragraphs

Paragraph 1 TRQSU
Paragraph 2 TRUQS
Paragraph 3 UQRTS

Logical Reasoning

10. D
11. J
12. A
13. F

Reading

14. B	20. E
15. H	21. J
16. A	22. B
17. F	23. G
18. D	24. E
19. K	25. G

Mathematics

26. D	31. F	36. E	41. F	46. E
27. H	32. B	37. H	42. D	47. J
28. C	33. G	38. A	43. H	48. A
29. F	34. E	39. K	44. B	49. G
30. C	35. K	40. C	45. J	50. A

ANSWER EXPLANATIONS
MINITEST 4

Scrambled Paragraphs

Paragraph 1   TRQSU
Chronological and transition clues are the keys to solving this one. The opening sentence introduces the subject of crows and gives a nighttime activity, roosting in groups of thousands. T moves forward to the morning and mentions the "thousands" traveling to feeding grounds. R follows T, telling how the crows spend the day and then flying to a "stopover" point. Q has the transitional "temporary station" and tells of smaller groups converging. S comes next, mentioning the "final lap" of their return. The chronology finishes with the day's end at "twilight."

Paragraph 2   TRUQS
T follows the opener, telling how the materials are handled. R is next, giving additional information about the mixture of the materials. U continues, telling how the "lead" strings are produced. Q begins with "these" referring to the strings and introducing blocks of wood. S with its transitional "the blocks" tells what happens to the blocks.

Paragraph 3   UQRTS
U follows the opener, connecting to both the destruction and the idea of profit, and it introduces the possibility of solutions. Next comes Q, giving an example of a solution. R must follow Q because the word "mined" refers to the solution in Q. T follows, referring to waste, which was mentioned in R, and giving another solution. S, with "these solutions," refers to the foregoing sentences and concludes the paragraph.

Logical Reasoning

Solutions in this section frequently involve techniques discussed in Skillbuilder B.

10,11. **(D,J)** Make several horizontal spaces (start with 4, but more will be needed shortly). Start with A in the first space and put B in the fourth space. (We could put B in the first space and A in the fourth, but this will lead to the same conclusions.) We must now place book C. Since there are two possible locations for C, make a second set of spaces, again putting A and B in positions 1 and 4. Now in the first set of spaces, put C to the left of B, in position 2. In the second set of spaces, put C to the right of B, in position 6 (you have to add some spaces). Finally, we must put D next to C. In the first set of spaces, D can go only in position 3. In the second set of spaces, D can go either in position 5 or position 7 (you do not have to draw another set of boxes at this time). We can now answer the questions.

10. **(D)** Among the given choices, only choice D is possible, coming from the second set of boxes.

11. **(J)** This comes from the second set of boxes, with *D* in position 7.

12. **(A)** Choice B is too general. Choice A is more specific. Choice E does not indicate the **relationship** between the words of each pair.

13. **(F)** Choice F explains why the coming of Uncle Ebeneezer guarantees that we will have roast beef. Choice G guarantees that we will have roast beef, but does not tie this to the coming of the uncle. Choice H does not say that the uncle eats roast beef on Fridays either. Choices J and K do not require our having roast beef at that Friday meal.

Reading

Passage I

14. **(B)** Main Idea   Since most of the passage discusses *Beowulf,* with only one other epic mentioned, the main idea must be related to the Beowulf legend. A places the emphasis on epics in general and thus is incorrect. C is too narrow, as only the last paragraph discusses the blood-feud culture. D is too extreme, as the passage does not attempt either to *prove* a

point or to cover *all* epics. E is also too narrow because the passage involves more than Beowulf's motives.

15. **(H)** The explanation is found in the last paragraph, in its second and third sentences (lines 48–54).

16. **(A)** Inference and Main Idea   The reference to the *Iliad* follows the statement that epics are a mixture of fact and fiction. Furthermore, it contains the phrase "for example" and states a factual basis for the *Iliad*. Therefore A is the correct answer. B and C contain some truth concerning the reference but do not relate to the main idea of the paragraph and therefore are incorrect choices. D and E contradict the language of the first paragraph.

17. **(F)** Inference   G is incorrect because "inhuman" destruction might suggest an animal of some kind, but not necessarily a mystery. H is incorrect because the last paragraph indicates that a reign of terror lasting for years was a familiar feature of the culture. J is incorrect because the Grendel of the epic is not known to carry a torch. K is an accurate detail, but may simply indicate an animal, not necessarily a mystery. The second paragraph places great emphasis on the fact that the Danes never see Grendel, and is followed by a paragraph speculating on the nature of Grendel. The inference can be drawn that the two topics are related.

18. **(D)** Detail   *Epic* is defined in the first sentence of the passage.

19. **(K)** Detail   The information is stated in the last sentence of the passage. F may be true, but according to the details given in the passage, it is "likely" but not certain (line 47).

FACT: An answer may be true but incorrect.

G is inaccurate because Beowulf is identified as an Anglo-Saxon hero; it is not suggested that he is also a hero of Denmark. H is incor-

rect because there is no evidence to support the idea that Beowulf gets a *clear* look, or even that he sees Grendel—they may have battled in the dark. J is inaccurate because Grendel dies *after* his arm is ripped off.

Passage II

20. **(E)** Main Idea   A misses the emphasis of the passage, which is damage and not salvation. B is too extreme, as there is no such suggestion. C is too narrow; the passage contains other topics. D is also too narrow, and the similarity is mentioned in only one sentence. Only E is both broad enough and accurate.

21. **(J)** Inference   The third paragraph explains that the top layers of the bottom that are scraped away are important to the ecology (lines 46–47), and the next paragraph says that the remaining population cannot quickly rebound because it loses (its usual) food and hiding places (lines 48–49). Thus J is the correct response. F, G, and K are not stated or suggested, and H contradicts the information given in lines 45–46.

22. **(B)** Detail   The correct answer is stated in the first three sentences of the last paragraph.

23. **(G)** Detail   The effect is given in the last sentence of the third paragraph (lines 45–49) and the first two sentences of the fourth paragraph (lines 50–54).

24. **(E)** Detail   A,B,C, and D are directly stated in the second paragraph. E is inaccurate and is therefore the correct choice as not stated. The paragraph says that nutritionists promoted the benefits of seafood but not that the benefits were newly discovered.

25. **(G)** Inference   F is too extreme. Overfishing is blamed, but banning is not suggested. H is incorrect because meat is not mentioned in the passage. J is inaccurate because it contradicts the detail given in lines 50–51. K is too extreme. The passage says that some

people *worry* that it may be too late, but the last sentence mentions hope. G is suggested in the last paragraph, which says that scientists are *beginning* to understand the impact (lines 70–71).

Mathematics

26. **(D)** According to the order of operations, we must multiply first. This produces $42 - 6 = 36$.

27. **(H)** Michael collected $150. 50% ($\frac{1}{2}$) of that is $75. Therefore Fred collected $150 + 75 = \$225$. Fred and Michael together collected $225 + 150 = \$375$.

28. **(C)** Multiplying by 10^4 moves the decimal point 4 places to the right (or just multiply 5,835 by 10,000).

29. **(F)** If $x = 9$, $y = 18$. Substitute these values in the expression, getting $|9 - 18| + |18 - 9|$.

> **TIP:** Combine the terms inside the absolute value signs before you compute the absolute value.

We have $|{-9}| + |9| = 9 + 9 = 18$.

30. **(C)** 54 must equal $13 \times N + R$. Since N is the divisor, R must be less than N. Trying $N = 4$, we get $R = 2$. Larger values of N don't work, and smaller values make R too big.

31. **(F)**

> **TIP:** $\sqrt{a+b}$ is generally not the same as $\sqrt{a} + \sqrt{b}$

First we must combine the numbers that are under the square root symbol. This results in $N = \sqrt{85}$, which is more than $9\ (= \sqrt{81})$ but less than $10\ (= \sqrt{100})$.

32. **(B)** Susan is 5 years older than Phen is now, so Phen is now $22 - 5 = 17$. In N years, Susan will be twice as old as Phen is now, so Susan will be 34. Since Susan is now 22, she will be 34 in 12 years.

33. **(G)** $\sqrt{1} = 1$ and $\sqrt{9} = 3$, so n can be any integer from 1 through 9 inclusive. That is 9 possible values for n.

34. **(E)** Angle *ABC* is also 70°, so angle *BEC* = 40°.

35. **(K)** Every 24 hours is a full day. The simplest solution is to go back 48 hours (to 12:00 noon, once again) and then go forward 8 hours. The time will then be 8:00 P.M.

36. **(E)** Those odd integers are 7, 9, 11, 13, 15, 17, 19, 21, and 23. One way to find the mean is to add those nine numbers (getting 135), then divide by 9. The answer is 15. Another way to add those numbers is to notice that they are "equally spaced," so we can add them more easily in pairs as follows: $7 + 23 = 30$, $9 + 21 = 30$, $11 + 19 = 30$, and $13 + 17 = 30$. The total is therefore $4 \times 30 + 15 = 120 + 15 = 135$.

37. **(H)** For $\frac{10x}{3}$ to be an integer, the number $10x$ must be divisible by 3. We quickly find that only two values of x satisfy this requirement, namely 1.2 and 4.2.

38. **(A)** Using single letters to represent chocolate bars and ice cream cones, we see that George can just buy $3c + 2i$. He can also just buy $9c$. Therefore, $3c + 2i = 9c$. Solving this for i, we get $2i = 6c$, so $i = 3c$. George can just buy $9c$, which is equivalent to $3i$. He can buy exactly 3 ice cream cones.

39. **(K)** $AB = 12$, so $RS = 6$. Since S is to the right of R, the coordinate of S must be $4 + 6 = 10$. The midpoint of $\overline{RS}$ is halfway between 4 and 10. That coordinate is the average of 4 and 10, which is $\frac{4+10}{2} = 7$.

40. **(C)** The side of the big square is 3, so its area is 9.

> **FACT:** The area of a right triangle is $\frac{1}{2}$ the product of its legs.

The area of each small triangle is $(\frac{1}{2})(2)(1)$ = 1. Subtracting the areas of the four small triangles from the area of the big square, we get the area of the small square. That is $9 - 4(1)$ = 5. Do not go on to find the side of the small square, as that is not what is called for.

41. **(F)** We must evaluate $8(30 - 16)$. That is $8(14) = 112$.

42. **(D)** If one-third the product is 24, then the entire product is $3(24) = 72$. Now one-half that product is 36.

43. **(H)** Let $CB = DA = h$. The sum of the areas of triangles CBF and DAF is $(\frac{1}{2})(h)(BF) + (\frac{1}{2})(h)(FA) = (\frac{h}{2})(BF) + (\frac{h}{2})(FA)$. We can factor $\frac{h}{2}$ out of both terms, getting the total area to be $(\frac{h}{2})(BF + FA)$. That is $(\frac{h}{2})(BA)$. Finally, notice that this is equal to $(\frac{1}{2})(h)(BA)$, which is $\frac{1}{2}$ the area of the rectangle. The answer is $(\frac{1}{2})(72) = 36$. The fact that $BF = 4$ is irrelevant.

Point F can be anywhere on side $\overline{AB}$, and the answer would be the same. Another approach is to realize that the area of triangle CFD is half the area of the rectangle. Therefore the required sum is the other half.

44. **(B)** If the number of boys is $2x$ and the number of girls is $5x$, then $2x + 5x = 28$. This produces $x = 4$, so there are 8 boys and 20 girls in the class. To make the ratio of boys to girls equal to 1:2, we need 10 boys total. Therefore we must add 2 boys.

45. **(J)**

> **FACT:** If a rectangle is "inscribed" in a circle, the diagonal of the rectangle will be the diameter of the circle.

The circumference of a circle equals πd, where d is the diameter of the circle. Therefore $\pi d = 64\pi$, so $d = 64$. Thus $AC = 64$.

46. **(E)** First realize that there are 10 cards to start with. Thinking that there are only nine is a common counting error. The numbers from 10 through 19 contain four primes (namely 11, 13, 17, and 19). Brian removes three of these, so only one is left. Therefore there is only one prime number among the 7 cards that go into the hat. The probability that the prime number will be drawn is $\frac{1}{7}$. None of the first four choices is correct.

47. **(J)** This is $(5 \cdot 9 - 1) + \frac{10}{2} = 44 + 5 = 49$.

48. **(A)** If we extend both inner vertical segments down to the base, the figure will be broken into three rectangles. The dimensions of those rectangles are 8×8, 4×2, and 6×2. The total of their areas is $64 + 8 + 12 = 84$.

49. **(G)** If there were n nickels and p pennies to start, their value in cents would be $5n + p$. When the coins are interchanged, their new value is $5p + n$. The difference between these is $(5n + p) - (5p + n) = 5n + p - 5p - n = 4n - 4p$. We know that this difference is 80¢, so $4n - 4p = 80$. Dividing both sides by 4, we get $n - p = 20$.

50. **(A)** In order to have 3 cards left over when they are arranged in groups of 10, the number of cards could be 73, 83, 93, 103, 113, 123, 133, or 143 (notice how these numbers differ by 10). To have 5 left over when they are arranged in groups of 9, the number of cards could be 77, 86, 95, 104, 113, 122, 131, 140, or 149 (notice how these numbers differ by 9). The only number common to both of these arrangements is 113. If these 113 cards are arranged in groups of 8, the number left over is the same as the remainder when 113 is divided by 8. That is 1.

Answer Sheet
MODEL TEST 1

Part I Verbal

Scrambled Paragraphs

Paragraph 1

The second sentence is   Q R S T U

The third sentence is   Q R S T U

The fourth sentence is   Q R S T U

The fifth sentence is   Q R S T U

The sixth sentence is   Q R S T U

Paragraph 2

The second sentence is   Q R S T U

The third sentence is   Q R S T U

The fourth sentence is   Q R S T U

The fifth sentence is   Q R S T U

The sixth sentence is   Q R S T U

Paragraph 3

The second sentence is   Q R S T U

The third sentence is   Q R S T U

The fourth sentence is   Q R S T U

The fifth sentence is   Q R S T U

The sixth sentence is   Q R S T U

Paragraph 4

The second sentence is   Q R S T U

The third sentence is   Q R S T U

The fourth sentence is   Q R S T U

The fifth sentence is   Q R S T U

The sixth sentence is   Q R S T U

Paragraph 5

The second sentence is   Q R S T U

The third sentence is   Q R S T U

The fourth sentence is   Q R S T U

The fifth sentence is   Q R S T U

The sixth sentence is   Q R S T U

Logical Reasoning

11 A B C D E

12 F G H J K

13 A B C D E

14 F G H J K

15 A B C D E

16 F G H J K

17 A B C D E

18 F G H J K

19 A B C D E

20 F G H J K

Reading

21 A B C D E

22 F G H J K

23 A B C D E

24 F G H J K

25 A B C D E

26 F G H J K

27 A B C D E

28 F G H J K

29 A B C D E

30 F G H J K

31 A B C D E

32 F G H J K

33 A B C D E

34 F G H J K

35 A B C D E

36 F G H J K

37 A B C D E

38 F G H J K

39 A B C D E

40 F G H J K

41 A B C D E

42 F G H J K

43 A B C D E

44 F G H J K

45 A B C D E

46 F G H J K

47 A B C D E

48 F G H J K

49 A B C D E

50 F G H J K

Answer Sheet
MODEL TEST 1

Part II Mathematics

51 Ⓐ Ⓑ Ⓒ Ⓓ Ⓔ	71 Ⓐ Ⓑ Ⓒ Ⓓ Ⓔ	91 Ⓐ Ⓑ Ⓒ Ⓓ Ⓔ
52 Ⓕ Ⓖ Ⓗ Ⓙ Ⓚ	72 Ⓕ Ⓖ Ⓗ Ⓙ Ⓚ	92 Ⓕ Ⓖ Ⓗ Ⓙ Ⓚ
53 Ⓐ Ⓑ Ⓒ Ⓓ Ⓔ	73 Ⓐ Ⓑ Ⓒ Ⓓ Ⓔ	93 Ⓐ Ⓑ Ⓒ Ⓓ Ⓔ
54 Ⓕ Ⓖ Ⓗ Ⓙ Ⓚ	74 Ⓕ Ⓖ Ⓗ Ⓙ Ⓚ	94 Ⓕ Ⓖ Ⓗ Ⓙ Ⓚ
55 Ⓐ Ⓑ Ⓒ Ⓓ Ⓔ	75 Ⓐ Ⓑ Ⓒ Ⓓ Ⓔ	95 Ⓐ Ⓑ Ⓒ Ⓓ Ⓔ
56 Ⓕ Ⓖ Ⓗ Ⓙ Ⓚ	76 Ⓕ Ⓖ Ⓗ Ⓙ Ⓚ	96 Ⓕ Ⓖ Ⓗ Ⓙ Ⓚ
57 Ⓐ Ⓑ Ⓒ Ⓓ Ⓔ	77 Ⓐ Ⓑ Ⓒ Ⓓ Ⓔ	97 Ⓐ Ⓑ Ⓒ Ⓓ Ⓔ
58 Ⓕ Ⓖ Ⓗ Ⓙ Ⓚ	78 Ⓕ Ⓖ Ⓗ Ⓙ Ⓚ	98 Ⓕ Ⓖ Ⓗ Ⓙ Ⓚ
59 Ⓐ Ⓑ Ⓒ Ⓓ Ⓔ	79 Ⓐ Ⓑ Ⓒ Ⓓ Ⓔ	99 Ⓐ Ⓑ Ⓒ Ⓓ Ⓔ
60 Ⓕ Ⓖ Ⓗ Ⓙ Ⓚ	80 Ⓕ Ⓖ Ⓗ Ⓙ Ⓚ	100 Ⓕ Ⓖ Ⓗ Ⓙ Ⓚ
61 Ⓐ Ⓑ Ⓒ Ⓓ Ⓔ	81 Ⓐ Ⓑ Ⓒ Ⓓ Ⓔ	
62 Ⓕ Ⓖ Ⓗ Ⓙ Ⓚ	82 Ⓕ Ⓖ Ⓗ Ⓙ Ⓚ	
63 Ⓐ Ⓑ Ⓒ Ⓓ Ⓔ	83 Ⓐ Ⓑ Ⓒ Ⓓ Ⓔ	
64 Ⓕ Ⓖ Ⓗ Ⓙ Ⓚ	84 Ⓕ Ⓖ Ⓗ Ⓙ Ⓚ	
65 Ⓐ Ⓑ Ⓒ Ⓓ Ⓔ	85 Ⓐ Ⓑ Ⓒ Ⓓ Ⓔ	
66 Ⓕ Ⓖ Ⓗ Ⓙ Ⓚ	86 Ⓕ Ⓖ Ⓗ Ⓙ Ⓚ	
67 Ⓐ Ⓑ Ⓒ Ⓓ Ⓔ	87 Ⓐ Ⓑ Ⓒ Ⓓ Ⓔ	
68 Ⓕ Ⓖ Ⓗ Ⓙ Ⓚ	88 Ⓕ Ⓖ Ⓗ Ⓙ Ⓚ	
69 Ⓐ Ⓑ Ⓒ Ⓓ Ⓔ	89 Ⓐ Ⓑ Ⓒ Ⓓ Ⓔ	
70 Ⓕ Ⓖ Ⓗ Ⓙ Ⓚ	90 Ⓕ Ⓖ Ⓗ Ⓙ Ⓚ	

Model Test 1

PART 1—VERBAL

45 QUESTIONS

SUGGESTED TIME: 75 MINUTES

Scrambled Paragraphs

Paragraphs 1–5

> **Directions:** Below are six sentences that can be arranged to form a well-organized and grammatically correct paragraph. The first sentence is provided, but the other five are listed in random order. Choose the order that will form the **best** paragraph. Each correct paragraph is worth two points, with no partial credit given.
>
> You may wish to put numbers in the blanks at the left of each sentence to help keep track of the order. When you finish the set, mark your answers on the answer sheet.

PARAGRAPH 1

In surgery to remove a tumor, a young boy lost most of his right humerus—the upper arm bone—but doctors saved the arm by means of a groundbreaking procedure.

_____ (Q) The surgeons at the Joe Dimaggio Children's Hospital combined the two procedures: They used the little boy's fibula and fused it to the cadaver's humerus to provide added strength.

_____ (R) However, even though this procedure does restore movement to the limb, the dead bone cannot grow.

_____ (S) As a result the young patient will have an arm that grows naturally with the rest of his body plus protection against frequent fractures.

_____ (T) Previous cases of this kind had been treated by replacing the lost bone with similar bone from a cadaver.

_____ (U) Another approach, transplanting part of the patient's own fibula and attaching it to the remaining bone, allows for growth but carries a severe risk of fracture because the fibula is so thin.

PARAGRAPH 2

It's amusing to watch a squirrel try to reach suet or seed in a feeder protected by a good baffle—the circular kind that tilts and twirls at the slightest touch.

_____ (Q) Frequently this maneuver lands him in an undignified heap on the ground, but, undaunted, he tries again—often from the other side—and is again defeated.

_____ (R) Typically the animal romps easily up the feeder pole until he reaches the barrier; then he scrambles frantically around, vainly looking for a foothold.

_____ (S) If the owners of the bird feeder have planned carefully, however, he makes a few comical false starts and then goes off to find a less challenging meal.

_____ (T) His next approach is to climb to a higher vantage point, perhaps atop a lawn chair or a shrub, where he appears to study the odds of his making a successful leap.

_____ (U) Squirrels have an especially keen sense of smell that allows them to detect food that is far away, even food that is kept out of sight high at the top of a feeder pole.

PARAGRAPH 3

Years ago, when knowledge of ecology was much more primitive than it is today, wetlands were considered useless stretches of unpleasant mud and dirty water.

_____ (Q) It was a common and approved practice in those days to fill in such areas and build upon them; such "made" land was considered a vast improvement to the local geography.

_____ (R) Wetlands are also significant flood-control features, and they are so important as water reservoirs that severe water shortages are likely to result when large marshy acreages are drained.

_____ (S) The city of Boston, Massachusetts, for example, contains several square miles of neighborhoods that were built upon "made" land in the nineteenth century.

_____ (T) Teeming with life, they provide habitat and food for countless numbers and varieties of animal life and also serve as "nurseries" for species that spend their immature stages in marshy areas.

_____ (U) Now, however, wetlands are to some extent protected from this casual destruction because their importance to both wild and human life has become known.

PARAGRAPH 4

People have typically feared and avoided the bat because they thought it was likely to annoy them by getting tangled in their hair and harm them by drinking their blood and spreading rabies.

_____ (Q) Bats serve as good neighbors in several ways: They pollinate plants and disperse seeds, and they devour enormous numbers of noxious insects every night.

_____ (R) As untruths about these little creatures' habits are corrected and truths about their usefulness are promoted, bat houses have become additions to many neighborhoods.

_____ (S) The truth of the matter, however, is that although some bats do drink cattle blood and some fruit-eating bats do damage crops, the bat is for the most part a beneficial neighbor.

_____ (T) These structures built to attract the helpful mammal can be made from scratch or purchased; some are even given away free of charge by bat conservation societies.

_____ (U) Furthermore, bats won't annoy people by getting in their hair, and they are no more likely to carry rabies than any other animal susceptible to the disease.

PARAGRAPH 5

Although the English theater of the Renaissance owed much to the drama of classical Greece and Rome, English drama was fundamentally a homegrown art form with roots in the liturgical drama of the Middle Ages.

_____ (Q) The end of that century saw the introduction of dark and violent "revenge plays" in which the main character takes bloody vengeance against a wrongdoer and, in the process, usually brings tragedy upon himself as well.

_____ (R) In the fifteenth century the mystery play was replaced by the morality play, in which characters represent virtues and vices and are used to teach a moral lesson to the audience.

_____ (S) Usually produced by the local trade guilds, or unions, the plays, called mystery or miracle plays, presented a Bible story or a story about a saint, usually with non-Biblical plot elaborations and a great deal of slapstick humor.

_____ (T) During this period, church services sometimes included simple dramatizations of the Gospels, which were so popular that when they were eventually banned from church, they were continued by the townspeople.

_____ (U) Thus when the Elizabethan playwrights began to write, they were fortunate enough to be able to work with a combination of elements: the vigorous and home-grown plus the sophisticated and classical.

LOGICAL REASONING

Questions 11–20

> **Directions:** For each of the following questions, select the **best** answer from the given choices. Bubble in the letter corresponding to your answer on the answer sheet. Your answer should be based **only on the given information.**
>
> Read the words carefully. For example, "The red book is **to the right** of the blue book" does not necessarily mean that there is no other book between them. Similarly, be careful when reading words such as **between, below, above, after, before, behind,** and **ahead of.**

Questions 11, 12, and 13 refer to the following information.

Table I has 5 seats around it. Table II has 3 seats around it, and is not near table I. Eight people sit in those seats in accordance with the following wishes:

(1) Patrick and Peg are twins, and must sit next to each other. Joe and Judeah are twins, and must sit next to each other.

(2) The two sets of twins want to sit at different tables.

(3) Geo does not want to sit next to any of the twins.

(4) Anne does not want to sit next to Geo.

(5) Beth and Neil are happy to sit anywhere.

11. Which one of the following **must** be at table II?

A. Joe
B. Geo
C. Anne
D. Beth
E. Neil

12. Which one of the following pairs of people **must** be at different tables from one another?

F. Patrick and Geo
G. Joe and Geo
H. Joe and Anne
J. Joe and Beth
K. Anne and Beth

13. Which one of the following pairs of people **cannot** be seated next to one another?

A. Peg and Anne
B. Peg and Beth
C. Geo and Beth
D. Geo and Neil
E. Beth and Neil

Questions 14 and 15 refer to the following information.

In the code below, (1) each letter represents the same word in all 4 sentences, (2) each word is represented by only one letter, and (3) in any given sentence, the letter may or may not be presented in the same order as the words.

    P   *Q*   *R*   *S*   means "Barney may work Monday."

    P   *T*   *S*   *Q*   means "Barney may work Tuesday."

    U   *P*   *S*   *V*   means "I work with Barney."

    W   *V*   *P*   *Q*   means "I may work today."

14. The letter that represents the word "may" is

F. *P*
G. *Q*
H. *R*
J. *S*
K. Cannot be determined from the information given.

15. Which word is represented by the letter *U*?

    A. today
    B. work
    C. with
    D. Barney
    E. Cannot be determined from the information given.

16. If Merrie is sleeping, then she is not a pest. No pest is likable.

    Based only on the information above, which of the following **must** be true?

    F. If Merrie is awake, then she is a pest.
    G. Merrie is not likable.
    H. Merrie is likable if she is not sleeping.
    J. No likable person is a pest.
    K. If a person is a pest, then they are not sleeping.

Questions 17 and 18 refer to the following information.

    Joel, Rick, Helen, and Lee each engage in one or more of the following activities: swimming, jumping, and running. Furthermore,

    (1) Joel swims and jumps.
    (2) people who can run can't jump.
    (3) Rick can't jump and Lee can't swim.

17. What is the smallest number of these people who are definitely engaged in running?

    A. 0
    B. 1
    C. 2
    D. 3
    E. All 4

18. What is the greatest number of these people who **could** be engaged in running?

    F. 0
    G. 1
    H. 2
    J. 3
    K. All 4

19. Below are two word pairs. The words in each pair are related in some way. The relationship between the words in the first pair is similar to the relationship between the words in the second pair.

    lightbulb—lamp
    battery—flashlight

    What is the relationship displayed in both word pairs?

    A. Inventions for lighting things
    B. Things that glow in the dark
    C. Objects that are found in homes and stores
    D. Things that are powered by electricity
    E. Components of objects that produce light

20. We will call a number "special" if it has property *S*. We will call a number "nice" if it has property *N*. The number 101 is a "special" number. Hannah said that 101 is also "nice."

    Which of the following choices, if true, guarantees that Hannah's statement is valid?

    F. A number having property *N* will always have property *S*.
    G. "Special" numbers can also be "nice."
    H. All numbers greater than 96 that have property *S* are also "nice."
    J. There is only one "special" number that is also "nice."
    K. The smallest number that is both "special" and "nice" is 97.

READING

Questions 21–50

Directions: Read each passage and answer the questions that follow it. Base your answers **only on the material contained in the passage.** Select the one **best** answer for each question. Bubble in the letter corresponding to that answer on the answer sheet.

Read each of the following passages and answer the questions that follow it. Base your answers only on the material contained in the passages. Do not rely on memory alone: verify each answer by checking the passage. Select the one best response for each question.

I. One of the most remarkable creatures ever to live on Earth is the despised cockroach. When people see cockroaches in
Line their homes, they stomp them, spray them
(5) with poison, set traps for them—anything to get rid of the hated brown insects. But the battle is often a losing one, and for good reason. Cockroaches have a superb ability to survive, an ability that has made them
(10) thrive on Earth for millions and millions of years.

Living fossils, cockroaches were crawling around on Earth 320 million years ago, about 150 million years before dinosaurs
(15) appeared. They even have an era named after them, the Age of Cockroaches, otherwise known as the Carboniferous period. Because of their adaptability, including their willingness to eat almost anything
(20) available, they have seen many species come and go.

The easygoing food habits of cockroaches are due to the variety of organisms dwelling in their digestive tract. These bacteria and
(25) protozoans enable the insects to eat a wide range of matter, including flower buds, leaf litter, feces, paper, glue, paint, soap, and wood. They will eat their own shed skin, cockroach eggs, and even other cock-
(30) roaches.

Unusual survival skills have promoted the success of this order of insects. Cockroaches have adapted to most of Earth's environments. They live in the desert, in the forest,
(35) in underground burrows, in electrical equipment, and in almost any kind of human habitation—including space capsules. They can live without food and water for a month and can survive on only water
(40) for two months. If they have dry food, they can go without water for five months. And they have good defenses against enemies. Their eyes are extremely sensitive and their bodies are equipped with extra warning
(45) devices—sense organs that detect the tiniest motion in the air. A fetid odor keeps some potential predators away and hard, compressible bodies make them amazingly tough.

(50) Although most human beings shudder at them, cockroaches play an important role in both natural and artificial settings. Most species prefer to live outdoors where they aid in decomposition of vegetable matter
(55) and animal feces. Furthermore, in spite of their built-in protection devices, they are significant in the food chain, being eaten by many animals, including (in some circumstances) human beings. In the laboratory
(60) they are docile and easy to handle, and they are cooperative research subjects in areas such as disease and nutrition studies.

21. Which of the following is the best title for this passage?

A. "The Amazing Eating Machine"
B. "Survivor and Contributor"
C. "The Pest and the Dinosaur"
D. "The Living Fossil"
E. "The Immortal Cockroach"

22. According to the passage, which of the following is **not** true of the cockroach?

 F. Most of them are outdoor insects.
 G. They lived on Earth at the same time as dinosaurs.
 H. They are used in scientific research.
 J. They can eat anything.
 K. They are well equipped for survival.

23. What does the passage suggest about cockroaches?

 A. Humans may find them bad-smelling.
 B. It would be good if they could be eradicated.
 C. They live everywhere on Earth.
 D. They are important in space research.
 E. They cause environmental damage.

24. What is meant by the expression "they have seen many species come and go" (lines 20–21)?

 F. They have lived on Earth before and after some extinct species.
 G. They have acute eyesight.
 H. They lived on Earth long before the dinosaurs and are still living on Earth.
 J. They can perceive approaching enemies and escape them.
 K. They can live in both artificial and natural habitats.

25. Which of the following best explains why cockroaches are such a successful insect?

 A. Most insects are amazingly successful creatures.
 B. They have excellent defense mechanisms.
 C. They are adaptable and well protected.
 D. They are significant factors in the ecology.
 E. They evolved long before most other creatures now living on Earth.

26. Why can cockroaches eat so many different kinds of foods?

 F. Their taste buds are adaptable.
 G. They live in a wide variety of habitats.
 H. They are basically easygoing, docile creatures.
 J. They do not have highly developed sensory organs except those for eyesight.
 K. Their bodies contain organisms that help them process a variety of matter.

II. In the centuries just before Rome converted to Christianity, two philosophies were very influential there. One was Epicur-
Line eanism, founded in Greece early in the
(5) fourth century B.C. by the philosopher Epicurus. The other was Stoicism, which originated in Cyprus around the same time. Both taught that the highest good in life is a state of inner tranquility that one can achieve
(10) by conquering anxieties and passions.

Both schools of thought were materialistic. That is, they taught that everything that exists is composed of matter. They did not recognize a spiritual world. The Epicurean
(15) universe contained empty space and matter composed of atoms and compounds. Not only the human body, but also the human soul was thought to be material. Epicurus taught that death brings an end to both. The
(20) Stoics also considered both body and soul to be composed of matter. However, they believed that there is a dynamic force they called the Logos. It also consists of matter, according to them, but it is the source of the
(25) human soul's ability to reason.

Epicureanism taught that pleasure is the ultimate goal of life. Some versions of this philosophy emphasized bodily pleasure and self-indulgence. But Epicurus argued that
(30) intellectual pleasure is a greater good than physical pleasure. According to Epicurus, true pleasure depends on inner serenity. People can achieve the serene state by controlling impulses and desires, behaving in
(35) moderation, and freeing themselves from

attachments and fears. It is especially important, he maintained, to conquer fear of death and of the gods. Epicurus explained that since death is merely the end (40) of existence, it should not be frightening. He also taught that the gods are too far removed from human life to affect it in any way.

Stoicism taught that one should strive for a (45) "tranquil soul" free of all anxiety and fear. The major key to the tranquil soul, according to the Stoics, is to be moderate in all things. Wisdom, courage, and justice, however, were also considered crucial. The (50) Stoics saw a divine order in the universe. They taught that people can live in harmony with the divine order by letting reason—that is, Logos—guide their lives.

Since Logos, the dynamic source of reason, (55) was thought to be a part of all human beings, all human souls are related. Each people should feel equal to all other people and connected to all others. A sense of equality and relatedness should lead a person to act (60) according to the rule of brotherly love.

27. Which of the following best states the author's purpose?

   A. To show contrasts between Epicureanism and Stoicism
   B. To explain the origin of the doctrine of brotherly love
   C. To demonstrate how philosophical teachings can be misunderstood
   D. To explain the basic teachings of two ancient philosophies
   E. To set forth the foundations of Christianity

28. Which of the following is not a principle of Epicureanism?

   F. Materialism
   G. The existence of Logos
   H. The importance of pleasure
   J. The need to achieve serenity
   K. The mortality of the soul

29. According to Stoicism, why should people treat others with brotherly love?

   A. Because there is a divine order in the universe
   B. Because wisdom and justice are important virtues
   C. Because love leads to intellectual pleasure
   D. Because there is no spiritual world, and people must depend on each other
   E. Because all people are related and equal

30. According to Epicurus, why should people not fear the gods?

   F. Because they are kind gods of brotherly love
   G. Because there is no afterlife and therefore no punishment for sin
   H. Because the gods have nothing to do with human life
   J. Because Logos joins humankind to the gods
   K. Because pleasure erases fear

31. Which of the following is a similarity between Epicureanism and Stoicism?

   A. Belief in a universal order ordained by the gods
   B. Rejection of the idea of a spiritual world
   C. Belief in Logos
   D. Belief that pleasure is the proper goal of life
   E. The ideal of brotherly love

32. Which of the following is an example of Stoic behavior?

   F. Avoiding excessive eating and drinking
   G. Striving for pleasures of the mind
   H. Developing the spiritual aspect of one's nature
   J. Giving away one's worldly goods
   K. Meditating upon Logos

III. For several decades the novels of Louisa May Alcott were a favorite among young readers, especially girls. Her most famous *Line* book, *Little Women,* is still popular in print (5) as well as in its three or four film versions. Most of her works tell of the trials and joys of young people in nineteenth-century New England. *Little Women,* for example, a novel based on her own early life and the (10) early lives of her three sisters, tells of the struggles of a close-knit family during and after the Civil War. To some modern readers Alcott's stories seem sentimental and moralistic, for she sometimes exaggerates (15) emotion, and she sprinkles her narratives with little sermons. But her emotional scenes can still make readers cry, and her heartwarming vignettes of domestic happiness can still bring smiles to their faces.

(20) The author was born in Germantown, Pennsylvania, but grew up in Boston. Her father, Bronson Alcott, was a well-known philosopher and educator with radical ideas. Dissatisfied with contemporary edu- (25) cational practices, he developed an innovative teaching method and put it into practice in his own school, which he opened in 1834. His method used conversation instead of drill and memorization in (30) the teaching of young children. In spite of much negative criticism of his system, he managed to keep the school open for five years.

Although Bronson Alcott went on to (35) become well known as a philosopher, lecturer, and leader in the movement for the abolition of slavery, he was a poor provider for his family. The family seldom had more than the basic necessities, and the female (40) members of the family had to work hard to provide those. In fact it is said that during one particularly hard winter they would have starved if friends had not given them food.

(45) Their poverty motivated Louisa to venture into a field that would startle some of her fans. Pulp magazines were good markets for thrillers—stories with plenty of action and suspense and, often, violence. Although the (50) magazines were cheap and of inferior quality, they paid well, and Louisa needed the money to help her family. She became a frequent contributor to this market, but always under assumed names. In *Little* (55) *Women,* Jo, the main character, helps her family financially by selling stories to the pulp magazines. She stops after a friend, not knowing who the author is, harshly criticizes one of her thrillers. Motivated to (60) write something better, she produces a warm and highly moral narrative based on her own family!

33. Which of the following best tells what this passage is about?

   A. The poor family of a famous man
   B. The motives of a famous author
   C. The background and work of Louisa May Alcott
   D. How *Little Women* came to be written
   E. The contrast between two kinds of fiction

34. What are pulp magazines?

   F. Nineteenth-century magazines using paper made from pulpwood
   G. A magazine of the kind that first published *Little Women*
   H. An inexpensive magazine produced for a young but well-educated audience
   J. A magazine of poor quality that published sensational fiction
   K. A bulky magazine containing many stories of various kinds

35. What does the passage suggest about the novels of Louisa May Alcott?

   A. They are not as popular today as they used to be.
   B. They are sensational but enjoyable.
   C. In their own day they were considered too sentimental.
   D. She wrote them because she could not make money any other way.
   E. Most of them are about her own life.

36. Which of the following is **not** stated about Bronson Alcott?

    F. He operated his own school for a time.

    G. He struggled unsuccessfully to support his family.

    H. He was a philosopher.

    J. He provided leadership for a social cause.

    K. He was a public speaker.

37. Why did Louisa May Alcott begin writing sensational fiction?

    A. She wanted to start out in a highly lucrative market.

    B. She needed the money it could provide.

    C. Such fiction had a large readership.

    D. She wanted to train for the writing of her first novel.

    E. She wanted to cheer up her family.

38. Which of the following is true about most of the main characters in the novels of Alcott?

    F. They are young.

    G. They are all based on her own family.

    H. They are sensationalized.

    J. They are immoral.

    K. They read sermons to each other.

IV. The land of Mesopotamia, centered around the valley of the Tigris and Euphrates rivers, has been called "the cradle *Line* of civilization." Western civilization had its
(5) beginnings there and in the surrounding areas, which produced the great cultures of Phoenicia, India, Persia, and Egypt. Even in earlier prehistoric times, Mesopotamia saw important beginnings, for it is thought that
(10) the people of this land were the first to develop agriculture. And ages ago a Mesopotamian people called the Sumerians gave the Western world its first system of writing.

(15) The Sumerians moved into the Tigris-Euphrates region six or seven thousand years ago and settled in the delta at the confluence of the two rivers. It was a muddy area, and over the centuries the Sumerians
(20) made the most of mud as a resource. They drained land to build on and channeled water into irrigation ditches. They turned the mud into bricks with which they built protective walls, dwellings and temples, and
(25) they also used it to create superior pottery and terra-cotta sculpture. The Sumerians even wrote on mud, shaping it into soft tablets on which they carved the first letters of Western civilization, wedge-shaped char-
(30) acters called *cuneiform*.

Each prosperous Sumerian city-state was built around an elevated temple dedicated to a god whose representative ruled the city. Sumerian gods were distant from the peo-
(35) ple and sometimes cruel, reflecting perhaps the harsh conditions in which their subjects lived. The floods, storms, and wild beasts that threatened the people and sometimes overwhelmed them must have seemed like
(40) manifestations of supernatural power. Nor did the Sumerians have the comfort of an afterlife to look forward to, for in their religion death brought only gloomy darkness.

A story in the Sumerian epic *Gilgamesh*
(45) reflects this people's beliefs about life and death. The hero Gilgamesh's beloved friend Enkidu has just died, and Gilgamesh is so inconsolable at his loss that for seven days and nights he refuses to give up his friend's
(50) body for burial. After he finally relents, he goes on a long journey to the underworld, seeking the goddess who he thinks can grant him immortality. But the answer given him by all those he meets on his jour-
(55) ney is "You will never find that life that you seek." He is told to go home and to make the best of his life. He is to love those close to him and to make them happy. When he returns home, he is reminded of his great
(60) achievements; and when he dies, he is cherished in the memory of his people.

39. Which of the following best tells what the passage is about?

   A. The invention of writing
   B. The history of "the cradle of civilization"
   C. A civilization that flourished in Mesopotamia
   D. The quest of the hero Gilgamesh
   E. Religion and customs of the ancient Sumerians

40. What is the most likely reason why Gilgamesh goes to the underworld?

   F. The death of Enkidu has made him afraid of dying.
   G. He thinks that as a hero he deserves special consideration.
   H. He wants one more achievement to add to his heroic deeds.
   J. He is a hero and wishes to go where no one has gone before.
   K. He is seeking the secret of happiness.

41. Why did the Sumerians make so many things out of mud?

   A. It was easier to work with than stone.
   B. They wanted to use it up.
   C. It was easy to write on.
   D. It made colorful pottery and sculpture.
   E. It was their most abundant material.

42. Which of the following best describes the Sumerians' attitude toward their gods?

   F. Mystical devotion and adoration
   G. Respect and fear
   H. Personal love
   J. Confident dependence
   K. Indifference

43. In addition to writing, what other Mesopotamian invention does the passage mention?

   A. Temples
   B. Pottery
   C. Terra-cotta sculpture
   D. Agriculture
   E. Irrigation

44. According to the passage, what kind of lives did the Sumerians live?

   F. Adventurous and bold
   G. Comfortable
   H. Helpless and terrified
   J. Happy and optimistic
   K. Prosperous but often difficult

V. French Impressionism was one of the most controversial artistic movements of modern times. The Impressionists were nineteenth-century painters who rebelled (5) against the strict rules of classical art laid down by the French Academy. According to eighteenth-century standards, acceptable paintings had to be executed in smooth, precise lines. Except for formal portraits, art (10) had to depict subjects above the level of common life—for example, mythology and history. The Impressionists cast off these restrictions, using experimental techniques to produce spontaneous-looking (15) representations of outdoor scenes and everyday life.

The aim of these rebels was to reproduce what the eye actually sees rather than to give an exact rendering of form. For this (20) reason they studied light and its effects on colors and shapes and strove to represent these effects on canvas. Some Impressionists would paint several pictures of a scene at different times of the day to catch the vary- (25) ing influences of the light. One of their discoveries was that shadows are not always tones of black or brown but tend to contain reflections of the colors in nearby objects. Another discovery was that light can soften (30) the outlines of objects, making shapes appear less precise to the eye than they actually are, and causing the eye to overlook some detail.

The resulting paintings embody techniques (35) drastically different from those used in classical art. Brushstrokes do not carefully outline a shape; rather they suggest it, often with short, side-by-side touches of different colors. These tints look separate only upon

(40) close examination, blending when viewed from farther away. Colors are especially radiant because the artists would lay two contrasting primary colors next to each other on the canvas instead of blending
(45) them beforehand on a pallette.

The Impressionists organized their first joint exhibition in 1874. Although some of the public were enthusiastic about this new kind of painting, the establishment was
(50) scornful of such radical work. In fact, the term "Impressionist" comes from an excoriating review of Claude Monet's painting *Impression: Sunrise,* in which the critic condemned the work as being not a work of
(55) art, but rather an art-less impression, and dubbed the painters not arists, but "impressionists." Rather than denouncing this label for their work, the new school adopted it. In 1877, for the third exhibition of their
(60) paintings, the artists themselves described their work as Impressionist. Appreciated at first by other artists and by a small segment of the public, Impressionism gradually gained ground, finally earning acceptance
(65) among both the general public and the critics.

45. Which of the following is the best title for the passage?

   A. "Light Effects in Art"
   B. "A Classical Style"
   C. "Success at Last"
   D. "A New Movement in Art"
   E. "The Influence of Impressionism"

46. Which of the following is **not** a feature of Impressionist art?

   F. Short strokes
   G. Contrasting colors side-by-side
   H. Precise outlines
   J. Brilliant color effects
   K. Outdoor scenes

47. Why did the public and the critics not like Impressionism at first?

   A. They thought it was too classical.
   B. It did not follow the established standards.
   C. They felt that there was too much study behind it.
   D. They felt it was too colorful.
   E. They felt it used too much light.

48. Which of the following best expresses what the Impressionists were trying to accomplish?

   F. To shake up the establishment
   G. To paint more realistic portraits
   H. To achieve unusual color effects
   J. To depict what the eye really sees
   K. To experiment with light

49. What is the meaning of "excoriating" (lines 51–52)?

   A. Harshly critical
   B. Puzzling
   C. Humorous
   D. Reluctant
   E. Admiring

50. Why did some Impressionists paint the same scene at different times of the day?

   F. They were trying to achieve perfection.
   G. They were trying to duplicate the blacks and browns of shadows.
   H. They liked painting outdoor scenes.
   J. They were trying to learn more about the effects of light.
   K. They were trying to create sharper images.

PART 2—MATHEMATICS

QUESTIONS 51–100

SUGGESTED TIME: 75 MINUTES

Directions: For each of the following questions, select the **best** answer from the given choices. Bubble in the letter corresponding to your answer on the answer sheet. **DO NOT PUT ANY OTHER WORK ON THE ANSWER SHEET.** All necessary work can be done in your test booklet or on scrap paper that is provided.

NOTE: Diagrams other than graphs might not be drawn to scale. Do not assume any relationships that are not specifically stated unless they are implied by the given information.

51. $(3 + 4)^2 =$

  A. 13
  B. 14
  C. 19
  D. 25
  E. 49

52. The exact value of $\sqrt{49} - \sqrt{24}$ is

  F. 2.
  G. between 2 and 5.
  H. 5.
  J. more than 5.
  K. The expression does not have an exact value.

53. 200% of 7 is

  A. .14
  B. 7
  C. 14
  D. 21
  E. 1,400

54. (All line segments are either horizontal or vertical, as shown.) The perimeter of the figure is

  F. 5
  G. 6
  H. 7
  J. 12
  K. 14

55. What is the value of N if $\frac{1}{5} - \frac{1}{6} = \frac{1}{N}$?

  A. 7
  B. 30
  C. $\frac{1}{30}$
  D. −30
  E. $\frac{-1}{30}$

56. Find the value of $(2^4 - 4^2) + (2^3 - 3^2)$.

  F. −11
  G. −8
  H. −1
  J. 0
  K. 1

57. On the number line shown, Q (not shown) is the midpoint of $\overline{PR}$. What is the midpoint of $\overline{QS}$?

  A. −5
  B. −4
  C. 0
  D. 1
  E. 8

58. The ratio of boys to girls at a dance was 2 to 3. If 45 girls attended, what is the number of boys who attended?

   F. 9
   G. 18
   H. 27
   J. 30
   K. 45

59. If the measure of angle A is 40°, then $x + y =$

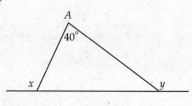

   A. 80°
   B. 120°
   C. 180°
   D. 220°
   E. 360°

60. If $6x$ is increased by $4y$, and the sum is divided by 2, the result is equivalent to

   F. $3x + 4y$
   G. $6x + 2y$
   H. $3x + 2y$
   J. $\dfrac{10x + y}{2}$
   K. $5(x + y)$

61. If $a*b$ means a^b, then $2*(3*2)$ is

   A. 512
   B. 256
   C. 81
   D. 64
   E. 12

62. Let n be an integer from 9 to 38. For *how many* values of n will $\dfrac{n}{5}$ be a prime?

   F. 3
   G. 4
   H. 6
   J. 8
   K. 29

63. $|2 - 8| - |7 - 3| =$

   A. −10
   B. −2
   C. 2
   D. 10
   E. none of these.

64. Mary is m years old now. Joe is 3 years younger than Mary. Express Joe's age 10 years from now in terms of m.

   F. $13 - m$
   G. $m - 3$
   H. $m + 7$
   J. $m + 10$
   K. $m + 13$

65. The smaller angle between the hands of a clock at 10:00 is

   A. 15°
   B. 30°
   C. 45°
   D. 60°
   E. 75°

66. Find the smallest positive integer that is a multiple of both 21 and 77.

   F. 7
   G. 33
   H. 98
   J. 231
   K. 1,617

67. Over which interval was the growth in the value of the stock of the ABC Company *most* rapid?

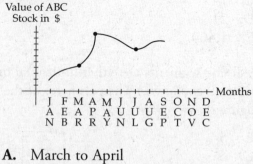

   A. March to April
   B. April to May
   C. May to June
   D. June to July
   E. July to August

68. Express the *sum* of 1.2×10^2 and 1.2×10^3 in scientific notation.

    F. 0.144×10^6
    G. 1.32×10^3
    H. 1.44×10^5
    J. 2.4×10^5
    K. 2.4×10^6

69. Today is Saturday. What day of the week will it be 65 days from today?

    A.   Sunday
    B.   Monday
    C.   Tuesday
    D.   Wednesday
    E.   Thursday

70. The circles are "tangent" to the rectangle and to each other, as shown. If the area of each circle is 16π, then the area of the rectangle is

    F.   32
    G.   48
    H.   96
    J.   128
    K.   512

71. Thirty of the fifty students who took an exam received a grade of 90% or greater. What percentage of those fifty students received a grade of less than 90%?

    A.   70
    B.   35
    C.   40
    D.   30
    E.   10

72. Let n be a number from -3 to 4 inclusive. What is the range of values of n^2?

    F. $-9 \leq n^2 \leq 16$
    G. $9 \leq n^2 \leq 16$
    H. $3 \leq n^2 \leq 4$
    J. $0 \leq n^2 \leq 2$
    K. $0 \leq n^2 \leq 16$

73. A is 3 times C. B is 8 less than C. For what value of C does $A = B$?

    A. -4
    B.   0
    C.   1
    D.   2
    E. $\dfrac{5}{2}$

74. In a class of 28 students, everyone likes math, English, or both. If 17 like math and 19 like English, how many like both?

    F.   2
    G.   8
    H.   16
    J.   20
    K.   28

75. Let $x = 3^2 \cdot 5^3 \cdot 7^4$ and $y = 2^3 \cdot 3 \cdot 5^2$. What is the greatest common factor of x and y?

    A. $2 \cdot 3 \cdot 5 \cdot 7$
    B. $2^3 \cdot 3^2 \cdot 5^3 \cdot 7^4$
    C. $3 \cdot 5$
    D. $3 \cdot 5^2$
    E. $3^2 \cdot 5^3$

76. The equation $2(3x + 8) = 3(2x + 4)$ is satisfied by

    F.   no value of x.
    G.   only negative values of x.
    H.   only $x = 0$.
    J.   only positive values of x.
    K.   all values of x.

77. In the formula $V = s^2h$, if s is doubled and h is tripled, then V is multiplied by

    A.   5
    B.   6
    C.   12
    D.   18
    E.   36

Model Test 1

78. You have 10 large boxes that can each hold 8 soccer balls, and 10 small boxes that can each hold 5 of the same soccer balls. If you have 99 soccer balls, what is the greatest number of boxes you can completely fill?

   F. 13
   G. 14
   H. 15
   J. 16
   K. 19

79. The straight line graph shows the relationship between number of hours worked and amount earned. How much would be earned for 50 hours of work?

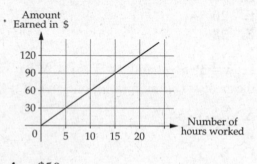

   A. $50
   B. $83
   C. $120
   D. $150
   E. $300

80. The perimeter of a triangle, all of whose sides have integer length, is 19. A possible length for the largest side is

   F. 6
   G. 8
   H. 10
   J. 15
   K. 17

81. A value of x that satisfies the inequality $2x - 10 > 3x$ is

   A. −11
   B. −10
   C. −1
   D. 0
   E. 12

82. The midpoints of the four sides of square *ABCD* are joined to form square *WXYZ* as shown. The area of square *WXYZ* is 16. The area of triangle *YCX* is

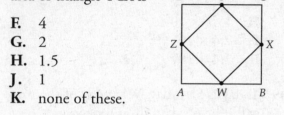

   F. 4
   G. 2
   H. 1.5
   J. 1
   K. none of these.

83. The mean of 3 numbers is 7. The mean of 4 other numbers is 8. The mean of 5 other numbers is 11. What is the mean of all 12 numbers?

   A. 4
   B. $4\frac{2}{13}$
   C. $8\frac{2}{3}$
   D. 9
   E. 36

84. There were 20 socks in a drawer. Of these, 8 were blue, 10 were black, and 2 were white. Someone then removed 4 blue socks. If one sock is now drawn at random, what is the probability that it is *not* white?

   F. $\frac{1}{10}$
   G. $\frac{9}{10}$
   H. $\frac{1}{8}$
   J. $\frac{7}{8}$
   K. None of these

85. Two sides of a right triangle are 3 and 4. The third side is

   A. 1
   B. 3
   C. 5
   D. 7
   E. not uniquely determined.

86. A cube 3 by 3 by 3 is painted red on all six faces and then cut into 27 smaller 1 by 1 by 1 cubes. How many of these new smaller cubes have exactly two faces that are painted red?

    F. 6
    G. 8
    H. 12
    J. 21
    K. 27

87. If 2 blobs = 3 glops and 3 blobs = 2 chunks, then 1 chunk =

    A. 1 glop

    B. $\frac{2}{3}$ glop

    C. $\frac{3}{2}$ glops

    D. $\frac{4}{9}$ glop

    E. $\frac{9}{4}$ glops

88. and 89. The two pie charts show the ice cream flavor preferences of the students at two high schools.

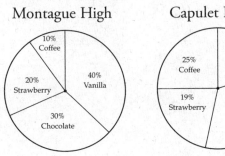

Montague High   Capulet High

88. The ratio of Montague students who prefer vanilla to Montague students who prefer chocolate is

    F. 10:9
    G. 4:3
    H. 3:10
    J. 3:4
    K. 2:5

89. If the *number* of Montague students who prefer vanilla is M and the *number* of Capulet students who prefer vanilla is C, then

    A. $M > 2C$
    B. $M = 2C$
    C. $M = C$
    D. $M < C$
    E. The relationship cannot be determined from the given information.

90. If x is an integer, which one of the following *must* be odd?

    F. $3x + 1$
    G. $3x + 2$
    H. $4x - 1$
    J. $4x - 2$
    K. $5x - 2x$

91. In the sequence of numbers 1, 2, 2, 3, 3, 3,. . . [assume the pattern of one 1, two 2s, three 3s, four 4s, and so on continues], the number in the 40th position will be

    A. 8
    B. 9
    C. 10
    D. 11
    E. 40

92. Each side of a square is an integral number of inches, and its area is 576 square inches. If each side of the square is increased by 1 *foot,* forming a new square, the area of the new square, in square *inches,* is

    F. 577
    G. 588
    H. 720
    J. 1,296
    K. not determined.

93. Let $P = \frac{18}{25}$, $Q = \frac{5}{7}$, and $R = \frac{3}{4}$. Then

    A. $P < Q < R$
    B. $P < R < Q$
    C. $Q < P < R$
    D. $Q < R < P$
    E. $R < P < Q$

94. A water container is $\frac{3}{4}$ full. After 20 ounces of water is removed, the container is $\frac{1}{4}$ full. How many ounces of water does a full container hold?

    F. 20
    G. 40
    H. 60
    J. 80
    K. 100

95. For *how many* integer values of n will the expression $\frac{n-10}{14-n}$ have a positive value?

    A. 0
    B. 1
    C. 3
    D. 4
    E. 5

96. A square of side 4 is topped by a semicircle, as shown. Point P is the center of the arc at the top. Then the shaded area is equal to

    F. $\pi + 2$

    G. $\frac{\pi}{2} + 2$

    H. $2\pi + 2$
    J. $2\pi - 4$
    K. $2\pi + 4$

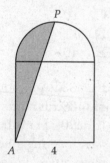

97. $\dfrac{4^{6} \times 3^{4} \times 2^{2}}{4^{2} \times 3^{4} \times 2^{6}} =$

    A. 1
    B. 2
    C. 8
    D. 16
    E. 24

98. Which one of the following numbers is *less* than $\frac{1}{3}$?

    F. $\frac{1111}{3333}$

    G. $\frac{299}{895}$

    H. $.1 \times 4$
    J. $.4 \times 1$

    K. $\frac{5!}{6!}$

99. The ratio of a to b is 3 to 4. The ratio of b to c is 5 to 6. The ratio of a to c is

    A. 9:10
    B. 5:8
    C. 1:2
    D. 2:5
    E. none of these.

100. (All lines shown are either vertical or horizontal.) If x and y are integers, and the shaded area is 52, then the perimeter of the figure is

    F. 20
    G. 24
    H. 52
    J. 56
    K. 196

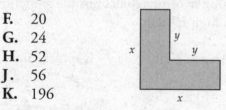

Answer Key
MODEL TEST 1

Scrambled Paragraphs

Paragraph 1 TRUQS
Paragraph 2 URQTS
Paragraph 3 QSUTR
Paragraph 4 SQURT
Paragraph 5 TSRQU

Logical Reasoning

11. C	16. J
12. K	17. A
13. E	18. J
14. G	19. E
15. C	20. H

Reading

21. B	29. E	37. B	44. K
22. J	30. H	38. F	45. D
23. A	31. B	39. C	46. H
24. F	32. F	40. F	47. B
25. C	33. C	41. E	48. J
26. K	34. J	42. G	49. A
27. D	35. A	43. D	50. J
28. G	36. G		

Mathematics

51. E	61. A	71. C	81. A	91. B
52. G	62. G	72. K	82. F	92. J
53. C	63. C	73. A	83. D	93. C
54. K	64. H	74. G	84. J	94. G
55. B	65. D	75. D	85. E	95. C
56. H	66. J	76. F	86. H	96. F
57. D	67. A	77. C	87. E	97. D
58. J	68. G	78. J	88. G	98. K
59. D	69. B	79. E	89. E	99. B
60. H	70. J	80. G	90. H	100. J

ANSWER EXPLANATIONS
MODEL TEST 1

Scrambled Paragraphs

Paragraph 1   TRUQS

All of the sentences involve arm bones in some way. The subject is introduced in the inital sentence along with "a young boy" who has lost bone. T has the transitional phrase "cases of this kind" and describes a procedure for replacing the lost bone. R tells about the drawback of the procedure.

> **TIP:** Look for transitional words and phrases.

U begins with another transitional phrase, "Another approach," and describes a second procedure with its drawback. Q logically follows because it describes a third operation, which "combines the two procedures." S concludes the paragraph with a result that has neither of the previously described drawbacks.

Paragraph 2   URQTS

U is the second sentence; it explains how the squirrel detects the food but does not yet describe how he attempts to reach it. R is the third sentence because it describes the squirrel confidently approaching the suet, discovering the problem, and making a first attempt at solving it. Q has the transitional phrase "this maneuver" referring to the squirrel's scrambling and searching for a foothold. T logically follows, giving a "next approach." S concludes the paragraph with the squirrel giving up and looking for other food.

Paragraph 3   QSUTR

U looks tempting as a second sentence with its transitional "now, however," but the second sentence has to be Q because Q tells of practices that resulted from the old idea. S, which provides an example of "made" land, is third.

> **TIP:** Read all the sentences before deciding on the order.

U with its "Now, however" comes fourth and gives the newer idea, that wetlands are important. T logically follows because it states important features of wetlands. R also gives important features, but the transitional word "also" indicates that R must follow T and conclude the paragraph.

Paragraph 4   SQURT

The sentences all concern bat behavior and relations between bats and people. S corrects the misconception in the initial sentence by giving "The truth of the matter—that the bat is a beneficial neighbor." "Beneficial neighbor" links S to the similar phrase "good neighbor" in Q.

> **TIP:** Look for words and phrases that serve as transitions.

Q states ways in which bats are good neighbors. U comes next because it contains other correct information about bat behavior. "Furthermore" is the connecting link to Q. R is next, bringing together the information in S, Q, and U and stating a new bat-human relationship. T concludes the paragraph with more information on bat houses.

Paragraph 5   TSRQU

This paragraph has clear chronological clues, but even if you don't know the chronology, there are enough transitions to guide you through the problem. T is linked to the initial sentence by two transitions, the phrase "this period" and the word "church," which links to "liturgical." S logically follows by specifying the townspeople who continued the dramatizations, or plays. S also calls the plays "mystery or miracles plays." R and Q move forward in time by giving later plays that replaced the mystery plays. U concludes with the transitional word "thus" and a shift back to the time period mentioned in the first sentence.

Logical Reasoning

Solutions in this section frequently involve techniques discussed in Skillbuilder B.

11–13. (C,K,E) Draw a 5-sided table and a 3-sided one. Using the first letter of each name to represent the people, we put *P* and *P* next to each other at one table, and *J* and *J* at the other. This satisfies requirements (1) and (2). Now because of (3), *G* must be at table I, not next to either twin. Requirement (4) makes *A* the final person at table II. This leaves two non-adjacent seats at table I for *B* and *N*. We can now answer all the questions. Note that we do not know which set of twins is at a particular table.

11. **(C)**

12. **(K)**

13. **(E)**

14–15. **(G,C)** Remember to **mark your sentences** in this type of logical reasoning problem.

14. **(G)** The word "may" is in sentences 1, 2, and 4. Letter *Q* is the only one in exactly those sentences, so the correct choice is G.

15. **(C)** The letter *U* is just in sentence 3. The only word that is in that sentence and no other is "with," so the correct choice is C.

16. **(J)** Let *S* represent "Merrie is sleeping," *P* represent "being a pest," and *L* represent "being likable."

    The given statements can now be written as *S* → ~*P* and *P* → ~*L*. The choices are (F) ~*S* → *P*, (G) a statement about Merrie that is not tied to her being asleep or awake, (H) ~*S* → *L*, (J) *L* → ~*P*, and (K) a statement about *P* that is tied to people in general sleeping, but not tied to *S*, which is Merrie sleeping. The correct choice is J, which is the contrapositive of the original second statement. In this example, the original first statement does not contribute to the final answer.

17,18. **(A,J)** Make a chart whose rows are labeled *J, R, H*, and *L* (for the people) and whose columns are labeled *swim, jump*, and *run* (using initial letters could confuse the activities with some of the people's initials). Mark your chart according to given facts. Be careful with (2). It tells you that an X must go into *J*'s run box (because if *J* could run, he could not

jump). Do not put anything in *R*'s run box. ("People who can run can't jump" is **not** the same as "people who can't jump can run.") We can now answer the questions.

17. **(A)** We don't know if anyone at all is engaged in running.

18. **(J)** It is possible that everyone but Joel is engaged in running.

19. **(E)** This is the only choice that relates the first word of each pair to the second word of that pair.

20. **(H)** If Choice F is true, then all "nice" numbers are also "special." That does not mean that all "special" numbers are also "nice," so 101 may be "special," but not "nice." Choices G, J, and K tell us nothing about the number 101. But choice H tells that all "special" numbers greater than 96 are also "nice." This describes the number 101 quite nicely.

Reading

Passage I

21. **(B)** Main Idea   A and C are too narrow: A relates only to one sentence in the second paragraph and to the third paragraph; C relates only to the first paragraph. E is incorrect because the individual cockroach is certainly not immortal, and the passage does not suggest that the species will last forever. D could be correct except that it does not cover the last paragraph. B is correct because every paragraph discusses either the survival or the contributions of the cockroach.

> **TIP:** Be sure the main-idea choice you select involves the entire passage.

22. **(J)** Detail   For a question that asks what is not true or not stated, you should work by a process of elimination. F can be eliminated because it is mentioned in the last paragraph (lines 52–53). The second paragraph says that cockroaches were on Earth before dinosaurs (line 14), and since they are still here they

must have been on Earth when the dinosaurs were, so G is an incorrect choice. The last sentence states their use in research, making H incorrect. The fourth paragraph tells of their good defense equipment, making K an incorrect choice. J is the right answer because it is too extreme. The passage says they will eat "almost anything available"; it does **not** say that they will eat anything.

> **FACT:** Answers that are more extreme than the stated information are inaccurate.

23. **(A)** Inference   A is correct because the fourth paragraph says that cockroaches have a fetid odor that keeps some predators away (line 46). It can be inferred that humans also might find them bad-smelling. B is wrong because although they are seen as pests, the passage says that they are important in more ways than one (line 51). C is too extreme. According to the fourth paragraph, they have adapted to "most" of earth's environments, not all (line 33). D is wrong because although it is mentioned that they can live in space capsules, no mention is made of their being used in space research. The last paragraph says that cockroaches aid the natural ecology (line 52), making E incorrect.

24. **(F)** Inference

> **TIP:** Always determine a definition answer by examining the context in which a word or phrase occurs.

The expression "they have seen many species come and go" occurs in the context of their long survival on Earth and their outlasting the dinosaurs, so F is the correct choice.

25. **(C)** Main Idea   This item requires you to summarize information. "Adaptable" and "well protected" cover every reason given in the paragraphs that discuss why they have survived for so long, paragraphs 2, 3, and 4. A may be true but is not given or suggested in the passage.

> **FACT:** An answer may be true but a wrong choice because it is not given or suggested in the passage.

B is true but too narrow, as it involves only one reason for survival, and more than one is given. D is true but not mentioned or suggested as being a reason for survival. E may also be true but is an incorrect choice for the same reason as D.

26. **(K)** Detail   The correct answer is clearly stated in the first sentence of the third paragraph (line 23).

Passage II

27. **(D)** Main Idea   A is incorrect because the passage doesn't focus on contrasts, and it also points out some similarities. B and C are both too narrow. Brotherly love (B) is mentioned only in the last paragraph, and misunderstanding (C) only in one sentence. E is incorrect because it is not stated or suggested that either of these philosophies is a foundation of Christianity. The first sentence says that they were influential just before Rome converted to Christianity but not that they influenced the religion. D is both broad enough and accurate.

28. **(G)** Detail   F is stated in the second paragraph (line 11). H and J are both stated in the third paragraph (line 26 and line 32). K is stated in the second paragraph (line 19). G is correct because Logos is a concept of Stoicism, not Epicureanism.

29. **(E)** Detail   The correct answer is stated in the last sentence of the passage.

30. **(H)** Detail   Paragraph three states Epicurus' teaching that people should not fear the gods (lines 37–38). The last sentence in the paragraph gives the reason stated in H.

31. **(B)** Detail   The correct answer is stated in the third sentence of the second paragraph (lines 13–14). A and C are given as concepts

of Stoicism only, and D as a concept of Epicureanism only.

32. **(F)** Inference   Although eating and drinking are not specifically mentioned, the fourth paragraph does say the Stoics taught moderation in "all things" (lines 47–48). "All things" includes eating and drinking, so it can be inferred that one should not be immoderate, or excessive, in these activities. G is an Epicurean concept. H is incorrect since Stoics do not believe in a spiritual world. J is not mentioned or suggested. Although Logos is important in Stoicism, meditation is not mentioned or suggested.

Passage III

33. **(C)** Main Idea   All of the other choices are too narrow. A does not include Louisa May Alcott's writing. B is mentioned only in the fourth paragraph, and the same is true of D. E is too narrow because it involves only the first and last paragraphs. It is also inaccurate because contrast is not stressed in the passage. C covers ideas in all paragraphs of the passage, so C is correct.

34. **(J)** Detail   The correct answer is stated in the second and third sentences of the last paragraph (lines 47–52).

35. **(A)** Inference   The first two sentences make the suggestion stated in A. The first sentence states the novels' popularity "For several decades" and uses the past tense verb "were." The second sentence indicates indirectly that only *Little Women* is still popular. B contradicts the information about the novels that is stated in the first paragraph, and also contradicts the suggestion of "something better" made in the last sentence of the passage. C is incorrect because the first paragraph says only that "some modern readers" find the stories too sentimental; no such suggestion is made for readers of the nineteenth century. D contradicts the fact that Alcott made money by writing stories for pulp magazines. Although the first paragraph says that *Little Women* is

based on Alcott's family, no such suggestion is made about the other novels.

36. **(G)** Detail   All of the other answers are stated in the second and third paragraphs. The third paragraph says that he was a poor provider and that the females in the family worked hard, but no suggestion is made that Alcott actually struggled or even cared about his family's poverty.

37. **(B)** Detail   The correct answer is stated in the first three sentences of the last paragraph.

38. **(F)** Detail   The correct answer is stated in the first paragraph (line 7). G is inaccurate because only the *Little Women* characters are stated as being based on her family. Neither H nor J is stated or suggested. K is incorrect because although the first paragraph says that Alcott "sprinkles" her fiction with "little sermons," nothing is said about the characters reading sermons.

Passage IV

39. **(C)** Main Idea   Only C is both accurate and broad enough. A is too narrow, as writing is mentioned in only two sentences. B is inaccurate because the passage discusses only one civilization of the "cradle" and doesn't attempt to give its history. D is too narrow because Gilgamesh is mentioned only in the last paragraph. E is also too narrow: Only two paragraphs give customs and religion.

40. **(F)** Inference   Several sentences make this suggestion. The third paragraph says that the Sumerian afterlife brought no comfort (line 43). The last paragraph says that after his friend's death Gilgamesh goes to the underworld looking for a goddess who can grant him immortality. The suggestion is that his friend's death made Gilgamesh fear death.

FACT: Sometimes it is necessary to read several sentences to draw a correct inference.

None of the other choices are stated or suggested.

41. **(E)** Inference   A is incorrect because the passage doesn't mention stone. Although the second paragraph says that mud was abundant, no suggestion is made that the people tried to "use it up," so B is incorrect. C is true but an incorrect choice, as it does not involve most of the things that were made of mud.

> **FACT:** A choice may be true but incorrect as an answer.

D is incorrect, as no statement or suggestion is made about color.

42. **(G)** Inference   The fact that every city was centered around a temple dedicated to a god indicates respect. The gods are called "sometimes cruel," suggesting that they were to be feared for what they sometimes did. F is wrong as mysticism and devotion are not stated or suggested. The gods are called "distant from the people," contradicting the devotion mentioned in F and the love mentioned in H. Confident dependence contradicts the idea that the gods were cruel and distant. The fact of temples dedicated to gods contradicts the indifference given in K.

43. **(D)** Detail   The answer is stated in the first paragraph (line 11).

44. **(K)** Detail   Two sentences in the third paragraph give the correct answer. The cities are described as "prosperous," suggesting that the citizens were also prosperous. Hardships and disasters are mentioned in this same paragraph (line 36). Adventure is mentioned only in connection with Gilgamesh, so F is wrong. "Comfortable" contradicts the disasters mentioned above, so G is wrong. H is wrong because although fear is suggested in the third paragraph, helplessness is not stated or suggested. J is incorrect because it contradicts the suggestions of fear and discomfort in the third paragraph.

Passage V

45. **(D)** Main Idea   A and C are too narrow, as they each involve information given in only one paragraph. B and E are inaccurate because Impressionism violates "classical" rules and because the passage says nothing about the influence of the movement.

46. **(H)** Detail   H is the correct choice because it contradicts the fact that Impressionist "brushstrokes do not carefully outline a shape" (lines 36–37) F, G, and J are all stated in the third paragraph, and K is stated in the first paragraph.

47. **(B)** Inference   The passage says that the "establishment" rejected the Impressionist style because it was "radical" (line 50), suggesting that this departure from the norm was why it was not popular at first. A contradicts the information given above and also in the first paragraph. C, D, and E are not stated or suggested in the passage.

48. **(J)** Detail   The correct answer is stated in the first sentence of the second paragraph.

49. **(A)** Inference   The context in which the word is used concerns condemnation and negative criticism (lines 53–55); thus "harshly critical" is the correct interpretation of the word. None of the other choices fits the tone indicated by criticism and condemnation.

50. **(J)** Detail   The correct answer is stated in the second paragraph (line 20).

Mathematics

51. **(E)** $7^2 = 49$.

52. **(G)** $\sqrt{24}$ is a little less than 5, so $\sqrt{49} - \sqrt{24}$ is a little more than $7 - 5$. The result is actually between 2 and 3, so the best choice is G.

> **TIP:** $\sqrt{a} - \sqrt{b}$ is generally not the same as $\sqrt{a-b}$.

Also note that $\sqrt{24}$ is an exact number, even though its decimal form never ends. The same is true of $\frac{1}{3}$, for example, which is an exact number even though its decimal form never ends.

53. **(C)** $\frac{200}{100} \cdot 7 = 14$. This is quite logical, since 100% of 7 is 7.

54. **(K)** The two unmarked vertical sides must add up to 3, and the two unmarked horizontal sides must add up to 4. Therefore the perimeter is $3 + 4 + 3 + 4 = 14$.

55. **(B)** The difference between the fractions on the left is $\frac{6}{30} - \frac{5}{30} = \frac{1}{30}$. Since this equals $\frac{1}{N}$, N must be 30.

56. **(H)** This is $(16 - 16) + (8 - 9) = 0 - 1 = -1$.

57. **(D)** The coordinate of Q is $\frac{(-8) + (2)}{2} = -3$. Then the midpoint of $\overline{QS}$ is $\frac{(-3) + (5)}{2} = 1$.

58. **(J)** Let $2x$ and $3x$ represent the number of boys and girls at the dance. Then $3x = 45$, so $x = 15$. Therefore, $2x = 30$ boys attended. Do not misread the problem to think that 45 people attended, or that the value of x is the answer to the problem.

59. **(D)** If we call the other interior angles of the triangle p and q, then $x + p + q + y = 180 + 180 = 360$. Since $p + q = 140$, then $x + y$ must equal 220°.

60. **(H)** The answer is $\frac{6x + 4y}{2} = 3x + 2y$.

61. **(A)** First compute $3*2 = 3^2 = 9$. Then $2*9 = 2^9 = 512$.

62. **(G)** The smallest integer value of $\frac{n}{5}$ occurs when $n = 10$, and is $\frac{10}{5} = 2$. The largest integer value occurs when $n = 35$, and is $\frac{35}{5} = 7$.

The only primes from 2 to 7 are 2, 3, 5, and 7. Thus, there are 4 values of n that produce primes. Don't forget that 2 is a prime number.

63. **(C)**

TIP: Combine the terms inside the absolute value signs before you compute the absolute value.

This is $|-6| - |4| = 6 - 4 = 2$.

64. **(H)** Joe's age is now $m - 3$. Ten years from now Joe's age will be $(m - 3) + 10 = m + 7$.

65. **(D)** At 9:00, the hands obviously form a 90° angle. At 10:00 the angle is $\frac{2}{3}$ as large, or 60°.

66. **(J)** The integer must be a multiple of both $3 \cdot 7$ and $7 \cdot 11$. The least common multiple of these is $3 \cdot 7 \cdot 11 = 231$.

67. **(A)** We must find the one-month interval where the graph rises most quickly. This is between March and April.

68. **(G)** We have $1.2 \times 10^2 = 120$ and $1.2 \times 10^3 = 1200$. Their sum is 1,320. In scientific notation, that is 1.32×10^3.

FACT: For a number to be in scientific notation, it must be of the form $A \times 10^B$, where $1 \le A < 10$ and B is an integer.

FACT: If you have difficulty remembering how to adjust the exponent of 10 when you move a decimal point, try using smaller numbers. For example, 25×10 is equal to 2.5×100 (that is 2.5×10^2).

69. **(B)** Every 7th day after Saturday is also a Saturday. Dividing 65 by 7 gives a remainder of 2, so it will be 2 days after Saturday, which is Monday.

70. **(J)** Using the fact that the area of a circle is πr^2, the radius of each circle is 4. That makes each diameter 8. Then the height and width of the rectangle must be 8 and 16, and the area of the rectangle is $(8)(16) = 128$.

71. **(C)** Twenty of the fifty students got less than 90%. That is $\frac{20}{50} \cdot 100 = 40\%$.

72. **(K)** The square of the given numbers can never be negative, and they cannot be more than 16.

73. **(A)** We have $A = 3C$ and $B = C - 8$. When $A = B$, we have $3C = C - 8$, so $C = -4$.

74. **(G)** Method 1. Make a Venn diagram showing two overlapping circles. Let one circle represent the students who like math and the other circle represent the students who like English. The overlapping section would represent students who like both. If x students like both, we can put an x in that center section. Then the other sections of the circles would be represented by $17 - x$ and $19 - x$. Since there are 28 students altogether, we can now add all three sections and get $(17 - x) + (19 - x) + x = 28$. This produces $x = 8$.
Method 2. Another method would be to add 17 and 19 to get 36. This is 8 more than the number of students in the class because the overlapping section (= 8) is counted twice.

75. **(D)**

> **FACT:** The greatest common factor (also called the greatest common divisor) of x and y consists of the primes common to both x and y, with each such prime raised to the smaller of the exponents it had in x or y.

In this case the answer is $3 \cdot 5^2$.

76. **(F)** When simplified, the equation becomes $6x + 16 = 6x + 12$, or $4 = 0$. This is impossible, so no value of x can satisfy this. Compare this with the equation $2(4x + 6) = 4(2x + 3)$, which leads to $8x + 12 = 8x + 12$. This equation is true for all values of x. Finally, compare these with an equation like $3x + 7 = 22$, which is only satisfied by one value of x.

77. **(C)** Replacing s by $2s$ and h by $3h$ produces $V = (2s)^2(3h) = 12s^2h$. The original V has been multiplied by 12.

78. **(J)** To maximize the number of boxes filled, start by filling the smaller boxes. The 10 small boxes hold 50 balls all together. We can use the remaining 49 balls to fill 6 large boxes, leaving one ball out. Thus, we can completely fill 16 boxes at most.

79. **(E)** Every 5 hours earns us $30, so 50 hours would earn us $10 \times \$30 = \$300$.

80. **(G)**

> **FACT:** The sum of the lengths of two sides of a triangle is greater than the length of the third side.

The sum of the three lengths is given as 19. If the longest side is 10, the sum of the other two sides would be 9, which is impossible. Therefore the longest side must be less than 10. On the other hand, if the longest side is only 6, then the perimeter cannot be more than 18. The only valid choice is G.

81. **(A)** If we subtract $2x$ from each side of the inequality, we get $-10 > x$. The only choice for x that is less than -10 is A.

82. **(F)** Each side of square $WXYZ$ must be 4. If we let CY and CX each equal x, then in right triangle YCX we have $x^2 + x^2 = 4^2 = 16$. Thus $2x^2 = 16$, so $x^2 = 8$. But the area of triangle YCX is $(\frac{1}{2})(\text{base})(\text{height}) = (\frac{1}{2})(x)(x) = (\frac{1}{2})x^2 = (\frac{1}{2})(8) = 4$.

83. **(D)**

> **TIP:** If the mean of n numbers is A, then the numbers add up to $n \times A$.

The sum of all 12 numbers is $3 \cdot 7 + 4 \cdot 8 + 5 \cdot 11 = 108$. The mean of those numbers is $\frac{108}{12} = 9$.

84. **(J)** After the 4 blue socks are removed, the drawer still contains 4 blue socks, 10 black socks, and 2 white socks. Of these 16 socks, 14 are *not* white. Therefore the probability of drawing a sock that is not white is $\frac{14}{16} = \frac{7}{8}$.

85. **(E)** If the 3 and 4 are the lengths of the legs of the triangle, the hypotenuse would be 5. But the 3 could be a leg and the 4 could be the hypotenuse. That would produce a different length for the missing leg. Thus, the third side is not uniquely determined.

86. **(H)** Only the small center cube on each *edge* of the original cube would be painted on exactly 2 faces. The original cube has 12 edges, so there are 12 such small cubes. The answer is H. Try figuring out how many of the small cubes have exactly 1 painted face. Finally, try for 3 (then 0) painted faces.

87. **(E)** Using single letters for the "nonsense words," we have $2b = 3g$ and $3b = 2c$. We can relate g and c if we can eliminate the bs. One easy way to do this is to change each equation to an equivalent one. Multiplying each side of the first equation by 3, and each side of the second equation by 2, we get $6b = 9g$ and $6b = 4c$. Therefore $4c = 9g$, so $c = \frac{9}{4}g$.

88. **(G)** If Montague High has N students, the ratio of vanilla preference to chocolate preference is $\frac{40}{100}N : \frac{30}{100}N$, which equals 4:3.

89. **(E)** We cannot compare 40% of one population with 20% of another because we do not know how large the populations are. For example, if Capulet High is very large, 20% of its population may be much larger than 40% of Montague's population.

90. **(H)** If x is an integer, $4x$ must be even. Then $4x - 1$ must be odd. Notice that $3x$ (or $5x$) could be odd or even.

91. **(B)** Counting numbers, we have 1 one + 2 of the twos + 3 of the threes + 4 of the fours + etc. Adding through the eights gives us a total of $1 + 2 + 3 + \ldots + 8 = 36$ numbers. The next set of numbers (nines) will include the 40th position.

92. **(J)** We first find the side of the original square. Since $20^2 = 400$ and $25^2 = 625$ the side of that square is between 20 and 25. Of those integers, only 24^2 could end in a 6. (You can check that 24^2 does equal 576.) Increasing each side of that square by 12 inches ($= 1$ foot) produces a new square with each side being $24 + 12 = 36$ inches long. Its area would be $36^2 = 1,296$ square inches.

93. **(C)** We could get a common denominator for each fraction, then compare them. However, it is easier to change each to a decimal and then compare. The decimal equivalents are $P = \frac{18}{25} = \frac{72}{100} = .72$, $Q = \frac{5}{7} = .714\ldots$, and $R = .75$. Clearly, $Q < P < R$.

94. **(G)** To reduce the contents of the container from $\frac{3}{4}$ full to $\frac{1}{4}$ full, we must have removed $\frac{3}{4} - \frac{1}{4} = \frac{1}{2}$ of what the container could hold. Since that was 20 ounces, the full container can hold 40 ounces.

95. **(C)** Method 1. If n is less than 10, the numerator will be negative and the denominator will be positive. That would give the fraction a negative value. If n is more than 14, the numerator will be positive but the denominator will be negative. That also gives the fraction a negative value. But when the numerator is between 10 and 14, the numer-

ator and the denominator (and the fraction) will be positive. That means n can be 11, 12, or 13. We must check $n = 10$ and $n = 14$ separately. The former makes the fraction equal to 0, which is not positive. The latter is not a permitted value of n because it would make the denominator equal to 0. Therefore there are 3 values of n that are acceptable.

Method 2. This problem can also be done using inequalities as follows: The fraction will be positive if the numerator and denominator are either both positive or both negative. That produces either $n - 10 > 0$ and $14 - n > 0$ (these lead to $14 > n > 10$), or else $n - 10 < 0$ and $14 - n < 0$ (these lead to $14 < n < 10$, which is impossible). We get the possibilities 11, 12, and 13 this way also.

96. **(F)** Drop a perpendicular from P to the base of the square, and let it hit that base at a point B. It will also go through the "center of the semicircle." Looking to the left of altitude $\overline{PB}$, we can see that the shaded area consists of one-fourth the area of a circle, plus one-half the area of a square, minus the area of right triangle PBA. Notice that each side of the square is 4, and the radius of the circle is 2. Then the

shaded area is $(\frac{1}{4})(4\pi) + (\frac{1}{2})(16) -$

$(\frac{1}{2})(2+4)(2) = \pi + 8 - 6 = \pi + 2$.

97. **(D)** Using the laws of exponents for division, the fraction is equal to

$$\frac{4^4}{2^4} = \frac{4^4}{16} = \frac{4^4}{4^2} = 4^2 = 16.$$

98. **(K)** If you quickly glance over the choices, you may see that K is the obvious answer,

since it is equal to $\frac{1}{6}$. You would then save

time by not bothering with the other choices. Otherwise, you must check out each of the choices. The first choice is equal to

$\frac{1111}{3(1111)} = \frac{1}{3}$. In the second choice, 3 times

the numerator is 897 (that is $900 - 3$); since

the denominator is smaller, the fraction is

larger than $\frac{1}{3}$. The third and fourth choices

each equal .4, which is more than

$\frac{1}{3}$ $(= .333 \ldots)$.

99. **(B)** We have $a:b = 3:4 = 15:20$. We also have $b:c = 5:6 = 20:24$. We have purposely gotten the same value into the "b" position, so we can now say that $a:b:c = 15:20:24$. Therefore, $a:c = 15:24$, which is also equal to 5:8.

100. **(J)** Method 1. Extend both "y" segments across the shaded region until they meet the "x" segments. Call each of the four unmarked segments "r" (they must all be equal). Then the shaded area will be $r^2 + ry + ry = r^2 + 2ry = 52$. Pick values for r, starting with $r = 1$, and see if there is a corresponding integer value for y. We quickly get a value at $r = 2$ ($y = 12$). Then, $x = r + y = 14$, and the perimeter is $2x + 2r + 2y = 56$.

Method 2. If we complete the square whose sides are of length x, we see that the shaded area is $x^2 - y^2$. Then we have $x^2 - y^2 = 52 = (x - y)(x + y)$.

FACT: If the product of two integers is even, at least one of them must be even.

Since x and y are integers, at least one of these factors must be even.

FACT: If the sum of two integers is even, the integers are either both even or both odd.

Therefore x and y are either both even or both odd. That further means that *both* factors will be even. The only way to factor 52 so that both factors are even is $(2)(26)$. Then $x - y = 2$ and $x + y = 26$. It is not hard to find that $x = 14$ and $y = 12$. Finally, we see that the two smaller horizontal segments of the figure must add up to x, and the two smaller vertical segments must also add up to x. Therefore the perimeter of the figure will be $4x$, which equals 56.

Answer Sheet
MODEL TEST 2

Part I   Verbal

Scrambled Paragraphs

Paragraph 1

The second sentence is   Ⓠ Ⓡ Ⓢ Ⓣ Ⓤ
The third sentence is   Ⓠ Ⓡ Ⓢ Ⓣ Ⓤ
The fourth sentence is   Ⓠ Ⓡ Ⓢ Ⓣ Ⓤ
The fifth sentence is   Ⓠ Ⓡ Ⓢ Ⓣ Ⓤ
The sixth sentence is   Ⓠ Ⓡ Ⓢ Ⓣ Ⓤ

Paragraph 2

The second sentence is   Ⓠ Ⓡ Ⓢ Ⓣ Ⓤ
The third sentence is   Ⓠ Ⓡ Ⓢ Ⓣ Ⓤ
The fourth sentence is   Ⓠ Ⓡ Ⓢ Ⓣ Ⓤ
The fifth sentence is   Ⓠ Ⓡ Ⓢ Ⓣ Ⓤ
The sixth sentence is   Ⓠ Ⓡ Ⓢ Ⓣ Ⓤ

Paragraph 3

The second sentence is   Ⓠ Ⓡ Ⓢ Ⓣ Ⓤ
The third sentence is   Ⓠ Ⓡ Ⓢ Ⓣ Ⓤ
The fourth sentence is   Ⓠ Ⓡ Ⓢ Ⓣ Ⓤ
The fifth sentence is   Ⓠ Ⓡ Ⓢ Ⓣ Ⓤ
The sixth sentence is   Ⓠ Ⓡ Ⓢ Ⓣ Ⓤ

Paragraph 4

The second sentence is   Ⓠ Ⓡ Ⓢ Ⓣ Ⓤ
The third sentence is   Ⓠ Ⓡ Ⓢ Ⓣ Ⓤ
The fourth sentence is   Ⓠ Ⓡ Ⓢ Ⓣ Ⓤ
The fifth sentence is   Ⓠ Ⓡ Ⓢ Ⓣ Ⓤ
The sixth sentence is   Ⓠ Ⓡ Ⓢ Ⓣ Ⓤ

Paragraph 5

The second sentence is   Ⓠ Ⓡ Ⓢ Ⓣ Ⓤ
The third sentence is   Ⓠ Ⓡ Ⓢ Ⓣ Ⓤ
The fourth sentence is   Ⓠ Ⓡ Ⓢ Ⓣ Ⓤ
The fifth sentence is   Ⓠ Ⓡ Ⓢ Ⓣ Ⓤ
The sixth sentence is   Ⓠ Ⓡ Ⓢ Ⓣ Ⓤ

Logical Reasoning

11 Ⓐ Ⓑ Ⓒ Ⓓ Ⓔ
12 Ⓕ Ⓖ Ⓗ Ⓙ Ⓚ
13 Ⓐ Ⓑ Ⓒ Ⓓ Ⓔ
14 Ⓕ Ⓖ Ⓗ Ⓙ Ⓚ
15 Ⓐ Ⓑ Ⓒ Ⓓ Ⓔ

16 Ⓕ Ⓖ Ⓗ Ⓙ Ⓚ
17 Ⓐ Ⓑ Ⓒ Ⓓ Ⓔ
18 Ⓕ Ⓖ Ⓗ Ⓙ Ⓚ
19 Ⓐ Ⓑ Ⓒ Ⓓ Ⓔ
20 Ⓕ Ⓖ Ⓗ Ⓙ Ⓚ

Reading

21 Ⓐ Ⓑ Ⓒ Ⓓ Ⓔ
22 Ⓕ Ⓖ Ⓗ Ⓙ Ⓚ
23 Ⓐ Ⓑ Ⓒ Ⓓ Ⓔ
24 Ⓕ Ⓖ Ⓗ Ⓙ Ⓚ
25 Ⓐ Ⓑ Ⓒ Ⓓ Ⓔ
26 Ⓕ Ⓖ Ⓗ Ⓙ Ⓚ

27 Ⓐ Ⓑ Ⓒ Ⓓ Ⓔ
28 Ⓕ Ⓖ Ⓗ Ⓙ Ⓚ
29 Ⓐ Ⓑ Ⓒ Ⓓ Ⓔ
30 Ⓕ Ⓖ Ⓗ Ⓙ Ⓚ
31 Ⓐ Ⓑ Ⓒ Ⓓ Ⓔ
32 Ⓕ Ⓖ Ⓗ Ⓙ Ⓚ

33 Ⓐ Ⓑ Ⓒ Ⓓ Ⓔ
34 Ⓕ Ⓖ Ⓗ Ⓙ Ⓚ
35 Ⓐ Ⓑ Ⓒ Ⓓ Ⓔ
36 Ⓕ Ⓖ Ⓗ Ⓙ Ⓚ
37 Ⓐ Ⓑ Ⓒ Ⓓ Ⓔ
38 Ⓕ Ⓖ Ⓗ Ⓙ Ⓚ

39 Ⓐ Ⓑ Ⓒ Ⓓ Ⓔ
40 Ⓕ Ⓖ Ⓗ Ⓙ Ⓚ
41 Ⓐ Ⓑ Ⓒ Ⓓ Ⓔ
42 Ⓕ Ⓖ Ⓗ Ⓙ Ⓚ
43 Ⓐ Ⓑ Ⓒ Ⓓ Ⓔ
44 Ⓕ Ⓖ Ⓗ Ⓙ Ⓚ

45 Ⓐ Ⓑ Ⓒ Ⓓ Ⓔ
46 Ⓕ Ⓖ Ⓗ Ⓙ Ⓚ
47 Ⓐ Ⓑ Ⓒ Ⓓ Ⓔ
48 Ⓕ Ⓖ Ⓗ Ⓙ Ⓚ
49 Ⓐ Ⓑ Ⓒ Ⓓ Ⓔ
50 Ⓕ Ⓖ Ⓗ Ⓙ Ⓚ

Answer Sheet
MODEL TEST 2

Part II   Mathematics

51 Ⓐ Ⓑ Ⓒ Ⓓ Ⓔ   71 Ⓐ Ⓑ Ⓒ Ⓓ Ⓔ   91 Ⓐ Ⓑ Ⓒ Ⓓ Ⓔ
52 Ⓕ Ⓖ Ⓗ Ⓙ Ⓚ   72 Ⓕ Ⓖ Ⓗ Ⓙ Ⓚ   92 Ⓕ Ⓖ Ⓗ Ⓙ Ⓚ
53 Ⓐ Ⓑ Ⓒ Ⓓ Ⓔ   73 Ⓐ Ⓑ Ⓒ Ⓓ Ⓔ   93 Ⓐ Ⓑ Ⓒ Ⓓ Ⓔ
54 Ⓕ Ⓖ Ⓗ Ⓙ Ⓚ   74 Ⓕ Ⓖ Ⓗ Ⓙ Ⓚ   94 Ⓕ Ⓖ Ⓗ Ⓙ Ⓚ
55 Ⓐ Ⓑ Ⓒ Ⓓ Ⓔ   75 Ⓐ Ⓑ Ⓒ Ⓓ Ⓔ   95 Ⓐ Ⓑ Ⓒ Ⓓ Ⓔ

56 Ⓕ Ⓖ Ⓗ Ⓙ Ⓚ   76 Ⓕ Ⓖ Ⓗ Ⓙ Ⓚ   96 Ⓕ Ⓖ Ⓗ Ⓙ Ⓚ
57 Ⓐ Ⓑ Ⓒ Ⓓ Ⓔ   77 Ⓐ Ⓑ Ⓒ Ⓓ Ⓔ   97 Ⓐ Ⓑ Ⓒ Ⓓ Ⓔ
58 Ⓕ Ⓖ Ⓗ Ⓙ Ⓚ   78 Ⓕ Ⓖ Ⓗ Ⓙ Ⓚ   98 Ⓕ Ⓖ Ⓗ Ⓙ Ⓚ
59 Ⓐ Ⓑ Ⓒ Ⓓ Ⓔ   79 Ⓐ Ⓑ Ⓒ Ⓓ Ⓔ   99 Ⓐ Ⓑ Ⓒ Ⓓ Ⓔ
60 Ⓕ Ⓖ Ⓗ Ⓙ Ⓚ   80 Ⓕ Ⓖ Ⓗ Ⓙ Ⓚ   100 Ⓕ Ⓖ Ⓗ Ⓙ Ⓚ

61 Ⓐ Ⓑ Ⓒ Ⓓ Ⓔ   81 Ⓐ Ⓑ Ⓒ Ⓓ Ⓔ
62 Ⓕ Ⓖ Ⓗ Ⓙ Ⓚ   82 Ⓕ Ⓖ Ⓗ Ⓙ Ⓚ
63 Ⓐ Ⓑ Ⓒ Ⓓ Ⓔ   83 Ⓐ Ⓑ Ⓒ Ⓓ Ⓔ
64 Ⓕ Ⓖ Ⓗ Ⓙ Ⓚ   84 Ⓕ Ⓖ Ⓗ Ⓙ Ⓚ
65 Ⓐ Ⓑ Ⓒ Ⓓ Ⓔ   85 Ⓐ Ⓑ Ⓒ Ⓓ Ⓔ

66 Ⓕ Ⓖ Ⓗ Ⓙ Ⓚ   86 Ⓕ Ⓖ Ⓗ Ⓙ Ⓚ
67 Ⓐ Ⓑ Ⓒ Ⓓ Ⓔ   87 Ⓐ Ⓑ Ⓒ Ⓓ Ⓔ
68 Ⓕ Ⓖ Ⓗ Ⓙ Ⓚ   88 Ⓕ Ⓖ Ⓗ Ⓙ Ⓚ
69 Ⓐ Ⓑ Ⓒ Ⓓ Ⓔ   89 Ⓐ Ⓑ Ⓒ Ⓓ Ⓔ
70 Ⓕ Ⓖ Ⓗ Ⓙ Ⓚ   90 Ⓕ Ⓖ Ⓗ Ⓙ Ⓚ

Model Test 2

PART 1—VERBAL

45 QUESTIONS

SUGGESTED TIME: 75 MINUTES

Scrambled Paragraphs

Paragraphs 1–5

> **Directions:** Below are six sentences that can be arranged to form a well-organized and grammatically correct paragraph. The first sentence is provided, but the other five are listed in random order. Choose the order that will form the **best** paragraph. Each correct paragraph is worth two points, with no partial credit given.
>
> You may wish to put numbers in the blanks at the left of each sentence to help keep track of the order. When you finish the set, mark your answers on the answer sheet.

PARAGRAPH 1

The traditional view of women's participation in the War Between the States is a picture of women keeping the home going, knitting socks, rolling bandages, and nursing the wounded.

_____ (Q) Some women traveled with the troops as helpmates of their husbands or as laundresses for the soliders.

_____ (R) These stay-at-home activities were important contributions of women but by no means indicate the limits of feminine activity.

_____ (S) Others did more dangerous work as smugglers, carrying important messages and sometimes scarce medicines across the lines.

_____ (T) So, no matter how most people remember women's participation today, it is clear that they played an important role during the war, supporting the troops in many different ways.

_____ (U) And there were women with even more perilous roles: Some women had to defend their homes against invading soldiers, and others actually donned uniforms and fought alongside their men.

245

PARAGRAPH 2

The "Father of the Steam Locomotive" is Richard Trevithick, a native of Cornwall in England, who built and operated the first railway locomotive in 1804.

_____ (Q) Trevithick learned about steam engines when working as a mining engineer, and he applied his knowledge to the design of a steam-driven road carriage.

_____ (R) A replica of the locomotive is now on display in a British railway station, and a special coin was issued in 2004 to commemorate the two-hundredth anniversary of Trevithick's famous train ride.

_____ (S) He subsequently adapted the principles of this vehicle to his rail locomotive, which he used to haul coal on a railway in South Wales.

_____ (T) For example, it demonstrated that steam traction was a feasible alternative to horsepower and that smooth wheels on smooth track could move forward without slipping.

_____ (U) This experiment was not entirely successful, as the locomotive and train were too heavy for the weak plateway on which they ran and so caused extensive damage, but the project did yield valuable information.

PARAGRAPH 3

One of the most colorful characters in the colorful history of San Francisco is Lillie Hitchcock Coit, who was born in the mid-nineteenth century and lived until 1928.

_____ (Q) She also enjoyed drinking with longshoremen, and she became an unofficial member of a volunteer fire company called the Knickerbocker Engine Company Number Five.

_____ (R) These behaviors were considered highly improper for women, so Coit, especially when visiting poker halls, would often disguise herself by dressing in men's trousers and wearing a short-haired wig.

_____ (S) In adulthood she liked to shock the more proper San Franciscans by such scandalous behavior as sticking her bare leg out a window, smoking in public, playing poker, and attending cock fights.

_____ (T) The less staid citizens of San Francisco loved her, and five years after her death the city honored her with Coit Tower, a striking memorial structure atop famous Telegraph Hill.

_____ (U) Her bizarre exploits began in girlhood, when one of her unusual pastimes was to slip from home and wander around the city, using a string baited with cheese to catch rats.

PARAGRAPH 4

A decade or so ago, Blythe, the owner of an imposing brick house near a busy intersection, began decorating her front lawn with pink flamingos, one at a time, until she had about a dozen.

_____ (Q) One October morning in the early '90s, commuters were startled to see the familiar birds wearing Halloween masks and carrying trick-or-treat bags.

_____ (R) Recently she learned that she had an appreciative audience when she withdrew the flamingos for a month for refurbishing; both she and the local news media were swamped with protests by commuters who missed their daily show.

_____ (S) A few weeks later, and just in time for Thanksgiving, they saw some of the birds wearing big black Pilgrim hats, whereas others sported colorful turkey tails.

_____ (T) Blythe must have liked the new look, for since then she has presented a seasonal show on her lawn: reindeer antlers for Christmas, green derbies for St. Patrick's Day, swimsuits for midsummer—her inventiveness never fails.

_____ (U) When friends informed her that pink flamingoes are not the epitome of style and elegance, Blythe decided to change the look of her yard and perhaps to needle the more proper folk at the same time.

PARAGRAPH 5

The history of Carnival glass goes back to 1905, when it first appeared as decorative pieces like bowls and vases and later also as tableware, toilet accessories, and almost anything else made of glass.

_____ (Q) Produced in a wide range of colors, from brilliant reds and rich orange-yellows to soft pastel pinks and greens, it was offered as a less expensive substitute for crystal and art glass.

_____ (R) Styles change, however, and by the late 1920s demand had dropped so drastically that manufacturers dumped their inventories wherever they could, often selling off large batches to bazaars, fairs, and carnivals.

_____ (S) Because its attractiveness and economy made it very popular, it was sold in many different kinds of stores and through mail order, and it was a frequent and popular prize for contests and promotions.

_____ (T) Three decades later collectors discovered the glassware, which now bore the "Carnival" title, and soon it was popular enough to be launched on a second life—Carnival reproductions.

_____ (U) Today, authentic Carnival glass is a favorite of antiques collectors, and, although much of it is still inexpensive, rare pieces can be worth thousands of dollars.

LOGICAL REASONING

Questions 11–20

Directions: For each of the following questions, select the **best** answer from the given choices. Bubble in the letter corresponding to your answer on the answer sheet. Your answer should be based **only on the given information.**

Read the words carefully. For example, "The red book is **to the right** of the blue book" does not necessarily mean that there is no other book between them. Similarly, be careful when reading words such as **between, below, above, after, before, behind,** and **ahead of.**

Questions 11 and 12 refer to the following information.

Whenever Mildred, Augusta, Fay, Sylvia, and Ruth run a race, the following always happens:

(1) Augusta beats Fay.
(2) Mildred is first or last.
(3) Ruth is first or last.
(4) There are no ties.
(5) Everyone finishes the race.

11. We can conclude that

A. Augusta can be 1st, 2nd, or 3rd.
B. Augusta can be 2nd or 3rd only.
C. Augusta is always 2nd.
D. Augusta is always 3rd.
E. Augusta could be 4th.

12. If Sylvia beats Mildred, then we can definitely determine who came in

F. 1st.
G. 2nd.
H. 3rd.
J. 4th.
K. None of the above

Questions 13, 14, and 15 refer to the following information.

In the code below, (1) each symbol represents the same word in all 3 sentences, (2) each word is represented by only one symbol, and (3) in any given sentence, the position of a symbol is **never** the same as that of the word it represents.

& $ @ # > means
  "Gavan and Carmen saw Vic."

! & $ @ # means
  "Vic and Gavan like Carmen."

* $ @ # ! means
  "Carmen and Diane like Gavan."

13. Which symbol represents "like"?

A. *
B. $
C. !
D. &
E. Cannot be determined from the information given.

14. Which word is represented by the symbol $?

F. Gavan
G. and
H. Carmen
J. saw
K. Vic

15. Which symbol represents "and"?

    A. &
    B. $
    C. @
    D. #
    E. Either @ or #, but cannot determine which one.

16. Below are two word pairs. The words in each pair are related in some way. The relationship between the words in the first pair is similar to the relationship between the words in the second pair

    yellow—caution
    red—stop

    What is the relationship displayed in both word pairs?

    F. Colors in the rainbow
    G. Types of road signs
    H. Traffic signal colors and what they mean
    J. Warning signs
    K. Road sign colors and questions on a test for drivers

Questions 17, 18, and 19 refer to the following information.

Rafael, Bonita, Chris, and Ludwig play the piano, violin, oboe, and trumpet, but not necessarily in that order. Each person plays exactly 2 of these instruments, but no one plays the exact same pair as anyone else. Furthermore,

(1) Rafael doesn't play piano.
(2) Bonita doesn't play violin.
(3) One person plays violin and oboe, and another person plays violin and trumpet.
(4) Chris plays oboe and trumpet.

17. Who plays piano?

    A. Rafael
    B. Ludwig
    C. Chris
    D. Bonita
    E. Cannot tell from the information given.

18. Who plays violin and oboe?

    F. Rafael
    G. Bonita
    H. Chris
    J. Ludwig
    K. Cannot tell from the information given.

19. How many of the instruments are played by **more** than 2 of the people?

    A. 0
    B. 1
    C. 2
    D. 3
    E. all 4

20. Judge Zhu Dee noted that Mr. Lee was driving a red sports car, and the last 12 red sports car drivers that had appeared before her were guilty of speeding. Therefore she concluded that Mr. Lee must be guilty of speeding.

    Which of the following uses reasoning that is most similar to that in the paragraph above?

    F. Tony missed his first class four days in a row because he got up late each day. When Tony missed that class on the 5th day, the teacher accused him of getting up late.
    G. Every man going to the concert had to wear a suit. Jerry saw that Dennis was not wearing a suit, and concluded that Dennis was not going to the concert.
    H. Although the speed limit on the highway is 50 mph, many drivers exceed that limit. Therefore the 50 mph limit is too low.
    J. Everyone in Ms. Perez's class is on the honor roll. Martin is in Ms. Perez's class, so Martin must be on the honor roll.
    K. Eve appeared before Judge Zhu Dee for speeding. The judge concluded that Eve must have been driving a red sports car.

READING
Questions 21–50

> **Directions:** Read each passage and answer the questions that follow it. Base your answers **only on the material contained in the passage**. Select the one **best** answer for each question. Bubble in the letter corresponding to that answer on the answer sheet.

I. A recent movie, *Shakespeare in Love,* tells the intimate story of the romantic relationship of young William Shakespeare and a
Line beautiful woman. The film is entertaining
(5) but not factual, for little is actually known about the young manhood of Shakespeare. The bare facts of his early life are available. He was born in Stratford-on-Avon in April of 1564 into a well-respected family. At the
(10) age of eighteen he married Anne Hathaway, who bore him three children in the next three years. However, there are few details to flesh out the story of his beginnings. Even the extent of his formal education is
(15) uncertain. He probably attended school in Stratford, but no official record confirms this assumption.

Literary historians know even less about his life from age twenty-one to age twenty-
(20) eight. No one knows exactly when he moved from Stratford to London or exactly how he became involved in the theater. In 1592 he was important enough to attract the public attention of a professional rival,
(25) whose jealous attack on Shakespeare reveals that the latter was at the time active as both actor and playwright.

Scholars have more information about his later career if not his private life. His theater
(30) career endured a two-year interruption caused by a shutdown of theaters during a time of plague. However, after this brief setback he achieved remarkable artistic and financial success as actor, playwright, and
(35) shareholder in the company that was the favorite of two monarchs, Elizabeth and James I. It is also known that he made considerable money in Stratford real estate and retired a wealthy man.

(40) Many gaps in his history remain. Most mysterious, perhaps, is the question of how he acquired some of the knowledge his plays display. For example, how did this middle-class man gain familiarity with aristocratic
(45) and even royal lifestyle? How did this product of the Stratford school acquire a complex understanding of the law? Questions such as these have led some scholars to believe that William Shakespeare is not the author of the
(50) works bearing his name. The scholar Francis Bacon, the playwright Christopher Marlowe, and the 17th Earl of Oxford, Edward de Vere, are three of the often-mentioned possible real authors.

(55) Most critics and literary historians, however, feel that the puzzle of authorship is likely to remain unresolved. Most think that it is less important to know with finality who wrote Shakespeare's works than it is
(60) to know and appreciate the author's wondrous genius.

21. Which of the following best tells what this passage is about?

    A. History versus legend
    B. The scarcity of biographical information about Shakespeare
    C. The mystery surrounding authorship of the works of William Shakespeare
    D. The question of how the writers of *Shakespeare in Love* knew so much about his private life
    E. The success of a great playwright

22. What does the passage suggest about the film *Shakespeare in Love*?

    F. It required painstaking research
    G. It gives private details of a real love affair.
    H. It has won many awards.
    J. It was one of the top money-making films of 1999.
    K. It is pure fiction.

23. What is the most likely reason for the written attack by Shakespeare's rival?

    A. He was envious of Shakespeare's success.
    B. Shakespeare had insulted or otherwise offended him personally.
    C. They were romantic rivals.
    D. He was the real author of plays produced under Shakespeare's name.
    E. He was trying to have the theaters shut down.

24. Which of the following is **not** given as a detail of Shakespeare's life?

    F. His birthplace
    G. His monetary success in his chosen career
    H. His poverty during a two-year period of plague
    J. A secondary source of income
    K. The name of his wife

25. Which of the following means about the same as "flesh out" (line 13)?

    A. Add information to
    B. Give a visual image of
    C. Contradict
    D. Detect
    E. Add imaginative ideas to

26. Why are literary researchers intrigued by Shakespeare's depictions of royalty and court life?

    F. They provide historical detail that would otherwise be unknown.
    G. They suggest the plays could not have been written by a member of the middle class.
    H. They suggest that William Shakespeare had important social contacts with the aristocracy.
    J. They explain the attack by the rival playwright.
    K. They suggest that Shakespeare spent the plague years in the court of Queen Elizabeth.

II. Just a few decades ago mushrooms were infrequently seen on the dinner tables of most American households, and those that
Line did find their way into home-cooked food
(5) were almost always the cultivated white "button" mushrooms. In recent years, however, mushroom popularity in America has burgeoned. This tasty vegetable is now a highly favored ingredient in numerous
(10) everyday recipes, and readily available to the consumer are several varieties of mushrooms ranging from common commercially grown types to the more expensive wild varieties favored by gourmets.

(15) Not everyone who enjoys mushrooms knows much about what they are or where they come from. They are members of a family of fungi that grow mainly underground. The part of the organism that
(20) appears above ground and is harvested is the fruiting body that sprouts from the underground part, the mycelium. In commercial cultivation they are grown in carefully

controlled environments, often in cellars or
(25) caves. In the wild they flourish in fields,
forests, lawns and backyards, some sprout-
ing from the ground and others growing on
decaying or decayed trees. At least one
important type grows entirely underground:
(30) Rare and costly truffles are harvested with
the help of pigs and other animals trained to
sniff them out.

Because some varieties are highly toxic, it is
unwise for an untrained person to gather
(35) wild mushrooms. Even experienced "mush-
roomers" can get in trouble because poisonous varieties in one region may resemble
edible varieties in another area. In a case
widely reported a few years ago, several peo-
(40) ple in California became gravely ill when an
experienced gatherer from the Far East mistook the deadly amanita for an edible Asian
type.

This element of danger has until recent
(45) years made the harvesting of the highly
favored wild varieties—chanterelles, shaggy
manes, morels, and others—a specialized
calling of the few. Nowadays, however, high
demand has encouraged so many entrepre-
(50) neurs in the field that competition among
them is fierce. Encounters of rival gatherers
are almost always unpleasant and sometimes
actually violent. Moreover, environmentalists as well as marketers worry about serious
(55) overharvesting, which could result in
scarcity or even complete elimination of the
most desirable kinds of this delectable
fungus.

27. Which of the following best tells what this
passage is about?

  A. The recent demand for mushrooms
  B. Edible and poisonous mushrooms
  C. Description and popularity of
  mushrooms
  D. Little-known facts about mushrooms
  E. An endangered species

28. Which of the following means about the
same as "burgeoned" (line 8)?

  F. Grown
  G. Become more available
  H. Declined
  J. Become more varied
  K. Been commercialized

29. According to the information given, which
of the following statements about
mushrooms is the most accurate?

  A. They need dark places like caves and
  cellars to grow.
  B. They achieved worldwide popularity
  only in the last few decades.
  C. Their fruiting bodies grow
  underground.
  D. It is sometimes hard to distinguish
  between toxic and nontoxic varieties.
  E. Overharvesting has caused the
  extinction of the most popular types.

30. What is the most likely reason that truffles
are costly?

  F. They are scarce.
  G. They must be grown by professionals
  under the most exacting conditions.
  H. They are not fruiting bodies but
  mycelia.
  J. They are difficult to find.
  K. Both F and J

31. What does the passage suggest about
mushroom gathering?

  A. It requires extensive classroom training.
  B. It is lucrative.
  C. It is a relatively new activity.
  D. Until recent years it involved only
  white "button" mushrooms.
  E. It usually requires extensive digging,
  which can damage the forest floor.

32. Why did the mushroom gatherer mentioned in the passage above make such a deadly mistake?

   F. She did not know what *amanita* means.
   G. She lacked professional training.
   H. She was unfamiliar with local mushroom varieties.
   J. She was careless.
   K. She was not well acquainted with the American countryside.

III. In recent years the word *Cajun* has become familiar to most Americans. Cajun food appears on restaurant menus across
Line the country, Cajun music entertains radio
(5) listeners, and Cajun festivals pop up in places remote from their more likely venues. However, relatively few people outside Louisiana and other Gulf states fully understand what a Cajun is.

(10) The word *Cajun* is a corruption of *Acadian,* the Acadians being a people of French ancestry who once lived in Acadia in eastern Canada. After the former French colony fell under British rule, its Catholic
(15) inhabitants were required to swear allegiance to Great Britain. In 1755, those who refused to take the required oath were expelled. After a period of wandering, the Acadians eventually found homes in scat-
(20) tered locations in Canada and what is now the United States. Several thousand settled in the bayou country of south Louisiana, and these are the people who came to be called Cajuns.

(25) Bayous, which would be called creeks in other parts of the country, are often associated with marshy or swampy areas. But bayou country includes rich, productive farmland as well. The Acadian settlers of
(30) this area became farmers, hunters, and fishermen. Because of their relatively isolated situation, they developed the distinctive culture that now charms so many Americans.

(35) The cuisine of these descendants of the Acadians features local seafood such as shrimp and oysters as well as the popular freshwater crawfish and such meats as tasso, a highly seasoned ham, and boudin, a kind
(40) of pork sausage. *Cajun* cooks have created the soup called gumbo and the rice-based mixture called jambalaya, which are favorites on tables across the country. And the Cajuns continue to be adventurous
(45) cooks. They were pioneers in the art of turkey frying, originally cooking the big birds in galvanized tubs filled with used vegetable oil from local fast-food restaurants.

(50) Cajun music often has the feel of bluegrass, but it has its own characteristic sound. The accordion, not featured in most contemporary music, is an integral part of this Cajun sound. Cajun songs are still frequently sung
(55) in French, another unique feature. And the music has its modern offshoots, including Zydeco, which is considered to be based on a combination of African-American and Cajun rhythms and instrumentation.

(60) Today, these people may live in San Francisco or Manhattan, and may be electrical engineers, psychologists, carpenters, or clerks. Irish names like Terrence O'Brien and English names like Mary Elizabeth
(65) Carter belong to people claiming Cajun descent. But in Louisiana there are still enclaves of Acadians who make their living off the land, speak the old language, and cling to an old way of life.

33. Which of the following best states the purpose of the author of the above?

   A. To explain the popularity of Cajun music and food
   B. To explain the derivation of the word *Cajun*
   C. To give a history of south Louisiana
   D. To describe a distinct culture
   E. To show how a way of life can change

34. What is the most likely reason for the expulsion of the Acadians?

    F. The British saw them as a threat.
    G. The British were carrying out "ethnic cleansing."
    H. The British wished to punish them.
    J. The British wished to make room for English settlers.
    K. It was an act of religious persecution.

35. According to the passage, which of the following is **not** true of the Cajuns?

    A. Some of them have intermarried with other ethnic groups.
    B. They remained a distinct group for so long because they were somewhat separated from people of other cultures.
    C. Some of them still speak a form of French.
    D. They lived in northern North America before migrating to the South.
    E. Their cooks stick to traditional recipes.

36. Which of the following means the same as *venues* as it is used in the passage (lines 6–7)?

    F. Sites
    G. Locations of courtroom trials
    H. Musicians
    J. Restaurants
    K. Customers

37. What is a bayou?

    A. An elevated piece of land in a swamp
    B. A lake
    C. A tidal creek
    D. A swamp
    E. Farmland watered by one or more creeks

38. Which of the following is most essential to the Cajun style of music?

    F. French rhythms
    G. Zydeco
    H. French lyrics
    J. The African-American influence
    K. The sound of an accordion

IV. A relatively recent discovery has given support to the theory that the dinosaurs became extinct because of a collision between Earth and a giant asteroid. (5) Scientists have discovered the element iridium and granules of shocked quartz in the late Cretaceous rock layer. The presence of the two substances indicates that a large asteroid or comet did indeed strike the earth (10) during the geologic era in which the dinosaurs became extinct. Such a collision could have drastic environmental consequences.

Such collisions are considered "common" in (15) terms of geologic time—time in the context of the earth's billions-year-old existence. Asteroids, after all, are our close neighbors. At one time they were considered the last remaining fragments of a destroyed planet. (20) Now, however, they are currently thought to be ancient matter that might have coalesced into a single planet if the gravity of the nearby planet Jupiter had not interfered. Classed as small planets, they behave like (25) their larger sisters in orbiting the sun. In one form or another they have been with us since the beginning of the solar system.

For most of our solar system's history, visitation between asteroids and Earth were one-(30) way. Particles of these bodies constantly shower the earth in the form of meteorites, and the much rarer big collisions do occur. In recent years, however, earthlings have turned the tables. In 1991 the *Galileo* space (35) probe passed near the asteroid 951 Gaspara and successfully photographed its surface. The NEAR (Near Earth Asteroid Rendezvous) project carried out a flyby of 253 Mathilde in 1997. NEAR is also plan-(40)ning a year-long orbit of Eros in the year 2000. A privately funded NEAP (Near Earth Asteroid Prospector) group is planning to send a vehicle to a nearby asteroid for the purpose of studying the composition (45) of its surface. NEAP intends to complete its mission at a cost minuscule in comparison with the costly ventures of NASA.

Line

Scientific curiosity aside, the inhabitants of Earth continue to be intrigued and
(50) sometimes frightened by the prospect of a catastrophic asteroid strike. In 1999 NASA announced that on August 7, 2027, asteroid 1999AN10 will pass by Earth. According to NASA, it could come as close
(55) as 19,000 miles, or it could pass by at a distance of 600,000 miles. In either case, say astronomers, it will not hit Earth. Most earthlings have seemed to take NASA's word for it. Some, however, fret over a pos-
(60) sible error in calculation or a shift in the asteroid's path. There is even an Internet website that flaunts a day-by-day Asteroid Doomsday Countdown Clock. But according to astronomers the chance of a cata-
(65) strophic collision occurring within the next several thousand years is remote.

39. What is the best title for the above passage?

    A. "Dinosaurs and Asteroids"
    B. "Disaster from the Stars"
    C. "Earth's Planetary Neighbors"
    D. "The Origins of Asteroids"
    E. "Close Encounters"

40. Which of the following means the same as "minuscule" (line 46)?

    F. Terrifying
    G. Reasonable
    H. Tiny
    J. Privately funded
    K. Understandable

41. Which of the following is the most likely result of the collision of a large asteroid with the earth?

    A. The extinction of human life
    B. The destruction of all life on Earth
    C. Fragmentation similar to that which produced the asteroids
    D. A gravitational shift changing the earth's orbit
    E. Ecological damage

42. Why is the word "common" (line 14) enclosed in quotation marks?

    F. It is being used in a special context.
    G. It is a direct quotation.
    H. It is an attempt at humor.
    J. It is a synonym of "close neighbors" in line 17.
    K. It is meant to suggest *crude* rather than *refined*.

43. Which of the following is **not** true about asteroids?

    A. They have collided with Earth many times in the past.
    B. They are responsible for most of the environmental changes on Earth.
    C. In other evolutionary circumstances, they would have been a single planet.
    D. They are considered planets.
    E. They fascinate many human beings.

44. Which of the following most accurately states why some people are worried about the approach of 1999AN10?

    F. They think NASA is lying to calm people's fears.
    G. They feel that such events are not entirely predictable.
    H. They detect a conflict between the interests of the International Astronomical Union and those of NASA.
    J. A distance of 600,000 miles is no protection from an asteroid.
    K. Information gathered by the NEAR and NEAP projects contradicts NASA's findings.

    V. The shorelines of Earth's continents have shifted and changed shape as long as there have been oceans to wash them. Offshore
Line currents carry sand along the coast, moving
(5) it from one beach to another. As one beach accretes, another erodes. Storms also play their part as they push huge waves against the dunes, carrying tons of sand out to sea. This continual movement and reshap-
(10) ing is a natural phenomenon that is

environmentally benign. Only when human beings invade the beach does trouble begin.

People are attracted to the beach.
(15) Beachfront property is highly desirable, valuable real estate. But when a shore is lined with houses, the inevitable sooner or later occurs. Natural erosion, often hastened by the removal of protective dunes, begins
(20) to eat away at the beach. Homeowners and local authorities scramble to put up protective devices. Either the devices don't work, or they work to protect one beach while increasing the erosion on others.

(25) Even the best modern technology does not control the sea. In 1998 a storm attacked Long Island and dumped a $750,000 house into the sea. In Galveston, Texas, an entire subdivision is in danger of being washed
(30) away. In a Virginia beach community a huge steel bulkhead erected in 1989 as a shield against ocean currents is now a useless wreck.

Historically, the battle against the sea has
(35) been a losing one. In the past jetties and groins—structures built out from the shore or offshore—were favorite remedies. Unfortunately, the engineers who built them did not understand what the long-range conse-
(40) quences of such hard devices could be. Not understanding the natural action of off-shore currents, they failed to take into consideration the effects of blocking the sand flow to other areas. Disastrous erosion has
(45) resulted from these ill-conceived projects. Today a favored approach is beach renourishment. Typically this process involves dredging sand from the ocean floor and pumping it onto the beach. It is expensive,
(50) and although does build up the beach, it is at best a temporary solution. The same currents that have washed it away once will wash it away again.

Some environmentalists, although acknow-
(55) ledging that beach renourishment does provide at least a stopgap solution, vigorously oppose it on several grounds. One is the huge cost to taxpayers, most of whom get no benefit from such projects. Another
(60) objection is based on its appearance of success. This, they say, will only encourage more beachfront building and more shoreline destruction. By the same logic they oppose federal subsidies for beachfront con-
(65) struction and federally subsidized flood insurance for such properties.

45. Which of the following best states the author's purpose?

   A. To explain why beachfront property is expensive

   B. To describe the intricate balance between ocean currents and shoreline

   C. To explain the detrimental effects of human meddling in a delicate ecosystem

   D. To present the best methods for beach protection

   E. To applaud a valiant battle against powerful forces

46. Which of the following is the most likely reason why some states now ban hard erosion-control devices?

   F. They have no effect on erosion.

   G. They encourage more beachfront building.

   H. They increase erosion in other areas.

   J. They require federal subsidies.

   K. They require dune removal.

47. For what purpose is the bulkhead in Virginia (line 31) mentioned?

    A. It provides an example of the futility of trying to control the ocean.

    B. It implies that the builder of the bulkhead was incompetent.

    C. It proves that stronger materials must be used in such projects.

    D. It suggests that a jetty would have been a better device.

    E. It suggests that "If at first you don't succeed," you must "try, try again."

48. Why was beach erosion in former times seldom a serious problem?

    F. Storm patterns were different.

    G. Communities would work together on a continual basis to combat erosion.

    H. Ocean currents were more stable without human interference.

    J. Dunes and forests prevented erosion from occurring.

    K. Erosion did not usually directly affect human beings.

49. With which of the following statements would the author probably agree?

    A. Many useful erosion-control devices have been invented.

    B. Beachfront building should be avoided.

    C. Federal subsidies for beachfront construction are to be encouraged as a way of controlling development.

    D. In previous centuries people did not live near the coast.

    E. New construction on beachfront is likely to come to a halt in the near future.

50. Which of the following does the passage not present as possibly detrimental to the stability of beach areas?

    F. Bulkheads

    G. Groins

    H. Jetties

    J. Beach renourishment

    K. Dunes

PART 2—MATHEMATICS

QUESTIONS 51–100

SUGGESTED TIME: 75 MINUTES

> **Directions:** For each of the following questions, select the **best** answer from the given choices. Bubble in the letter corresponding to your answer on the answer sheet. **DO NOT PUT ANY OTHER WORK ON THE ANSWER SHEET.** All necessary work can be done in your test booklet or on scrap paper that is provided.

> **NOTE:** Diagrams other than graphs might not be drawn to scale. Do not assume any relationships that are not specifically stated unless they are implied by the given information.

51. One-half of one-sixth is equal to

   A. one-third of one-fourth
   B. one-third
   C. one
   D. two
   E. three

52. The areas of triangles *ABC* and *XYZ* are each 10. The area of the shaded region is 14. Then the area of triangle *XWC* is

   F. 12
   G. 8
   H. 6
   J. 3
   K. 2

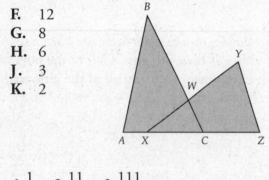

53. $1\frac{1}{10} + 2\frac{11}{100} + 3\frac{111}{1000} =$

   A. 6.111
   B. 6.123
   C. 6.111111
   D. 6.321
   E. 6.6

54. If *x* is positive and $x^2 + x = 50$, then *x* is a number between

   F. 6 and 7
   G. 7 and 8
   H. 8 and 9
   J. 9 and 10
   K. 10 and 11

55. In the figure, *C* is a point on line segment $\overline{AE}$. If *AB = BC*, what is the measure of angle *DCE*?

   A. 80°
   B. 75°
   C. 60°
   D. 25°
   E. 20°

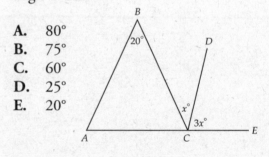

56. Barbara is 7 years older than Carole is now. Katie is half as old as Carole is now. If Katie is now 16 years old, how many years old is Barbara now?

   F. 15
   G. 23
   H. 32
   J. 39
   K. 46

57. $3.4 \times 10^2 + 3.4 \times 10^2$ is equal to

A. 6.8×10^2
B. 6.8×10^4
C. 3.4×10^4
D. 3,400
E. 3,434

58. The points *S, P, Q,* and *R* are on the sides of rectangle *ABCD* such that $\overline{SQ}$ is perpendicular to $\overline{PR}$. *APXS* is a square whose side is 3. The area of *SXRD* is 12 and the area of *PBQX* is 27. What is the perimeter of rectangle *ABCD*?

F. 84
G. 72
H. 38
J. 36
K. 18

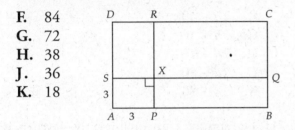

59. Kobi has $9.83, made up of nickels and pennies only. Which of the following *could not* be a possible value for the number of pennies?

A. 208
B. 113
C. 93
D. 88
E. 85

60. If $\dfrac{2x-3}{4} = 8$, then $2x + 3 =$

F. 41
G. 38
H. 35
J. 29
K. 28

61. Five apples and 6 bananas together cost as much as 8 bananas and 9 pears. One apple costs as much as 2 pears. For the same price as 1 pear, how many bananas could be bought?

A. 1
B. 2
C. 3
D. 4
E. 6

62. Let $R = 8 \cdot 9 \cdot 7 \cdot 13$ and $S = 4 \cdot 6 \cdot 11 \cdot 49$. The greatest common factor of *R* and *S* is

F. 12
G. 24
H. 56
J. 168
K. 504

63. What is the value of $4|x - y| - 3|xy|$ if $x = -5$ and $y = 2$?

A. −42
B. −18
C. −2
D. 42
E. 58

64. In the following sequence of eight numbers, each number has one more "1" than the number before it:

2, 12, 112, 1112, . . . ,11111112

What is the hundreds digit in the sum of all eight of these numbers?

F. 0
G. 6
H. 7
J. 8
K. 9

65. In Ms. Hsiao's class there are twice as many boys as there are girls. Half of the boys are in the math club and all of the girls are in the math club. What percent of Ms. Hsiao's class is in the math club?

A. 25%
B. $33\frac{1}{3}\%$
C. 50%
D. $66\frac{2}{3}\%$
E. 75%

66. $(16 + 5x) - (8 - 2x) =$

    F. $8 + 3x$
    G. $8 - 3x$
    H. $8 - 7x$
    J. $8 + 7x$
    K. $24 - 7x$

67. The three lines shown intersect in a point. The value of x

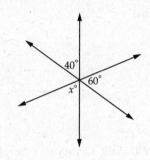

    A. is 100.
    B. is 80.
    C. is 50.
    D. is 20.
    E. cannot be determined from the given information.

68. The straight line graph shows how many people are in a large cafeteria eating lunch at different times. If the people leave at a steady rate, at what time will only 150 people remain?

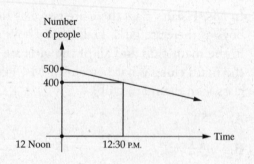

    F. 1:15 P.M.
    G. 1:30 P.M.
    H. 1:45 P.M.
    J. 2:15 P.M.
    K. 3:30 P.M.

69. Two congruent circles have centers P and Q as shown. What is the measure of angle PXQ?

    A. 30°
    B. 45°
    C. 55°
    D. 60°
    E. 75°

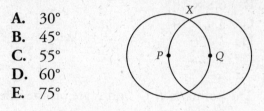

70. Andrew has d dollars. He has one-third as many dollars as Bruce has. Carlos has $80 less than half the total of Andrew's and Bruce's dollars. In terms of d, how many dollars does Carlos have?

    F. $4d - 40$
    G. $2d - 40$
    H. $2d + 40$
    J. $2d + 80$
    K. $2d - 80$

71. The sum of 7 unequal positive integers is 61. What is the largest possible value that any of those integers can have?

    A. 55
    B. 40
    C. 39
    D. 13
    E. 9

72. In the set $\{1, 5, x, 10, 15\}$, the integer x is the median. The mean of the five numbers is one less than x. The value of x is

    F. 6
    G. 7
    H. 8
    J. 9
    K. none of these.

73. If $\dfrac{7}{50} < \dfrac{1}{x} < \dfrac{8}{51}$ where x is an integer, then $x =$

    A. 8
    B. 7
    C. 6
    D. 5
    E. 4

74. Half of 2^8 is

   F. 2^7
   G. 2^6
   H. 2^4
   J. 1^8
   K. 8

75. If x is greater than $\frac{1}{2}$ but less than 1, which of the following has the largest value?

   A. $2x - 1$
   B. x^2
   C. $\dfrac{1}{x}$
   D. $1 - x$
   E. x^3

76. Maria, Anoki, and Boris are teenagers, and the sum of their ages now is 49. The sum of their ages 8 years from now will be F, and the sum of their ages 10 years ago was P. The value of $F - P$ is

   F. 54
   G. 18
   H. 17
   J. 6
   K. 2

77. If $\dfrac{1}{4} + \dfrac{1}{x} = 1$, then $x =$

   A. $\dfrac{1}{8}$
   B. $\dfrac{2}{3}$
   C. $\dfrac{4}{3}$
   D. 2
   E. 3

78. When the integer N is divided by 7, the quotient is Q and the remainder is 5. When $N + 24$ is divided by 7, the remainder is

   F. 4
   G. 3
   H. 2
   J. 1
   K. 0

79. Point B is on line segment $\overline{AD}$, and point E is on line segment $\overline{BC}$. The value of x is

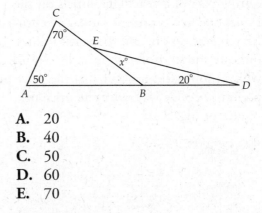

   A. 20
   B. 40
   C. 50
   D. 60
   E. 70

80. Three-fourths of a number is equal to L. What is three-halves of that original number, in terms of L?

   F. $\dfrac{4}{3}L$
   G. $\dfrac{3}{2}L$
   H. $2L$
   J. $3L$
   K. $4L$

81. For *how many* positive integer values of N will the expression $\dfrac{18}{N+2}$ be an integer?

   A. 1
   B. 2
   C. 3
   D. 4
   E. 5

82. In the figure, numbers are to be placed in each of the nine small squares such that the sum of the numbers in any row, column, or diagonal must be the same. The number x

	13	
		x
10	9	14

   F. will be 1.
   G. will be 7.
   H. will be 9.
   J. will be 11.
   K. cannot be determined from the given information.

83. The two straight line graphs indicate the change in the price per pound of coffee and the change in the price per pound of sugar during part of a year. The initials on the horizontal axis represent January, February, March, and so on, and the vertical lines indicate the start of each month. During which month did it occur that the price per pound of coffee was twice the price per pound of sugar?

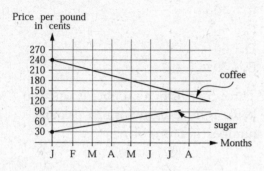

A. March
B. April
C. May
D. June
E. July

84. The pie chart shows the yearly expenses of the Jones family. Each expense is indicated as a percent of the total money they spent. Which one of the following bar charts, which indicate actual money spent in each area, best represents the data in the pie chart?

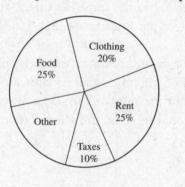

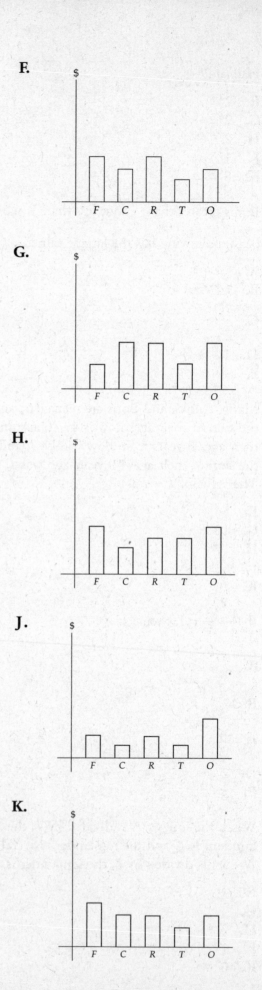

85. A fence encloses a triangular field. There is a vertical wooden fence post at each corner (vertex) of the field, and vertical posts all along the fence, placed 5 feet apart. If the sides of the field measure 20 feet by 35 feet by 25 feet, how many posts are there altogether?

A. 13
B. 14
C. 15
D. 16
E. 17

86. The longest side in the figure (which need not be drawn to scale) must be

F. $\overline{BC}$

G. $\overline{BD}$

H. $\overline{CD}$

J. $\overline{AB}$

K. $\overline{AD}$

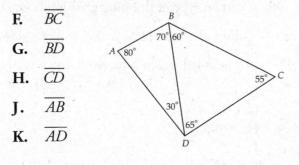

87. $(x^2y^3)(xy^2) =$

A. x^2y^6
B. x^3y^6
C. $2x^3y^6$
D. x^3y^5
E. $2x^3y^5$

88. The smallest positive integer value of n that will make $12n$ exactly divisible by 56 is

F. 7
G. 12
H. 14
J. 21
K. 24

89. If $2x + 2y + 2z = 110$ and $x + y = 11$, then $z =$

A. 99
B. 50
C. $49\frac{1}{2}$
D. 49
E. 44

90. Suppose $a \oplus b$ means $a^2 - ab$. (For example, $3 \oplus 2 = 9 - 6 = 3$ and $5 \oplus 3 = 10$.) Which of the following has the smallest value?

F. $19 \oplus 18$
G. $15 \oplus 14$
H. $17 \oplus 15$
J. $14 \oplus 11$
K. $15 \oplus 10$

91. Box A contains exactly four cards, numbered 3, 5, 6, and 9. Box B contains exactly three cards, numbered 1, 4, and 7. One card is selected at random from Box A, and one card is selected at random from Box B. What is the probability that the *sum* of the numbers on the two selected cards is even?

A. $\dfrac{1}{4}$

B. $\dfrac{1}{3}$

C. $\dfrac{5}{12}$

D. $\dfrac{1}{2}$

E. $\dfrac{7}{12}$

92. Gil is now 80 miles ahead of Larry. Gil is traveling at a constant rate. Larry is traveling in the same direction, at a rate 5 miles per hour faster than Gil. In how many hours will Larry catch up to Gil?

F. 16
G. 15
H. 12
J. 10
K. Larry cannot catch up to Gil

93. If $\dfrac{3x + 3}{3} = 2.5$, then $x =$

A. $-.5$
B. $.5$
C. $.75$
D. 1
E. 1.5

Model Test 2

94. On Thursday, the ABC Company stock lost 60% of its value. On Friday it lost another 10% of its remaining value. The total loss for the two days would have been the same if the stock had lost x% of its value the first day and x% of its remaining value the second day. Then $x =$

   F. 30
   G. 35
   H. 38
   J. 40
   K. 64

95. The area of triangle *AOE*

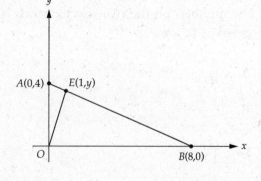

   A. is 1.
   B. is 2.
   C. is 2.5.
   D. is 4.
   E. cannot be determined from the given information.

96. Given triangles *ABC* and *DEB* as shown, the value of y in terms of x is

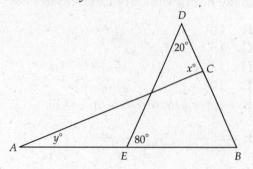

   F. $y = x + 120$
   G. $y = x - 120$
   H. $y = 100 - x$
   J. $y = 80 - x$
   K. $y = x - 80$

97. Here are two sequences:

Sequence *F*: 2, 7, 12, 17, 22, . . .
Sequence *S*: 3, 10, 17, 24, 31, . . .

The numbers in sequence *F* increase by fives. The numbers in sequence *S* increase by sevens. The first number that occurs in both sequences is 17. What is the next number that occurs in both sequences?

   A. 87
   B. 85
   C. 72
   D. 65
   E. 52

98. A certain type of drinking glass holds exactly $\frac{5}{8}$ liter of water. How many of those glasses can be filled if you have 40 liters of water?

   F. 72
   G. 64
   H. 30
   J. 25
   K. 24

99. $5^4 + 5^4 + 5^4 + 5^4 + 5^4 =$

   A. 5^5
   B. 5^{20}
   C. 25^{20}
   D. 25^4
   E. 10^4

100. Points *C*, *D*, *E*, and *H* lie on the sides of rectangle *ABFG* as shown. $AB = 8$ and $AG = 15$. What is the mean of the areas of the three triangles *ACG*, *ADH*, and *HEG*?

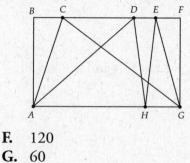

   F. 120
   G. 60
   H. 40
   J. 30
   K. There is more than one possible answer.

Answer Key
MODEL TEST 2

Scrambled Paragraphs	Logical Reasoning		Reading			
Paragraph 1 RQSUT	11. B	16. H	21. B	29. D	37. C	44. G
Paragraph 2 QSUTR	12. F	17. D	22. K	30. K	38. K	45. C
Paragraph 3 USRQT	13. C	18. K	23. A	31. B	39. C	46. H
Paragraph 4 UQSTR	14. H	19. B	24. H	32. H	40. H	47. A
Paragraph 5 QSRTU	15. E	20. F	25. A	33. D	41. E	48. K
			26. G	34. F	42. F	49. B
			27. C	35. E	43. B	50. K
			28. F	36. F		

Mathematics

51. A	61. B	71. B	81. D	91. E
52. H	62. J	72. J	82. G	92. F
53. D	63. C	73. B	83. D	93. E
54. F	64. G	74. F	84. F	94. J
55. B	65. D	75. C	85. D	95. B
56. J	66. J	76. F	86. F	96. K
57. A	67. B	77. C	87. D	97. E
58. H	68. H	78. J	88. H	98. G
59. E	69. D	79. B	89. E	99. A
60. G	70. K	80. H	90. G	100. H

Model Test 2

ANSWER EXPLANATIONS
MODEL TEST 2

Scrambled Paragraphs

Paragraph 1   RQSUT
All of the sentences tell about how women participated in wartime activities. The progression is from the safer and more traditional roles to the more untraditional and dangerous. R comes second, with its transitional reference to "stay-at-home activities" referring to the knitting socks, etc. R ends with an indication that other activities will be named. The next two sentences begin with "some" and "others" respectively. Q begins with "some" and gives less traditional roles involving traveling with the troops. "Others" signals that S is next, and introduces "more dangerous" work. The next sentence, U, tells about "even more perilous" work. Sentence T ends the paragraph by summarizing the role of women during the war.

Paragraph 2   QSUTR
S might seem to come second, because of the transitional "this vehicle" seeming to refer to the rail locomotive, but the sense of the sentence shows that "this vehicle" must be an earlier model, with the rail locomotive coming later.

TIP: Read the sentences carefully.

Q is the second sentence because it gives Trevithick's background and his first invention, the steam-driven road carriage. S comes next, the "subsequently" indicating a later development, and "this vehicle" referring to the steam-driven road carriage. U has the transitional "this experiment" and the word "locomotive" referring to S. U ends with "valuable information," and T with its "for example" gives an example of the information gained from the railway locomotive experiment. Sentence R concludes the paragraph by providing examples of two ways that Trevithick is remembered today.

Paragraph 3   USRQT
The pattern of this paragraph involves the introduction of a colorful character followed by a summary of her colorful activities in chronological order. U is the second sentence, with "Her bizarre exploits" referring to the colorful Lillie and an example of colorful behavior at an early time, childhood. S moves the time forward to adulthood and gives examples of her behavior. R provides a commentary on this behavior. Q with its transitional "also" goes on to give more adult behavior. T ends the paragraph with information about what happened after Lillie died.

Paragraph 4   UQSTR
This paragraph has some chronological clues, but the sentences require careful attention to transitions and development. Q could logically come second, but the sense of U indicates that it is second because it tells about friends criticizing the "pink flamingoes" mentioned in the first sentence and introduces the idea of changing the way her yard looks. Q and S are third and fourth, respectively, describing the change that Blythe made (the addition of costumes) first for Halloween and then, "a few weeks later," for Thanksgiving. T continues telling about the change, describing other costumes. R brings the time forward with its "recently," and concludes with a statement about the public reaction to Blythe's "show."

Paragraph 5   QSRTU
This paragraph offers a convenient chronology but requires some careful reading to determine the second and third sentences. S could be the second sentence if Q didn't produce a more logical development. Q describes the glassware and tells about its "less expensive" quality. S begins with a reference to the description—"its attractiveness"—and the less expensive price—its "economy." Therefore, S logically follows Q. S also introduces the idea of the popularity of the glass, which leads logically to R. R begins with "Styles change," indicating a fall from popularity, and moves the time forward to the late 1920s. T is next, telling about a "second life" for Carnival glass three decades later. U concludes the paragraph by describing the popularity of Carnival glass in the present time.

Logical Reasoning

Solutions in this section frequently involve techniques discussed in Skillbuilder B.

11–12. **(B,F)** Make 5 horizontal spaces, representing how the racers finish (with the fastest on the right). Using the first letter of each name to represent the people, we see from requirements (2) and (3) that *M* and *R* must occupy the first and last positions, although we don't know which of them is in each of those spots. Requirement (1) puts *A* to the right of *F*. Person *S* can finish in any of the three inner positions. We can now answer the questions.

11. **(B)** Although the position of *S* affects the position of *A*, *A* can only be 2nd or 3rd.

12. **(F)** If *S* beats *M*, then *M* must be in the leftmost position; that means *R* must be 1st.

13–15. **(C,H,E)** Remember to **mark your sentences** in this type of logical reasoning problem.

13. **(C)** The word "like" is in sentences 2 and 3 only. Only the ! symbol is in exactly those sentences. Notice that, in each of these sentences, the word and the symbol are never in the same position as one another. The correct choice is C.

14. **(H)** The $ symbol is in all three sentences. The words "Gavan," "and," "Carmen" are also in all three sentences. But because of the **restriction** (that the position of a symbol is never the same as that of the word it represents), you should have immediately eliminated "Gavan" (because of its position in sentence 2) and "and" (because of its position in either sentence 1 or sentence 3). Therefore, the only possible answer is "Carmen" (choice H). Always do this elimination in problems with this restriction.

15. **(E)** The word "and" is in all three sentences. Immediately eliminate the symbols & and $ because of the **restriction** (by the way, from

the previous question we also know that $ represents "Carmen"). It seems that "and" can be represented by either @ or #. However, it is possible that one of these must represent some other word. This tricky situation can only arise in the restricted type of code problem. The only other word (aside from "Carmen") that is also in all three sentences is "Gavan." Must a specific one of the symbols @ or # represent "Gavan" because the restriction eliminates the other? If so, the remaining symbol would represent "and." However, neither is eliminated. That confirms that these two symbols represent "and" and "Gavan," but we cannot determine which is which. The correct choice is E.

16. **(H)** This is the only choice that relates the first word of each pair to the second word of that pair.

17–19. **(D,K,B)** Make a chart whose rows are labeled *R*, *B*, *C*, and *L* (for the people) and whose columns are labeled *p*, *v*, *o*, and *t* (for the instruments). Mark your chart according to given facts (1), then (2), then (4). Notice that you know which instruments *C* plays, so put X's in the other two boxes in row *C*. Also note that *B* cannot play the oboe and trumpet since *C* already plays that pair. Therefore one of *B*'s instruments must be the piano. Now (3) tells you that one person plays violin and oboe, while another plays violin and trumpet. Those people must be *R* and *L*, since the chart already shows that *B* and *C* do not play the violin. It may be easiest now to make a second chart with all the information from (1), (2), and (4).

On the first chart, let *R* be the violin and oboe player and let *L* be the violin and trumpet player. On the second chart, let *R* be the violin and trumpet player and let *L* be the violin and oboe player. You can now fill in the missing X's in the rows for *R*, *C*, and *L*. Although *B* plays piano, you cannot tell what *B*'s second instrument is. We can now answer the questions.

17. **(D)**

18. **(K)** Either Rafael or Ludwig could play violin and oboe.

19. **(B)** Bonita must play either the oboe or the trumpet as her second instrument. Whichever one of those instruments you check off (on either chart) will be played by 3 different people. This will only be the case for one instrument.

20. **(F)** In the paragraph, the judge is taking 12 specific occurrences about speeding in red sports cars, and generalizing to include *all* those who drive red sports cars. This is "going from the specific to the general." (Such generalizations are often wrong, even when many similar specific cases occur. We are not interested in whether any of the statements employ valid reasoning or not, but rather in finding which choice parallels the *type* of reasoning used in the original statement.)

Choice **F** parallels this type of reasoning.

Choice **G** makes a statement, then uses the contrapositive of that statement to conclude that Dennis was not going to the concert. Even though that reasoning is valid, it does not parallel the original example.

Choice **H** does not draw a general conclusion about all drivers from specific information about some drivers.

Choice **J** illustrates logical reasoning, but does not parallel the original statement.

The judge concluded that driving a red sports car implied that the driver was speeding. Choice **K** states that speeding implies that the car driven was a red sports car. This is not even the contrapositive of the judge's conclusion. It is certainly not generalizing from specific occurrences.

Reading

Passage I

21. **(B)** Main Idea   A is incorrect because while history is given in the passage, no reference is made to legend. B is correct because it is broad enough to cover all the information in the passage, and it is also accurate as every

paragraph mentions the scarcity of information. C and E are too narrow. D contradicts the statement (line 5) that the movie is not factual.

22. **(K)** Inference   K is correct because while the passage does not state that the movie is pure fiction, it states (line 5) that it is not factual. F and G contradict the statement that the film is not factual. Neither H nor J is stated or suggested in the passage.

23. **(A)** Inference   A is correct because the rival is described as "jealous," and his attack reveals Shakespeare's activity in the theater, suggesting that his jealousy was professional. C might be correct if there were any suggestion that his attack mentions an affair, but there is no such suggestion. B, D, and E are incorrect because there is no information in the passage that would support them.

24. **(H)** Detail   H is the correct answer because the passage does not say that Shakespeare endured poverty during the plague, only that his theater career was interrupted. F, G, and K are directly stated, and J is incorrect because it is stated (line 38) that he made money in real estate—a secondary source of income.

25. **(A)** Inference   The context (line 13) involves a lack of information, leading to the definition given in A. None of the other choices is consistent with the topic of this part of the passage.

26. **(G)** Detail   The passage asks how a middle-class man could have been familiar with aristocratic and court life and calls this knowledge "mysterious." None of the other choices are mentioned or suggested by any detail in the passage.

Passage II

27. **(C)** Main Idea   Only C is broad enough to cover all the information in the passage. A is incorrect because only the first and last paragraphs mention recent demand. B is also too

narrow. D and E are both too narrow and also inaccurate. There is no suggestion made that the information given is "little-known," and the passage says that the "most desirable" kinds may be endangered, not the entire species.

28. **(F)** Inference   The sentence using the word (line 6) is followed by details that exemplify how mushroom popularity has grown; thus *grown* is the correct choice. H contradicts the context. The other choices are unsuitable because *burgeoned* modifies *popularity,* and the other choices do not refer to popularity.

29. **(D)** Detail   A contradicts the information given in (lines 26–27). The word *worldwide* makes B incorrect since the passage refers only to mushroom popularity in America. C contradicts the statement that the fruiting body appears above ground (line 20). D is stated in lines 36–38. E is inaccurate because it is too extreme; it is stated (line 54) that people worry that some varieties may become extinct, but not that any have become extinct.

30. **(K)** Inference   It is stated that truffles are "rare and costly" (line 30) and that animals are trained to find them; it can be inferred that both the scarcity and the difficulty in finding them contribute to their cost. G contradicts the statements (lines 30–33) about where they grow and how they are harvested. H may be true according to the information given in the passage, but there is no suggestion in the passage that cost would be affected by the part of the mushroom harvested.

31. **(B)** Inference   A is incorrect because although training is stated as important (line 34), there is no suggestion of a classroom setting. The statement that "high demand" encourages "enterpreneurs" suggests that mushroom gathering must be profitable; therefore B is correct. C and D contradict the statement in the last paragraph that mushroom gathering took place before recent years (lines 44–45). E is incorrect because the fruiting bodies—the ones gathered—grow above the ground (line 20).

32. **(H)** Detail   It is stated that the Asian gatherer mistook a local variety for an Asian type; therefore she was not familiar with the local deadly amanita. F and J are not stated or suggested in the passage. G contradicts the fact that she was experienced (line 35). K might be true, but her mistake is more likely to have been caused by unfamiliarity with mushroom varieties than countryside, so H is the better answer.

Passage III

33. **(D)** Main Idea   A, B, and E are too narrow, and C is too broad, as the passage focuses only on Cajuns, not other people and cultures of south Louisiana. Although the second paragraph does give history, that history is related to the description of culture since it explains the French influence as well as the early separation of the group, so D is correct.

34. **(F)** Inference   The reason stated for expulsion is refusal to sign a loyalty oath. One can infer that a person who made such a refusal might be rebellious and thus a threat. H might be correct if F were not given, but F is clearly the more logical answer of the two. G, H, and K are neither stated nor suggested.

35. **(E)** Detail   A, B, C, and D are all stated in the passage. E is correct because it not only is not stated, but contradicts the statement that Cajun cooks are adventurous.

36. **(F)** Inference   The context compares remote places with "more likely venues," indicating that a venue is a place. G is one definition of the word venue but does not fit the context in which the word is used.

TIP: Don't rely on a known definition of a word; rely on context.

37. **(C)** Detail   The third paragraph says that another name for a bayou is a creek (line 25).

38. **(K)** Detail   French rhythms are not mentioned, so F is incorrect. Choices G, H, and J

are mentioned as "frequent" (line 54) in the music or related to the music as an "offshoot" (line 56). Only the accordion is stated to be "integral" (line 53) or essential.

Passage IV

39. **(C) Main Idea** A is mentioned only in the first paragraph. Most of the passage does not involve collisions, choices B and E. Only one paragraph discusses origins. A, B, D, and E are all too narrow. Only C is broad enough to incorporate all the content of the passage.

40. **(H) Inference** The "minuscule" cost of the NEAP project is compared with the "costly" projects of NASA; therefore the cost of the NEAP project must be small, making H the correct choice. None of the other choices are words that compare or contrast with "costly," so they cannot be correct definitions.

41. **(E) Detail** The first paragraph says that the collision of a large asteroid could have "drastic environmental consequences." No other consequences are mentioned in the passage, so E must be the correct answer.

> **TIP:** Base your answer only on the information in the passage. Do not rely on outside knowledge or suppositions.

42. **(F) Inference** *Common* means occurring frequently, but the passage says that such collisions are frequent or "common" only in the context of billions of years. So the word is being used in a different or special context, and F is the correct answer. G is incorrect; the word is not used earlier in the passage, and there is no indication that the author is quoting anyone. H might possibly be an acceptable choice if F were not clearly correct. J is incorrect according to grammar and context, and K is not suggested by the context.

43. **(B) Detail** Although it is stated that a big collision could cause environmental change, there is no mention of such change except in this one statement. There is no statement or

suggestion that they have caused most of Earth's environmental changes. A, C, and D are directly stated in the passage, and E is implied (line 50) in the last paragraph.

44. **(G) Detail** It is stated that people worry about a collision because of a possible "shift in the asteroid's path" or an "error in calculation." In other words, such events are not entirely predictable. The other choices are not stated or suggested in the passage.

Passage V

45. **(C) Main Idea** This item is an example of the need sometimes to recognize tone in determining main idea. E might be correct if the tone of the passage were different. But there is no congratulatory or approving language used in discussing the efforts to hold back the sea. E, then, cannot be correct. All of the defensive efforts against the sea are presented negatively. A and B are too narrow. D is inaccurate, as none of the methods are presented as being desirable. Only C is acceptable since the entire passage focuses on various detrimental effects of building on the beach.

46. **(H) Inference** The passage says that hard devices block the sand flow to other areas and cause erosion (lines 43–45), this is the most likely reason for banning the devices. The other choices are not suggested or stated in the passage.

47. **(A) Main Idea** The topic of the paragraph in which the bulkhead is mentioned is that technology cannot control the ocean; the bulkhead is used as an example of this concept. B, C, and D are not mentioned or suggested in connection with the bulkhead. E contradicts the negative tone of the passage.

48. **(K) Detail** The first paragraph states this idea (line 11). F, G, and H are not stated or suggested in the passage, and J contradicts the information in the first paragraph.

49. **(B)** Main Idea   Again, tone is important. The author paints a negative picture of the results of building on the beach. Thus A is not a good choice. Nowhere are federal subsidies supported in the text; they are mentioned only once, in the last paragraph (line 63) and in a negative context, so C is incorrect. Nothing in the passage supports D or E as a good choice.

50. **(K)** Detail   Dunes are called "protective" of the beach. All the other choices are presented in the passage as harmful.

Mathematics

51. **(A)** Multiplying $\frac{1}{2}$ by $\frac{1}{6}$ produces $\frac{1}{12}$. That is the same as $\frac{1}{3}$ times $\frac{1}{4}$.

52. **(H)** Adding the areas of the two large triangles (= 20) counts the overlapped region twice. Subtracting that region once must produce 14, so its area is 6.

53. **(D)** Adding, $1.1 + 2.11 + 3.111 = 6.321$.

54. **(F)** One approach is to try values for x. When $x = 6$, $x^2 + x = 36 + 6 = 42$, so 6 is too small. Letting $x = 7$ turns out to be too large, so x is between 6 and 7.

55. **(B)** Since the triangle is isosceles, angle BCA must be 80°. Then angle $BCE = 100° = 4x°$, so $x = 25$ and $3x = 75$.

56. **(J)** Start with Katie's age = 16. That makes Carole 32, so Barbara is 39.

> **TIP:** When simple but specific numerical values are given in a problem, that is often a good starting point for analysis.

57. **(A)** If we think of 3.4 as p and 10^2 as q, we have $pq + pq$. This is $2pq$, or $2 \times 3.4 \times 10^2 = 6.8 \times 10^2$. It is sometimes easier to manipulate letters (symbols) than numbers.

58. **(H)** The area of $SXRD$ is 12, so $SD = 4$. The area of $PBQX$ is 27, so $PB = 9$. Then $AD +$

$AB = 7 + 12 = 19$, and the perimeter of $ABCD$ is 38.

59. **(E)** Start to test the choices. If Kobi has 208 pennies, the remaining $7.75 must be made up of nickels. This is certainly possible. So long as the difference between $9.83 and the number of pennies is a multiple of 5, that difference can be made up of nickels. Only 85 pennies will not work.

60. **(G)** $2x - 3 = 32$. Rather than solve for x, we can add 6 to both sides producing $2x + 3 = 38$. Notice that you do not always have to solve for x (although that would be another way to do the problem).

61. **(B)** We wish to compare pears with bananas, knowing that 1 apple = 2 pears. Putting this information into the first sentence (and using letters to represents the fruits) produces $10p + 6b = 8b + 9p$. Therefore, $1p = 2b$, and the answer is 2. Another approach would be to set a price for one pear. For example, if one pear costs 10¢, then one apple costs 20¢, and so on.

62. **(J)** We have $R = 2^3 \cdot 3^2 \cdot 7 \cdot 13$ and $S = 2^3 \cdot 3 \cdot 7^2 \cdot 11$. The greatest common factor (sometimes called the greatest common divisor) must contain every prime that is in *both* R and S, and each of those primes must be raised to the smallest exponent that it originally had in either R or S. Therefore, the greatest common factor is $2^3 \cdot 3 \cdot 7 = 168$.

63. **(C)** Substitution produces $4|-5 - 2| - 3|-10| = 4|-7| - 3|-10| = 4(7) - 3(10) = 28 - 30 = -2$.

> **TIP:** Combine the terms inside the absolute value signs before you compute the absolute value.

64. **(G)** List the numbers vertically. There are eight 2s in the units column, for a total of 16. Thus, we must carry 1 into the tens column. There are seven 1s in that column, for a total (including the "carry") of 8. There are six 1s

in the hundreds column (and no "carry"), so that total is 6.

65. **(D)** If we let g represent the number of girls, we can express everything in terms of g. There would be $2g$ boys and g girls, so the class has $3g$ members. Half of the boys plus all of the girls would be $g + g$, so $2g$ students are in the math club. Changing this to a percent, we have $\frac{2g}{3g} \cdot 100 = \frac{2}{3} \cdot 100 = 66\frac{2}{3}\%$.

66. **(J)** Removing all parentheses produces $16 + 5x - 8 + 2x$, so the answer is $8 + 7x$.

67. **(B)**

> **FACT:** When two straight lines intersect, the "vertical angles" formed are equal.

We can fill in the values of all the vertical angles, producing $x + 40 + 60 + x + 40 + 60 = 360$, leading to $x = 80$. If you prefer, just add the angles on one side of a straight line, getting $x + 40 + 60 = 180$. This also produces $x = 80$.

68. **(H)** Each half hour we are losing 100 people. To lose 350 people would take three half-hours plus another 15 minutes. That is 1 hour and 45 minutes. Measuring from noon, this would bring us to 1:45 P.M.

69. **(D)** Draw triangle PXQ. Each side is actually a radius of one of the circles. Since the circles are congruent, all three sides are equal. That makes this an equilateral triangle, so each of its angles is $60°$.

70. **(K)** Since Andrew has d dollars, Bruce must have $3d$ dollars. Carlos has $\$80$ less than half of $(d + 3d)$, so Carlos has 80 less than $2d$, or $2d - 80$ dollars.

71. **(B)** If six of the integers are as small as possible, the seventh would have to be as large as possible. Since the integers must be positive and unequal, let the first six be 1, 2, 3, 4, 5,

and 6. Their sum is 21, so the seventh integer would be 40.

72. **(J)** Using algebra would give us $\frac{1 + 5 + x + 10 + 15}{5} = x - 1$. That means $31 + x = 5(x - 1)$, leading to $x = 9$. Another method would be to use "trial and error." That is, try each choice until you find the correct answer. Note that since x is supposed to be an integer, the mean (which is 1 less than x) must also be an integer. For example, if $x = 6$, the mean would be $\frac{31 + 6}{5}$. That is not 1 less than 6 (and isn't even an integer).

73. **(B)**

> **FACT:** For positive numbers a, b, c, and d, $\frac{a}{b} < \frac{c}{d}$ if and only if $ad < bc$.

$\frac{7}{50} < \frac{1}{x}$ tells us that $7x < 50$ so $x < 7\frac{1}{7}$. Also, $\frac{1}{x} < \frac{8}{51}$ tells us that $51 < 8x$, so $6\frac{3}{8} < x$. Putting these together produces $6\frac{3}{8} < x < 7\frac{1}{7}$. Since x is an integer, it can only be 7.

74. **(F)** $\frac{2^8}{2} = 2^7$ Remember that 2 is the same as 2^1. Notice how choice J is testing whether anyone would try to cancel the 2s. That choice is a wonderfully absurd answer since 1^8 is simply 1, which is certainly not half of 2^8.

75. **(C)** Each choice must be tested. Since x is between $\frac{1}{2}$ and 1, $2x - 1$ is between 0 and 1. x^2 is between $\frac{1}{4}$ and 1. $\frac{1}{x}$ is between 2 and 1. $1 - x$ is between $\frac{1}{2}$ and 0. x^3 is between $\frac{1}{8}$

and 1. The largest value occurs for $\frac{1}{x}$. The problem does not actually allow x to have the value $\frac{1}{2}$ or the value 1. Another approach would be to choose an appropriate number for x (such as $\frac{3}{4}$) and evaluate each choice.

76. **(F)** In eight years, the sum of their three ages will be $49 + 24$. Ten years ago, the sum of their three ages was $49 - 30$. Then $F - P = (49 + 24) - (49 - 30) = 54$.

77. **(C)** Clearly $\frac{1}{x} = \frac{3}{4}$, so $x = \frac{4}{3}$.

78. **(J)** $N = 7Q + 5$. Then $N + 24 = 7Q + 29$, which is 1 more than a multiple of 7.

79. **(B)**

> **FACT:** An exterior angle of a triangle is equal to the sum of the two remote interior angles.

Angle $DBE = 70 + 50 = 120$, so the third angle of triangle DBE is $40°$.

80. **(H)** Since $\frac{3}{2}$ is $2 \times \frac{3}{4}$, the answer is $2L$.

81. **(D)** The numerator 18 is divisible by the positive integers 1, 2, 3, 6, 9, and 18. The only positive integer values of N that produce any of these are $N = 1, 4, 7,$ and 16. The *number* of values is 4.

82. **(G)** To find x, we must fill in several other boxes first. Since the "constant sum" is 33, the center box must be 11. Then the upper right box must be 12, so x must be 7.

83. **(D)** We must locate the approximate position on the horizontal axis where the height of the coffee graph is twice the height of the sugar graph. At the start of June, the coffee graph is $5\frac{1}{2}$ boxes high, while the sugar graph is only $2\frac{2}{3}$ boxes high. By July, the coffee graph is too low. The correct heights occurred during June.

84. **(F)** "Other" occupies 20% of the pie chart. The correct bar graph must have the same heights for F and R, the same (but lower) heights for C and O, and a still lower height for T.

85. **(D)** Start with a post at one corner. We have 4 more posts along the 20 foot side, then 7 more along the 35 foot side, then 5 more along the 25 foot side. However, that final post is the same as the starting post. Therefore the answer is $1 + 4 + 7 + (5 - 1) = 16$. A carefully drawn picture is very helpful.

86. **(F)**

> **FACT:** The longest side of a triangle is opposite the largest angle of the triangle.

In triangle ABD, $\overline{BD}$ is the longest side. Now in triangle BCD, $\overline{BC}$ is the longest side, making it longer than $\overline{BD}$. The longest side of the figure is $\overline{BC}$.

87. **(D)** Remember the rules of exponents for multiplication, and that multiplication can be done in any order. Then we have $x^2 \cdot x \cdot y^3 \cdot y^2 = x^3 \cdot y^5$.

88. **(H)** $\frac{12n}{56} = \frac{3n}{14}$. For this fraction to be an integer, 14 must exactly divide n. The smallest n that works is 14.

89. **(E)** Dividing both sides of the first equation by 2 and then replacing $x + y$ with 11, we have $11 + z = 55$. Then $z = 44$.

90. **(G)** The easiest way to test each choice is to first rewrite $a^2 - ab$ as $a(a - b)$. Then, for example, choice F equals $19 \cdot 1 = 19$. We quickly find that G is the answer.

91. **(E)** An even sum comes from two odd or two even numbers. The 3, 5, or 9 could each go with the 1 or 7; that produces six possibilities. The 6 could only go with the 4, producing one more possibility. Therefore there are seven satisfactory pairs. Since there are 12 possible pairings all together, the probability is $\frac{7}{12}$.

92. **(F)** Distance = rate × time, or $t = \frac{D}{r}$.

    Therefore Larry will make up the 80 miles in $\frac{80}{5}$ hours.

93. **(E)** Dividing each term in the numerator by 3 produces $x + 1 = 2.5$, so $x = 1.5$.

94. **(J)** It is easiest to consider how much value remains each day. If we started with $\$N$ worth of stock, at the end of the first day we have 40% of N, or $\frac{40}{100}N$, left. At the end of the second day we have $\frac{40}{100} \cdot \frac{90}{100} N$ left. That is 36% of N. If $y\%$ were to *remain* each day, we would have $\frac{y}{100} \cdot \frac{y}{100} N$ left. Thus $\frac{y^2}{10000} = \frac{36}{100}$, so $y^2 = 3600$ and $y = 60$. Retaining 60% each day is equivalent to losing 40% each day.

95. **(B)** When using the formula Area $= \frac{1}{2} hb$ to get the area of a triangle, any side of the triangle can be considered its base, so long as the altitude goes to that base. For triangle AOE, let $\overline{OA}$ be the base and draw an altitude from E to that base. Since point E is 1 unit to the right of the y-axis, the length of that altitude is 1. Base $\overline{OA}$ is 4, so the area of the triangle is $\frac{1}{2} \cdot 1 \cdot 4 = 2$. There is no need to find the y-coordinate of point E. Do not let yourself be distracted by that missing coordinate.

96. **(K)** In triangle DEB, angle EBD must be 80°. Now look at triangle ABC.

    FACT: An exterior angle of a triangle is equal to the sum of the two remote interior angles.

    $x = y + 80$, so $y = x - 80$.

97. **(E)** Sequence F contains every 5th integer after 17. Sequence S contains every 7th integer after 17. Therefore both will contain every 35th integer after 17. The next common number will be $17 + 35 = 52$.

98. **(G)** We must figure out how many times $\frac{5}{8}$ goes into 40. That is $\frac{40}{\frac{5}{8}} = 40 \cdot \frac{8}{5} = 64$.

99. **(A)** This is $5 \times 5^4 = 5^5$.

100. **(H)** Let $AH = p$ and $HG = q$. Note that $p + q = 15$. Also notice that the altitude for each triangle is equal to 8 (= AB). The three areas are $\frac{1}{2} \cdot 8 \cdot 15$, $\frac{1}{2} \cdot 8 \cdot p$, and $\frac{1}{2} \cdot 8 \cdot q$. Then their mean is $\frac{60 + 4p + 4q}{3}$. Since $p + q = 15$, $4p + 4q = 60$. The mean is now $\frac{60 + 60}{3} = 40$.

Answer Sheet
MODEL TEST 3

Part I   Verbal

Scrambled Paragraphs

Paragraph 1

The second sentence is   Ⓠ Ⓡ Ⓢ Ⓣ Ⓤ
The third sentence is   Ⓠ Ⓡ Ⓢ Ⓣ Ⓤ
The fourth sentence is   Ⓠ Ⓡ Ⓢ Ⓣ Ⓤ
The fifth sentence is   Ⓠ Ⓡ Ⓢ Ⓣ Ⓤ
The sixth sentence is   Ⓠ Ⓡ Ⓢ Ⓣ Ⓤ

Paragraph 2

The second sentence is   Ⓠ Ⓡ Ⓢ Ⓣ Ⓤ
The third sentence is   Ⓠ Ⓡ Ⓢ Ⓣ Ⓤ
The fourth sentence is   Ⓠ Ⓡ Ⓢ Ⓣ Ⓤ
The fifth sentence is   Ⓠ Ⓡ Ⓢ Ⓣ Ⓤ
The sixth sentence is   Ⓠ Ⓡ Ⓢ Ⓣ Ⓤ

Paragraph 3

The second sentence is   Ⓠ Ⓡ Ⓢ Ⓣ Ⓤ
The third sentence is   Ⓠ Ⓡ Ⓢ Ⓣ Ⓤ
The fourth sentence is   Ⓠ Ⓡ Ⓢ Ⓣ Ⓤ
The fifth sentence is   Ⓠ Ⓡ Ⓢ Ⓣ Ⓤ
The sixth sentence is   Ⓠ Ⓡ Ⓢ Ⓣ Ⓤ

Paragraph 4

The second sentence is   Ⓠ Ⓡ Ⓢ Ⓣ Ⓤ
The third sentence is   Ⓠ Ⓡ Ⓢ Ⓣ Ⓤ
The fourth sentence is   Ⓠ Ⓡ Ⓢ Ⓣ Ⓤ
The fifth sentence is   Ⓠ Ⓡ Ⓢ Ⓣ Ⓤ
The sixth sentence is   Ⓠ Ⓡ Ⓢ Ⓣ Ⓤ

Paragraph 5

The second sentence is   Ⓠ Ⓡ Ⓢ Ⓣ Ⓤ
The third sentence is   Ⓠ Ⓡ Ⓢ Ⓣ Ⓤ
The fourth sentence is   Ⓠ Ⓡ Ⓢ Ⓣ Ⓤ
The fifth sentence is   Ⓠ Ⓡ Ⓢ Ⓣ Ⓤ
The sixth sentence is   Ⓠ Ⓡ Ⓢ Ⓣ Ⓤ

Logical Reasoning

11 Ⓐ Ⓑ Ⓒ Ⓓ Ⓔ
12 Ⓕ Ⓖ Ⓗ Ⓙ Ⓚ
13 Ⓐ Ⓑ Ⓒ Ⓓ Ⓔ
14 Ⓕ Ⓖ Ⓗ Ⓙ Ⓚ
15 Ⓐ Ⓑ Ⓒ Ⓓ Ⓔ
16 Ⓕ Ⓖ Ⓗ Ⓙ Ⓚ
17 Ⓐ Ⓑ Ⓒ Ⓓ Ⓔ
18 Ⓕ Ⓖ Ⓗ Ⓙ Ⓚ
19 Ⓐ Ⓑ Ⓒ Ⓓ Ⓔ
20 Ⓕ Ⓖ Ⓗ Ⓙ Ⓚ

Reading

21 Ⓐ Ⓑ Ⓒ Ⓓ Ⓔ
22 Ⓕ Ⓖ Ⓗ Ⓙ Ⓚ
23 Ⓐ Ⓑ Ⓒ Ⓓ Ⓔ
24 Ⓕ Ⓖ Ⓗ Ⓙ Ⓚ
25 Ⓐ Ⓑ Ⓒ Ⓓ Ⓔ
26 Ⓕ Ⓖ Ⓗ Ⓙ Ⓚ
27 Ⓐ Ⓑ Ⓒ Ⓓ Ⓔ
28 Ⓕ Ⓖ Ⓗ Ⓙ Ⓚ
29 Ⓐ Ⓑ Ⓒ Ⓓ Ⓔ
30 Ⓕ Ⓖ Ⓗ Ⓙ Ⓚ
31 Ⓐ Ⓑ Ⓒ Ⓓ Ⓔ
32 Ⓕ Ⓖ Ⓗ Ⓙ Ⓚ
33 Ⓐ Ⓑ Ⓒ Ⓓ Ⓔ
34 Ⓕ Ⓖ Ⓗ Ⓙ Ⓚ
35 Ⓐ Ⓑ Ⓒ Ⓓ Ⓔ
36 Ⓕ Ⓖ Ⓗ Ⓙ Ⓚ
37 Ⓐ Ⓑ Ⓒ Ⓓ Ⓔ
38 Ⓕ Ⓖ Ⓗ Ⓙ Ⓚ

39 Ⓐ Ⓑ Ⓒ Ⓓ Ⓔ
40 Ⓕ Ⓖ Ⓗ Ⓙ Ⓚ
41 Ⓐ Ⓑ Ⓒ Ⓓ Ⓔ
42 Ⓕ Ⓖ Ⓗ Ⓙ Ⓚ
43 Ⓐ Ⓑ Ⓒ Ⓓ Ⓔ
44 Ⓕ Ⓖ Ⓗ Ⓙ Ⓚ
45 Ⓐ Ⓑ Ⓒ Ⓓ Ⓔ
46 Ⓕ Ⓖ Ⓗ Ⓙ Ⓚ
47 Ⓐ Ⓑ Ⓒ Ⓓ Ⓔ
48 Ⓕ Ⓖ Ⓗ Ⓙ Ⓚ
49 Ⓐ Ⓑ Ⓒ Ⓓ Ⓔ
50 Ⓕ Ⓖ Ⓗ Ⓙ Ⓚ

Answer Sheet
MODEL TEST 3

Part II   Mathematics

51 Ⓐ Ⓑ Ⓒ Ⓓ Ⓔ   71 Ⓐ Ⓑ Ⓒ Ⓓ Ⓔ   91 Ⓐ Ⓑ Ⓒ Ⓓ Ⓔ
52 Ⓕ Ⓖ Ⓗ Ⓙ Ⓚ   72 Ⓕ Ⓖ Ⓗ Ⓙ Ⓚ   92 Ⓕ Ⓖ Ⓗ Ⓙ Ⓚ
53 Ⓐ Ⓑ Ⓒ Ⓓ Ⓔ   73 Ⓐ Ⓑ Ⓒ Ⓓ Ⓔ   93 Ⓐ Ⓑ Ⓒ Ⓓ Ⓔ
54 Ⓕ Ⓖ Ⓗ Ⓙ Ⓚ   74 Ⓕ Ⓖ Ⓗ Ⓙ Ⓚ   94 Ⓕ Ⓖ Ⓗ Ⓙ Ⓚ
55 Ⓐ Ⓑ Ⓒ Ⓓ Ⓔ   75 Ⓐ Ⓑ Ⓒ Ⓓ Ⓔ   95 Ⓐ Ⓑ Ⓒ Ⓓ Ⓔ

56 Ⓕ Ⓖ Ⓗ Ⓙ Ⓚ   76 Ⓕ Ⓖ Ⓗ Ⓙ Ⓚ   96 Ⓕ Ⓖ Ⓗ Ⓙ Ⓚ
57 Ⓐ Ⓑ Ⓒ Ⓓ Ⓔ   77 Ⓐ Ⓑ Ⓒ Ⓓ Ⓔ   97 Ⓐ Ⓑ Ⓒ Ⓓ Ⓔ
58 Ⓕ Ⓖ Ⓗ Ⓙ Ⓚ   78 Ⓕ Ⓖ Ⓗ Ⓙ Ⓚ   98 Ⓕ Ⓖ Ⓗ Ⓙ Ⓚ
59 Ⓐ Ⓑ Ⓒ Ⓓ Ⓔ   79 Ⓐ Ⓑ Ⓒ Ⓓ Ⓔ   99 Ⓐ Ⓑ Ⓒ Ⓓ Ⓔ
60 Ⓕ Ⓖ Ⓗ Ⓙ Ⓚ   80 Ⓕ Ⓖ Ⓗ Ⓙ Ⓚ   100 Ⓕ Ⓖ Ⓗ Ⓙ Ⓚ

61 Ⓐ Ⓑ Ⓒ Ⓓ Ⓔ   81 Ⓐ Ⓑ Ⓒ Ⓓ Ⓔ
62 Ⓕ Ⓖ Ⓗ Ⓙ Ⓚ   82 Ⓕ Ⓖ Ⓗ Ⓙ Ⓚ
63 Ⓐ Ⓑ Ⓒ Ⓓ Ⓔ   83 Ⓐ Ⓑ Ⓒ Ⓓ Ⓔ
64 Ⓕ Ⓖ Ⓗ Ⓙ Ⓚ   84 Ⓕ Ⓖ Ⓗ Ⓙ Ⓚ
65 Ⓐ Ⓑ Ⓒ Ⓓ Ⓔ   85 Ⓐ Ⓑ Ⓒ Ⓓ Ⓔ

66 Ⓕ Ⓖ Ⓗ Ⓙ Ⓚ   86 Ⓕ Ⓖ Ⓗ Ⓙ Ⓚ
67 Ⓐ Ⓑ Ⓒ Ⓓ Ⓔ   87 Ⓐ Ⓑ Ⓒ Ⓓ Ⓔ
68 Ⓕ Ⓖ Ⓗ Ⓙ Ⓚ   88 Ⓕ Ⓖ Ⓗ Ⓙ Ⓚ
69 Ⓐ Ⓑ Ⓒ Ⓓ Ⓔ   89 Ⓐ Ⓑ Ⓒ Ⓓ Ⓔ
70 Ⓕ Ⓖ Ⓗ Ⓙ Ⓚ   90 Ⓕ Ⓖ Ⓗ Ⓙ Ⓚ

Model Test 3

45 QUESTIONS

SUGGESTED TIME: 75 MINUTES

Scrambled Paragraphs

Paragraphs 1–5

> **Directions:** Below are six sentences that can be arranged to form a well-organized and grammatically correct paragraph. The first sentence is provided, but the other five are listed in random order. Choose the order that will form the **best** paragraph. Each correct paragraph is worth two points, with no partial credit given.
>
> You may wish to put numbers in the blanks at the left of each sentence to help keep track of the order. When you finish the set, mark your answers on the answer sheet.

PARAGRAPH 1

In the fifteenth century Christopher Columbus and his crew introduced a West Indian plant that they called "pepper" to Spain.

_____ (Q) In Spain it became popular mainly as an ornamental plant, and it was as an ornamental that Spain's next-door neighbor Portugal took the plant to North Africa, India, and Indonesia.

_____ (R) In these places it became important as food, and as food it spread to the Ottoman Empire and eventually to Britain.

_____ (S) Both the sweet and hot varieties were eaten, the latter producing a burning sensation that many eaters valued highly.

_____ (T) But it is a versatile species, and today peppers have a remarkable array of uses in cooking, ornamental gardening, medicine—even in insect and animal control!

_____ (U) They called it this because the plant's berries reminded them of East Indian black pepper.

PARAGRAPH 2

During World War II it was obvious that to win the war the Allies would have to invade France and drive back the German army entrenched there.

_____ (Q) Even after Allied troops took the beach at Normandy on June 6, 1944, Hitler stubbornly declared the Normandy landing a diversion and sent all available reinforcements to the Seine area.

_____ (R) He had immense fortifications built to protect the major ports in that area and sent thousands of troops to guard them, but he left the beaches unprotected.

_____ (S) In part because of the Fuehrer's blunder, by the end of June the Allies had 850,000 men and 150,000 vehicles securely on Normandy soil.

_____ (T) Hitler believed that the major attack would come north of the Seine River and therefore maintained a large defensive force there.

_____ (U) Where in France the invasion would take place was a major question, for although the Allied command had chosen Normandy, the choice was shrouded in secrecy.

PARAGRAPH 3

The black-and-white keys of a grand piano may look simple, but each one is actually a lever in a complex arrangement of levers that both produces sound and cuts it off.

_____ (Q) A finger striking a key depresses a lever—the key itself—that raises another, the "wippen," which in turn acts upon a jack to lift a felt-tipped hammer.

_____ (R) As the damper rises, the hammer quickly strikes the wire and falls back, and the wire vibrates to produce the piano's musical sound.

_____ (S) When the finger is lifted, however, the damper falls back onto the wire, stopping its vibration and cutting off the sound.

_____ (T) As long as the finger holds down the key, the damper remains raised, and the wire will continue to vibrate—and sound—for up to 30 seconds.

_____ (U) Simultaneously, the key-lever also elevates the damper, which in its resting position presses lightly against a wire to prevent vibration.

PARAGRAPH 4

You may think that when you turn on a faucet, you are turning on a flow of water, but actually the faucet's basic purpose is to block a strong flow of water driven by a powerful pumping system.

_____ (Q) A misaligned washer, however, or one that no longer fits tightly inside the pipe because of corrosion or chemical buildup, will allow some leakage to occur even when the faucet is in the *off* position.

_____ (R) The precisely fitting shape of the washer and the force with which it is driven down prevent leakage, and once it is in place, friction prevents its being dislodged.

_____ (S) When you turn the faucet *off*, you are blocking that water—which you would not be able to do on your own—with the aid of a machine that maximizes the slight effort it takes to turn the handle.

_____ (T) So when you turn the faucet *on*, what you are doing is almost effortlessly removing a tightly set plug so that the pressurized stream of water is no longer blocked.

_____ (U) This machine is the rotary faucet, which consists of a wheel with axle and screw; when your hand rotates the wheel, the axle-screw drives down a washer to block the flow of water.

PARAGRAPH 5

Although the United Nations' Population Division declared October 12, 1999, as the day Earth's population reached the six-billion mark, the United States Census Bureau pinpointed July 19 of the same year as the big day.

_____ (Q) If you wonder how two scholarly and respected agencies can differ three months in measuring such a milestone, you probably think their measurements are more precise than they actually are.

_____ (R) In fact, the two agencies use figures that are not only more than ten years old but also come from countries using methods of varying accuracy.

_____ (S) Some error remains when all adjustments are done, but both agencies are confident that their figures are valid for all practical purposes.

_____ (T) Furthermore, although they both have methods for making adjustments based on the rates and kinds of error in each country, the methods are not perfect.

_____ (U) Some countries, for example, take a limited door-to-door census that is used to estimate the total population, whereas others mail out questionnaires to households, only some of which may be returned to the census bureau.

LOGICAL REASONING

Questions 11–20

> **Directions:** For each of the following questions, select the **best** answer from the given choices. Bubble in the letter corresponding to your answer on the answer sheet. Your answer should be based **only on the given information.**
>
> Read the words carefully. For example, "The red book is **to the right** of the blue book" does not necessarily mean that there is no other book between them. Similarly, be careful when reading words such as **between, below, above, after, before, behind,** and **ahead of.**

Questions 11 and 12 refer to the following information.

Four books of different colors are in a stack. They are numbered 1, 2, 3, and 4, from *top to bottom*. The red book is below the white book. The red book is below the yellow book, and there is no book between these two.

11. The only position(s) the blue book **cannot** be in

    A. is 1.
    B. is 2.
    C. is 3.
    D. is 4.
    E. are 3 and 4.

12. The yellow book can be in positions

    F. 1 or 2.
    G. 2 or 3.
    H. 1 or 3.
    J. 1, 2, or 3.
    K. 1, 2, 3, or 4.

Questions 13, 14, and 15 refer to the following information.

In the code below, (1) each letter represents the same word in all 3 sentences, (2) each word is represented by only one letter, and (3) in any given sentence, the letters may or may not be presented in the same order as the words.

L A R R Y means "Two seniors helped two juniors."

H E A R D means "The two juniors used Barron's."

L A T E R means "The juniors helped two sophomores."

13. Which word is represented by *A*?

    A. two
    B. seniors
    C. helped
    D. juniors
    E. Either "two" or "juniors," but cannot determine which one.

14. What letter represents "the"?

    F. *L*
    G. *R*
    H. *H*
    J. *D*
    K. *E*

15. What letter represents "used"?

   A. Either *H* or *D* but cannot determine which one.

   B. Either *H*, *E*, or *D*, but cannot determine which one.

   C. *H*

   D. *D*

   E. *E*

16. If Ahmal gets a job, Bing will buy a car. If Bing buys a car, Charles will go to school. If Charles goes to school, Ahmal will get a job.

Based only on the information above, which of the following statements **must** be true?

   I. If Ahmal gets a job, Charles will go to school.

   II. If Charles does not go to school, Bing will not buy a car.

   III. If Ahmal does not get a job, Bing will not buy a car.

   F. I only

   G. II only

   H. I and II only

   J. II and III only

   K. I, II, and III

Questions 17 and 18 refer to the following information.

Paul likes Joyce and all people whose names start with the letter L. Sean likes Lucia and all people whose names start with the letter V. Antonio likes Velma, but does not like Joyce. No one person is liked by Paul, Sean, *and* Antonio.

17. We can conclude that

   A. Paul likes Velma.

   B. Paul does not like Velma.

   C. There is not enough information to know if Paul likes or does not like Velma.

   D. Velma likes Paul.

   E. Velma does not like Paul.

18. We can conclude that

   F. Sean likes Joyce.

   G. Sean does not like Joyce.

   H. There is not enough information to know if Sean likes or does not like Joyce.

   J. Joyce likes Sean.

   K. Joyce does not like Sean.

19. Below are two word pairs. The words in each pair are related in some way. The relationship between the words in the first pair is similar to the relationship between the words in the second pair.

tree—wood
pyramid—stone

What is the relationship displayed in both word pairs?

   A. Natural things and man-made things

   B. Objects and what they are made of

   C. Objects that are very old

   D. Large things and their smaller counterparts

   E. Ways to build things

20. Jimmy said, "Teenagers are not influenced by advertising as much as people think they are. What they actually buy is different from what advertisers think they buy."

Which of the following statements, if true, would most **weaken** Jimmy's point?

   F. Teenagers buy a wide variety of brands of the same product.

   G. Teenagers, as a group, collectively outspend any other age group.

   H. Teenagers are confused by having too many choices.

   J. A survey indicated that when Brand Y began to advertise to teenagers, its sales to them increased dramatically.

   K. Research has shown that teenagers' buying patterns are not very predictable and tend to vary considerably.

READING

Questions 21–50

I. The English language has undergone many changes in its long history and in fact is still evolving, although more slowly now
Line than it did in the past. Its story began in the
(5) fifth century A.D. when tribesmen later called Anglo-Saxons brought their dialects to the island now named England.

Anglo-Saxon, or Old English, was an inflected language—that is, one in which
(10) the endings of words indicate grammatical function. For example, the Old English word meaning *stones* would be spelled *stanas* if it were the subject, but *stanum* if it were the direct object. Between the fifth
(15) and fourteenth centuries, most of these endings disappeared.

Another major way in which the language has changed is in its vocabulary. The original inhabitants of England, the Celts, con-
(20) tributed only a few words to English, as did the eighth- and ninth-century Danish invaders, who spoke Old Norse. But after the Anglo-Saxons were converted to Christianity, many Latin words entered the
(25) language, and scholars continued to add Latin words for several hundred years. The major change in English vocabulary, how-ever, came with the Norman Conquest of 1066. The Normans brought their Norman
(30) French dialect with them, and in the three hundred years following the Conquest thousands of French words entered the English language.

The most mysterious development in English
(35) had to do with pronunciation. Between the late fourteenth and the late sixteenth century, English speakers, for some reason, began to pronounce their long vowels differently. This phenomenon is called the Great Vowel Shift,
(40) and it radically changed the sound of spoken English. The word sheep, for example, for-merly had a sound closer to the modern shape, while the word mouse used to sound somewhat like moose.

(45) Our language has altered much less in the last five hundred years than it did in the previous five hundred. The spelling of English is now standardized, and there have been no dramatic changes in vocabulary or
(50) pronunciation. But the language does con-tinue to develop. Although the rules of gram-mar are established, those rules are not immutable, and some formerly "unbreak-able" laws have changed in recent years. For
(55) example, sentences may now end in prepo-sitions, and infinitives may be split.

Vocabulary is still a factor in the ongoing evolution of our language. *Macho* from Latin America and *blitz* from Germany show that
(60) English remains hospitable to outside influ-ences. Another important influence is tech-nology. The familiar *laptop* does not appear in fifteen-year-old dictionaries, and the noun *mouse* appears, but only as a rodent or an
(65) undereye bruise. Our fifteen-hundred-year-old language continues to grow.

21. Which of the following best tells what this passage is about?

    A. The reason why English is the earth's most influential language
    B. The evolution of the English language
    C. How new words come into a language
    D. Grammar and vocabulary changes in English from the beginning to the present
    E. The early history of English

22. What is the meaning of "immutable" (line 53)?

    F. Contradictory
    G. Unacceptable
    H. Flexible
    J. Unchangeable
    K. Trivial

23. Which of the following is true of an inflected language?

    A. It has a varying pronunciation.
    B. Professional grammarians determine the endings of its words.
    C. Words have varying meanings depending on their spellings.
    D. The endings of some words change according to how they are used in a sentence.
    E. The endings of most words have been dropped.

24. According to the passage, which of the following has had the most influence on English vocabulary?

    F. Latin
    G. French
    H. Old Norse
    J. Modern technology
    K. The Great Vowel Shift

25. Why does the author call the Great Vowel Shift "mysterious"?

    A. No one knows why it happened.
    B. No one knows how the different vowel sounds are produced.
    C. There are no recordings to indicate the earlier sounds.
    D. No one knows when it happened.
    E. English is the only language that ever underwent such a change.

26. Which of the following is an example of what the author of the passage calls the English language's being "hospitable to outside influences"?

    F. The English word *futon,* adopted from the Japanese language
    G. The word *pulsar,* introduced by astronomers in the late 1960s
    H. The Great Vowel Shift
    J. The dropping of inflections
    K. The technological term *fiber optics*

II. A Greek myth tells of the engineer Daedalus, who used wax and feathers to fashion wings for himself and his son Icarus.
Line According to the story the two were able to
(5) escape from the island where they were held prisoner by flapping their wing-enhanced arms. In the fifteenth or sixteenth century, the great Leonardo da Vinci, perhaps intrigued by the Daedalus myth, investi-
(10) gated the possibility of human flight. His notebooks and sketches indicate that he studied aerodynamics and learned much about the design requirements of a workable wing.

(15) Earthbound human beings have always been fascinated by the bird's ability to fly. No one knows how many other inventors like Daedalus and Leonardo thought that they might be able to figure out the mysteries of
(20) successful wing design for human flight. But even if Leonardo or some other genius had designed the perfect wing, the human body's bulky, uneven shape and cumbersome weight would have kept it on the ground.

(25) A bird's body, unlike a human's, is a true marvel of aerodynamic engineering. Unlike the denser bones of Homo sapiens, many of the bones of a bird are hollow, and thus the bird's body is light enough to be wing (30) borne. It is also designed for maximum flight efficiency, with most of the weight carried below the wings and a tapered shape that minimizes air resistance.

The wings of a bird are aerodynamic won-(35) ders. A complex muscle system makes the essential flapping motion possible, and the shape of the wing makes it an excellent air-foil. The forward part of the wing is curved in such a way that air is pushed downward (40) with each wing stroke, increasing the air pressure under the wing. At the same time, the air moving across the upper part of the wings flows freely, decreasing the pressure above the wing. The pressure differential (45) creates the lift needed for flight. Once aloft, birds can decrease drag, or air resistance, by altering their angle of flight.

Feathers are another bird exclusive that con-tribute to flight. The tapered lines of a bird's (50) body are accentuated by the smooth surface of its contour feathers, and the tail and wings have flight feathers that assist in tak-ing off, navigation, and landing. On the wings' downstroke, the wing flight feathers (55) move in such a way that they provide a propeller-like effect for thrust and maneu-verability. Tail feathers act as rudders, steer-ing the bird in the direction it wishes to go as it flies. For the complicated task of land-(60) ing, the bird raises its body until it is almost vertical and fans out its tail feathers. As its rate of motion slows, feathers (called the alula), folded back until now, move forward to act as stabilizers, producing a smooth landing.

27. Which of the following best states the author's purpose?

A. To explain why flight has always fascinated humankind
B. To explain why the Daedalus myth cannot be true
C. To create a feeling of admiration for the wonders of the animal world
D. To describe the body of a bird
E. To explain the complex design that makes bird flight possible

28. According to the passage, why could a human body not fly even with well-designed wings?

F. Its muscles are not strong enough.
G. It does not have feathers.
H. It is too heavy and awkward.
J. It is too large.
K. It does not have a tail.

29. How do contour feathers assist flight?

A. They make the bird's body lighter.
B. They provide insulation.
C. They help reduce air resistance.
D. They assist in takeoff, navigation, and landing.
E. They act as stabilizers.

30. What is the function of the wing's curved shape?

F. It creates lift by altering the angle of flight.
G. It increases pressure under the wing and lessens the pressure above.
H. It directs the faster-moving air above the wing downward.
J. It makes the flapping motion possible.
K. It eliminates drag.

31. Which of the following is **not** given as part of the landing maneuver?

    A. Decrease in speed
    B. "Rudder" action of the tail feathers
    C. Change in the position of the bird's body
    D. Movement of tail feathers
    E. Deployment of certain specialized feathers

32. What does the passage suggest about Leonardo da Vinci?

    F. He was ignorant of the structure of the human body.
    G. His notebooks were hard to decipher.
    H. He tried unsuccessfully to build a flying machine.
    J. He did not understand the importance of feathers.
    K. He did not master all the principles of aerodynamics.

III. In 1969 scientists made a discovery destined to revolutionize the medical world's thinking about disease and its causes. The
Line discovery was a copper protein that makes
(5) possible the body's use of oxygen. Further study identified many substances of this type, whose interactions with other molecules in the body trigger a variety of useful reactions. Some, for example, stimulate
(10) hormones active in fighting harmful bacteria and viruses. Free radicals, as these substances are called, had been identified before 1969, but until this time their functions had not been thoroughly understood.

(15) Ironically, this biochemical group also includes molecules that trigger harmful reactions. Today's medical experts are accusing the harmful free radicals of biological mayhem ranging from wrinkled skin to
(20) cancer and Alzheimer's disease. And a problem is that some of the same processes that produce the helpful molecules also create their harmful opposites.

A free radical is a molecule with a free or
(25) unpaired electron. The unpaired electron seeks a stable bond with available molecules. If it finds and bonds with a molecule in a nearby cell, it causes cell injuries including damaged walls, weakened DNA,
(30) and altered chemistry. Thus crippled, cells can no longer function adequately to maintain the body's health. A host of illnesses that used to be considered a natural part of aging are now known to be associated with
(35) the action of free radicals.

Fortunately, human beings can defend their bodies against the ravages of free radicals. It is known that many external factors are linked to free radical damage: cigarette
(40) smoke, alcohol, ultraviolet light, and pesticides are some examples. Obviously, then, one thing people can do for the health of their bodies is to avoid substances and radiation that lead to the production of these
(45) harmful particles. At this time, though, total protection is not possible. Is the body, then, helpless against attack?

The welcome answer is "no." In addition to maintaining a healthful lifestyle, people can
(50) fight free radical damage with a group of chemicals called antioxidants. Antioxidants are able to make free radicals harmless by altering their molecular structure. Nutritionists therefore recommend a diet
(55) high in vitamins A, C, and E. Furthermore, some experts also recommend supplemental doses of these as well as of melatonin and selenium.

As scientists learn more about free radical
(60) harm and antioxidant protection, some are predicting that medicine will change course in the next century. The treatment and prevention of disease, say these experts, will rely heavily on the use of antioxidants to
(65) control free radicals. Drugs, which now lead the fight against illness, will be relegated to a secondary role.

33. Which of the following best expresses the author's purpose?

    A. To give medical advice on a little-known problem in the area of disease prevention
    B. To explain the difference between similar molecules produced in the human body
    C. To inform the reader of relatively recent discoveries concerning disease and its prevention
    D. To explain why medicine will be revolutionized in the near future
    E. To explain the dangers of cigarette smoking, alcohol abuse, overexposure to the sun, and environmental pollutants

34. Which of the following is **not** true concerning free radicals?

    F. A healthful lifestyle will prevent the formation of free radicals in the human body.
    G. They are attracted to other molecules or atoms.
    H. Some are important to the body's healthy functioning.
    J. Antioxidants prevent them from attacking other cells.
    K. They were discovered before 1969.

35. What are the harmful opposites mentioned in (line 23)?

    A. Molecules that cause cell damage
    B. Harmful external factors such as smoking
    C. Diseases caused by free radicals
    D. Antioxidants
    E. Molecules having no unpaired electrons

36. How do free radicals cause disease?

    F. They cripple the disease-fighting "good" free radicals.
    G. They stimulate hormones that strengthen bacteria and viruses.
    H. They increase the intensity of ultraviolet light.
    J. They weaken the cells that they attack.
    K. They chemically bond with beneficial antioxidants.

37. What does the passage suggest about antioxidants?

    A. They destroy free radicals in the human body.
    B. They can eliminate disease in human beings by controlling the action of free radicals.
    C. They will completely destroy the pharmaceutical industry.
    D. They can eliminate some of the ills of aging.
    E. A well-balanced diet provides adequate amounts of antioxidants.

38. What aspect of the molecular structure of a free radical causes its damaging effects?

    F. One of its components causes it to invade nearby cells.
    G. It contains environmental toxins.
    H. Its free electron upsets the hydrogen balance in the body.
    J. The unpaired electron results in electrolyte imbalance within the healthy cell.
    K. Its free electron causes it to bond with other free radicals.

IV. Light pollution is not new, but it has been widely recognized as a serious problem only in recent years. With the spread of *Line* urban areas has come the invasion of night-
(5) time lighting in areas that used to be dark after sundown. In the suburbs, too, the night is brighter, lit by glaring street lights, home security lamps, and massive shopping centers beaming upward at the sky. It is
(10) harder and harder to find a spot where a person can gaze upward at a star-filled sky.

Environmentalists worry because too much nighttime light can upset natural patterns in both plant and animal life. For example,
(15) endangered sea turtles will not lay their eggs on brightly lit beaches. Cultures such as the Inuit, to whom the constellations have strong significance, find the transmission of their legends hampered. Amateur skygazers
(20) can see little because the ambient light is brighter than all but the brightest stars. Even professional astronomy, with all its advanced technology, is suffering from the interference of this noxious pollution.
(25) Important observatories such as Mount Wilson and Goethe Link can no longer see as much as they did in former years, and in fact the earth's light is so strong that it actually interferes with signals from space.

(30) The earth is not doomed, however, to live with an orange night sky. Shielding the upper regions from unwanted light is not forbiddingly difficult. One simple approach is to design fixtures so that their light is
(35) directed downward, adequately illuminating the target area without spilling unwanted brightness outward and upward. Lamps that produce excessive glare, like mercury vapor fixtures, can be replaced by
(40) less glaring appliances. Such measures are practical as well as being environmentally friendly. Experts argue that much home-security lighting is poorly designed in that it is too diffuse and inappropriately
(45) directed, sometimes actually providing handy shadows for a lurking burglar! More careful design and placement not only avoid polluting the sky but offer better protection. Also, since better-designed
(50) systems for every purpose would put light only where it is needed, they would be economical and energy efficient.

Action is being taken to deal with the situation. Some state and local governments
(55) have passed antilight-pollution laws. Maine and New Mexico are leading the way for other states, and counties and cities across the nation are following suit. Environmental and astronomical groups such as the
(60) International Dark-Sky Association are working to restore a more natural night. And in July 1999, the International Astronomical Union convened in Austria to consider the extent of the problem and possible
(65) solutions. Perhaps in the next millennium, Earth dwellers will once again have a night sky brightened only by celestial lights.

39. Which of the following best tells what this passage is about?

A. A serious technological problem for astronomers
B. A new form of pollution
C. Improvements in lighting design and how to implement them
D. Urban sprawl
E. Causes, results, and possible solutions of a problem

40. All of the following are mentioned in the passage as effects of light pollution **except**

F. difficulty in passing on cultural traditions.
G. interference in astronomical studies.
H. negative impact on biological processes.
J. fewer opportunities for watching the night sky.
K. closing down of some important observatories.

41. According to the passage, which of the following is true about the reduction of light pollution?

    A. It is expensive but worth the investment.
    B. It yields significant incidental benefits.
    C. It requires technology not presently available.
    D. It results in an orange night sky.
    E. Most state and local governments now have some useful ordinances.

42. In what sense is light pollution a penalty paid for growth?

    F. It is inevitable in large urban and suburban areas.
    G. It encourages urban sprawl by providing well-lighted areas
    H. Light pollution exists only in densely populated regions.
    J. It mainly develops because of security concerns.
    K. It tends to increase as populated areas grow.

43. What is the meaning of the word "noxious" (line 24)?

    A. Harmful
    B. Unusual
    C. Subtle
    D. Urban
    E. Natural

44. How do brightly lit beaches threaten the survival of the sea turtle?

    F. They force female sea turtles to lay eggs in dangerous open water.
    G. They prevent the sea turtles from mating.
    H. They interfere with reproduction.
    J. They interrupt the balance between time in the ocean and time on dry land.
    K. They drive the sea turtles inland.

V. Even before her death in September 1997, it was widely assumed that Mother Teresa of Calcutta was destined for official
Line sainthood in the Roman Catholic Church.
(5) She had become a worldwide hero through her dedication to the poor. Moreover, her prayerful lifestyle and adherence to Catholic teaching marked her as a true daughter of her Church.

(10) Mother Teresa was born in 1910 of Albanian parents in the town of Shkup, in what is now the Former Yugoslav Republic of Macedonia. At the age of eighteen she joined the Sisters of Loreto and was sent to
(15) Darjeeling, India, to serve her years as a novice. In 1931 she began teaching at Loreto House, a Calcutta girls' school for the daughters of the elite. But Sister Teresa was drawn to a different kind of ministry, and fif-
(20) teen years later she left the upper-class world for the slums of Calcutta. In the next four years she recruited others—Indian women—to assist her in her work on the streets, and in 1950 the Missionaries of
(25) Charity was given official recognition by the Vatican.

It took the citizens of Calcutta several years to trust this woman who, by Indian standards, behaved so strangely. One of her spe-
(30) cial ministries was to the dying poor and homeless who, in "normal" circumstances, would die alone, without care or comfort. The 1952 opening of the Nirmal Hriday ("Pure Heart") Home for Dying Destitutes
(35) was a puzzle for Hindus. They did not understand why Mother Teresa was so determined to soften what they saw as a welcome escape from earthbound existence. They were also cynical about her interest in
(40) destitute children. The order called itself "Missionaries," after all, and sheltering ignorant children could be seen as an easy way to pick up converts to Christianity. Furthermore, with India so plagued by
(45) overpopulation, her teachings against abortion and birth control seemed both wrong-headed and subversive.

Mother Teresa proved her sincerity when she opened a facility to provide care for (50) lepers, the outcasts of India. Skeptics finally acknowledged that the Missionaries of Charity were indeed dedicated to the service of the destitute and abandoned.

Mother Teresa's stature grew both in (55) Calcutta and throughout India. In 1963 the government of India recognized her work with an official award, the Padmashri. Her fame spread until she achieved worldwide recognition as a holy person devoted to the (60) service of God and others. The Nobel Peace Prize in 1979 seemed a fitting reward for such a woman. In later life, until her health began to fail, Mother Teresa traveled widely, establishing her ministry on other conti- (65) nents. She was welcomed with honor wherever she went, and when she died, the Earth mourned the loss of a holy person.

45. Which of the following best tells what this passage is about?

- **A.** How Mother Teresa won the hearts of the people of India
- **B.** The wretched conditions of the poor of Calcutta
- **C.** A change of direction in the life of a nun
- **D.** Sainthood for a servant of the poor
- **E.** The life of a twentieth-century holy woman

46. Why were the people of Calcutta skeptical about Mother Teresa's work?

- **F.** They didn't like Roman Catholics.
- **G.** They doubted that her main goal was to serve the poor.
- **H.** They thought that her attentions to the dying were insincere.
- **J.** They thought that her work with lepers was a scheme to gain converts.
- **K.** They suspected her of abusing destitute children.

47. What does the passage suggest about Mother Teresa?

- **A.** She disliked working with children.
- **B.** She was reluctant to leave the comforts of "upper-class" life.
- **C.** She thought that overpopulation was manageable without resorting to artificial birth control.
- **D.** She was ambitious for fame and honor.
- **E.** She was somewhat of a "rebel" in the Roman Catholic Church.

48. Which of the following is the meaning of the word "novice" as it is used in line 16?

- **F.** Servant of the poor and destitute
- **G.** Citizen of Calcutta
- **H.** Child
- **J.** New member of a religious order
- **K.** One who is skeptical of the actions of another

49. Which of the following is not stated in the passage?

- **A.** Mother Teresa was publicly honored by her adopted country.
- **B.** As a young woman Mother Teresa joined an order of nuns.
- **C.** Mother Teresa was officially named a saint of her Church.
- **D.** Mother Teresa extended her missionary work beyond India.
- **E.** In her earlier years Mother Teresa worked among the upper classes.

50. Which of the following most closely parallels the work of Mother Teresa?

- **F.** Providing free medical care to the poor
- **G.** Establishing a religious school for young children
- **H.** Operating a health education clinic
- **J.** Campaigning for population control
- **K.** Teaching prayer and meditation

PART 2—MATHEMATICS

QUESTIONS 51–100

SUGGESTED TIME: 75 MINUTES

Directions: For each of the following questions, select the **best** answer from the given choices. Bubble in the letter corresponding to your answer on the answer sheet. **DO NOT PUT ANY OTHER WORK ON THE ANSWER SHEET.** All necessary work can be done in your test booklet or on scrap paper that is provided.

NOTE: Diagrams other than graphs might not be drawn to scale. Do not assume any relationships that are not specifically stated unless they are implied by the given information.

51. $\dfrac{3^3 + 3^2 + 3}{3} =$

A. 9
B. 12
C. 13
D. 18
E. 21

52. After Richard gave 10% of his money to charity, he had $180 left. How much money did he have originally?

F. $216
G. $200
H. $195
J. $172
K. $144

53. $(a - 1) - (a - 2) + (a - 3) =$

A. $-a + 4$
B. $a + 4$
C. $a - 6$
D. $a - 2$
E. $3a - 2$

54. $.\overline{3} + \dfrac{1}{6} =$

F. .4
G. .6
H. $\dfrac{2}{3}$
J. $\dfrac{5}{6}$
K. $\dfrac{1}{2}$

55. In Mr. Chin's math class there were g girls and b boys. The number of girls was 5 less than twice the number of boys. Which of the following represents the value of g in terms of b?

A. $5 + 2b$
B. $5 - 2b$
C. $2b - 5$
D. $b + 10$
E. $b - 10$

56. On line segment $\overline{AB}$, $AY = XB = 30$ and $XY = 7$. What is the length of $\overline{AB}$?

F. 44
G. 53
H. 60
J. 67
K. 74

57. If $4(x - 3) = 3(x - 4)$, then $x =$

A.   0

B.   −24

C.   24

D. $\dfrac{24}{7}$

E. $-\dfrac{24}{7}$

58. The least common multiple of 2, 3, 4, 5, and 6 is

F. $2 \times 3 \times 4 \times 5 \times 6$

G. $2 \times 3 \times 4 \times 5$

H. $2 \times 3 \times 5$

J. $3 \times 4 \times 5$

K. 2^5

59. $(6)(6) + (-6)(-6) =$

A.   0

B.   24

C.   72

D.   180

E.   none of these

60. A room is 20 feet long, 15 feet wide, and 12 feet high. If it costs 20¢ per square foot to paint walls, 30¢ per square foot to paint a ceiling, and 10¢ per square foot to paint a floor, how much does it cost to paint just the four walls of the room?

F. $48

G. $84

H. $96

J. $168

K. $480

61. $.26 \times .37$ is closest to

A. $\dfrac{1}{4}$

B. $\dfrac{3}{32}$

C. $\dfrac{3}{5}$

D. $\dfrac{2}{3}$

E. $\dfrac{2}{10}$

62. The mean of a, b, and c is 80. The mean of a, b, c, d, and e is 84. What is the mean of d and e?

F.   82

G.   87

H.   88

J.   89

K.   90

63. As shown in the straight line graph, the ABC Telephone Company charges an initial fee of $5 per month and then charges a fixed amount for each minute of phone call time. *What is that fixed amount charge* for each minute of phone call time?

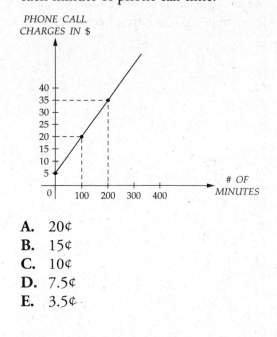

A.   20¢

B.   15¢

C.   10¢

D.   7.5¢

E.   3.5¢

64. The area of square *ABCD* is 9. The area of trapezoid *CDEF* is 24. The area of square *EFGH* is 81. Then the height of the trapezoid is

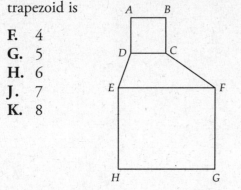

   F. 4
   G. 5
   H. 6
   J. 7
   K. 8

65. During a dull football game, $\frac{1}{4}$ of the spectators left after 1 hour. During the next hour another 20,000 spectators left. There were now $\frac{1}{12}$ of the original number of spectators still watching the game. How many spectators were originally present?

   A. 120,000
   B. 60,000
   C. 40,000
   D. 30,000
   E. 24,000

66. What is the smallest prime number that is 2 more than a positive multiple of 7?

   F. 9
   G. 19
   H. 23
   J. 37
   K. 41

67. One-third of the sum of *P, Q,* and *R* is 21. If $P + Q = 46$, then $R =$

   A. −25
   B. 17
   C. 25
   D. 50
   E. 75

68. In the figure, point *B* is on line segment $\overline{AC}$ and point *D* is on line segment $\overline{AE}$. The value of $x + y$ is

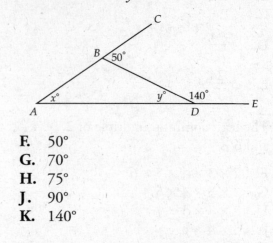

   F. 50°
   G. 70°
   H. 75°
   J. 90°
   K. 140°

69. If $709 - x = 199$, then the value of $720 - x$ is

   A. 520
   B. 510
   C. 210
   D. 189
   E. 11

70. The figure shows two circles, one entirely within the other. The area of the entire large circle is 9 times the area of the small circle. Then the ratio of the *shaded* area to the *unshaded* area is

   F. 1:9
   G. 1:8
   H. 1:18
   J. 1:16
   K. 1:17

71. Let *x* represent a positive integer. Which of the following *must* be true?

   A. If 5*x* is even, then *x* must be even.
   B. If 5 + *x* is odd, then *x* must be odd.
   C. If 3*x* + 7 is even, then *x* must be even.
   D. If *x* + 1 is even, then *x* + 12 must be even.
   E. If $\frac{x}{3}$ is an odd integer, then *x* must be even.

72. For any positive integer *n*, let ◊*n*◊ represent the *number of odd factors* of *n*. For example, ◊15◊ = 4 because 15 has exactly 4 odd factors [1, 3, 5, and 15]. Which of the following has the largest value?

    F. ◊10◊
    G. ◊12◊
    H. ◊25◊
    J. ◊27◊
    K. ◊36◊

73. In the figure, rectangle *ABCD* is drawn in the coordinate plane with its sides parallel to the axes. The area of *ABCD* is

    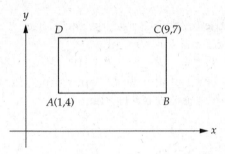

    A. 4
    B. 6
    C. 24
    D. 30
    E. 63

74. In a scale diagram, 1 inch represents 5 feet. On the same diagram, how many square inches would represent 1 square foot?

    F. 25
    G. 4
    H. .4
    J. .25
    K. .04

75. On the number line, point *R* (not shown) is to the right of *Q*, and *PQ* is $\frac{1}{5}$ of *PR*. What is the coordinate of *R*?

    A. 7
    B. 15
    C. 23
    D. 25
    E. 40

76. $-3x(7y - 5) =$

    F. $21xy - 15x$
    G. $-10xy + 8x$
    H. $-21xy + 15x$
    J. $10xy + 8x$
    K. $4xy - 8x$

77. In writing the integers from 1 to 50 inclusive, how many times is the digit "2" written?

    A. 5
    B. 13
    C. 14
    D. 15
    E. 16

78. Let $x = 3y$ and $y = 3z$. If $y = 30$, then the value of $(x + y + z)$ is

    F. 390
    G. 130
    H. 90
    J. $43\frac{1}{3}$
    K. 41

79. If *M* and *N* are positive integers, then the statement "One-ninth of *M* is greater than one-eighth of *N*" is equivalent to

    A. $\frac{N}{M} > \frac{8}{9}$
    B. $MN > 72$
    C. $N - M > 1$
    D. $9N > 8M$
    E. $8M > 9N$

80. The sum $2^{10} + 1^{10} + (\frac{1}{2})^{10} + (\frac{1}{3})^{10} + (\frac{1}{4})^{10}$ is closest to

    F. 21
    G. 32
    H. 513
    J. 1,025
    K. 2,000

81. If $2x(x - y) = 54$ and $x = 9$, then $y =$

    A. 6
    B. 3
    C. 2
    D. 1
    E. 0

82. What is the acute angle formed by the hands of a clock at 2:00?

    F. 30°
    G. 36°
    H. 45°
    J. 60°
    K. 75°

83. In the figure, the area of the entire circle is twice the area of the entire rectangle. If the shaded area is removed, then the remaining area of the circle would be 9 more than the remaining area of the rectangle. The area of the rectangle

    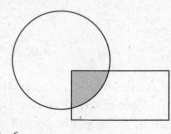

    A. is 6.
    B. is 9.
    C. is 12.
    D. is 18.
    E. cannot be determined from the given information.

84. In rectangle *ABCD*, *E* is a point on $\overline{DC}$. The area of rectangle *ABCD* is 120. The area of triangle *AEB*

    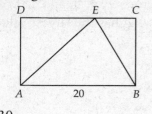

    F. is 30.
    G. is 50.
    H. is 60.
    J. is 90.
    K. cannot be determined from the given information.

85. In the following pattern, each letter represents some number:
    P   Q   6   R   S   T   10
    The sum of any three consecutive numbers in the pattern is 21. Then

    A. *Q* is 11.
    B. *Q* is 10.
    C. *Q* is 6.
    D. *Q* is 5.
    E. there is more than one possible value for *Q*.

86. Six bleeps equal 13 floops, and 2 floops equal 5 geebles. Based on this, 1 bleep is equal to *N* geebles. The integer closest to *N* is

    F. 1
    G. 2
    H. 3
    J. 4
    K. 5

87. If the base and the height of a rectangle are each doubled, the area of the original rectangle will be multiplied by

   A. 2
   B. 4
   C. 8
   D. 16
   E. The answer depends on the lengths of the sides of the original rectangle.

88. Alan ran $\frac{5}{6}$ the distance run by Ilayne.

Alan ran $8\frac{1}{3}$ miles. How many miles did Ilayne run?

   F. $6\frac{17}{18}$
   G. 7
   H. $7\frac{5}{18}$
   J. $9\frac{14}{15}$
   K. 10

89. If $\frac{a}{b} = \frac{1}{3}$, where a and b are each greater than 3, which one of the following must also equal $\frac{1}{3}$?

   A. $\frac{3ab}{a+b}$
   B. $\frac{a+b}{3ab}$
   C. $\frac{a+b}{3a}$
   D. $\frac{b}{3a}$
   E. $\frac{b}{9a}$

90. The probability that Roberto wins is $\frac{1}{3}$ the probability that Roberto loses. What is the probability that Roberto loses?

   F. $\frac{1}{4}$
   G. 1
   H. $\frac{1}{3}$
   J. $\frac{3}{4}$
   K. $\frac{4}{3}$

91. x and y are positive integers and $x + y = 11$. What is the largest possible value of $\frac{1}{x} - \frac{1}{y}$?

   A. $\frac{1}{30}$
   B. $\frac{9}{10}$
   C. 1
   D. 9
   E. 11

92. What is the *smallest* prime p such that one-fifth of p is greater than 12?

   F. 3
   G. 13
   H. 49
   J. 59
   K. 61

93. Express the product of 8×10^2 and 8×10^4 in scientific notation.

   A. 6.4×10^7
   B. 64×10^6
   C. 6.4×10^6
   D. 6.4×10^5
   E. 8×10^6

94. In the figure, a square with perimeter 20 is contained within a square of perimeter *P*. The area of the shaded region is 56. Then the *perimeter* of the larger square is

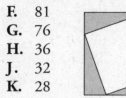

F. 81
G. 76
H. 36
J. 32
K. 28

95. The table shows what two different companies charge for shipping packages, based on the weight of the package. How many pounds does a package weigh if the charge for shipping that package is the same by both companies?

SHIPPING COMPANY	FIRST POUND	EACH ADDITIONAL POUND
AERO FREIGHT	$9.50	$3.95
BETTER EXPRESS	$8.00	$4.10

A. 101
B. 51
C. 31
D. 21
E. 11

96. The total value of some coins is $1.20. The coins contain nickels, dimes, and quarters only (*at least one of each kind*). What is the fewest number of coins possible?

F. 5
G. 6
H. 7
J. 8
K. 9

97. It takes 12 men 4 hours to do a certain job. Working at the same rate, how many hours would it take 8 men to do that job?

A. 2
B. $\frac{8}{3}$
C. 3
D. 6
E. 24

98. In the diagram, *O* is the center of the circle. What is the area of the shaded region?

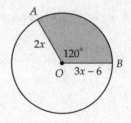

F. 48π
G. 12π
H. 8π
J. 4π
K. Cannot be determined from the given information.

99. Which of the following points is closest to the point (4, 5)?

A. (4, 0)
B. (0, 5)
C. (0, 0)
D. (−4, 5)
E. (4, −5)

100. Which one of the following *cannot* be the product of two consecutive integers?

F. 9,900
G. 15,750
H. 20,448
J. 38,612
K. 49,506

Answer Key
MODEL TEST 3

Scrambled Paragraphs	Logical Reasoning		Reading			
Paragraph 1 UQRST	11. C	16. K	21. B	29. C	37. D	44. H
Paragraph 2 UTRQS	12. G	17. B	22. J	30. G	38. F	45. E
Paragraph 3 QURTS	13. D	18. H	23. D	31. B	39. E	46. G
Paragraph 4 SURQT	14. K	19. B	24. G	32. K	40. K	47. C
Paragraph 5 QRUTS	15. A	20. J	25. A	33. C	41. B	48. J
			26. F	34. F	42. K	49. C
			27. E	35. A	43. A	50. F
			28. H	36. J		

Mathematics

51. C	61. B	71. A	81. A	91. B
52. G	62. K	72. J	82. J	92. K
53. D	63. B	73. C	83. B	93. A
54. K	64. F	74. K	84. H	94. H
55. C	65. D	75. A	85. D	95. E
56. G	66. H	76. H	86. K	96. H
57. A	67. B	77. D	87. B	97. D
58. J	68. F	78. G	88. K	98. F
59. C	69. C	79. E	89. E	99. B
60. J	70. G	80. J	90. J	100. H

ANSWER EXPLANATIONS
MODEL TEST 3

Scrambled Paragraphs

Paragraph 1   UQRST
Q could serve as the second sentence if U were not part of the paragraph, but U must be second, as it continues the thought of the first sentence, commenting on the name "pepper" and referring to the West Indies. Furthermore, it begins with the pronoun "they" referring to Christopher Columbus and his crew.

> **FACT:** Pronouns frequently serve as transitional words.

Q comes after U, with "In Spain" serving as a transitional expression linking it to the topic sentence. It ends with a reference to North Africa, India, and Indonesia, and R begins with the transition "In these places," so R comes next. R mentions a change in the use of the pepper plant from mere ornament to food, and S elaborates on the uses of pepper as food. T continues the idea of other uses for the plant and concludes the sentence.

Paragraph 2   UTRQS
Although T could logically come second, U must be the second sentence because it lays the groundwork of the paragraph's topic, Hitler's mistake.

> **FACT:** The topic of a paragraph is not always indicated in the first sentence.

U begins with a reference to the location of the invasion of France and states that the location was secret. T comes next, giving the first mention of Hitler and his mistake, R provides some additional details about this mistake, and Q moves the paragraph along chronologically to the actual invasion on June 6 and Hitler's refusal to admit his mistake. S concludes the paragraph with a later date and the result of Hitler's mistake.

Paragraph 3   QURTS
This is an example of a paragraph containing complex and possibly confusing information. It is basically a "process" paragraph, however, and so the trick to arranging the sentences is careful attention to the nouns and the transitional expressions. Q moves the paragraph along, repeating the word "key" and starting the process of sound production. U is the only logical sentence to follow Q because the transitional "Simultaneously" and "key-lever" begin a sentence that tells about another early step in the process. U also introduces the damper and its elevation, to which R refers with "As the damper rises." R says that the wire vibrates, and T and S conclude the paragraph with statements about the continuation of the vibration.

Paragraph 4   SURQT
The initial sentence ends with a reference to a "strong flow of water." S comes next, with the transitional idea of turning the faucet off rather than on.

> **TIP:** A transition may be a phrase indicating contrast.

The transitional phrase "that water" in S is a strong clue linking to the "strong flow of water" in Q. U comes next because "This machine" links to the machine mentioned in S. U ends with a statement about a washer, and R follows, giving additional information about the washer and describing it as fitting tightly to block the water and prevent leakage. S explains the leakage that can occur with a washer that is, "however," not fitting tightly. T concludes by explaining how the washer, or "plug," is removed when one turns the faucet on.

Paragraph 5   QRUTS
Q is second, referring to the difference and introducing the idea of lack of precision. R begins with the transitional "In fact" and goes on to offer two reasons for the lack of precision. U elaborates on the inaccurate methods that some countries use. T gives another reason introduced by "furthermore," which suggests the continuation of a previous

idea—reasons for the error. S ends the paragraph, referring to the "adjustments" mentioned in T and concluding with an acknowledgment of error and a rationalization about validity.

Logical Reasoning

Solutions in this section frequently involve techniques discussed in Skillbuilder B.

11,12. **(C,G)** Draw a set of four vertical boxes. We are given that the red book is "immediately" below the yellow book, and the white book is somewhere above them. We need another set of four vertical boxes. In one set of boxes we put yellow in box 3 and red in box 4 (thus white can be in 1 or 2, and blue can be in 2 or 1). In the other set of boxes we put yellow in box 2 and red in box 3; here white must be in box 1, leaving box 4 for blue. We can now answer the questions.

11. **(C)**

12. **(G)**

13,14,15. **(D,K,A)** Remember to **mark your sentences** in this type of logical reasoning problem. Also, notice that there are two R's in sentence 1, so R must represent the word "two." This is important to the analysis.

Question 13: The letter A is in all three sentences. The words "two" and "juniors" are also in all three sentences. You might be tempted to pick choice E as the answer, but (as pointed out earlier) the word "two" must be represented by the letter R. Therefore the letter A must represent the word "junior." The correct choice is D.

Question 14: The word "the" is in sentences 2 and 3. Only letter E is in exactly those sentences. The correct choice is K.

Question 15: The word "used" is only in sentence 2. Both H and D occur only in those sentences, so the correct choice is A.

16. **(K)** Let A represent "Ahmal gets a job," B represent "Bing buys a car," and C represent "Charles goes to school."

The given statements can now be written as A → B, B → C, and C → A. Now look at statements I, II, and III.

Statement I says A → C. This is a consequence of the original first two statements (by Principle 2), so it is true.

Statement II says ~C → ~B. This is the contrapositive of the original second statement, so it is true.

Statement III says ~A → ~B. You probably looked at the original first statement and realized that statement III is <u>not</u> the contrapositive of that first statement. You might have been tempted to think, therefore, that statement III need not be true. However, some more careful reasoning is needed here. Notice that the original second and third statements lead (by Principle 2) to B→A. The contrapositive of this is ~A→ ~B. So statement III is true after all. Thus the correct choice is K.

17,18. **(B,H)** After studying the problem, you will find it most convenient to make a 3-by-3 chart whose rows are labeled *P*, *S*, and *A* (for the men) and whose columns are labeled *J*, *L*, and *V* (for the women). Mark your chart according to the given information. You can now put X's in the remaining box under *V* and the remaining box under *L* (because no one person can be liked by all three men). There should be only one box still empty. We can now answer the questions.

17. **(B)** Notice that "Paul does not like Velma" gives us no information regarding Velma's feelings about Paul.

18. **(H)** We have no information regarding Joyce's feelings about Sean, but that is not one of the choices.

19. **(B)** This is the only choice that relates the first word of each pair to the second word of that pair.

20. **(J)** Choices F, G, and H do not link advertising to teenagers' buying habits. Choice K indicates that the buying patterns are not very predictable, so perhaps they are not much

influenced by advertising. This seems to strengthen Jimmy's point. Choice J indicates that advertising influenced sales in a positive way, thus weakening Jimmy's point.

Reading

Passage I

21. **(B)** Main Idea   This question requires a broad answer that incorporates all the information in the passage. A involves information that is neither stated nor implied in the passage. While it may be true that the changes English has undergone contribute to its influence, you must base your answer only on the information given. B is correct because the entire passage is about changes in the language from its beginning to the present, and the word *evolution* is general enough to include all the changes. C involves only part of the passage. D involves most of the passage but does not cover the paragraph on pronunciation changes. E mentions only the language's early history, but the passage gives history up to the present.

22. **(J)** Inference   Questions on word meanings will ask you to rely on the context in which the word is used. F is incorrect because there is no idea of contradiction in the context. G is wrong because the context concerns grammar development, and the sentence containing the word *immutable* is followed by examples of development or change, not of acceptance. H is incorrect because the context actually suggests some flexibility in the rules. J is correct because the context shows that the grammar rules do change and thus are not unchangeable. K is wrong for the same reason as F—there is no idea of triviality in the context.

23. **(D)** Detail   A is an example of the need to rely on the context. Inflection, which involves tone or pitch, may seem to involve pronunciation; however, the sentence gives a definition of an inflected language that clearly limits the term to grammar.

FACT: When a word has more than one meaning, context determines meaning.

B is wrong because there is no statement or implication about professional grammarians deciding upon word endings. C might possibly be an acceptable answer if the word *meanings* is interpreted very loosely, however, D is clearly the best answer because grammar, as the example involving *stanas* clearly illustrates, involves how words are used in a sentence. E contradicts the sentence that defines *inflected*.

24. **(G)** Detail   G is the only possible correct response because the passage clearly states that the "major change in English vocabulary" occurred when the Normans brought French to England.

25. **(A)** Inference   A is the correct answer because the sentence following the one that calls the Great Vowel Shift "mysterious" says that "for some reason" people started changing their pronunciation. B is incorrect because there is no statement or suggestion about how vowel sounds are produced. C is true, but it provides a good example of why you must base your answers on the content of the passage. There are, of course, no recordings of speech that were made at that time, but the passage does not mention or suggest this fact. E is incorrect for the same reason.

FACT: An answer may be true but incorrect.

26. **(F)** Inference   F is correct because the Japanese language is an "outside" factor and "hospitable" implies giving a welcome; so the English language welcomed this "outsider," a Japanese word. Furthermore, the sentence involved gives two examples of this hospitality, and they are both foreign words. G and K give examples of new words from technology, which the passage identifies as a separate category of influence on vocabulary. H and J are incorrect because nothing in the passage states or suggests that outside influences affected

the Great Vowel Shift or the dropping of inflections.

Passage II

27. **(E) Main Idea** Determining the author's purpose can be difficult because it involves recognizing the main idea of a passage and, in some cases, the author's attitude as well. A is a tempting response because the second paragraph states that human beings are fascinated by birds' flying ability. The passage, however, does not dwell on this idea of fascination or even mention it again after this paragraph. B is true for the same reason; the information probably does show that Daedalus could not have flown, but the passage does not stress this idea. C is too broad; birds are the only animals discussed. D is incorrect because the passage describes not the entire body but only those parts involved in flight. E is correct because most of the passage carries out the purpose of explaining how a bird can fly. Paragraphs one and two, while not giving such explanation, lead up to it, and both mention the form requirements of flight.

28. **(H) Detail** The correct answer is stated clearly in the last sentence of paragraph two.

29. **(C) Detail** The correct answer is clearly stated, but in two different places in the passage. It is stated in lines 49–50 that contour feathers accentuate the bird's tapered shape. In line 33 it is stated that the bird's tapered body minimizes air resistance.

30. **(G) Detail** F is incorrect because nothing in the passage connects angle of flight to wing shape. The fourth paragraph states that the curved shape of the wing creates the air-pressure difference, so G is correct. H is incorrect because while the shape of the wing does push air downward, the air pushed is not the air above the wing. J is incorrect because it contradicts the second sentence of paragraph four. The last sentence in the paragraph links drag reduction to angle of flight, not shape, making K incorrect.

31. **(B) Detail** The last two sentences in the passage explain landing. The rudder action of tail feathers is not mentioned in these sentences, but in the sentence just before, which explains steering, not landing.

32. **(K) Inference** Although an inference question requires you to understand ideas or facts that are suggested rather than stated, you still must base your response on the passage. You cannot rely on anything you know or think unless it is stated in the passage. K is correct because the passage states (line 12) that Leonardo learned "much" about the requirements of a wing. The word "much" indicates that there are things he did not learn. None of the other choices are mentioned in connection with Leonardo.

Passage III

33. **(C) Main Idea** Although the passage does suggest ways of avoiding free radical damage, A is too narrow. Most of the passage does not involve advice. B, D, and E are also too narrow. Only the first two paragraphs consider the similarity and difference of the molecules, so B is incorrect. Only the last three sentences in the passage mention the revolutionizing of medicine, making D incorrect. And E cannot be right because only one paragraph discusses the dangers of these factors. Only C covers all the information given in the passage.

34. **(F) Detail** A question asking what is *not* true requires you to locate details in the passage.

> **TIP:** The correct answer choice may be worded differently from the wording in the passage.

F is correct because the passage states (line 46) that a healthful lifestyle cannot offer "total protection" against free radicals. G is given in the words "seeks a stable bond with available molecules" (lines 26–27). H summarizes information given in the first paragraph. J is stated in line 52, in the words "able to make free radicals harmless." Since the radicals harm cells by attacking them, this statement about antioxidants is true.

35. **(A)** Detail   A is correct because the pronoun *their* (line 23) refers to helpful molecules. The opposite of helpful molecules is harmful molecules—the free radicals that damage cells.

36. **(J)** Detail   The third paragraph describes cells attacked by free radicals as "crippled" (line 30). Thus J is correct.

37. **(D)** Inference   A is incorrect because the passage states that antioxidants make free radicals "harmless" (line 52). This language does not suggest destruction of the free radicals. B and C are both too exaggerated. The passage states that many illnesses (line 32) are caused by free radicals, not all illnesses. Thus controlling the free radicals will not eliminate all disease.

TIP: Be very careful about choosing an answer including "all," "every," "always," and so on. Such an answer may be correct, but it may well be a trap.

The word "completely" in C makes it too extreme. Drugs will still have a "secondary" role, and so the pharmaceutical industry will still be in existence. D is correct; the suggestion is made in two different sentences. The passage states (lines 51–52) that antioxidants make free radicals harmless and also (line 34) that free radicals "are associated" with illness of aging. It can be inferred that antioxidants can "eliminate some of the ills of aging."

38. **(F)** Detail The correct answer is found in the third paragraph. The "component" mentioned is the free radical's unpaired electron.

Passage IV

39. **(E)** Main Idea

FACT: The correct answer to a main idea question must be broad enough and also accurate.

A is too narrow, as the passage discusses light pollution as a problem in several areas, not just astronomy. B is broad enough but not accurate, as the word "new" contradicts the first sentence of the passage. D is too narrow as the passage mentions urban sprawl only once. E is correct because it names every topic covered in the passage.

40. **(K)** Detail   The other choices are all mentioned in the second paragraph. K is inaccurate as the passage mentions problems of two observatories but not their being closed down.

41. **(B)** Detail   This question requires you to summarize details. The third paragraph discusses the reduction of light pollution. B is correct because the paragraph mentions as incidental benefits better security, economy, and energy efficiency. A contradicts the paragraph's statement (line 52) that such measures are economical. C contradicts the information given in the paragraph. D is inaccurate as the "orange sky" (line 31) is the light-polluted sky. E is too extreme; the last paragraph (line 34) refers to *some,* not "most" state and local governments.

42. **(K)** Inference   F contradicts the passage's information on pollution reduction. G is not stated in the passage; the passage says (lines 4–5) that urban sprawl produces light, not that light produces or encourages urban sprawl. H is too extreme. The word "only" contradicts the information (line 6) that suburbs, which are not always densely populated, can also be light polluted. J is also too extreme; security lighting is mentioned as being polluting, but not as a *main* cause of light pollution. K is correct according to the information on the growth of urban areas (lines 3–4) and its effect on lighting.

43. **(A)** Inference   You must depend on the context to determine a word's definition. The passage says that astronomy suffers from "noxious" (line 24) light pollution. A factor

that causes suffering can be called "harmful." You should check the other choices, however. B is wrong because the passage make it clear that light pollution is common today. C is wrong because it is unrelated to the context, which involves a problem. D is too limited, as light pollution has been stated as involving the suburbs also (line 6). E is incorrect because light pollution is man-made and artificial.

44. **(H)** Detail.   The passage states that light pollution affects egg-laying. Only H refers to egg-laying.

Passage V

45. **(E)** Main Idea   A, B, and C are all too narrow because they each involve only one part of the passage. D is also too narrow because it does not involve the facts about Mother Teresa's early life; furthermore, while the passage states that people expected Mother Teresa to be made an official saint, it does not state that this has happened. E is the only choice both broad enough and accurate.

46. **(G)** Inference   F is wrong because it is not stated or suggested in the passage. G is correct because the passage states that the citizens were cynical about Mother Teresa's work with children because such work could result in converts (line 43). In other words, that she had an ulterior motive for working with the poor. H is inaccurate because the passage states that the citizens did not understand her work with the dying, but does not suggest that they thought it was insincere. J is also inaccurate because Mother Teresa's work with lepers is what finally convinced the citizens of her sincerity. K is not mentioned or suggested by anything in the passage.

47. **(C)** Inference   A is not supported by the passage. Mother Teresa left her teaching job because she was "drawn to a different kind of ministry"; furthermore, this new ministry involved working with children. B contradicts the statement that she was "drawn,"

attracted away, from the upper-class life. C is correct although the inference is subtle. Mother Teresa preached against abortion and artificial birth control, and yet she was deeply concerned for the welfare of the people; therefore, she must have thought that the problem of overpopulation was somehow manageable by other means. D is incorrect because while she gained fame and honor, nothing in the passage states or suggests that she sought it or even enjoyed it. E is contradicted by the official recognition given her order by the Vatican and by the expectation of official sainthood. While she changed her ministry, nothing in the passage says that she did this in a rebellious way.

48. **(J)** Inference   The second paragraph states (line 13) that Mother Teresa joined the religious order and was sent to India for her years as a novice. The suggestion is that she went to India right after joining; this context clue implies that a novice must be a new member of an order. F is wrong because she was not yet serving the poor. G contradicts the information given, as she went to Darjeeling. H is wrong because she was eighteen at the time, not a child. K has no connection with the context.

49. **(C)** Detail   All of the other choices are stated in the passage. C is correct because while it is stated that she was expected to be made an official saint, it is not stated that this has happened.

> **TIP:** Marking details as you read can help you locate the correct answer.

50. **(F)** Main Idea   F is the best choice because the main idea in the description of Mother Teresa's work is that she cared for the poor. None of the other choices are parallel to anything stated in the passage about Mother Teresa's work, and J actually contrasts her teachings against abortion and artificial birth control.

Model Test 3

Mathematics

51. **(C)** Divide each term of the numerator by 3, getting $3^2 + 3 + 1 = 13$. Alternatively, combine the terms of the numerator first, getting 39, then divide by 3.

52. **(G)** $180 must be 90% of what he started with. Dividing both numbers by 9, we see that $20 is 10% of his starting money, so he started with $10 \times \$20 = \$200$.

53. **(D)** Removing parentheses produces $a - 1 - a + 2 + a - 3 = a - 2$.

54. **(K)** This is $\frac{1}{3} + \frac{1}{6} = \frac{3}{6} = \frac{1}{2}$.

55. **(C)** Twice the number of boys is represented by $2b$, so 5 less than that is $2b - 5$.

56. **(G)** Subtracting 7 from 30 shows that $AX = 23$ and $YB = 23$. Then $AB = 23 + 7 + 23 = 53$. Another approach would be to add AY and $XB = 60$, then realize that XY was counted twice. Subtracting 7 once produces the correct answer.

57. **(A)** Multiplying out, we have $4x - 12 = 3x - 12$, so $x = 0$.

58. **(J)** These numbers, expressed in terms of their prime factors, are 2, 3, 2^2, 5, and $2 \cdot 3$. The least common multiple is $2^2 \cdot 3 \cdot 5$.

59. **(C)** The sum is $36 + 36 = 72$.

60. **(J)** The total area of the four walls is $12 \cdot 15 + 12 \cdot 20 + 12 \cdot 15 + 12 \cdot 20 = 840$ square feet. The cost of painting is $840 \cdot 20¢ = \$168$.

61. **(B)** This product is a little more than $\frac{1}{4} \times \frac{1}{3}$, which is $\frac{1}{12}$. The respective choices are approximately (or exactly) $\frac{1}{4}, \frac{1}{10}, \frac{1}{2}, \frac{2}{3}$, and $\frac{1}{5}$. The closest to $\frac{1}{12}$ is B.

62. **(K)**

> **TIP:** If the mean of n numbers is A, then the numbers add up to $n \times A$.

$a + b + c + d + e = 5 \times 84 = 420$, while $a + b + c = 3 \times 80 = 240$. Subtracting these equations produces $d + e = 180$, so the mean of d and e is $\frac{180}{2} = 90$.

63. **(B)** Eliminating the initial $5 fee, we see that 100 minutes of phone call time costs $15. Therefore each minute of phone call time costs 15¢.

64. **(F)**

> **FACT:** The area of a trapezoid is $\frac{1}{2}h(b_1 + b_2)$, where h is its height, and b_1 and b_2 are the lengths of its bases.

From the areas of the squares, we see that DC must be 3 and EF must be 9. Applying the formula for the area of a trapezoid, we have $24 = \frac{1}{2} \cdot h(3 + 9) = 6h$. Therefore, $h = 4$.

65. **(D)** $\frac{11}{12}$ of the spectators left during the first two hours. Since $\frac{1}{4} (= \frac{3}{12})$ left during the first hour, the other $\frac{8}{12}$ left during that second hour. Therefore, $\frac{8}{12} (= \frac{2}{3})$ of the spectators is 20,000. Then $\frac{1}{3}$ is 10,000 and $\frac{3}{3}$ is 30,000. If you prefer, you can use algebra as follows: If x is the original number of spectators, then $\frac{x}{4} + 20,000 = \frac{11}{12}x$. Multiplying both sides of this equation by 12

produces $3x + 240{,}000 = 11x$, leading to $x = 30{,}000$. A third approach would be to try each of the choices.

66. **(H)** Trying small multiples of 7 and adding 2 to each quickly produces $21 + 2 = 23$, which is a prime.

67. **(B)** $P + Q + R = 3 \times 21 = 63$. Subtracting $46 (= P + Q)$ from both sides of the equation produces $R = 17$.

68. **(F)**

> **FACT:** An exterior angle of a triangle is equal to the sum of the two remote interior angles.

The fact above immediately produces the answer 50. The 140° is not needed.

69. **(C)** Instead of solving for x, just add 11 to both sides of the equation. This produces $720 - x = 210$.

70. **(G)** If the area of the small circle is x, then the area of the large circle is $9x$. The unshaded area is $9x - x = 8x$. Then the ratio of the shaded area to the unshaded area is $x : 8x$, which is 1:8.

71. **(A)** This is the type of problem where you examine each choice. However, it is immediately clear that choice A is correct!

> **FACT:** If the product of two integers is even, at least one of them must be even.

There is no need to waste time looking at the other choices. You should go right on to the next problem.

72. **(J)** Here we *must* examine all of the choices. The number 10 has two odd factors (1 and 5). The number 12 also has two. The number 25 has three (1, 5, and 25). The number 27 has four. The number 36 has three. The answer is J.

73. **(C)** The height (above the x axis) of point D is the same as the height of point C (=7), so $AD = 7 - 4 = 3$. The length of $\overline{AB}$ is $9 - 1 = 8$. Therefore the area of the rectangle is $3 \times 8 = 24$.

74. **(K)** If 1 inch represents 5 feet, then 1 square inch represents 25 square feet. Therefore $\frac{1}{25}$ (=.04) square inches represents 1 square foot. Did you spend too much time on this problem?

> **TIP:** If a problem gives you too much trouble, move on!

75. **(A)** $PQ = 3$, so PR must equal 15. Now 15 more than -8 is $+7$.

76. **(H)** Multiplying, and being careful of signs, we get $-21xy + 15x$.

77. **(D)** Writing the integers from 1 through 9 requires writing the digit "2" only 1 time. The same is true each time when we write the integers from 10 through 19, 30 through 39, and 40 through 49. So far we have written the digit "2" 4 times all together. The tricky part is counting the digit "2" when we write the integers from 20 through 29. This requires writing that digit 11 times (try it). The final total is $11 + 4 = 15$.

78. **(G)** If $y = 30$, then $x = 90$ and $z = 10$. The value of $x + y + z$ is 130.

79. **(E)** The statement, when written in symbols, says $\dfrac{M}{9} > \dfrac{N}{8}$.

> **FACT:** For positive numbers a, b, c, and d,
> $\dfrac{a}{b} > \dfrac{c}{d}$, if and only if $ad > bc$.

Then $8M > 9N$. That is choice E.

80. **(J)** The first two terms add up to 1,025. The other three terms are extremely small [for example, $\left(\frac{1}{2}\right)^{10} = \frac{1}{1024}$] and barely affect the total. The correct choice is J.

81. **(A)** Substituting $x = 9$ into the equation, we have $18(9 - y) = 54$. Therefore $9 - y = 3$, so $y = 6$.

82. **(J)** At 3:00, the hands form a 90° angle. The angle at 2:00 is $\frac{2}{3}$ of 90° = 60°, so the answer is J. A much harder problem is to find the angle between the hands at 2:05 or 2:15. For example, at 2:05 the minute hand would be on the 1, but the hour hand would have gone *past* the 2! That hour hand would have traveled $\frac{1}{12}$ of the distance from the 2 to the 3, which is $\frac{1}{12}$ of 30°. The angle between the hands at 2:05 would be $32\frac{1}{2}°$.

83. **(B)** If the area of the rectangle is R, then the area of the circle is given to be $2R$. If the shaded area is x, then we have $2R - x = (R - x) + 9$. This is $2R - x = R - x + 9$, so $R = 9$.

84. **(H)** Since the area of the rectangle is 120, its height must be 6. But in triangle AEB, that would be the same as the length of an altitude from point E to base $\overline{AB}$. The area of a triangle is $(\frac{1}{2})$(height)(base) = $(\frac{1}{2})(6)(20) =$ 60. No matter where E is located along $\overline{DC}$, the area of triangle AEB will be half the area of the rectangle.

85. **(D)** The sum of R, S, and T is the same as the sum of S, T, and 10. Therefore R must equal 10. Then $Q + 6 + R = Q + 6 + 10 = 21$, so $Q = 5$.

86. **(K)** Using single letters to stand for the "nonsense words," we have $6b = 13f$ and $2f = 5g$. We can relate b and g if we can eliminate the fs. One easy way to do this is to change each equation to an equivalent one. Multiplying each side of the first equation by 2, and each side of the second equation by 13, we get $12b = 26f$ and $26f = 65g$. Therefore

$$12b = 65g, \quad \text{so} \quad 1b = \frac{65}{12}g. \quad \text{That means}$$

$N = \frac{65}{12} = 5\frac{5}{12}$. The integer closest to N is 5.

87. **(B)** If the base and height of the original rectangle are b and h, then its area is $(b)(h)$. The base and height of the new rectangle are $2b$ and $2h$, so its area is $(2b)(2h)$, which equals $4bh$. Thus the new area is 4 times the original area.

88. **(K)** If the distance run by Ilayne is D, then $8\frac{1}{3} = \frac{25}{3} = \frac{5}{6}D$. Multiplying each side of this equation by 6 produces $50 = 5D$, so $D = 10$.

89. **(E)** If $\frac{a}{b} = \frac{1}{3}$, then $b = 3a$. Replacing b with $3a$ in each of the choices allows us to evaluate them more easily. The choices become $\frac{9a^2}{4a}, \frac{4a}{9a^2}, \frac{4a}{3a}, \frac{3a}{3a}$ and $\frac{3a}{9a}$. The last choice is the only one that must equal $\frac{1}{3}$. This problem can also be done by choosing a simple value for a, such as 4. Then $b = 12$, and only the last choice equals $\frac{1}{3}$ (if more than one choice became $\frac{1}{3}$ you must try another value for a).

90. **(J)**

> **FACT:** The probability of winning plus the probability of losing must equal 1.

Let L be the probability that Roberto loses. The probability that he wins is given as $\frac{1}{3}L$.

Then $\frac{1}{3}L + L = 1$. Multiplying each side of this equation by 3, we get $L + 3L = 3$. Then

$4L = 3$, so $L = \frac{3}{4}$.

> **FACT:** The probability of an event can never be more than 1.

91. **(B)** The fraction $\frac{1}{x}$ will be largest when the positive integer x is as small as possible. Similarly, $\frac{1}{y}$ will be smallest when the positive integer y is as large as possible. Therefore the greatest difference will occur when $x = 1$ and $y = 10$.

That difference will be $\frac{1}{1} - \frac{1}{10} = 1 - \frac{1}{10} = \frac{9}{10}$.

92. **(K)** Since one-fifth of p is greater than 12, then p is greater than $(5)(12) = 60$. The smallest prime greater than 60 is 61.

93. **(A)** The product is $(8)(10^2)(8)(10^4)$. Rearranging terms before multiplying, we get $(8)(8)(10^2)(10^4) = (64)(10^6) = 6.4 \times 10^7$.

> **FACT:** For a number to be in scientific notation, it must be of the form $A \times 10^B$, where $1 \le A < 10$ and B is an integer.

> **TIP:** If you have difficulty remembering how to adjust the exponent of 10 when you move a decimal point, try using smaller numbers. For example, 25×10 is equal to 2.5×100 (that is 2.5×10^2).

94. **(H)** The side of the smaller square is 5, so its area is 25. Adding on the shaded area produces the area of the larger square. Therefore the area of the larger square is $25 + 56 = 81$. Then the side of the larger square must be 9, so its perimeter is 36.

95. **(E)** If the package weighs $x + 1$ pounds, then the first company will charge (in dollars) $9.50 + 3.95x$. The second company will charge $8.00 + 4.10x$. Setting these expressions equal to one another, we have $9.50 + 3.95x = 8.00 + 4.10x$. The easiest way to solve for x is to first multiply both sides by 100 to eliminate all decimal points. We then solve $950 + 395x = 800 + 410x$. This leads to $150 = 15x$, so $x = 10$. *But this is not the final answer to the problem.* The weight of the package is $x + 1 = 11$ pounds.

> **TIP:** The value of x is not always the answer to the problem!

Trying choices and finding out what the companies would charge in each case is very time consuming, and not an efficient way to do this problem.

96. **(H)** We are required to have at least one nickel, one dime, and one quarter. These 3 coins total 40¢. We still have 80¢ to go. The fewest coins that total 80¢ would be 3 quarters and 1 nickel. That makes a total of 7 coins needed.

97. **(D)** The job takes $12 \times 4 = 48$ man-hours to do. If there are only 8 men, they must work for 6 hours (because $8 \times 6 = 48$) to get the job done.

98. **(F)** The angle at the center of the circle is $\frac{1}{3}$ of 360°, so the shaded region is $\frac{1}{3}$ of the entire circle. We must find the area of the circle. All radii of a circle are equal, so we set $2x = 3x - 6$. This produces $x = 6$, so the radius ($= 2x$) is 12.

> **TIP:** The value of x is not always the answer to the problem!

The area of the circle is equal to πr^2, which is 144π. Therefore the shaded area is $\frac{1}{3}(144\pi) = 48\pi$.

99. **(B)** The distance between $(4, 5)$ and $(4, 0)$ is 5 units. The distance between $(4, 5)$ and $(0, 5)$ is 4 units. Now consider the rectangle with vertices $(0, 0)$, $(4, 0)$, $(4, 5)$, and $(0, 5)$. We have already found that the lengths of two sides of that rectangle are 5 and 4. The line

segment joining (0, 0) and (4, 5) is a diagonal of the rectangle, so it is longer than either side. The final two choices are clearly more than 4. The answer is B.

100. **(H)** This is an unusual problem. When two consecutive integers are multiplied, the product can only end in 0×1, 1×2, 2×3, 3×4, 4×5, 5×6, 6×7, 7×8, 8×9, or 9×0 (those are the possible final digits of the numbers we are multiplying together). These products only end in 0s, 2s, or 6s! Therefore such a product cannot end in an 8 (that is choice H). What can the product of three consecutive integers end in? How about four consecutive integers?

NINTH-GRADE
MATH SUPPLEMENT

Practice Problems

This section provides a brief sampling of some of the types of problems that can appear on the ninth-grade form of the admissions test.

Topics covered on the 9th-year test may vary as curricula change. Problems marked with an asterisk (*) represent topics that have not appeared recently.

1. If $6! + 7! + 8! = (n)(6!)$, then the value of n is

    A. 15
    B. 16
    C. 63
    D. 64
    E. 15!

2. $\dfrac{x \cdot x^2 \cdot x^3 \cdot x^4 \cdot x^5}{x^8 \cdot x^{15}} =$

    F. x
    G. x^{-8}
    H. x^8
    J. $\dfrac{5}{2}$
    K. 1

3. The volume of a cube is 64. What is its total surface area?

    A. 128
    B. 96
    C. 72
    D. 64
    E. 48

4. Which of the following ordered pairs (x, y) satisfies *both* of the inequalities $y \geq 3x + 8$ and $y < x$?

    F. $(2, 1)$
    G. $(2, -1)$
    H. $(8, -1)$
    J. $(-8, -9)$
    K. $(-8, 9)$

5. The value of $\dfrac{12!}{9!}$ is

    A. $\dfrac{4}{3}$
    B. 3
    C. 3!
    D. 4
    E. 1320

6. Which of the following is the only one that can be (and is) the sum of 5 consecutive integers?

    F. 43,210
    G. 43,211
    H. 43,212
    J. 43,213
    K. 43,214

*7. In right triangle ABC, hypotenuse $AB = 25$. If $\cos A = .28$, then $AC =$

    A. 2.4
    B. 7
    C. 15
    D. 24
    E. 26.04

8. For which of the following values of *L* will the lines whose equations are $3x + 4y = 10$ and $12x + 16y = L$ be parallel?

    I. $L = 0$
   II. $L = 10$
  III. $L = -10$

    F. I only
    G. II only
    H. III only
    J. I and II only
    K. I, II, and III

9. The product of the ages of three teenagers is 3705, and their ages are integers. The sum of their ages

    A. is less than 45.
    B. is 45.
    C. is 47.
    D. is 51.
    E. Cannot be determined from the information given.

10. What is the smallest integer *x* for which the sides of a triangle can be $2x$, $4x + 10$, and $6x - 21$?

    F. 1
    G. 2
    H. 7
    J. 8
    K. 10

11. A jar contains only white and black marbles. The probability of picking a black marble is $\frac{1}{10}$. One red marble is added to the original jar. Now the probability of picking a black marble

    A. is $\frac{1}{3}$
    B. is $\frac{1}{10}$
    C. is $\frac{1}{11}$
    D. is $\frac{1}{20}$
    E. Cannot be determined from the information given.

12. In the diagram, the lines $y = ax - 10$ and $x + 3y = 20$ intersect at the point (n, n). What is the value of *a*?

    F. 1
    G. 2
    H. 3
    J. 4
    K. 5

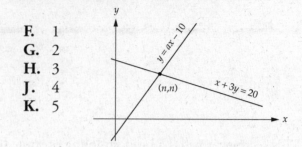

13. A pyramid has a triangular base whose sides are 3, 4, and 5 meters. If the volume of the pyramid is 24 cubic meters, what is the height (to that base) of the pyramid, in meters?

    A. 12
    B. 8
    C. 6
    D. 4
    E. 2

*14. A polyhedron is made up of 10 triangular faces. How many vertices does the polyhedron have?

    F. 7
    G. 10
    H. 15
    J. 22
    K. 30

*15. In right triangle *ABC*, $AC = 6$ and $BC = 8$. The sine of angle *y* is

    A. .6
    B. .75
    C. .8
    D. 1
    E. 1.25

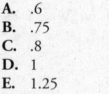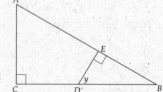

16. The measure of each interior angle of a regular polygon is 156°. How many sides does the polygon have?

    F. 12
    G. 15
    H. 24
    J. 156
    K. Cannot be determined from the information given.

17. If $x + y = 10$ and $xy = 20$, then $\dfrac{1}{x} + \dfrac{1}{y} =$

    A. $\dfrac{1}{10}$
    B. 10
    C. $\dfrac{1}{2}$
    D. 2
    E. $\dfrac{1}{5}$

18. Let x be a number greater than 10. Which of the following is closest to $x(x-1)$?

    F. x^2
    G. $(x-1)^2$
    H. x
    J. $x-1$
    K. $x+1$

19. Two vertices of a square are (12, 0) and (12, 12). What is the smallest possible area the square can have?

    A. $24\sqrt{2}$
    B. 36
    C. 48
    D. 72
    E. 144

20. In triangle ABC, $AB = AC = 18$, and $BC = 10$. If $\overline{PQ} \parallel \overline{AC}$ and $\overline{RQ} \parallel \overline{AB}$, then the perimeter of quadrilateral $APQR$ is

    F. 18
    G. 20
    H. 23
    J. 36
    K. 46

21. If $\dfrac{a}{b} = -6$, then $\dfrac{a+b}{a-b}$

    A. $-\dfrac{7}{6}$
    B. -1
    C. $\dfrac{5}{7}$
    D. $\dfrac{7}{6}$
    E. $\dfrac{7}{5}$

22. Let x, y, and z be positive numbers such that $5x = 3y = 7z$. Which one of the following inequalities must be true?

    F. $x < y < z$
    G. $x < z < y$
    H. $y < x < z$
    J. $z < x < y$
    K. $z < y < x$

23. In the diagram, line segment $\overline{AC}$ is a diagonal of square $ABCD$ and triangle ABE is equilateral. What is the measure of $\angle AFE$?

    A. 120°
    B. 105°
    C. 75°
    D. 60°
    E. 45°

24. An equivalent value of $\left(4\dfrac{1}{4}\right)^2$ is

    F. $8\dfrac{1}{2}$
    G. $16\dfrac{1}{16}$
    H. $16\dfrac{1}{4}$
    J. $16\dfrac{1}{2}$
    K. $18\dfrac{1}{16}$

25. Let $M = .\overline{35} + \frac{1}{11}$. The value of M may

also be expressed as

A. $.\overline{36}$

B. $.\overline{46}$

C. $\frac{4}{99}$

D. $\frac{4}{9}$

E. $\frac{51}{99}$

26. The point $A(3,4)$ is rotated about the origin to point $A'(x,y)$. Which one of the following **cannot** be a possible value for x?

F. 6

G. 4

H. 2

J. −3

K. −4

27. The original price of an item is discounted by 30%. In order to restore this discounted price to the original price, the discounted price must be increased by x%, where x is **closest** to

A. 23

B. 30

C. 35

D. 43

E. 50

28. If $\frac{4^4 + 4^4}{4} = 2^x$, then $x =$

F. 7

G. 14

H. 16

J. 20

K. 24

29. Line segment $\overline{AB}$ in the xy-coordinate plane has endpoints $A(1,1)$ and $B(9,13)$. *How many* points, **both** of whose coordinates are integers, are on segment $\overline{AB}$? Include points A and B in the total count.

A. 2

B. 3

C. 5

D. 8

E. 9

30. A formula for converting temperature from degrees Centigrade (Celsius) to degrees Fahrenheit is $F = \frac{9}{5} C + 32$. Which of the following graphs *best* represents this relation?

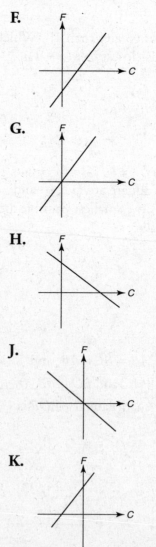

F.

G.

H.

J.

K.

31. The sum of two nonnegative numbers A and B is 20. Let P represent the product of A and B. Which one of the following graphs best represents the relationship between A and P?

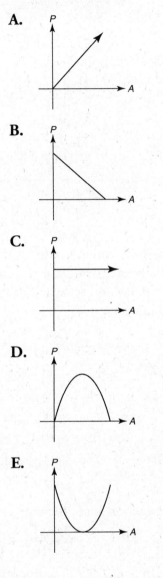

A.

B.

C.

D.

E.

32. In how many different ways can a team of 3 boys and 2 girls be formed if there are 4 boys and 5 girls from which to select and Robert (one of the boys) **must** be on the team?

F. 6
G. 20
H. 30
J. 40
K. 80

33. The graph of a certain relation is known to be symmetric about the line $x = 3$. If the point $A(8,7)$ is on this graph, which one of the following points **must** also be on the graph?

A. $(-8,7)$
B. $(-2,7)$
C. $(-3,7)$
D. $(3,7)$
E. $(8,-1)$

34. In $\triangle ABC$, altitudes $\overline{BD}$ and $\overline{CE}$ intersect at F as shown in the figure. $\angle ABD$ is labeled 1, $\angle CBD$ is labeled 2, $\angle BCE$ is labeled 3, $\angle ACE$ is labeled 4, and $\angle CFD$ is labeled 5. Which one of the following pairs of angles **must** be congruent?

F. 1 and 4
G. 2 and 3
H. 3 and 4
J. 3 and 5
K. 4 and 5

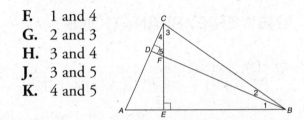

35. Each edge of a rectangular box has integer length. If the volume of the box is 72 cubic inches and one face is a square, what is the *smallest* possible total surface area of the box (in square inches)?

A. 100
B. 114
C. 120
D. 152
E. 290

Answer Key
PRACTICE PROBLEMS

1. D	8. K	15. C	22. J	29. C
2. G	9. C	16. G	23. B	30. K
3. B	10. J	17. C	24. K	31. D
4. J	11. E	18. G	25. D	32. H
5. E	12. H	19. D	26. F	33. B
6. F	13. A	20. J	27. D	34. F
7. B	14. F	21. C	28. F	35. B

ANSWER EXPLANATIONS

1. **(D)** Factoring out 6! from each term produces $6!(1 + 7 + 7 \cdot 8) = 6!(64)$. Therefore $n = 64$.

2. **(G)** Applying the laws of exponents, we get $\dfrac{x^{15}}{x^{23}}$, which equals x^{-8}.

3. **(B)** The edge of the cube must be 4. Therefore each face has an area of 16. Since there are six congruent faces, the total surface area is $6(16) = 96$.

4. **(J)** The choices in which $y < x$ are F, G, H, and J. Substituting each pair of values into the first inequality shows that only choice J works: $-9 \geq 3(-8) + 8 = -16$.

5. **(E)** The numerator is $12 \cdot 11 \cdot 10 \cdot 9 \cdot 8 \cdots 3 \cdot 2 \cdot 1$. Dividing by 9! leaves us with $12 \cdot 11 \cdot 10$, which equals 1320.

6. **(F)** If the smallest integer is represented by x, then the others are $x + 1$, $x + 2$, $x + 3$, and $x + 4$. The sum of these five numbers is $5x + 10$, which must be a multiple of 5. The only choice that is a multiple of 5 is F. An alternate representation for a set of five consecutive integers is $x - 2$, $x - 1$, x, $x + 1$, and

$x + 2$. Their sum is $5x$, which is also a multiple of 5. It is usually easier to use a representation similar to this second set when dealing with consecutive integers.

7. **(B)** $\cos A = \dfrac{AC}{AB} = \dfrac{AC}{25} = .28$. Then $AC = (25)(.28) = 7$.

8. **(K)**

> **FACT:** The slope of the line whose equation is $y = mx + b$ is the number m. If two lines have the same slope, the lines are parallel.

If we solve each equation for y, the equations become $y = -\dfrac{3}{4}x + \dfrac{10}{4}$ and $y = -\dfrac{12}{16}x + \dfrac{L}{16}$. Each of these lines has a slope of $-\dfrac{3}{4}$, so they are parallel regardless of the value of L. Thus, the lines are parallel for all three given values for L.

9. **(C)** Since the product of the ages is 3,705, we must factor that number. Clearly 5 and 3 are factors, producing $3,705 = 5 \times 3 \times 247$. To factor 247, we try dividing by prime numbers: 2, 3, 5, 7, and 11 don't work (you should know divisibility tests for 2, 3, 4, 5, 9, 10, and 11; for 7, just do the division). But 13 does, giving $247 = 13 \times 19$. Thus $3705 =$

$3 \times 5 \times 13 \times 19$. The teenagers must be 15, 13, and 19 years old, so the sum of their ages is 47. If they did not have to be teenagers, then the three ages (and their sum) would not have been uniquely determined.

10. **(J)**

> **FACT:** The sum of the lengths of two sides of a triangle is greater than the length of the third side.

Adding different pairs of sides and making each sum greater than the third side produces three different inequalities, each of which must be true. These inequalities are $6x + 10 > 6x - 21$, $8x - 21 > 4x + 10$, and $10x - 11 > 2x$. The first inequality, when simplified, becomes $10 > -21$; this is always true. The second inequality becomes $4x > 31$; the smallest integer x for which this is true is $x = 8$. The third inequality becomes $8x > 11$; the smallest integer x for which this is true is $x = 2$. The smallest x that works for all three inequalities is $x = 8$.

11. **(E)** If there are n black marbles, then there are $9n$ white marbles, for a total of $10n$ marbles to start with. After adding a red marble, the probability of picking a black marble becomes $\dfrac{n}{10n + 1}$. The value of this fraction depends on the value of n, so the answer is E.

12. **(H)** The point (n, n) is on both lines, so the ordered pair (n, n) must satisfy both equations. Substituting n for both x and y in the second equation, we get $4n = 20$, so $n = 5$. Substituting 5 for both x and y in the first equation produces $5 = 5a - 10$, so $a = 3$.

13. **(A)**

> **FACT:** The volume of a pyramid is given by $V = \dfrac{1}{3}Bh$, where B represents the area of the base of the pyramid, and h represents the length of the altitude to that base.

The base is a right triangle whose area is $\dfrac{1}{2}(3)(4) = 6$. Therefore we have $24 = \dfrac{1}{3}(6)(h)$, so $h = 12$.

14. **(F)**

> **FACT:** Euler's Formula states that $V - E + F = 2$, where V is the number of vertices the figure has, E is the number of edges, and F is the number of faces.

Clearly $F = 10$. Each triangular face has three edges (total = 30). However, each edge is shared by exactly two faces; therefore every edge has been counted twice. There are really only 15 different edges, so $E = 15$. The formula gives us $V = 7$.

15. **(C)** Using the Pythagorean Theorem in triangle ABC, we find that $AB = 10$. Now notice that angle y and angle A must be equal since each is the complement of angle B.

Therefore, $\sin y = \sin A = \dfrac{8}{10} = .8$.

16. **(G)** Method 1.

> **FACT (Method 1):** The measure of each interior angle of a regular polygon of n sides is equal to $\dfrac{(n-2) \cdot 180}{n}$ degrees.

$\dfrac{(n-2) \cdot 180}{n} = 156$. Then $(n-2) \cdot 180 = 156n$, leading to $24n = 360$. Thus, $n = 15$.

Method 2.

> **FACT (Method 2):** The sum of the measures of the exterior angles of *any* polygon is 360°.

Since each interior angle is 156°, then each exterior angle must be 24°. Then $24n = 360$, so $n = 15$.

17. **(C)** $\dfrac{1}{x} + \dfrac{1}{y} = \dfrac{x+y}{xy} = \dfrac{10}{20} = \dfrac{1}{2}$.

18. **(G)** Method 1. Trying choice F, we see that the difference between x^2 and $x(x-1)$ is $x^2 - (x^2 - x) = x$. Trying choice G, we see that the difference between $x(x-1)$ and $(x-1)^2$ is $x - 1$. Thus choice G is closer to the original expression. The other choices are much further away, especially when x is a large number.

Method 2. The problem implies that the result will be true for any value of x that is greater than 10. Choose a value for x, such as $x = 11$. Then $x(x - 1) = 110$. Trying the choices quickly leads to G as the closest.

19. **(D)** The given vertices are either consecutive vertices of the square or opposite vertices of the square. Draw a figure for each case. If the two given vertices are consecutive vertices of the square, then the side of the square is 12. Its area would be 144. But if the given vertices are opposite vertices of the square, we can connect both pairs of opposite vertices, forming four congruent right triangles. Each leg of each right triangle is 6, so the area of each right triangle is $\frac{1}{2}(6)(6) = 18$. That produces $(4)(18) = 72$ for the area of the square. That is the smallest possible area the square can have.

20. **(J)** Triangle ABC is isosceles, so angle $B \cong$ angle C.

> **FACT:** If two parallel lines are crossed by a transversal, the "corresponding angles" formed must be equal.

Since $\overline{PQ} \parallel \overline{AC}$, angle C = angle PQB. But that means that angle B = angle PQB. This tells us that triangle PBQ is isoceles. Thus, $PQ = PB$. We now see that $PQ + PA = PB + PA = AB = 18$. By similar reasoning, we find that $RQ + RA = RC + RA = AC = 18$. Therefore, the perimeter of quadrilateral $APQR$ is $18 + 18 = 36$. The length of $\overline{BC}$ has no bearing on the solution, and is simply a "distracter" that the student must pay no attention to.

21. **(C)** Method 1. If $\frac{a}{b} = -6$, then $a = -6b$. Therefore $a + b = -6b + b = -5b$ and $a - b = -6b - b = -7b$. Then $\frac{a+b}{a-b} = \frac{-5b}{-7b} = \frac{5}{7}$.

Method 2. Choose suitable values for a and b that reflect the given condition. For example, choose $a = -6$ and $b = 1$. Then $\frac{a+b}{a-b} = \frac{-6+1}{-6-1} = \frac{-5}{-7} = \frac{5}{7}$.

22. **(J)** Method 1. Let $5x = 3y = 7z = T$ and notice that T is positive. Thus $x = \frac{1}{5}T$, $y = \frac{1}{3}T$, and $z = \frac{1}{7}T$. Since $\frac{1}{7} < \frac{1}{5} < \frac{1}{3}$, we have $z < x < y$.

Method 2. Since $z = \frac{5}{7}x$, that means $z < x$. Since $x = \frac{3}{5}y$, that means $x < y$. Thus $z < x < y$.

23. **(B)** Equilateral $\triangle ABE$ is also equiangular, so $\angle BAE = \angle AEB = 60°$. Notice that $\triangle ABC$ is an isosceles right triangle, so $\angle BAC = 45°$. Thus in $\triangle AEF$, $\angle EAF = 60° - 45° = 15°$ and $\angle AEB = 60°$. Thus $\angle AFE = 180° - (15° + 60°) = 180° - 75° = 105°$.

24. **(K)** One approach is to express $4\frac{1}{4}$ as $\frac{17}{4}$. Then $\left(4\frac{1}{4}\right)^2 = \left(\frac{17}{4}\right)^2 = \frac{289}{16} = 18\frac{1}{16}$.

25. **(D)** Let us first consider $x = .\overline{35} = .353535...$ After multiplying both sides of this equation by 100, we get

$$100x = 35.3535... = 35.\overline{35}$$

Since $x = .3535... = .\overline{35}$, subtracting $100x - x$ produces $99x = 35$. So $x = \frac{35}{99}$.

Notice that multiplication by 100 (= 10^2) shifts the decimal point 2 places to the right. The number of digits in the repeating part of the decimal, in this case 2, motivates the choice of 10^2 as the multiplier.

> **FACT:** If a and b represent any of the digits 0, 1, 2, ..., 9 , then $.\overline{a} = \dfrac{a}{9}$ and $.\overline{ab} = \dfrac{ab}{99}$, where "ab" represents a two-digit number.

However, we want the value of $M = .\overline{35} + \dfrac{1}{11}$. By expressing $\dfrac{1}{11}$ as $\dfrac{9}{99}$, we have $M = \dfrac{35}{99} + \dfrac{9}{99}$ $= \dfrac{44}{99}$. After looking at the choices, we see that $\dfrac{44}{99}$ does not appear in this form. Be careful to consider the choices! Note that $\dfrac{44}{99} = \dfrac{4 \times 11}{9 \times 11} = \dfrac{4}{9}$. (Alternatively, using the FACT shown above, $\dfrac{44}{99} = .\overline{44} = .444444... = .\overline{4} = \dfrac{4}{9}$.) You can gain much understanding from carefully reviewing this problem.

26. **(F)** First observe that as point A is rotated about the origin, its distance from the origin remains the same. Point $A(3,4)$ is 5 units from the origin. To see this, let d be the distance from A to the origin. Drawing a perpendicular from A to the x-axis creates a right triangle with hypotenuse d and legs 3 and 4. By the Pythagorean Theorem, $d^2 = 3^2 + 4^2 = 25$, so $d = 5$. Thus all possible images of $A(3,4)$, when rotated about the origin, lie on a circle of radius 5 and center $(0,0)$, which is the origin. Any point whose x-coordinate is 6 would lie *outside* of this circle.

27. **(D)** Choosing a specific number for the original price will not affect the answer. For case of computation, choose \$100 as the original price. The discounted price is then (\$100) − (30% of \$100) = \$100 − \$30 = \$70. You must now increase \$70 by \$30 to obtain the original price. Therefore you need to find what percent of \$70 is \$30. Thus $x\% = \dfrac{x}{100}$ $= \dfrac{30}{70}$. Solving for x gives $x = \dfrac{300}{7} = 42\dfrac{6}{7}$, which is closest to choice D.

28. **(F)** Express 4^4 and 4 as powers of 2. Since $4 = 2^2$, the value of $4^4 = (2^2)^4 = 2^8$. (Note that $(2^2)^4 = 2^2 \times 2^2 \times 2^2 \times 2^2 = 2^8$.) Therefore $\dfrac{4^4 + 4^4}{4} = \dfrac{2^8 + 2^8}{2^2} = \dfrac{2 \cdot 2^8}{2^2} = \dfrac{2^9}{2^2}$ $= 2^7$, so $x = 7$.

29. **(C)** The slope of $\overline{AB}$ is $\dfrac{13-1}{9-1} = \dfrac{12}{8} = \dfrac{3}{2}$. This tells us that on this line, 2 units of motion in the positive x direction corresponds to 3 units of motion in the positive y direction. Starting at $A(1,1)$, the next "integer" point is $(1 + \mathbf{2}, 1 + \mathbf{3})$, which is $(3,4)$. Continuing, we reach $(5,7)$, then $(7,10)$, and then $(9,13)$, for a total of 5 such points. (Making a good sketch would be quite helpful.)

30. **(K)** When $C = 0$, $F = 32$. Therefore the point $(0,32)$ is on the graph. Choices F, G, and J are eliminated. Notice from the formula that if C increases, F also increases. This eliminates choice H. You could use many other approaches to solve this problem.

31. **(D)** Making a brief table of selected values is quite revealing.

A	B	P
0	20	0
2	18	36
4	16	64
6	14	84
8	12	96
10	10	100
12	8	96
14	6	84
16	4	64
18	2	36
20	0	0

Notice that as A increases, P increases and then decreases. (The values of P are symmetric about $A = 10$.) Choice D "best" illustrates this behavior.

32. **(H)** From 5 girls (*a, b, c, d, e*) we can select 2 girls in 10 different ways: *ab, ac, ad, ae, bc, bd, be, cd, ce,* and *de.* Since Robert must be on the team, we must select 2 more boys from the remaining 3 boys (*x, y, z*). This can be done in 3 different ways: *xy, xz,* and *yz.* Selecting the girls is independent of selecting the boys. So the total number of different team selections is 10 × 3 = 30.

33. **(B)** The sketch reveals the solution quite clearly.

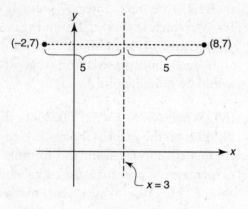

34. **(F)** Triangle *ACE* and triangle *ABD* are right triangles. Therefore $\angle 4 + \angle A = 90°$ and $\angle 1 + \angle A = 90°$. Thus $\angle 1$ and $\angle 4$ must be congruent. The word **must** rules out cases in which a pair of angles **may** be congruent but do not have to be congruent. Can you show why $\angle 5$ cannot be congruent to $\angle 3$?

35. **(B)** Let the dimensions of the square face be *x* by *x*. Without loss of generality, let this face be the base of the box. Let *y* represent the height. The volume of a rectangular box is *V* = length × width × height, which leads to $72 = x^2 y$. Remember that *x* and *y* are integers, so x^2 must be a factor of 72. The only possible square factors of 72 are 1, 4, 9, and 36, leading to *x* = 1, 2, 3, or 6. The total surface area is $4xy + 2x^2$. Compute the value of this expression for each *x*. If *x* = 1, *y* = 72, so the surface area would be 290. If *x* = 2, *y* = 18; if *x* = 3, *y* = 8; and if *x* = 6, *y* = 2. The corresponding surface areas are, respectively, 152, 114, and 120. The answer is 114.

Appendix:
Progress Charts

PROGRESS CHART: RESULTS ON PRACTICE TESTS

Date	Starting Time / Ending Time	Test	Number Correct (For scrambled paragraphs, enter the number correct times the multiplier shown in the box.)				TOTAL (*see note below about Minitests)	Circle Number of Each Incorrect Math Problem
			Scrambled Paragraphs	Logical Reasoning	Reading	Math		
	- - - - - - - - - -	Minitest 1	x3					26 27 28 29 30 31 32 33 34 35 36 37 38 39 40 41 42 43 44 45 46 47 48 49 50
	- - - - - - - - - -	Minitest 2	x3					26 27 28 29 30 31 32 33 34 35 36 37 38 39 40 41 42 43 44 45 46 47 48 49 50
	- - - - - - - - - -	Minitest 3	x3					26 27 28 29 30 31 32 33 34 35 36 37 38 39 40 41 42 43 44 45 46 47 48 49 50
	- - - - - - - - - -	Minitest 4	x3					26 27 28 29 30 31 32 33 34 35 36 37 38 39 40 41 42 43 44 45 46 47 48 49 50
	- - - - - - - - - -	Model Test 1	x2					51 52 53 54 55 56 57 58 59 60 61 62 63 64 65 66 67 68 69 70 71 72 73 74 75 76 77 78 79 80 81 82 83 84 85 86 87 88 89 90 91 92 93 94 95 96 97 98 99 100
	- - - - - - - - - -	Model Test 2	x2					51 52 53 54 55 56 57 58 59 60 61 62 63 64 65 66 67 68 69 70 71 72 73 74 75 76 77 78 79 80 81 82 83 84 85 86 87 88 89 90 91 92 93 94 95 96 97 98 99 100
	- - - - - - - - - -	Model Test 3	x2					51 52 53 54 55 56 57 58 59 60 61 62 63 64 65 66 67 68 69 70 71 72 73 74 75 76 77 78 79 80 81 82 83 84 85 86 87 88 89 90 91 92 93 94 95 96 97 98 99 100

*Minitests each total 50 points. The distribution of points on those tests does not exactly parallel the distribution used on the Model Tests. Specifically, to simplify calculations, the Verbal section (Scrambled Paragraphs, Logical Reasoning, Reading) is weighted slightly differently on the Minitests.

Appendix: Progress Charts 323

SECOND PROGRESS CHART

Date	Starting Time / Ending Time	Test	Number Correct (For scrambled paragraphs, enter the number correct times the multiplier shown in the box.)				TOTAL	Circle Number of Each Incorrect Math Problem (for comparison with the previous chart)
			Scrambled Paragraphs	Logical Reasoning	Reading	Math		
	– – – –	Minitest 1	x3					26 27 28 29 30 31 32 33 34 35 36 37 38 39 40 41 42 43 44 45 46 47 48 49 50
	– – – –	Minitest 2	x3					26 27 28 29 30 31 32 33 34 35 36 37 38 39 40 41 42 43 44 45 46 47 48 49 50
	– – – –	Minitest 3	x3					26 27 28 29 30 31 32 33 34 35 36 37 38 39 40 41 42 43 44 45 46 47 48 49 50
	– – – –	Minitest 4	x3					26 27 28 29 30 31 32 33 34 35 36 37 38 39 40 41 42 43 44 45 46 47 48 49 50
		Model Test 1	x2					51 52 53 54 55 56 57 58 59 60 61 62 63 64 65 66 67 68 69 70 71 72 73 74 75 76 77 78 79 80 81 82 83 84 85 86 87 88 89 90 91 92 93 94 95 96 97 98 99 100
	– – – –	Model Test 2	x2					51 52 53 54 55 56 57 58 59 60 61 62 63 64 65 66 67 68 69 70 71 72 73 74 75 76 77 78 79 80 81 82 83 84 85 86 87 88 89 90 91 92 93 94 95 96 97 98 99 100
	– – – –	Model Test 3	x2					51 52 53 54 55 56 57 58 59 60 61 62 63 64 65 66 67 68 69 70 71 72 73 74 75 76 77 78 79 80 81 82 83 84 85 86 87 88 89 90 91 92 93 94 95 96 97 98 99 100

RESULTS ON MATH DIAGNOSERS AND FOLLOW-UPS

Date	Diagnosers (15-minute time limit) and Follow-Ups	Number Correct	Circle Number of Each Incorrect Problem (compare results of <u>same</u> tests; work on problems gotten wrong both times)
	Diagnoser A		1 2 3 4 5 6 7 8 9 10
	Follow-Up A		1 2 3 4 5 6 7 8 9 10
	Diagnoser B		1 2 3 4 5 6 7 8 9 10
	Follow-Up B		1 2 3 4 5 6 7 8 9 10
	Diagnoser C		1 2 3 4 5 6 7 8 9 10
	Follow-Up C		1 2 3 4 5 6 7 8 9 10
	Diagnoser D		1 2 3 4 5 6 7 8 9 10
	Follow-Up D		1 2 3 4 5 6 7 8 9 10
	Diagnoser E		1 2 3 4 5 6 7 8 9 10
	Follow-Up E		1 2 3 4 5 6 7 8 9 10
	Diagnoser F		1 2 3 4 5 6 7 8 9 10
	Follow-Up F		1 2 3 4 5 6 7 8 9 10
	Diagnoser A		1 2 3 4 5 6 7 8 9 10
	Follow-Up A		1 2 3 4 5 6 7 8 9 10
	Diagnoser B		1 2 3 4 5 6 7 8 9 10
	Follow-Up B		1 2 3 4 5 6 7 8 9 10
	Diagnoser C		1 2 3 4 5 6 7 8 9 10
	Follow-Up C		1 2 3 4 5 6 7 8 9 10
	Diagnoser D		1 2 3 4 5 6 7 8 9 10
	Follow-Up D		1 2 3 4 5 6 7 8 9 10
	Diagnoser E		1 2 3 4 5 6 7 8 9 10
	Follow-Up E		1 2 3 4 5 6 7 8 9 10
	Diagnoser F		1 2 3 4 5 6 7 8 9 10
	Follow-Up F		1 2 3 4 5 6 7 8 9 10

NOTES

Really. This isn't going to hurt at all . . .

Learning won't hurt when middle school and high school students open any *Painless* title. These books transform subjects into fun—emphasizing a touch of humor and entertaining brain-tickler puzzles that are fun to solve.

Bonus Online Component—each title followed by (*) includes additional online games to challenge students, including Beat the Clock, a line match game, and a word scramble.

Each book: Paperback